Modernity and Identity

Edited by
Scott Lash
and
Jonathan Friedman

BLACKWELL
Oxford UK & Cambridge USA

First published 1992
Reprinted 1992, 1993, 1996

Blackwell Publishers Ltd
108 Cowley Road, Oxford, OX4 1JF, UK

Blackwell Publishers Inc.
238 Main Street
Cambridge, Massachusetts 02142, USA

British Library Cataloguing in Publication Data
A CIP catalogue record for this book is available from the British Library.

Library of Congress Cataloging in Publication Data
Modernity and Identity / edited by Scott Lash and Jonathan Friedman.
     p.   cm.
    Includes index.
    ISBN 0–631–17585–7 — ISBN 0–631–17586–5 (Pbk)
    1. Group identity.   2. Civilization, Modern — 20th century.
   3. Postmodernism.   I. Lash, Scott.   II. Friedman, Jonathan.
HM131.M567   1991
303.4—dc20
                                                   90–27629
                                                    CIP

Typeset in 10½ on 12pt Garamond
by Graphicraft Typesetters Ltd, Hong Kong
Printed in Great Britain by T. J. Press Ltd, Padstow

This book is printed on acid-free paper

Contents

Contributors

Nicholas Abercrombie is Professor of Sociology at Lancaster University, England.

Marshall Berman teaches comparative literature and popular culture at the City University of New York, USA.

Christa Bürger is Professor of German Literature at the Johann Wolfgang Goethe University, Frankfurt am Main, Germany.

Peter Bürger is Professor of French and Comparative Literature at Bremen University, Germany.

Peter Burke is a Fellow of Emmanuel College, Cambridge University, England.

Mike Featherstone is Reader in Social Studies at Teeside Polytechnic in Middlesbrough, England.

Jonathan Friedman teaches anthropology at Lund University, Sweden.

Dieter Hoffmann-Axthelm is a freelance philosopher and urban analyst in Berlin, Germany.

Martin Jay is Professor of History at The University of California, Berkeley, USA.

Douglas Kellner is Professor of Philosophy at the University of Texas at Austin, USA.

Scott Lash teaches sociology at Lancaster University, England.

Brian Longhurst is Lecturer in Sociology at Salford University, Greater Manchester, England.

George Marcus is Professor of Anthropology at Rice University, Houston, Texas, USA.

Paul Rabinow is Professor of Anthropology at the University of California, Berkeley, USA.

Richard Rorty is Kenan Professor of Humanities at the University of Virginia, Charlottesville, Virginia, USA.

Sharon Zukin is Professor of Sociology at the City University of New York, USA.

Acknowledgements

This book has been, as they say, a long time coming. The ideas that led to its initiation were first formulated at the University of Lund in Sweden as early as 1984. After countless discussions between the two editors, long into dark winter nights, over countless bottles of wine and quantities of good food, we decided on a common project. Following some abortive attempts to organize an international conference on the themes of modernity and identity, we finally ended up with two conferences in close succession in October 1988. The first of these was held at the Institute of Contemporary Arts in London and dealt with the City. Co-organizers were John Thackera, Jan Abrams and Erica Carter. The second, just a few days later, was held at the Center for Research in the Humanities in Copenhagen. Its theme was 'Modernity as History'. Mogens Trolle Larsen, Director of the Center, as well as the staff who helped organize and participated in the conference, were instrumental in making this conference a success. We are most grateful to those who contributed to the funding of these activities, the University of Lancaster, and the Center for Research in the Humanities.

Not all of the papers presented at those conferences were included in the present volume and we would like to take this opportunity to thank all the participants for a truly intensive week of discussions. We would also thank those few who were unable to participate in the conferences but who nevertheless did get in their contributions.

Introduction: subjectivity and modernity's Other

Scott Lash and Jonathan Friedman

This is a book about 'modernity'. Such books have now become rather a tradition. This tradition, of course, is that of the now well-known and quite institutionalized genre of debates on modernism and postmodernism. This book's thrust, however, is rather specific and well defined within the parameters of such debates. For most of the otherwise quite diverse writers in this book modernity is a matter of *movement*, of *flux*, of *change*, of *unpredictibility*.

Such an understanding of the modern is significantly at variance with the now conventional conceptions of both modernism and postmodernism, and especially the central, dominant notions, not of movement, but of *stasis*, of *fixity*. The paramount figure in modernism is that of the static and abstract model separated from the dynamic ebb and flow of reality. This figure is that of the Cartesian 'I', of the abstract natural rights of the French Revolution, of Kantian reason, of the unsuccessful blueprints of the worst of orthodox Marxism, of city grids, of Corbusier's *machine à habiter*, of Habermas's ideal speech situation.

The dominant figure in *post*modernism is equally static and abstract. Postmodernism annuls movement and change through its disavowal of avant-gardes. It posits a mediascape, an 'astral empire of signs', whose powers of social control over individuals and collectivities is so absolute that no change is possible. It posits an end to history, an end to art and an end to 'the subject', whose individual and collective action makes meaningful change possible. Even the postmodern utopia is one which cancels movement by emphatically privileging space over time. Utopian postmodernism is thus a vision of a neo-tribal paradise in which a set of spatially set forms of life carry on experiments, each in their own culture. In this vision, however, communication is impossible between tribes. The overwhelming spatiality of the tribes seems to suffocate the temporal dimension. Subject-less signifiers remain fixed in the absence of any sort of forward-propelling pulsions. There is no future.

The vision in this book is that of *another* modernity. One not of Rousseau's Geneva of natural rights and *volonté générale*, but instead of Baudelaire's Paris of the fleeting, the transient. This modernity signals not the destruction of the particular by the universality of the Cartesian *cogito* but the reassertion of the sensual in baroque allegory. This is not the early modernism of quattrocento perspective, but that of the disruption of classicisms and neo-classicisms by Hieronymus Bosch. It is not *la moderne* of the abstract (and positivist) individualism constituted by Durkheim's *conscience collective* in turn-of-the-century France but that of Simmel's aestheticization of everyday life in turn-of-the-century Berlin. It is a modernity which most of contemporary social theory – be it structuralist, poststructuralist, critical theory, positivist or rational choice – rather emphatically rejects.

This other face of the modern has been best instantiated in the 1980s in the work of Marshall Berman. In the 1980s Berman, on the one hand, and Jürgen Habermas, on the other, have provided a necessary point of reference for resistance to the excesses of postmodernism's onslaught. But there is as much which separates Berman from Habermas as there is that separates both from the postmoderns. Habermas gives us the (albeit sophisticated) blueprint of the ideal speech situation, where Berman intones that all that is solid, including blueprints, must melt into air. Habermas proffers a discursive modernism, of the achievement of the enlightenment project, through speech acts backed by rational discourse. Berman, like Walter Benjamin, proffers a *figural* vision of the *flâneur*, looking out onto the black kids playing basketball on the corner on Fourth Street near Sixth Avenue, and at the murals on the once again falling derelict building.

Habermas gives us a modernism of 'the ought'; his is a highly moral vision, based on a very abstract and general morality. Berman's instead is a modernism of 'the is'; the here and now, *la vie quotidienne*. It does hold promise of an ethics, but it is primarily an *aesthetic* vision, in both senses of the aesthetic: on the one hand as art, on the other as sense perception. Finally Habermas's modernism is fully utopian in its hope for a communicative paradise. It is in every meaningful sense of the word a *high* modernism. Berman's modernism is to the contrary populist. It is a modernism not of the elite opinion makers of *Öffentlichkleit* (public sphere), but of the popular, of – in a thoroughly globalized context – *das Volk*. It talks not of disembodied communications, of abstract signifiers, but of 'the signs in the street'. It transports the vulgarity of Bakhtinian carnival onto New York's Upper West Side, LA's Compton, Berlin's Kreuzberg. It is not a high, but rather a *low* modernism.

This 'low modernism', a 'modernism in the streets', at the same time disputes *post*modernism's rejection of history, movement, change; disputes its irrationalist anti-ethics and its neo-tribalist and localist rejection of any universalism; denies its pronouncements on the end of art and the end of theory. Yet low modernism's embrace of history is equally a disparagement of teleology. Its advocacy of movement and change is a denial of the *grands récits*. For low modernism art lives as experimentation, and persists in the absence of avant-gardes. Theoretical innovation takes on new life in the absence of the excesses of abstraction. Low modernism wants to work towards an ethics, but an ethics without blueprints. Its universalism is one which fosters cosmopolitanism, but cosmopolitanism *without* emancipation.

This book is also about *identity*. In social theory, structuralism has often been likened to modernism and poststructuralism to postmodernism. In this sense both modernists and postmodernists have had as the cornerstone of their theory some notion of the irrelevance of identity, of subjectivity, of the social actor or agency. Thus Barthes spoke of the death of the author; and Foucault in his inaugural lecture spoke of subject positions which only were created by discourse. Lyotard persists, even in 1983 in *Le Différend* (despite his anarchist anything-goes agonistics which would seem to hypervalue the individual), in refusing to ascribe any substance to the subject. As opposed to these orthodoxies of the last decade or two, the language of the analysts throughout this book is the language of subjectivity, the language of (individual and collective) identity.

This is a book in culture studies or cultural theory, in the very broadest sense of these words. It is fully interdisciplinary, with six disciplines – sociology, anthropology, history, philosophy, modern languages and urban studies – prominently represented. The main thrust, however, comes from two conferences that we as editors co-organized: one a conference in urban studies, and another whose main thrust came from anthropology. Urbanism as culture studies – and in particular the lineage that connects Baudelaire through Simmel to Benjamin and Marshall Berman – lends to this book its notion of modernity; however, it is anthropology – in a tradition from

Mauss and Durkheim through Bourdieu to contemporary analyses in world systems and 'writing culture' – which gives to it a notion of identity.

Anthropology and in particular Durkheim and the *Année Sociologique* group developed a tradition that is continued in the structuralism of Lévi-Strauss. And while Bourdieu takes issue with the Durkheimian model, the social determinism that works via the formation of individual habitus indicates a continued fascination with what might be called Kantian subjectivity, and with the social bases of cultural classification. Certainly, the generation of schemes of classification and of social distinction in the practice of social relations is an essential ingredient in the formation of social and individual identity.

This French tradition has thus had a long-standing and central concern with issues of collective representation and with how to give cultural content to and explain the social bases of cognitive, moral and aesthetic judgement. On such accounts collective representations not only constitute but define individual and collective identity. That is, structures of collective representation, whether conceived as binary oppositions in the mind, as habitus, or as group and grid, tell us how subjects in any culture classify the world. Further, judgement of any type is impossible without classification; and cognitive, moral and aesthetic judgement are main parameters of identity, even as they are produced and elaborated in practical fields of social interaction.

It is helpful to think of identity in terms of the cultural and social content of the Kantian subject; in terms of cognitive, moral and aesthetic judgement; and in terms of Kant's distinction between all three forms of judgement, on the one hand, and perception – with which we intuit objects through categories of time and space – on the other.[1] Just as there is among the writers in this volume a surprising degree of consensus as to what is modernity, there seems to be a rather broad, at least implicit consensus on this sort of framework as well as on the sort of periodization of identity one might expect. Thus pre-modern identity can be very generally understood as externally (or in Kant's sense 'heteronomously') determined. In 'tribal' societies it is kinship-ordered cosmologies that define identity in terms of deciding *who* someone is. In the archaic civilizations of the world religions, it is a transcendent godhead or pantheon or hierarchy of deities which take on these nominating powers, though the secular realm is clearly on the rise.

In modernity, heteronomous definition of identity persists. As Foucault suggested, however, powers of social control in this process of 'subjectivization' pass from the 'body of the king' to the social and enter via the capillaries of everyday life the veins and arteries of the subject. But also in modernity, with the demise of both God and Caesar, social space opens up the way for an autonomous definition of identity. In modernity we are fated to be free. Max Weber gave us the high modernist concept of this sort of identity in his 'ethics of responsibility'. With God, Caesar and the certainties of Kant's categorical ethics swept away, the onus is on us to forge our own subjectivity. Weber recognized the extent to which our subjectivity was de-centred by increasing demands from a plurality of life spheres. Mature modernist identity or *Persönlichkeit* for Weber meant a coherent and measured acceptance and taking on of these plural demands. It also included two temporal elements. First, responsibility in the modern meant responsibility for the consequences of one's actions, a more and more difficult task in an increasingly complex society. Identity also had to do with the temporality of our existence. Our *Lebensführung* (life-course), which previously was decided heteronomously for us by the ascetic Protestant sacred, now had to be ordered by us ourselves.

But this Weberian high modernist version of identity, which Habermas (1984) concurs with in *Theory of Communicative Action*, carries with it a certain amount of very questionable baggage, and this is registered by many of the contributors to this book. High modernist subjectivity gives extraordinary privilege, for example, to judgement and especially to cognition. It correspondingly devalues the faculty of perception, so that vision itself is so to speak colonized by cognition. The modern predominance of reading fosters epistemologies of representation, of a visual paradigm in the sphere of art (see Martin Jay, chapter 7; Dieter Hoffmann-Axthelm, chapter 8). High modernist subjectivity seems furthermore to privilege the cognitive and moral over the aesthetic and the libidinal, the ego over the id, the visual over touch, and discursive over figural communication. It gives primacy to culture over nature, to the individual over the community. As an ethics of responsibility, high modernist personality and *Lebensführung* it allows the individual to be somehow 'closed', instead of open; to be somehow obsessed with self-mastery and self-domination.

In the face of this, the writers in this book point to a whole range of what might be again called 'low modernist' alternatives. Dieter Hoffmann-Axthelm (chapter 8), for instance, optimistically sees a reassertion of perception against the previous modernist colonization of perception by our logical faculties. Martin Jay points to an alternative baroque regime of modernity, a tactile and allegorical alternative to the visual and cognitivist assumptions of quattrocento perspective (chapter 7). Mike Featherstone (chapter 11) in his account of the aestheticization of everyday life suggests that the carnivalesque itself has in a recast form provided a template for the modern unconscious, which has recently begun to reassert itself against the high modernist civilizing process. Paul Rabinow (chapter 10) in his panorama of a Brazil whose modernization and modernity is propelling it forward at breakneck speed proffers – in contradistinction to the closed nature of high modernist identity – a wide open, fully Wild West notion of the modern individual, in which anything can happen and usually does. Rabinow suggests, against Weberian self-mastery, a self of Faustian self-infinitization. But Rabinow's (and the Berman low modernist) vision is *not* postmodernist. It comprises a forward self-propulsion that is unacceptable to directionless postmoderns. It speaks not of 'dead signifiers' but of aesthetically energized forms of sociality.

Fourteen chapters were prepared for this book. The authors are many of the leading figures in the modernity/postmodernity debates. About half of these analysts are conventionally seen as moderns, about half as postmoderns. Yet almost every one of these writers, when asked to write about modernity and identity, has proffered, explicitly or implicitly, notions that in some important sense are *aesthetic*. Thus George Marcus (chapter 13) argues that ethnology should be about 'writing culture'. This means partly that the anthropologist should break with the model of scientific objectivity and him/herself write in a more experimental, aesthetic vein. It is also a question of enabling the Other (that is, the ethnologist's subjects) to partake in the writing. It is about taking ethnologists from their position in the Same and displacing them into the space of the Other.

But what about *post*modern identity? Here the outlook seems altogether more pessimistic. Sharon Zukin (chapter 9), for example, paints a bleak picture, more Baudrillard than Baudelaire. For Zukin, postmodern landscapes, whether in older cities such as New York, London or Paris or in new cities like Miami, LA and Houston, function as mechanisms of social control. They effectively constitute identities to function in the reproduction of transnational postindustrial capital. These landscapes – her prime example Disney World – take on the status of signifiers, of sign-values functioning in the reproduction of capital. Responsibility for social control – and its definition and normalization of identities – has passed on such an account from the modern norms of Foucault's social to the postmodern simulacra in Baudrillard's astral empire of signs.

Jonathan Friedman (chapter 14) offers a different, though equally bleak, slant on postmodern identity. Drawing on psychoanalysis and the cultural psychology of personhood, Friedman argues that both pre- and postmodern forms of identity are equally founded upon a primary narcissism. He unpacks the notion of narcissism and radically periodizes it historically. Here modern identity formation and the modern ego stem from the internalization of the Lacanian mirror stage, in which the mother's (Other's) identification of the child is internalized and transformed into a process of self-identification. In 'pre-modern' societies, holistic cosmologies and symbolic networks take the place of the Other that the 'father' occupies in modernity. And the mirror identification process is never internalized. Hence pre-moderns are dependent on the external world for identification. They are in formal terms narcissistic, if secondarily embedded in a meaningful universe. Postmodern conditions of identity are similar. The mirror stage is only weakly internalized and once again we are narcissistically dependent on the Other in order to become ourselves. Only this Other comprises the commodities and sign-values of consumer capitalism. Now the 'mirror' is not only externalized, it is fractured as well, and the narcissism is 'clinical'.

But there are alternative, more optimistic renderings of postmodern identity. Mike Featherstone in *Lifestyle, Postmodernism and Consumer Culture* (1991) provides the counterpart to Weber's self-mastered, modern *Lebensführung*, and points to a temporal fragmentation of the postmodern life-course, which though it can be anxiety-provoking, can also open up important possibilities for life-style innovation. Doug Kellner in chapter 6 shows that the quintessentially postmodern TV series *Miami Vice* offers a number of positive and politically progressive subject positions for viewers to identify with. Kellner observes that identity formation is displaced from the sphere of production to consumption and leisure in the transition to postmodernism. But he sees such identity formation as a chance for not less but greater intensity of reflexivity. Modernism called for reflexivity in the sense of balancing a plurality of role demands. Postmodernism is on the other hand much more aware of identity choice. Individuals can consciously experiment with identity. They can make identity choices entailing far greater risk than under modernism. Being a lesbian, being a single parent, running through a series of marriages, going off to live in an ecological commune outside of Rio were choices that one was much less able to make under modernism. And these choices entail great identity risks. Postmodern innovation of identity can, Kellner realizes, be akin to game-playing. But the risks involved can be dead serious.

All this said, the book divides into four parts: Cosmopolitan narratives; Representation and the transformation of identity; Spaces of self and society; and Modernity and the voice of the Other.

PART I: COSMOPOLITAN NARRATIVES

A number of theorists have in recent years attempted to work towards a sort of 'third way' between the blueprint-like abstraction of high modernism and the extremes of postmodern irrationalist anti-ethics. This has been the case in both German and French social theory. Thus probably the most influential book in German sociology in the 1980s was Ulrich Beck's (1986) *Risikogesellschaft* (Risk Society), which is subtitled *Auf dem Weg in eine andere Moderne* (Towards Another Modernity). Beck speaks of a 'paradox of modernization'. For him, like Habermas, modernization is a learning process (*Lernprozess*); hence it should be increasingly possible to achieve meaningful social change. The paradox, however, lies in that modernization also is a process of individualization. Hence we are unable to organize collectively to bring about this social change.

Klaus Eder (1988), also writing in the Habermasian tradition, in his *Vergesellschaftung der Natur* (Societalization of Nature) effectively picks up this thread. In as much as the new social movements which would bring about such social change tend to organize on a localist and decentralized basis, any new ethics would have to break with the abstraction of Habermasian communicative rationality and move towards a more particularist and localist basis. Habermas's notion, as is well known, favours the normative dimension over the cognitive and aesthetic and hence parallels Kant's second critique, of *Practical Reason*. Eder suggests that we must move towards the third critique, the *Critique of Judgement* (that is, through a Kantian aesthetics) in order to form a new, particularist ethics.

On the other side of the Rhine a similar development has been taking place. In Lyotard's *Différend*, again, the search has been for a localist ethics, and again the method – Lyotard had already been using Kant's beautiful/sublime distinction for his own aesthetics – was to be via Kant's third critique. Also from the French postmodernist camp, the sociologist Michel Maffesoli, influenced by Simmel and Henri Lefebvre, conjured up such localist forms of collective organization in his evocations of 'neo-tribalism' in *Les Temps des tribus* (1988). Maffesoli as well has come to stress the ethical underpinnings of these collectivities, and the aesthetic dimension of such ethics features again in his *Ethique esthétique* (1989).

The point is that of Kant's three forms of judgement, two – the cognitive and ethical – presume the subsumption of a particular by a universal. The third, aesthetic judgement presupposes the subsumption of a particular by a particular, but with reference to a universal. How a particular can subsume a particular is a problematic issue. It does, however, make sense to think in terms of *more or less highly mediated* universals, each of which can subsume particular entities or events. In Kant, for example, the categories of perception, time and space, are quite minimally mediated universals. The logical categories of the understanding are much more highly mediated. And the ideas of reason are the most highly mediated of all.

To think productively about these unmediated universals, as some of these analysts have noted, is to think anthropologically. Pierre Bourdieu's *Distinction* (1979) is appropriately subtitled – in contrast to the title *Critique du jugement* of Kant's aesthetic critique – *Critique sociale du jugement*. Bourdieu's distinction leads us in a direction charted by Durkheim and Mauss's *Primitive Classifications* (1913).

The primitive classifications are the least mediated universals. That is, when things, animals and people (for example, ancestors) are central enough to the everyday practices of a collectivity, they take on ritual and symbolic status. They take on nominating and classificatory powers; they become the unmediated universals. As such they constitute identity and give shape to the ethics of localist collectivities.

This sort of particularist ethics can at the same time be quite rational. It can potentially solve Beck's paradox of rationalization on the one hand and individuation on the other. That is, implicit in this new communitarian ethic is the claim that we have become *so* rational that we can overcome the problem of individuation. We have become *so* rational that we can understand the cultural conditions of formation of the sort of new communities that can then organize effectively for social change. We have become *so* rational that we can reflexively help shape these sorts of particularist and localist ethics. Increased rationality would thus become the basis of such a 'post-traditional Gemeinschaft'.

Intellectually intriguing. Politically promising. But does this sort of ethical–aesthetic localism, however rational, go far *enough* in the direction of rationality? Of universality? For the analysts – Marshall Berman, Richard Rorty, Christa and Peter Bürger – in Part I of this book the answer would seem to be rather emphatically in the negative.

In *All that Is Solid Melts into Air* Marshall Berman (1982) had already distanced himself, not just from the abstract universalism of Corbusier and the *tabula rasa* of the new town planners, but also from the localism of the urban village and exclusively immediate neighbourhood-orientated urbanism of Jane Jacobs. To be sure, Berman wanted to start from a localism of 'place' – whence his impassioned *j'accuse* against the carving up of his native Bronx to build freeways. But then starting from this very anti-temporal situatedness of spatiality, Berman *opens up and opens out space in the direction of the universal*. Such is his treatment of St Petersburg and especially of Baudelaire's Paris. This is the space of the local, of the tribalisms, which is then opened out onto the boulevards of the *flâneur*. In contrast to the Cartesian assumptions of high modernism, Berman's modernity moves from the ground up.

But Berman's vision is modern, and not the space of pre- or post-modern tribalism. This is true in two senses. First, as just noted, it moves in the direction of the universal, metaphorically from the Bronx to the avenues of the Upper West Side. From the Faubourg St Antoine to the boulevards. But second it has a very strong *temporal* element. Numerous commentators have spoken of the construction of boulevards in the major European cities as the destruction of space by time. That is, with modernization, space becomes a locus through which to get from A to B, rather than a place to live in. The street here is displaced from life-world to system. Whether for work or latterly in leisure, space becomes instrumental or a means rather than an end. This has opened up quite a debate recently in urban studies. Analysts such as Ed Soja and Fredric Jameson have on the one hand argued that postmodernity is the reassertion of space against time. On the other hand, writers such as David Harvey and Sharon Zukin (see chapter 9) view the postmodern only as an intensified replay of modernism's conquest of space by time.

Now whatever separates these analysts, there seems to be normative agreement that the conquest of space by time is a bad thing. Here is where Berman is different. He views temporality *positively*. It is integral to his view of modernity and indeed is the title of his benchmark book, *All that Is Solid . . .* But Berman's is another sort of temporality. Berman's time is not the abstract, homogeneous time of E. P. Thompson's 'work-discipline', nor that of Daniel Bell's railroad modernism in his *Cultural Contradictions* (1989), nor the overloaded airpaths and PC networks of David Harvey's *Condition of Postmodernity* (1989). Berman's time is somehow substance. It could also be the time of the winding medieval street. It is the self-constructed time of the *flâneur* whose only stake is to *se balader* through Parisian streets. It can be construed as *subjective* duration.

And the *flâneur's* temporality and the Bergsonian view are not so far apart. Berman's time is not homogeneous but *irregular* and *unpredictible*, as part of what was solid and melted into air includes abstract regular temporality. Berman's time is thus clearly not the abstract homogeneous time of system but is a temporality of the life-world. It is reminiscent of Henri Lefebvre's aestheticization of everyday life and his notion of spatialization.

In chapter 1 of this book Berman extends these views in arguing 'why modernism still matters'. Here, in a lengthy discussion of contemporary high and popular culture, the temporal sense is further reinforced. Berman argues against the 'no future' attitude of the postmodernists, whose proclamation by punk and by Baudrillard was foreshadowed already in New York in the early 1960s in the music of the East Village rock group The Fugs. Though these figures are either on the left or apolitical, Berman argues that, historically, the escape from freedom, from self-responsibility in the flow of temporality, was a motivation for fascism. But he fortunately sees much of just the opposite happening in the culture of the end of the twentieth century, in which important forces may be opening up with a pronounced historical consciousness and responsibility. Thus straight out of what is conventionally viewed as postmodernism there is a substantial thrust of the modern: in Anselm Kiefer's 'painting the Holocaust', in Salman Rushdie's 'throwing of himself into history'. This goes hand in hand with an intensification of universalism, of the positive side of globalization, instantiated in international cultural figures like Kiefer, Rushdie and Laurie Anderson. Against claims as to the 'fall of public man', Berman concludes that 'now is an exciting time to be alive'.

Richard Rorty has often been attacked as a postmodernist following his powerful arguments against foundationalism in *Philosophy and the Mirror of Nature* (1979). But in chapter 2, Rorty follows a tack very similar to Berman's in making the case for a nuanced form of modernity. Again the issues are time and universalism. And here Rorty like Berman wants to preserve these crucial elements of modernity without falling into the abstraction of the high modernists. Rorty takes this up in a pragmatist challenge to Lyotard's recent work. For Lyotard a '*différend* is a case in which the plaintiff is deprived of the means of arguing'. For Lyotard, history – and Auschwitz is the case he always comes back to – is a sequence of *différends*, a succession of such experiences by 'silent', or better silenced minorities.

The positive side of this – and here *Le Différend*, as noted by Christa Bürger in chapter 3, makes common cause with Lyotard's earlier writings such as *Instructions païennes* (1977) – is not critique but a set of 'minority affirmations' of 'la petite vie'. A politics not of metanarratives, but of 'little narratives', what Deleuze and Guattari in their book on Kafka (1972) have called a 'minor literature', of '1,000 little stories'. And *cultures* made up of stories which are assembled in series'. Bürger stresses how Lyotard – and the logic of postmodernism – is opposed to critical social theory. To critical social theory, postmodernism and Lyotard counterpose a theory of affirmation. Critical theory, for example, propounds that 'alienation' must be the subject of critique and dialectic sublation. Lyotard maintains to the contrary that we should not bemoan alienation, but 'affirm it'. This makes sense of Lyotard's politics of 'minority affirmations'. Such a politics could take the form of semiotic re- clamations by minorities such as, for example, today's reclamation – and symbolic reversal – of signifiers such as 'dike' by lesbian femin- ists and 'nigger' by rap musicians.

As promising as is such a semiotic politics, there are enormous problems with Lyotard's views. Minority affirmations still leave the Jews without an attorney at Auschwitz, and American and English blacks still live in a white man's society. But litigation – and hence a fair trial, not to mention juridical equality – is not possible on Lyotard's account, because of the radical separateness, the in- commensurability between his forms of life and language. In *Le Différend* Lyotard time and again stresses the radical incommensur- ability of 'phrase regimes' and 'discourse genres'. What this means is that communication, hence litigation, is impossible across space or between language communities. Richard Rorty in chapter 2, dissa- tisfied with such a state of affairs, makes the case for a limited universalism in his argument that certain levels of translatability do exist between speech communities. Drawing on his own pragmatist tradition in philosophy, he argues that only thus can we 'convert *différends* into processes of litigation'. Lyotard's assumptions of incompatibility between phrase regimes and discourse genres reduces speech or *parole* itself to a disconnected series of linguistic 'events'. Hence the temporal element of *parole* is for him nullified. Pragmat- ism, in the tradition of Peirce, Dewey and James, has always coun- terposed – as C. Wright Mills noted in his Ph.D. dissertation on pragmatism and Marxism – an 'ought', however circumscribed, to the 'is'. Hence pragmatism has always implied a built-in temporality. In such a vein Rorty proposes, in counterposition to the high mod- ernist 'narratives of emancipation', a set of 'narratives of increasing cosmopolitanism'.

Christa Bürger's critique of Lyotard takes a different tack. She, in accord with Rorty against Lyotard's implicit neo-tribalism, argues that the French philosopher's project is not in any significant sense postmodernist, but rather *hyper*modernist. She draws a parallel between Lyotard and Marinetti and the futurists. Both futurists and Lyotard proposed, in the place of historical memory, a philosophy of forgetting. Futurists, Lyotard and the 1980s postmodern trans-avantgarde have proposed – unlike, say, expressionists and neo-expressionists – a semiotics of non-meaning. Both futurists and Lyotard (think, for example, of the latter's *Immatériaux* installation at Beaubourg) proffer an uncritical, virtual worship of technology. Both use machine metaphors for human beings. Implicit hyper-modernism is also registered in a statement in *Le Différend* that postmodernism is just the extension of the self-reflexive content of modernist painting to the whole of social life.

Peter Bürger in his coda to chapter 3 and in chapter 4 also searches for an alternative to high modernism and Lyotard's hypermodern-ism. This he attempts to find in the notion of 'allegory', which was central to the argument in his *Theory of the Avant-Garde*, Manchester (1984). For Bürger the avant-gardes of the 1920s (Dada, surrealist, *neue Sachlichkeit*) were important in transgressing high modernism and its associated 'institutions of art'. And allegory or its equivalent was the key to these avant-gardes, and especially to surrealism.

Bürger's claim here is radical. It is effectively that high modernism (of, say, Mondrian or Pollock) is only an extension of the principles of early nineteenth-century idealist aesthetics. For Bürger idealist aesthetics is 'at the core of art as an institution'. What this means is that only with idealist aesthetics does the aesthetic sphere become fully separate from the everyday life of the social. Only with the idealist and romantic views of creativity and the author is art fully 'auratic'.

To Bürger, thus, idealist art would exemplify Theodor Adorno's 'identity-thinking' in its unity of form and content, of the particular and the universal, of sensibility and spirit, sensibility and meaning. It is quite clear that this was the crux of idealist aesthetics for, say, Hegel and Goethe. Hans-Georg Gadamer has written at length about this. Gadamer has noted that Hegel's aesthetic is based on a three-stage periodization of archaic (Greek), classical and modern; and that the opposition between sensibility and meaning has only been dialectically resolved in the last of these. In an article on the baroque Gadamer contrasts Goethe's idealist endorsement of 'symbol' as against his castigation of baroque 'allegory'. In idealist aesthetics, symbol was defined by the unity of sensibility and meaning.

And the problem with allegory was that sensibility or form slipped out from under meaning and appeared on stage all by itself.

Bürger propounds that a similar sort of identity-thinking also is present in modernist art. This is confusing at first glance because modernism seems to designate only self-referentiality: for example, truth to the aesthetic materials and flatness of the picture surface. Bürger would not deny this, but he argues that such a form–content unity is present, not on the level of reference to reality, but on a second, deeper level of meaning. Thus Brechtian theatre would latch onto a deeper set of social contradictions. It is also true that non-representational artists as diverse as Klee, Kandinsky, the *Blaue Reiter* painters and Picasso and Cézanne (not to mention the young Corbusier and other architects influenced by Owen Jones's philosophy of natural geometry) have all claimed a certain correspondence between their forms and another level of content, be it spiritual or, more commonly, natural (i.e. in nature). This unity of form and content, and art as a (separate) institution, are challenged by surrealist allegory, in which 'signs are no longer necessary', and in which form is not (or only tangentially is) motivated by content.

Bürger then speculates that if postmodernism (as an aesthetics of the unrepresentable) is just an intensification of high modernist aesthetics, then perhaps postmodernism itself fits quite well the mould of the institutions of art. He considers further that postmodernism is perhaps a mere interpretation of art works by critics active in the art institution. In this light he considers in chapter 4 the work of three putatively postmodern authors, Michel Tournier, Botho Strauss and Peter Handke. His conclusion is that these authors are truly post-modern in that their work achieves a rather full meaninglessness. Here Bürger seems to be suggesting a sort of hierarchical continuum of high modernism, allegory and postmodernism in terms of descending meaningfulness. Thus a modernist like Beckett, as Adorno claimed, did designate a second level of meaning, in the sense that his work was a 'cipher of his age'. Kafka's work would come under allegory in that it contained some reference to reality. But this is not the case for Tournier, Strauss and Handke. Tournier presents what looks like a traditional realist unity of form and content, while in the end the content fully escapes from the form and is rather fully indeterminate. Strauss exemplifies a creative mixture of genres, yet ultimately his allegory refers only to writing itself, while Handke, like the clinical schizophrenic, sees meaning everywhere. Yet this meaning leads nowhere and life, finally, appears as an endless chain of signifiers.

PART II: REPRESENTATION AND THE TRANSFORMATION
OF IDENTITY

While the first Part of this book deals largely with philosophical
issues, the second deals with the problem of representation.

The first two essays in the section, chapters 5 and 6 by Abercrombie et al. and by Kellner, are discussions of popular culture. In
chapter 5 Nicholas Abercrombie and his colleagues argue, against the
grain, that the problem particularly in need of explanation today is
not so much social change as stasis and continuity. They argue –
drawing on a wide range of popular culture sources, from cinema to
TV to pop music – that realism, the heir of timeworn quattrocento
perspective and the nineteenth-century novel is, despite all the hubbub over modernism and postmodernism, still the predominant form
in popular culture. They also claim continuity in their outline, of a
sociological periodization of culture forms, largely based in the work
of Raymond Williams. The operative model here is effectively of a
sort of *trans*modernity which comprises epochs of realism, modernism and postmodernism. The connecting thread among the three
is realism itself as an aesthetic *discourse*. That is, not just realist,
but also modernist and postmodernist art are grounded in realist
legitimations. Hence aesthetic discourse legitimates the value of
the stream of consciousness in Joyce's (modernist) *Ulysses* as well
as the value of (postmodern) punk music by arguing that both
these are very much like the real world. This was not the case before
modernity, in that aesthetic reference was much more commonly
other-worldly.

Douglas Kellner, discussed above, takes a more positive view of
the creative possibilities of postmodern identity. In chapter 6 he
discusses at some length the TV police series *Miami Vice* and Marlboro and Virginia Slims advertisements. Detectives Crockett and
Tubbs in *Miami Vice*, are seen as distinctive and very contemporary
in their apparently gleeful assumption of multiple identities. Kellner
thus contrasts modern and postmodern identity. That is, the multiplication of identity-tasks that led to anxiety and the experience of
alienation in the modern individual, is *affirmed* by the postmodern
self. Yet a set of caveats must be entered here. Crockett and Tubbs,
as well as the villains in *Miami Vice*, think of themselves and speak
of themselves as 'players'. In the series roles are theatrically constituted and played. Identities are disposed of at lightning speed. This
is surely a far cry from the seriousness of Nietzschean views of

affirmation of the self. Are we then really innovating in this post-modern identity construction? Or are we instead involved in a risk-less process in which no sort of substantial meaning is at stake?

In chapter 7 Martin Jay argues that modern culture is distinctively 'scopic'. He claims thus that, grounded in quattrocento perspective and the Cartesian *cogito*, a *visual* model is paradigmatic in modernity. Pre-modern culture, notes Jay, following Norman Bryson, was largely aural. Painting largely told a story to the unlettered masses – and was thus 'discursive', while the autonomy of the image in painting beginning from the Renaissance was correspondingly 'figural'. Note that the use of 'discourse' and 'figure' here, while based on Lyotard's *Discours, figure* (1971), is arguably rather divergent from Lyotard's notions. Jay suggests that postmodern culture is likely to be increasingly tactile in nature. In Lyotard, however (see Featherstone, chapter 11), the discursive would have a lot in common with the cognitivist (for Lyotard the secondary processes of the conscious mind) assumptions of Jay's scopic regime of modernity. By contrast the figural in Lyotard has to do with images in the unconscious mind, and thus for Featherstone and others it would provide a model for the image and spectacle like nature of postmodernism.

In medieval painting, light was conceived as 'divine *Lux* rather than perceived *Lumen*'. In the modern regime light was displaced from the religious objects in the picture onto the spatial relations of the canvas. Space became 'geometrically isotropic, rectilinear, abstract and uniform'. The Renaissance pictorial aesthetic presupposed 'the coldness of the perspectival gaze' and its characteristic absence of emotion and desire, whence the deficit in erotic energy from its nudes. Jay's modern scopic regime is also Cartesian, in that the 'intellect inspects entities modelled on retinal images'; it is thus 'representations which are in the mind'. On Cartesian and quattrocento accounts 'the eye' is effectively outside of time and space. All of which deviated vastly, as Foucault noted in *The Order of Things* (1970), from pre-moderns 'reading the world hermeneutically as a divine text'.

Jay also speaks of two other regimes of modernity, which are progressively less scopic and more tactile in character. The first of these is seventeenth-century Dutch painting which, as Svetlana Alpers has written, lacked the Renaissance's totalizing effect and presupposition of a clearly situated viewer. The deductivist paradigm of the Renaissance can be contrasted with the 'Baconian empiricism' of this Northern art with its very descriptive nature working towards a flatness of the picture surface. Jay's third modern regime is instantiated in baroque art, which deviates even more from the high modernist scopic assumptions, only this time in the direction of allegory. Drawing on the work of Christine Buci-Glucksmann, Jay concludes that baroque art is opaque, non-linear and throws up a 'hermeneutic challenge to the scopic regimes', daring the observer to 'read the texture of the Other'.

In chapter 8 Dieter Hoffmann-Axthelm, philosopher of perception and urbanist, addresses modernity in the context of change in the definition both of identity and reality. Hoffmann-Axthelm analyses identity through the metaphoric prism of the passport. The passport, he notes, combines two forms of (external) construction of identity. One of these, the measure of assigning names, is archaic; the other, numbering and picturing, is modern. Identities have always been defined for individuals externally – for example, in medieval times titles and heraldry symbolized the name. Subsequently the absolutist state took upon itself these functions of nomination, first through passports where the only proofs of one's self were the signature and fingerprints. Only later came the shift to photos and especially to numbering. It is only with modernization that an opposing process of self-identification arises. The market, as variously Adorno and Sohn-Rethel observed, served as condition for 'the subjective emancipation of the identity project'. Markets, as Polanyi wrote, are socially embedded, yet they give rise to forms of sociation (including 'carnival'; see chapter 9) that are increasingly cosmopolitan in nature and call for new powers of choice, risk-taking, responsibility and reflexivity.

Hoffman-Axthelm understands this dialectic of external determination and self-nomination of identity via the figure of the 'philosophical immigration officer'. Thus the 'philosophic concept of identity in each historical era is an attempt to mediate between a visible societal identity in the face of which individuals are nothing and a dispersed individuality that is free of coercion, clarity, entirety – but also void of the necessity of selfhood'. In this context philosophers such as Parmenides saw human identity as the predication of a deity. Aquinas claimed that 'being could not be attributed to the human individual as essence . . . but only as an externally assigned name'. Baudelaire and Nietzsche for their part celebrated the 'impossibility of self-fixing of identity'.

Received notions of 'the real' and 'reality' are important in this changing definition of identity. Here Hoffman-Axthelm stakes out claims conflicting with Martin Jay's position. Whereas Jay argued that in modernity a visual paradigm establishes hegemony over culture and hence cognition, Hoffman-Axthelm argues instead that a particular 'scriptural' model appropriates *vision* and perception more generally. Hoffmann-Axthelm observes that with the development of print-culture, vision becomes subordinate to cognition; the eye is now primarily used in such functions as investigating documents and accounts. Hearing also becomes reconstituted on a scriptural basis, and sensuality in general becomes dependent on script and legibility. Importantly, the ego's very self-identification project begins – through its reflexivity – to destroy the perceptual world. Cognition's hegemony is simultaneously, for Habermas and for Kant, the hegemony of instrumental rationality and the principle of labour; as labour power and its reproduction become dominant in modern identity-formation.

The several crises of modernity have thoroughly confounded this sort of identity formation. The shift from producer to consumer capitalism has meant its disruption, which on the negative side has brought the transience of new styles, the introduction of a new 'flattening' temporality and a reduction of the self to the mere politics of presentation. More positively, however, this at the same time signals a shift to a notion of the real in which a sensualist paradigm begins to replace the intellectualist one. Here communication itself operates through immediate perception. In an increasingly computerized work life, for example, the turnover of symbols is simply too fast for reflexive cognition. Thought becomes perceptual and 'the glance' replaces 'the gaze'. What all of this finally means for better or for worse – and Hoffmann-Axthelm is writing in Berlin in winter 1989–90 – is 'the end of the philosophical immigration officer'.

PART III: SPACES OF SELF AND SOCIETY

Sharon Zukin's understanding of postmodern culture also foregrounds the perceptual. Her analyses in chapter 9 work from the counterposition of two canonical types of the built environment, on the one hand 'landscape' and on the other 'vernacular'. 'Landscapes' here are always constituted by asymmetrical power. 'Vernacular' is the built environment of the powerless. Landscape somehow always forms around 'institutions' such as markets. Vernacular is more immediate and entails a sense of 'place'. Landscape is public and *gesellschaftlich*. Vernacular space is private space.

Through modernization and concomitant processes of zoning, landscape and vernacular undergo a process of differentiation from one another. But with postmodernization, and the reassertion of what Venturi called 'complexity' in the built environment, landscape and vernacular begin effectively to de-differentiate. Zukin recognizes two main types of such postmodernization in the built environment – one in older cities, of gentrification, the heritage movement, the conversion of docklands, of city-centre factories into lofts and the like. In these locations the 'remaining vernacular becomes landscape and is invested with cultural power'. The other is in newer cities such as Houston, Miami, Los Angeles and their ex-urban areas like Orange County and Orlando, where postmodernization takes place signally in theme parks and shopping malls. In such places, vernacular – like the recurrent Main Street motif – is 'lifted from its own historic time and space', and again 'incorporated into landscape and invested with cultural power'.

Who will win the battle between landscape and vernacular is not at issue for Zukin. Their implosion proceeds invariably under the sign of landscape. In both old cities and new cities, institutions consistently erode locality and 'market' consistently outdoes 'place'. Cultural postmodernization in the built environment comes about through the victory over 'place' of a very specific type of market. This is the triumph of postindustrial capital, which is simultaneously (1) international – hence the traffic in goods, tourists, gentrifiers and unskilled foreign workers; (2) dominated by finance – hence the importance of money flows and the 1980s postmodern architecture of the new finance centres; and (3) consumer capital – hence the centrality of shopping malls, theme parks and the like.

This de-differentiation, this new complexity of the built environment creates a set of new 'liminal spaces'. Liminality on Zukin's account is a 'transitional space', 'between individual introspection and the products of commercialized collective fantasy'. This is a comparatively unstructured space that in various combinations mixes, or more appropriately in the language of the record industry 're-mixes' private (vernacular) and public (landscape) space. Liminality is often a question of symbolic inversion of identities. In the old cities an 'inversion of socio-spatial identities by cultural categories' and in the new ones 'the transformation of cultural categories by socio-spatial appropriation'. Note the fundamentally dystopic, even Kafka-esque, cast of Zukin's take on liminality. This has nothing to do with Bakhtinian 'carnival' and little to do with spatialization à la Henri Lefebvre. In each case local distinctions are eroded and individuals are 'detached from place'. For Zukin we can never recover the experience of the carnivalesque (see chapters 10, 11 and 12 of this book) which begins from place and opens out in a cosmopolitan spatialization. Today it is only possible to *simulate* place. Liminality itself would then just be simulated and illusive, with social control the reality, as locality is eroded 'through capital's imposition of multiple perspectives'.

To use Pierre Bourdieu's categories in such a context, there would seem to be two modes of circulation of symbolic goods: one in which the goods, such as TV broadcasts, records, videos, magazines circulate among viewers; and the second, that of the built environment, in which the viewers circulate among the symbolic goods. In the circulation of the first type of ordinary symbolic goods, capital, rather straightforwardly, metes out symbolic violence in the social field. And this capitalist symbolic power operates via the specialist cultural fields in which symbolic goods (such as records, magazines, etc.) are produced. But the symbolic violence meted out through the built environment is doubly insidious, because doubly unannounced: first because the built environment appears as 'natural', 'material' and 'functional' to the viewer in a way that other symbolic goods do not; and secondly because previously landscapes effectuated their symbolic social control directly in their role as landscapes. Now they do so in the mask of vernacular.

Further, the balance of roles between the economic- and cultural-capital fractions of the dominant class are vastly different in old and new postmodern landscapes. In the old cities the cultural-capital fraction plays a leading role. That is, artists, designers, students, musicians and the like first impose landscape on what had been the vernacular of say SoHo, London's East End, Islington, Paris-Malakoff or Berlin-Kreuzberg. These urban scenes are landscape and not vernacular in the sense that their culturati inhabitants are so to speak 'distantiated' from the built environment. That is, they do not relate to it with the immediacy of place. Subsequently people from other cultural fields come into the area and start to set up galleries, alternative restaurants and theatres, clothes shops and the like, and in effect establish a sort of 'liminal scene'. At this point it is as if what had been the vernacular of the 'social field' were literally imploded into a sort of general cultural field. The cultural field which operates only on a spatial *metaphor* in Bourdieu's theory becomes here *literally* a field of *concrete* urban space. But it is still not yet a field of capital class power. It is only later with full-scale gentrification and the conquest of this space by the urban development corporations that hegemony is displaced onto the (international) economic-capital fraction of the dominant class.

In the new cities, however, the economic-capital fraction is in the driving seat from the start. Culture and public space – and Zukin quotes Rayner Banham on LA – is already a 'commercial fantasy of restaurants and drive-ins'. Disney World (i.e. Walt Disney's World, Orlando, Florida) and the shopping malls may exercise their power through symbolic goods, but these symbolic goods are not those of the specialist cultural fields; they are already part of the *social* field as commercialized, popular culture. This is Robert Venturi's (as opposed to, say, Aldo Rossi's) postmodernism. This is why, as Zukin notes, the consumption of the (high) cultural goods in the old city landscapes takes a 'didactic' form, whereas that of the popular culture goods in the new ones and ex-urban areas takes the form of 'entertainment'.

Zukin's always thought-provoking analysis is, as we mentioned, in the tradition of David Harvey. Thus postmodernization is fully the conquest of space by time. Postmodernization is, thus, hyper-modernization. Christa Bürger argued in chapter 3 that this was the direction of Lyotard's work. It is surely also the direction of Baudrillard's. For Lyotard and Baudrillard, unlike those following the Lefebvrian tradition, the postmodern takes place through de-differentiation, but *not* in the direction of the particular, the local, community or nature. Instead implosion is into a further realm of abstraction, a process that had already, for some, gone too far with *modern*ization. Thus Baudrillard implodes an already abstract social into the more abstract semio-scape. For him exchange-value, already a simulacrum in the modern, is imploded into sign-value, a second-order simulacrum in the postmodern. The same is true of Deleuze and Guattari, for whom the modern de-territorialization of Oedipus identity does not go far enough. For them only a fully abstract anything goes, complete de-territorialization of postmodern libidinal flows must be the answer. The only difference is that what Harvey and Zukin see as dystopic, Baudrillard and Deleuze celebrate.

In chapter 10 Paul Rabinow indeed does celebrate the vibrant modernity of Brazil. Rabinow reminds us of how modern Brazil really is: not fully of the Third World, with the globe's eighth-highest gross national product; and more like California than Morocco, India or Europe – as a country without a past. Margaret Thatcher proclaimed in the 1980s that there was no alternative to the type of modernization she and President Reagan were proffering. Brazil is a bit the Thatcherite dream let fully loose, in which deregulation extends to a breakdown of legality itself. More like *Robocop* (and its privatized police force) than English everyday life, Rabinow's Brazil features private police, private systems of blood donation, private guards outside suburban houses. And if the rent-a-cops are pervasive, the robbers are ubiquitous, as gangs on beaches mug tourists, gangs on bridges waylay cars. Near Salvador, Rabinow visits a squatter town, self-planned as it were, without electricity and running water. Fully high modernist planners and architects laid down the main lines of Rio and especially the overly modern, efficient, planned and zoned Brasilia. But the Cartesian framework has been helpless against the innovation and thrust of Brazilian modernity with its anarchic and privatized public life.

Rabinow's figural evocation of Brazilian modernism in the streets is recast theoretically and discursively by Mike Featherstone in chapter 11. Featherstone enumerates three types of 'aestheticization of everyday life'. In the first, modelled on the 1920s avant-gardes, art becomes more like life. The second is the paradigm of Baudelaire's *flâneur*, in which life becomes like art. And the third carries the imploding images of Baudelaire's semio-scape. Featherstone's focus is very much on the second of these, around which, drawing on the signal work of Stallybrass and White, he constructs a notion of the 'carnivalesque'. At issue here is not the simulated liminality of *Miami Vice* and perhaps Miami Beach, but what, evoking Bakhtin, Stallybrass and White have called 'liminoid symbolic repertoires'.

This, like Marshall Berman's 'low modernism', is a spatialized rather than a temporal (or simulated) liminality in the sense that carnival starts from the situs of 'place' (that is, in local markets and local fairs) and opens up into the cosmopolitan, with the admission of travellers from outside, of gypsies, of exotic people. The carnivalesque breaks down the structured rule-boundedness of locality as space is flooded with strange signs. Symbolic inversions are the rule, as the signifier of the 'grotesque body' is reclaimed as against that of the 'classical body'. From the standpoint of space liminality might be conceived as 'anti-structure'. But from the viewpoint of agency it is also a time/space of choice, of aesthetic-expressive reflexivity, in which agents previously structured by tradition are now free to choose from 'symbolic repertoires', free to try on masks, to try on identities.

Featherstone suggests a genealogy of the carnivalesque, extending from fifteenth-century popular culture and forking out in several directions – into literature and theatre, as observed by Richard Sennett in *The Fall of Public Man* (1976); in the direction of the world's fairs; and perhaps quintessentially in the direction of the *flâneur*, the arcades and nineteenth-century Paris Bohemia. This lineage extends to the contemporary thrust of cultural-capital Bohemians into today's vernacular areas of living space. It encompasses arguably the general colonization of urban space by the various art, green and alternative *Szenen*. Running parallel and opposed to this, Featherstone notes, is a sort of civilizing process which regulates, rationalizes and opposes the inversions of the carnivalesque. The upshot of this might, he speculates, be the effective displacement of the carnivalesque and aestheticization, on the one hand through repression into the unconscious imagery of *libidinal drives* and on the other through 'sublimation' into the simulacra of Baudrillard's semio-scape.

PART IV: MODERNITY AND THE VOICE OF THE OTHER

This section addresses similar issues, only in a more anthropological vein. Peter Burke thus picks up in chapter 12 where Featherstone left off. Burke's carnivalesque, however, is recast as the Other of popular culture and popular identity. Burke considers two nearly parallel – though politically counterposed – historical rediscoveries of the popular. There was on the one hand the romantic rediscovery of folk culture, which was mobilized in the interest of creation of national identity and nationalism. Thus anthologies of folk-songs were published in country after country from the early nineteenth century. Folk interest was apparent too in the writers of the great national histories of this century. On this view, the peasant, as the least corrupted by foreign influence, was seen to incorporate best the virtues of the national collectivity. These romantic intellectuals posed as poetic bearers of *Kultur* against the ravages of positivist and rationalizing *Zivilisation*. But such *Kultur* – just as much as *Zivilisation* – was itself irretrievably modern and hence an integral part of the Self engaged in reflection on the popular culture and carnival of the Other.

In a parallel trend the heirs of the Enlightenment tended to understand 'the popular', not as nation, but in terms of Third Estate, of Saint-Simonian industrial classes, of the making of the working class.

Burke points to a perhaps partly wishful sixteenth-century past in which the bourgeois Self and popular Other were not separate; to a space of popular culture of songs, tales, and festivals that was open to all alike, in tavern and piazza, in which living spaces and central space were shared by elites and masses. Burke also counterposes Elias to Bakhtin as historically civilizing European elites gradually withdraw from the street festivals and carnival. This is reflected in the division of public houses in nineteenth-century England. The fall of bourgeois public man would have been bad enough, had he not then tried to impose his civilizing values on the masses. This is instantiated in the banning of football from the town centre of

Derby in 1840; or in the process in all the West's great cities of Haussmanization and working-class dispersion to the suburbs. The bourgeois imposition of the civilizing process on the proletarian, on *his* workman was a dominant moral element in what Antonio Gramsci called 'Fordism'. Once the Self had separated himself from and disciplined the Other, the ground was prepared for the former to appropriate the latter in knowledge, either poetically and philologically in romanticism and relativism or through classification and dissection as positivism and developmentalism.

George Marcus proposes an antidote to such cultural pessimism in his notion of 'writing culture'. 'Writing culture' and the whole literary turn set off by 'postmodern' anthropologists such as Marcus and James Clifford has in some quarters been written off as a Derridean indulgence in asocial and ahistorical textuality. In chapter 13, however, what Marcus is proposing is a good deal stronger than this. He is proposing to situate writing culture and the new ethnography itself in the context of a changing world system. Jonathan Friedman (see chapter 14) has written extensively about the effects on culture of such global de-centring. Marcus argues that the struggle between core and periphery, between dominant Self and Other is not a struggle over whether there is to be global integration, but over the terms of such global integration; and in particular over what, or who, is to define the identity of social groups.

In his view the relations between core and periphery are not just relations of struggle, but of negotiation and, with globalization, increasingly of *shared* categories. These changes, Marcus notes, have substantially altered the experience of ethnographer and subject, so that on both sides 'distinctive identities have been created from turbulence, fragments, intercultural reference and the localized intensification of global possibilities and associations'.

In the face of this real historical deconstruction and reconstruction of identities, the structural and structural-functional assumptions of mainstream anthropology are thrown radically into doubt. Prior to intensified globalization, the prevailing paradigm of objective observer, on the one side, and social object to be investigated, on the other, may have been valid. The structuralists may also have been correct in their method of tracing the dense symbolic web of their subjects' life-world back to an underlying and governing 'indigenous structure', and then of reinterpreting the whole of their discourses and practices on this basis. But with raised stakes in globality, the relationship of observer to subject, of *Gesellschaft* to *Gemeinschaft* is *empirically* deconstructed. Modernity, that is as change and process, is perhaps occurring faster in the Third World than in the old core. With these raised international stakes, static notions of key symbols and deep structures (*la langue*) – and their concomitant assumptions of totality – lose their purchase on everyday reality. *Langue* incessantly deconstructs and reconstructs itself, both symbolically and linguistically. *Parole* becomes increasingly reflexive regarding the (re)constitution of its own rules. The *langue/parole* distinction thus falls asunder in its empirical contradictions. *Ecriture* or 'writing culture' becomes, not Derridean fantasy, but *social fact*, endowed, that is, with potential political power.

The ethnographer's subject, then, is now faced with a whole set of competing and complementary sources – the locality, the economy, his or her national state, the global context, the media, popular culture, the ethnographer him/herself, the subject's own increasing self-reflexivity – which define his identity. The ethnographer too is subjected to a not dissimilar array of identificatory sources. In this context Marcus wants to encourage a truly 'dialogic' anthropology. This means that ethnographies are to come about through a dialogue between ethnographer and subject(s), in which change in the categories and mentalities of both sides are presumed. Ethnography on this account is in fact 'the juxtaposition of two identity predicaments' and ethnographers must realize the implications of their work for their own identity processes. Given this dialogic process, 'writing culture' becomes at the same time a more literary anthropology: The texts are the everyday life of the ethnographer's subjects; the give and take between ethnographer and subject; and the recognition of the ethnographer as another Other, figuring him/herself as another subject in his or her own written ethnography.

In chapter 14, the concluding essay, Jonathan Friedman develops in some depth his theses on the cultural logics of a disintegrating world system. The disintegration carries with it the breakdown of its characteristic ordered hierarchy of identities, as Other rejects the identifying project of self. Exactly what the cultural reaction to this will be depends on where one is situated in this metamorphosing globality. At the core, in which capital accumulation has turned fictitious as finance and services, in which the abstraction of industrialization and modernization have become radicalized in post-industrialization and postmodernization, the reaction is likely to be a search for 'roots', in a new communitarianism, in ecology movements, in ethnicity and new nationalisms. Semi-peripheral NICs (Newly Industrializing Countries), increasingly taking the manufacturing and industrializing baton from the core, are likely to be infused with *modern*izing ideologies such as neo-Confucianism (which Weber saw as abstract and rationalist) or the sort of Faustian ethos of modernity that Rabinow described in Brazil in chapter 10.

Friedman looks in detail at two examples. First he discusses the Hawaiian movement, which has constituted itself around roots and communitarian identity in response to the postindustrial pastiche of the islands' booming tourist industry. Secondly he examines the phenomenon of the Congolese *sapeur*. The *sapeurs* are lower-class Brazzaville males whose prestige depends on wearing Paris haute couture clothes which they obtain by scrimping and saving for their long-planned and dreamt-of trip to Paris. The contrast is enormous: on the one hand Hawaii, in which roots and Hawaiian ethnicity have been practically destroyed by massive modernization; on the other the Congo, where Western influence was integrated but did not destroy kinship-based cultural strategies. In Hawaii, the cultural movement rejects modernity and opts for the re-establishment of tradition. In Brazzaville there is an ostensible worship of all things modern and Western. The Hawaiian movement lives a precarious existence amidst a powerful regime that would turn its self-image into a tourist commodity. Its members may depend on tourist industry incomes and many are caught up in the *Miami Vice* existence that pervades the state. Their traditionalist strivings are initiated from well within the bounds of modernity. The Congolese *sapeurs'* heroic quest for the modern is quite the converse of that. Their haute couture designs are not at all inscribed in the Western cultural mode of meaningless rapid turnover, but in the cosmology and symbolic nexus of traditional Congolese cultural strategies.

This volume, unlike others that have dealt with modernity, contains significant contributions by anthropologists. But there is also a convergence in the chapters here in so far as they combine a distance to the problem of modernity with an interest in its cultural organization. The discussion, in other words, has become increasingly focused on the question of culture and identity in modern and postmodern contexts. It might be argued that the growing concern with culture is itself an indicator of the decline of modernity. No longer is progress and infrastructurally-led development a self-evident reality. The denaturalization of doxa naturally leads to its relativization. And relativization substantialized is culture. We are now engrossed in the specificity of capitalist reality, in its cultural properties, be they the constitution of perception, of residential space, of rationality or national identity. These phenomena are no longer what they are because they are modern, but require a new kind of understanding whose point of departure is their relativity.

Anthropology is situated at the interface of Western modernity and its peripheries and has traditionally participated in a significant way in the establishment of Western selfhood via its otherness; modern versus traditional, developed versus underdeveloped, civilized versus primitive. The decline of modernist identity in anthropology has most recently been characterized as the demise of 'ethnographic authority', the impossibility of a univocal representation of the Other, who, as Marcus says in this volume, has begun to vie with the ethnographer in an emergent arena of competitive identification. Now if this obviously entails problems of anthropological identity, it is part and parcel of a more general disintegration of Western modernism whose self-definition depended upon its central place in a world of pre-modernities. If the evolutionary identity of the West has declined, if the hierarchical model of occidental civilization can no longer be upheld, nor can the hierarchical model of rational opposed to pre-logical discourse nor ego as opposed to primary processes be maintained. Anthropology is positioned at the outer edge of these self-reinforcing identities, and in a general sense can be said to encompass them. This may account for the inordinate number of references to ethnography when scientific knowledge is opposed to traditional wisdom, or when modern linear thinking is opposed to primitive holism. Even the fascination with the psychologically 'primitive', with the wild man within, is registered in the strongest terms in the often misapprehended ethnographica of cannibalism, witchcraft, acts of dismemberment and magical power. From urban Indians to the pop violence of devil cults it is apparent that such considerations are not mere intellectual pastimes, but resonate to the depths of Western existence.

In one sense, classical anthropology, as a reflection upon the difference between us and them, is a displacement of our own selves, divided between the civilized and the primitive. As such, its vicissitudes are bound to echo throughout modern identity as a whole. In other words, it is not some special privileged capacity of anthropology that comes to the fore here, but its privileged position in the identity-space of Western capitalist civilization. Anthropologists have, for the most part, been notoriously uninterested in the problems raised by books such as these and by the interest bestowed upon them by other disciplines. On the contrary the interest, where recognized, may have sometimes contributed to a false sense of satisfaction in a subject that supposes itself to have a monopoly on the concept of culture. The euphoria induced by academic survival can have blinded anthropology to the source of its own popularity. On the other hand, the discipline does provide the kind of discourse that is eminently suitable to the current social situation. For once the relativization, and not merely the historicization, of modernity is established, it becomes possible to understand it as a cultural phenomenon. The anthropological focus on the construction of identity, on the production of culture, on the specifics of socialization and its resultant habitus and strategies (*pace* Bourdieu), provides ample baggage for understanding the fragments of a fragmenting world. But it is not merely the fragments, for a globally orientated anthropology has important contributions to make to an understanding of global cultural transformations, to globalizations and localizations, to modernizations and traditionalizations. It has direct access to emergent modernities in other parts of the world, in Canton, Tokyo, Hong Kong and Delhi, and even to the apparent postmodernity of Rio. It may enable us to probe more deeply into the structural phenomena that may have occurred several times in the past that we, without any sense of history, have impetuously dubbed modernity and postmodernity. It may enable us to grasp variations on these themes, such as a modernity without the hyper-individualism of the Occident, or a modernity based entirely on consumption of Western goods while entirely ignorant of production. In the end the concepts of modernity and postmodernity and their concomitants may well be dissolved in favour of more structurally neutral terms. Such terms might truly elucidate the family resemblance between, for example, the baroque and the postmodernist, and allow us to look further into the contextual regularities involved in their emergence. The ultimate historicization of these terms is essential in any attempt to grasp the contours of the present. Anthropology, as a global yet culturally informed perspective, further affords us the possibility of penetrating other and less familiar strategies of social reproduction in their articulation with world economic and political – as well as cultural – processes.

Powerful and vastly dissimilar social forces are interlocked with one another in the global arena. Anthropologists must become cognizant of such large-scale processes if they too are to reach an adequate understanding of what is happening. Anthropology, as a social science, has traditionally been weak at both extreme macro- and micro-levels.

Has anthropology something to contribute here or has it with self-satisfaction merely 'waddled in', as Geertz (1985) suggests. Here we might argue that while anthropology is indeed a gold mine for postmodernity, its advantages in this respect are also quite genuine. Cultural sociology, the new anthropological history, literary criticism, among other endeavors, owe a great deal to anthropology in general. And the convergence of interests represented here may be evidence of a trend toward a more unified social science, or human science, in some distant future, one that is truly holistic. There is no necessity for our schemes of intelligibility to slavishly imitate the fragmentation of social reality.

NOTE

1 It should be noted here that the libidinal component that invests such parameters with energy provides them with a dynamic force capable of engaging the subject. This has been underscored by several contributors to this book, and takes us beyond the Kantian framework into issues of relations between everyday life on the one hand and the constitution of the self on the other. Here the cognitive and the moral are implicated in strategies of power and desire, and the aesthetic is embedded in the kinaesthetic.

REFERENCES

Beck, Ulrich 1986: *Risikogesellschaft*. Frankfurt a.M.: Suhrkamp.

Bell, D. 1976: *The Cultural Contradictions of Capitalism*. London: Heinemann.

Berman, M. 1982: *All that Is Solid Melts into Air: The Experience of Modernity*. New York: Simon & Schuster; 1983: London: Verso; 1988 (2nd edn): Harmondsworth: Penguin.

Bourdieu, P. 1979: *La Distinction: critique sociale du jugement*. Paris: Minuit. 1984 (Eng. tr. R. Nice) London: Routledge and Kegan Paul as *Distinction*.

Bürger, P. 1984: *Theory of the Avant-garde*. Manchester: Manchester University Press.

Deleuze, G., and Guattari, F. 1972: *L'Anti-Oedipe: capitalism et schizophrenie*. Paris: Minuit. 1977 English tr. New York: Viking, as *Anti-Oedipus*.

Durkheim, E., and Mauss, M. 1913: *Primitive Classifications*. London: Cohen & West.

Eder, K. 1988: *Vergesellschaftung de Natur*. Frankfurt a.M.: Suhrkamp.

Featherstone, M. 1991: *Consumer Culture and Postmodernism* London: Sage.

Foucault, M. 1970: *The Order of Things*. New York: Pantheon.

Geertz, C. 1985: 'Waddling in', *Times Literary Supplement*, 7 June: 623–4.

Habermas, J. 1984: *Theory of Communicative Action*, vol. 1 Cambridge: Policy Press.

Harvey, D. 1989: *The Condition of Postmodernity*. New York: Blackwell.

Lyotard, J.-F. 1971: *Discours, figure*. Paris: Klincksieck.

Lyotard, J.-F. 1977: *Instructions païennes*. Paris: Galilée.

Lyotard, J.-F. 1983: *Le Différend*. Paris: Minuit 1988 English tr. Manchester: Manchester University Press, as *The Differends Phrases in Dispute*.

Maffesoli, M. 1988: *Les Temps des tribus*. Paris: Klincksieck.

Maffesoli, M. 1989: *Ethique esthétique*. Paris, Klincksieck.

Rorty, R. 1979: *Philosophy and the Mirror of Nature*. Princeton: Princeton University Press.

Sennett, R. 1976: *The Fall of Public Man*. New York: Knopf.

Part I

Cosmopolitan narratives

1

Why modernism still matters

Marshall Berman

In 1968, when the students at my alma mater, Columbia University, rebelled and occupied the campus, the critic Lionel Trilling, one of Columbia's distinguished professors, described their actions as 'modernism in the streets'. I believed then, and I still believe, that this phrase got to the heart of things: in the troubles of those days, which at once tore up the streets of our cities and gave them new life, modernism was alive and well. This was the modern movement I set out to explore and chart in the book that eventually became *All that Is Solid Melts into Air*. That book, first published in 1982, shows some of the ways in which modern society, although racked with pain and misery and riven with uncertainty, nevertheless enables men and women to become freer and more creative than men and women have ever been.

Modernists, as I portray them, are at once at home in this world and at odds with it. They celebrate and identify with the triumphs of modern science, art, technology, economics, politics: with all the activities that enable mankind to do what the Bible said only God could do: to 'make all things new'.[1] At the same time, however, they deplore modernization's betrayal of its own human promise. Modernists demand deeper and more radical renewals: modern men and women must become the subjects as well as the objects of modernization; they must learn to change the world that is changing them, and to make it their own. Modernists know this is possible: the fact that the world has changed so much is proof that it can change still more. They can, in a striking phrase of Hegel's, 'look the negative in the face and live with it' (Hegel 1910: 92–3).[2] The fact that 'all that is solid melts into air' is a source of strength and affirmation, not of despair.[3] If everything must go, then let it go: modern people have the power to create a better world than the world they have lost.

Most of my book is about the past. It pays special attention to Marx, Baudelaire and Dostoevsky, the great modernists of the generation of 1848. (Wagner belongs with them, but I lacked the musical vocabulary.) But my argument is pointed toward the present and the future. 'Going back can be a way to go forward,' I wrote; 'remembering the modernisms of the 19th century can help us gain the vision and courage to create the modernisms of the 21st' (Berman 1982/1988: 36). Thus I hoped to take social thought back to the future.

When I started work on *All that Is Solid Melts into Air*, early in the 1970s, it seemed to me that the project and the problems of modernism were in the foreground of American and European intellectual life. By the time the book came out, however, in the early 1980s, modernism wasn't even in the background. If people used the word at all, they spoke of it as something from another century – if not, indeed, from another planet. Meanwhile, there was an inexhaustible flow of critical discourse asserting that we live in the postmodern world.[4] Had I really been asleep for so long? Had the structures and dynamics of life, thought and art changed so much so fast?

In this essay, I will sharpen and deepen my paradigm of modernism. I will try to understand why many intelligent people have come to believe modernism is out of date, and to explain why they are wrong. My argument unfolds in three phases. First, I recapitulate some of the central themes of modernism, as they emerged in what is generally considered its classic age, from the 1840s to the aftermath of the First World War. (Here I will elaborate some themes that my book does not develop adequately.) Second, I suggest how the recent movements that call themselves postmodern only re-enact, rather than overcome, modernism's deepest troubles and impasses. Finally, I will discuss a number of ways in which modernism can still be creative in the present and the future.

MODERN HOPES AND FEARS

Many of the abiding modern themes are unveiled with great flair in the first part of the *Communist Manifesto*, which appeared at the beginning of 1848, at a moment when, all over Europe, revolutions were in the air. Marx saw the bourgeois as the first really revolutionary class, and 'the first to show what man's activity can bring about'. Their obsessive and insatiable activism, which they have enforced first on their own workers and then (with increasing effectiveness) on the whole world, 'has created more massive and more colossal productive forces than have all the preceding generations put together'. Marx offers a short list:

> Subjection of nature's forces to man, machinery, application of chemistry to industry and agriculture, steam navigation, railways, electric telegraphs, clearing of whole continents for cultivation, canalization of rivers, whole populations conjured out of the ground – what earlier century had even a presentiment that such productive powers slumbered in the womb of social labor? (*Marx and Engels 1848/1959: 12*)

A century later, we would be likely to add automobiles, electronics (including an amazing array of electronic forms of communication), nuclear energy, cybernetics and the computerization of everyday life, flight through the air and into outer space, genetics and biotechnology, great breakthroughs in public health that have more than doubled the average lifespan from Marx's time to our own, and much more. What makes all these changes distinctively modern is not the inventions themselves, but a process of incessant enquiry, discovery and innovation, and a shared determination to transform theory into practice, to use all we know to change the world. Marx gives the bourgeoisie credit for starting this process. Like every other modernist, however, he expects the process to go a lot further than the bourgeoisie would like, and indeed further than it can even conceive.

Another great bourgeois achievement, which should also lead beyond bourgeois horizons, is the internationalization of daily life. 'The need for a constantly expanding market for its products,' Marx says, 'chases the bourgeoisie over the whole surface of the globe. It must nestle everywhere, settle everywhere, establish connections everywhere.' Moreover, Marx notes, internationalization goes on not only in economic matters, but in people's most intimate inner lives. 'And as in material, so also in intellectual production. The spiritual creations of individual nations become common property. National one-sidedness and narrow-mindedness become more and more impossible, and from the numerous local literatures there arises a world literature' (Marx and Engels 1848/1959: 11). Thus the modern bourgeoisie, interested only in its own profits, inadvertently creates a world culture whose creations are public property. We can see, more than a century later, that this is the culture of modernism itself. Although it has embraced the world horizons of modern capital, it ends up subverting capitalism, not necessarily because it sets out to (though it frequently does), but simply because, as an array of 'spiritual creations', it cannot help expressing values radically opposed to the profit-and-loss calculus of the bourgeois bottom line.

One of the central themes in modernist culture, starting in the 1840s, is the drive for free development. Goethe, in *Faust*, was probably the first to suggest the connection between the modern desire for self-development and the modern movement toward economic development. Marx conceptualizes this relationship in the *Manifesto*:

> The bourgeoisie cannot exist without constantly revolutionizing the instruments of production, and thereby the relations of production, and with them all the relations of society … Constant revolutionizing of production, uninterrupted disturbance of all social relations, everlasting uncertainty and agitation, distinguish the bourgeois epoch from all earlier ones. All fixed, fast-frozen relations, with their venerable train of prejudices and opinions, are swept away, all new-formed ones become antiquated before they can ossify. All that is solid melts into air, all that is holy is profaned, and man at last is forced to face with sober senses his real conditions of life and his relations with his fellow men. (*Marx and /Engels 1848/1959: 10*)

Under the pressure of the market, modern men and women are forced to grow in order to survive. But their growth is channelled and twisted into narrow, strictly marketable, directions. Still, Marx believes, the inner dynamism that capitalism creates in its subjects is bound to recoil against bourgeois rule. Sooner or later, modern men and women will come to feel that the boundaries of the capitalist bottom line are fencing them in; after lifetimes of forced and distorted development, they will begin to clamour for free development. This desire, more than any merely economic need, will propel the modern masses into movements for radical change. Indeed, when communism finally arrives, Marx says in the *Manifesto*, its gift to humanity will be 'an association in which the free development of each is the condition of the development of all' (Tucker 1978: 491).

Free development is celebrated by Marx's whole generation of modernists. It is what Baudelaire's 'Le Voyage' is about: 'to drown in the abyss – heaven or hell, who cares? Through the unknown, we'll find the new' (Lowell 1962). Free development is also what the hero of Dostoevsky's *Notes from Underground* has in mind when he says, 'I want to live, in order to satisfy all my faculties for life' (Dostoevsky 1864/1960). And it plays a crucial role in the thought of even so square a modernist as John Stuart Mill (1859), who declares in his *On Liberty* that 'not symmetry [of character] but bold, free expansion in all directions is demanded by the needs of modern life and the instincts of the modern mind'.

More than a century later, the drive for free development has spread all over the world, and has energized millions of people to demand shorter work hours, universal education, freedom of expression, and support for what Mill in *On Liberty* called 'experiments in living'. An amorphous but passionate public, open and responsive to any activity or creation that appears to be authentically new, has helped to keep many modes of modernism alive. It has encouraged several generations of artists and scientists and quite ordinary men and women to believe that, if they aren't transcending themselves, they aren't really alive. (Ironically, this public has also become the primary audience for postmodernism, which represents itself as the newest modern movement in town.)

The ideal of free development, elaborated in the 1840s, soon brought about a powerful undertow. From then till now, this undertow has been a primary source of anxiety and despair in modern life. I will call this undertow what Nietzsche called it at the start of *The Will to Power*: the problem of nihilism. Nietzsche himself, along with Baudelaire, Rimbaud, and other modernist 'bad boys', are often blamed for nihilism, which is said to spring from their drugged and overheated imaginations.[5]

Marx addressed a similar problem from a different angle. One of his bitterest complaints against bourgeois society is that it has 'resolved all standards of personal worth into exchange value': anything becomes morally permissible if it is economically profitable. Marx indicts the bourgeoisie as the first nihilistic ruling class in history. He looks forward to a socialist revolution, and eventually to a communist society, that will deliver modern men and women from the capitalist bottom line. But we could well ask: if free development for everybody is going to be the basic norm of the new society, won't such a norm engender new modes of nihilism that will be deeper and more thorough than the mode they replace?

The modernists of the 1840s created a vocabulary that made it possible to ask such questions. They didn't have answers, but they had faith in the capacities of modern men and women in the process of development to generate answers. Hence they could accept modern nihilism as what Nietzsche called it: 'a great clearing away', 'a simplification for the sake of life', 'a pathological transitional state', a prelude to the creation of new and better values (Nietzsche 1888/1968).

Meanwhile, however, came the counter-attack: the catastrophic ruin of the revolutions of 1848, and, in France, the new despotism of Napoleon III. 'The struggle seems to be settled,' Marx wrote in *The Eighteenth Brumaire of Louis Bonaparte*, just after Bonaparte's coup d'etat of December 1851, 'in such a way that all classes, equally mute and equally impotent, fall on their knees before the rifle butt ... France seems to have escaped the despotism of a class only to fall beneath the despotism of an individual, and, what is more, beneath the authority of an individual without authority' (Tucker 1978: 606). The dreadful denouements of 1848–51 revealed that there was a very large modern public – no one knew just how large – which, far from yearning for a future of free development, was fighting to flee from a present that already felt much too free.

For Marx, the collective desire to escape from freedom was a subject for comedy, though indeed a black comedy. (The humour of *The Eighteenth Brumaire of Louis Bonaparte* is actually much more typical of our century than of Marx's own. It belongs on the same shelf as Lenny Bruce and *Catch-22*.) Thirty years later Dostoevsky (1864/1960: 119–41), in his 'Legend of the Grand Inquisitor', brought out the tragic gravity of this theme. Dostoevsky's parable is told by the modernist intellectual Ivan Karamazov. Ivan imagines a very modern and humanistic Jesus, one who is concerned above all with freedom of conscience. The Grand Inquisitor judges this sort of freedom subversive and dangerous: it is too much, he believes, for mere human beings to handle. He pays a midnight visit to Jesus in the prison where he has thrown him, and entreats Jesus to slip away in the darkness, before the Inquisition burns him for heresy. Doesn't he understand that he is making life too hard? 'I tell you,' the Inquisitor says, 'man is tormented by no greater anxiety than to find someone to whom he can hand over the gift of freedom with which this ill-fated creature was born.' Jesus lacks true mercy and charity: he fails to see 'that man prefers peace, and even death, to freedom of choice in the knowledge of good and evil. Nothing is more seductive for man than his freedom of conscience, but nothing is a greater cause of suffering.'

The Inquisitor now steps out of his medieval setting and addresses Dostoevsky's modern audience: 'Look,' he says, 'now, today, people are persuaded that they are freer than ever before, yet they have brought their freedom to us and laid it humbly at our feet.' The masses rebel, but they 'lack the courage to carry through their own rebellion'. They are like schoolchildren who riot and drive their teacher from the room, only to recoil in fright when they see that there is no one in charge but themselves. Then they will throw themselves on the mercy of 'the three powers that alone are able to hold captive the conscience of these impotent rebels' – a modernist anti-Trinity of 'miracle, mystery and authority' – rather than take responsibility for their own lives.

Dostoevsky is dreadfully apt, here and elsewhere, as a prophet of twentieth-century fascist and totalitarian movements. He comes closest to home, not so much in his portrait of the leadership of these movements as in his vision of the followers: modern men and women who grow up in a state of partial freedom, but who find this freedom such a dreadful burden that they will gladly sign over their lives to any leader or movement that will take the weight away. The parable of the Grand Inquisitor can teach modernists that they are in a far more precarious and vulnerable position than they may think. Marx's generation, the makers (and victims) of 1848, had canonized Prometheus as their culture hero. The Grand Inquisitor can remind them how many people out there are rooting for Zeus, how many would give back the fire and apologize to the gods, if only they could.

Dostoevsky's parable has a remarkably contemporary ring, but in one important way it was anachronistic from the start. In all but a few parts of the world (Iran is currently most prominent), the primary source of 'miracle, mystery and authority' is not the church, but the state. A powerful strain in modern culture, springing from the 1840s generation – Stirner and Proudhon, Tocqueville and Thoreau – sees this as the basic fact of modern political life, strives to unmask and denounce the modern state, even as that state entrenches itself everywhere in the world and incessantly expands. 'The New Idol', Nietzsche scornfully called it in 1883, in the glory days of the Bismarkhian Reich:

> State is the name of the coldest of all monsters. Coldly it tells lies; and this lie crawls out of its mouth: 'I, the state, am the people...'
>
> Where there is still a people, it does not understand the state, and hates it as the evil eye and the sin against customs and rights...
>
> It will give you everything if you'll adore it, this new idol: thus it buys the splendor of your virtues and the look of your proud eyes. It will use you as bait...
>
> My brothers, do you want to suffocate? Rather break the windows and leap to freedom.

Escape from the bad smell! Escape from the steam of these human sacrifices. (*Nietzsche 1883: 160–3*)[6]

We needn't share Nietzsche's optimism about a great leap (where could one go, after all, except into another state's jurisdiction?) to get the critical point. Indeed, we could even argue – as Max Weber did a couple of decades later – that the more indispensable the state is to all modern people and peoples, the more oppressive and dangerous it is bound to be. Nietzsche might well have agreed. His aim was not to promote any particular escape route. Rather, it was to convince his readers that they didn't have to let themselves be absorbed by gigantic institutions: to strengthen these readers to the point where they could believe in their own inner strength. If powers of social control grew strong, men and women could grow even stronger. If people found themselves devalued, they had the capacity to create new values. Thus Nietzsche affirmed and deepened the modernist faith.

Two of Nietzsche's striking images in the passage above – the tragic image of human sacrifice to vicious gods, and the black-comic image of men used as bait (and dying like flies) – hurtle us into the trenches of 1914–18, and into the depths of what Gertrude Stein called 'the Cubist War' (cited in Kern 1983: 288). Actually, the self-awareness implicit in these Nietzschean images belongs to the second phase of World War I, after both sides had made murderous but futile attempts to break through enemy lines. During the first phase, August 1914 and its aftermath, the days of dancing in the streets, modernists from every country in Europe marched naively off to the war (or danced their nearest and dearest off to war), happy for once to belong to their national masses, identifying themselves with all the newly discovered modes of speed, flight, bursts of light and energy, explosive firepower (they called their avant-garde magazines *Bomb* and *Blast!*), yearning to see modernism put into practice on a spectacular scale. French cubists and German expressionists mobilized all their talents to create ingenious camouflage, apparently proud to help their respective armies kill each other. Proust's Baron Charlus stood on Paris roofs during air raids, singing Wagner arias and saluting a spectacle that was at once primeval and high-tech. As the war dragged on and on, however, many of the modernists who were still alive (so many of the most creative were killed) came to feel and understand its full horror: far from being an arena for heroism and heightened creativity, it had transformed subjects into objects, reduced its participants to helpless passivity, shivering in the trenches while waiting to be shot. The poet Edmund Blunden, after surviving the disastrous Battle of the Somme in July 1916 (the British lost 60,000 men on the first day of their attack), wrote: 'Neither race had won, nor could win, the War. The War had won, and would go on winning.'[7]

If the Italian futurists of 1914–16 typified the modernism of the war's start, the Central European Dadaists of 1917–21 best expressed the modernism of the war's endlessness, and then of its absurd end. Their outrages and provocations were meant to shock people – and peoples – into reflecting on what was being done to them, and imagining what they might do in return. Dada didn't last long, but it helped to expand people's minds, often against their will, to the point where angry but hopeful peoples pulled down several predatory empires, and fought fiercely, for a few years at least, to create the modern world anew.[8]

One of the great works of modernist self-education, written in the war's first dreadful year, was Freud's essay (1915) 'Thoughts for the times on war and death'. Freud was stunned by the war: not so much by the clash of armies, as by the eruptions of hatred on both sides; by the willingness, even eagerness, of intellectuals and scientists to hand their minds and consciences over to their propaganda bureaus; and by the eruptive, frenzied character of mass hatred all over Europe, as if there were no tomorrow coming, as if the peoples of Europe were not going to have to find ways to live together again. He tried to understand what forces had exploded inside modern men and women that could lead them to press all their energy and creativity into the service of mutual assured destruction. His conclusion was that the scientific, artistic and organizational triumphs of modern civilization were made possible by impossibly stringent ethical standards, which eventually extracted devastating psychic costs. In the respectable world of the pre-war European middle class, men and women were forced to repress their strongest and deepest feelings – not only sexual feelings, but, just as important, feelings of violent anger, of displacement, of nameless dread – and therefore, as Freud put it, 'to live psychologically beyond their means'.

In August 1914 the respectable façades had finally cracked. The war made it clear, Freud said, that 'the state forbids wrongdoing and violence, not, however, in order to abolish it, but in order to monopolize it'. Modern states enlisted subjects who were seething with rage – rage against parents, children, siblings, lovers, spouses, friends, authorities – and mobilized them to displace their repressed private enmities onto socially sanctioned public enemies. Freud's clinical work had taught him how many people there were in modern societies whose psyches were like bombs ready to explode;

World War I taught him how willing and able the modern state was (or could easily become) to supply detonators and targets. In uniform, normally peaceable and decent men could perpetrate unthinkable atrocities, and not only avoid arrest, but win medals and praise in the daytime – and moreover, because the state assumed responsibility for their actions, sleep well at night.

Freud's insight into the dynamics of patriotic gore is developed and deepened a decade later, in his most important late work, *Civilization and Its Discontents* (1930, 1931). The book reaches a climax with what may be a definitive vision of the inner contradictions and ultimate fragility of modern life: 'Men have gained control of the forces of nature to such an extent that, by using them [nature's forces], they would have no difficulty in exterminating one another to the last man. They know this, and hence comes a large part of their current unrest, their unhappiness, and their mood of anxiety.' Modern men and women are in urgent need of self-knowledge, if we are ever going to gain the power to protect us from the powers we have gained already.

But it is not enough merely to defuse ourselves: we must find ways to live. After summing up the profound destructive powers around and inside us, Freud adds, and ends his book this way: 'And now we may expect that the other of the two primal forces, eternal Eros, will assert his strength, so as to affirm himself in the struggle against his immortal antagonist.' (In 1931, a year later, the shadows a little longer, he gave the book a new and more melancholy ending: 'But who can foresee with what success and with what result?') Thus, the drive for self-knowledge that forces us to see through our world and our place in it, and brings us face to face with our inner darkness, may also have the power to bind us together in a new, more viable life. The dreaded negative powers of modernism may yet turn out to be driven by the power of love. Freud's lifelong quarrel with the modern world ends in a fragile but real dialectic of hope.

IMPASSES OF THE POSTMODERN

If my reading of modernity is right, it is a condition that at once empowers people and constrains them. They can face it more or less honestly, more or less confidently, more or less bravely, more or less imaginatively. But they can't face away from it, or stand beyond it: right now, it's the only world we have got. Nevertheless, since the end of World War II, all sorts of people have insisted that they are expressing a postmodern sensibility, and that all of us are living in a distinctively postmodern age. Postmodern claims have actually come in two waves: the first in the early 1960s, coming from all over America; the second in the 1970s and 1980s, coming at first from France.

The first wave of postmodernism emerged around 1960 in America's universities and Bohemian enclaves. It sprang from the people who invented happenings, assemblages, environments, and the art that would come to be called Pop – people who, without knowing it, were inventing the 1960s. For the most part, they were too busy to worry about labels. But they were at least occasionally willing to answer to the label 'postmodern' because they all deplored the cultural orthodoxy that, in the 1950s, seemed to pre-empt the label of modernism. This orthodoxy, hard to recapture today, was narrow, solemn and hieratic. Its high priest was T. S. Eliot, not the revolutionary poet who wrote 'The Love Song of J. Alfred Prufrock' and *The Waste Land*, but the grey eminence 'Mr Eliot', a clerical personage who presided over culture as over a sepulchre, and demanded that art be treated with the hushed reverence due to the dead.

The world-view of this orthodoxy was characterized aptly by Norman O. Brown, in *Life against Death*, a book that helped to shatter it, as 'the politics of sin, cynicism and despair' (1959: 7). Its overseers were ever vigilant in warding off threats to 'high art' from 'mass culture', as if art were a delicate antique that could be shattered by any loud noise or strong vibration. Moreover, these overseers demanded that practitioners of any art should foresake all others and concern themselves only with the essence of their particular form. Thus the only legitimate subject of painting was the nature of painting, poetry had to be about the nature of poetry, and so it went.

Nothing would have appalled the 1950s trustees of culture more than the idea that serious art could make you laugh. In dramatic contrast, the new wave of artists in the early 1960s struggled to make art fun. They mixed media, styles and genres, incorporated large chunks of the industrial world and mass culture in their work, and brought art out of the studios and galleries and into the streets. The critic Leslie Fiedler's formula for this new wave was 'Cross the border, close the gap'. Claes Oldenburg (1970: 25, 33), in the notes for one of his first shows, said, 'I am for an art that tells you the time of day, or where such and such a street is. I am for an art that helps old ladies across the street.'

The new faces of the early sixties were more active politically, and more militant in the demands they made on life, than were the modernists of the cold war years. At the same time, they were in love with the world they wanted to change. These artists broke culture open, opened it up to the amazing variety and richness of images, materials and ideas brought forth by the worldwide post-war economic boom; Marshall McLuhan's metaphor of a 'global village' seemed to come to life. The spirit of those times still lives in Allen Ginsberg's poem 'America', in James Rosenquist's mural *F–111*, in Bob Dylan's song 'Desolation Row'. Jean-Luc Godard captured it perfectly in a phrase from *La Chinoise*: 'the children of Marx and Coca-Cola'. This generation often thought of itself as postmodern, and compared with the curators of 1950s modernism, it was. But the children of Marx and Coca-Cola have a far better claim than their predecessors to the spirit and honour of modernism: they engaged the contradictions of their times, struggled to make the teeming and boiling society of the 1960s their own.[9]

If the first wave of postmoderns was composed of the people who invented the 1960s, the second wave, still flowing today, is a strange combination of people who were born too early to participate actively in the sixties, and people who were born too late and missed the sixties. This postmodernism was created by Parisian academics who spent their whole lives as members of the enviably privileged French mandarin caste. For two minutes, in May 1968, their lives were transfigured, a terrible beauty was born; in two minutes more, all their hopes were dead. The postmodernisms of the past twenty years grew out of this trauma, and also out of a collective refusal to confront it.

Instead, the Left Bank exploded with all the feverish rhetoric and sectarian fanaticism that typify radical politics at its worst, combined with a total abdication of concern for political issues and relationships in the grubby real world. (Indeed, it was typical of Parisian postmodernism to say it made no sense even to talk about a real world: there was 'nothing outside the text', as Jacques Derrida liked to say.) Derrida, Roland Barthes, Jacques Lacan, Michel Foucault, Jean Baudrillard, and all their legions of followers, appropriated the whole modernist language of radical breakthrough, wrenched it out of its moral and political context, and transformed it into a purely aesthetic language game. Eros, revolution, terrorism, diabolical possession, apocalypse, were now simply ways of playing with words and signifiers and texts. As such, they could be experienced and enjoyed – *jouir, jouissance*, Roland Barthes's favourite words – without engaging in any action, taking any risks, or paying any human costs. If modernism had found both its fulfilment and its ruin in the streets, this postmodernism saved its devotees the trouble of ever having to go out at all. The thinker could be ultraradical without ever leaving his desk. If this is nihilism (and these postmoderns are always invoking Nietzsche and Heidegger to show that it is), then it is a radically new form: nihilism without tears. The first time it was tragedy, the second time it's farce.

When this production crossed the Atlantic with great fanfare, and played to full houses of people who instead of laughing bowed their heads in awe, I was mystified at first. Then I noticed that the most reverent followers of postmodernism were rather younger than I was, and in fact were people who were too young for the 1960s. Coming of age in the 1970s, they inherited all the rage and bitterness of the Vietnam generation, without any of our experience of protracted struggle leading to limited but important changes in the world. Their generation appropriated and deepened our radical negations, without ever having shared our radical hopes. The most impressive achievement of this 1970s generation, I have always thought, is punk rock: a medium that proclaims and dramatizes radical negation without radical hope, and yet manages to create some sort of hope out of its overflow of energy and honesty and the communal warmth it ignites.

I have recently been reading Jean Baudrillard, the most recent postmodern pretender and object of cultic adoration in art scenes and universities all over America today. Here is his voice:

> The end of the dialectic signifier/signified, which permitted an accumulation of knowledge and meaning... The end of ... capital accumulation and social production. The end of linear discourse. The end of the classic era of the sign. The end of the era of production...
>
> Power is no longer present except to conceal the fact that there is none... Illusion is no longer possible because reality is no longer possible. (*Baudrillard 1984*)

As I read these words, I began thinking. Where have I heard all this before? Then I remembered. I turned to my record collection. It was the Fugs' 'January nothing, February nothing, March and April nothing ... / Capital and labor, still more nothing, / Agribusiness nothing' (Kupferberg 1965). It was the Sex Pistols' 'No Future', shouted all night till everybody dropped (Rotten et al. 1977). It was Flipper's 'Not to believe what you believe, / Nothing. Nothing. Nothing. Nothing' (Lose, 1981). It was the Minutemen's 'No heart/ soul, no working at that goal ... / Not living/dying, life just means surviving ... / No world/no fair, lost hope, I no longer care' (Watt and Watt 1985).

We can feel the metaphysical affinities here, yet they speak in such different voices! The punks put themselves on the line; the desolation of their world fills them with dread; they open up their inner wounds, in the vein of Rousseau and Baudelaire, Artaud and Billie

Holliday, Jackson Pollock and Sylvia Plath; in their musical and emotional contortions they are trying (as Nietzsche urged us all to try) to break the windows and leap to freedom. They are modernists, whether they know it or not.

The voice of the postmodern mandarins seems to emanate from a very different and distant space. They don't shriek, 'We are the future / There is no future!' – maybe because the alleged death of the subject would preclude it – but they manage to sound like they mean it. They announce the end of all things in tones of serene aplomb, proclaim incoherence in elegant neoclassical antitheses, and assert with dogmatic self-certainty the impossibility of truth and the death of the self. Where is this voice coming from? It sounds as if, after the failure of their one great leap into actuality, back in May 1968, they resolved never to go out again, and dug themselves into a grand metaphysical tomb, thick and tight enough to furnish lasting comfort against the cruel hopes of spring. Their postmodern world makes a sensible retirement community, a fine place to stay cool. But is this whole generation really ready for early retirement? And will the youth of the eighties and nineties be willing to die spiritually before they have even begun to live? We should not be surprised to find that, even in this vault of dead air, modernism is born again.

MODERNISM IN THE 1980s

The artists I will discuss briefly here – Maya Lin, Laurie Anderson, Les Levine, Anselm Kiefer, Salman Rushdie – come from very disparate backgrounds, work in different media, speak out of diverse temperaments and sensibilities, align themselves with contradictory and clashing ideologies. I have no idea whether they are aware of one another; they certainly do not constitute an artistic movement, in any ordinary sense of the word. But they are alike, not only in the scope and the seriousness of their work, but in their shared desire to reach across national, class, racial, religious and sexual boundaries. They have all developed new ways to communicate with people, even people at each other's throats, and to bring them together, even force them together, in dialogue. Their work has extended and deepened the human capacity for dialogue, both within cultures and between them; it has helped the world of the 1980s move tentatively, hesitantly, toward a genuine world culture. Without (so far as I know) doing any theorizing about modernism, they have nourished the progressive drives and universalistic hopes that are close to modernism's heart. The fact that modernist work can go on thriving in so many different modes is a sign that the modernist project is as viable and fruitful as ever.

Laurie Anderson's world seems to bear some of the marks of post-modernism: landscapes as cold and lifeless as outer space (they often are outer space, courtesy of NASA), with images of cold and dark-ness enveloping us all; people engaging in incessant arguments with their shadows, mirror images, magnifications, memory traces, com-puter clones; hypnotic trance music, electronically created; photo-graphs, shadows, drawings, simulations and montages, layered and blended with three-dimensional 'real' things and people; com-munication that seems cryptic and erratic at best – the Brooklyn Academy of Music feels like a high-tech version of Plato's cave. But Anderson's stance toward this universe is radically different from any postmodern perspective. When she brings her multi-media uni-verse, United States, to life, she is always in or near the centre of the stage, gliding or rushing about from microphone to synclavier, from vocoder to electric violin. She is the subject of everything that is said or sung, played or portrayed: incestuous families, farmers' barns that turn into missile silos, tigers breaking into family picnics (and, surprise, becoming part of the family), amorous encounters with the President (Carter), flights from stranglers on Hollywood freeways, Indians confessing to anthropologists that they never really knew their tribal chants, travellers in search of towns that are purely hypothetical, and far more.[10]

So she goes, propelled by an immensely rich imagination: *United States* is the sort of thing James Joyce might have created if he had had cybernetics to work with. The enormous world that rotates around Anderson suggests an update of Chaplin's *Modern Times* – only this time the human controls the machines. 'There are ten million stories in the Naked City,' she says (echoing a radio show of the 1940s and a TV show of the 1960s), as slab-shaped skyscrapers flash on and glide across the screen, 'but no one can remember which is theirs.' She is determined to find out, both for herself and for us all. *United States* ends with a brilliant update – ironic, maybe quixo-tic, but the more determined for all that – of the archetypally modern romance of Enlightenment: Anderson is onstage alone, sur-rounded by smoke (or smog?) and darkness; she looks toward us intensely, through the deep night, with powerful fog lights shining from her eyes.

Maya Ying Lin's Vietnam Veterans Memorial in Washington, dedi-cated in 1982, shows how the idioms of the modernist movement in architecture, so often criticized for their supposed indifference to history, may be uniquely qualified to tell the truth about contemporary history. The memorial's design, chosen in an open competition with more than 1,400 entries, is distinguished by its purity of form, its open and gently flowing space; it displays an austere honesty in its use of materials and in the directness and simplicity of its gestures. Furthermore, the memorial is as remarkable for what it leaves out as for what it says. It leaves out all the grandiloquence, pomposity and vainglory that have poisoned so many monuments – and, indeed, so many wars – through the ages. Lin's rejection of patriotic bombast gives visible form to Hemingway's insight that, for the men who were under fire in the Great War, 'abstract words such as glory, honor, courage or hallow were obscene beside the concrete names of villages, the numbers of regiments and the dates' (1929: 191; cited in Fussell 1975: 21). This memorial tells us virtually nothing but the names and the dates, and reminds us how, in design as in writing, the sparsest and most abstract modes of modernism can set us free from lies, and give us space to make a fresh start, so we can at least try to construct personal and public lives we won't have to be ashamed of.

The memorial, as it stands today on the Mall, creates a protected space in the most unlikely place: the heart of the United States capital. We move down a gentle slope in the landscape, drawn forward by the giant extended wings that form the memorial's walls. As we get closer to the thousands of names etched in bright black granite, we see ourselves interfaced with them, reflected with a startling vividness: have we ever seen ourselves so clear? Lin has given us a sanctuary without walls, an enclosure where even as we feel for our dead, we can honestly think about our lives. Regardless of what we felt or what we did about the war, even those born after it ended, everybody who goes through this space cries. This memorial shows how modernism can help a culture look the negative in the face and live with it. If Americans can learn to examine the wounds we have inflicted on others, along with those we have inflicted on ourselves, maybe we can begin to heal.[11]

I have focused so far on modernism's capacity to heal. But this emphasis shouldn't lead us to think that today's modernists have lost the flair for making trouble. Some of the most fruitful trouble in the art of the 1980s was made by the New York conceptual artist Les Levine, when the Institute of Contemporary Art in London invited him in 1985 to create a series of giant billboards that would be installed all over London's streets. Levine, a Jew born in Dublin, but living and working in New York for most of the last thirty years, found a theme in his own past and England's present. He went up to Derry, Northern Ireland, where he took a series of photos of Irish Catholics and Protestants threatening each other and brandishing their banners and guns. Levine turned the photos into huge paintings, rendered in strong industrial colours and flat, crude advertising-poster tones. He made people who were dreadful to look at, in ways that evoke the post-World War I caricatures of Georg Grosz. But his captions, in huge block letters, are even more disturbing: all the words, in different but inescapable ways, accuse and implicate God.

Thus, overlaid on a caricature of a grim and worn old lady and an undernourished boy, Levine inscribed a command: STARVE GOD. Over a huddled squad of British soldiers in battle fatigues: ATTACK GOD. Over loyalist patriots waving their flags (one actually turned himself into a living flag) and grimacing at the camera, PARADE GOD. Over a squad of border guards beaming lights at us through barbed wire, BLOCK GOD. Over a soldier prodding a blanketed corpse with his gun, while an old man turns his face away in shock, KILL GOD. Over an urban ruin, BOMB GOD. So it goes.

Mounted together and shown as paintings in an art gallery, these works were devastating, in the vein of Leon Golub's 'Mercenaries and Interrogations' sequence of paintings. Displayed as billboards along the London streets (as they were in September 1985), incorporated into the mass media, sandwiched in among ads for cigarettes, tyres, and *Rambo*, they carried an even more explosive force. London's ICA has reproduced some of the many letters and editorials that express unmediated hysterical panic. The posters seem to have forced a large assortment of people to think quickly and seriously, not only about their relationship to the troubles in Ireland, but about the meaning of history and human life itself. For many people, having to think this way seems to have been just too hard. These people were not consoled by the hopes expressed in some of Levine's posters: hopes that they, or people like them, might have (or could gain) the capacity to PROTECT GOD, and even to CREATE GOD. Works like these should make it clear to us what modernism is for: to force modern men and women to face their real conditions of life, to bring buried realities into the open, out on the street.[12]

This enterprise has a special gravity and urgency in Germany, where some of the most dreadful mass murders in all history were systematically organized, and then, a little later, systematically forgotten. In the 1950s and 1960s, with massive American aid, West Germany quickly became not only one of the world's leading industrial nations, but also, for the first time in German history, a stable bourgeois democracy. But it was a weird stability, built on an inability to remember where it had come from, or to mourn what it had done. One of the primary drives that animated the youth of the 1960s counter-culture in Germany was a need to force their parents' generation to face the Nazi past and accept responsibility for their complicity in mass murder. The work of the painter Anselm Kiefer, born in 1943, suggests the imaginative power and fruitfulness of this drive, but also some of its innate dangers and ambiguities.

Since he changed his career from law to art, in the late 1960s, Kiefer has taken it as his mission to saturate his work with fascist imagery, to flood German culture with the monstrous mythology and iconography that it had so skilfully repressed. One of his first ambitious works, entitled *Occupations* (1969), was a conceptual piece, a series of photographs of the artist occupying his studio, the mountains, the ocean, the Roman Colosseum, the ruins at Pompeii, etc., and giving the Nazi salute. Much of the German public seems to have been outraged by this, although (here as elsewhere) those most angry were also least willing to think about why. In the 1970s Kiefer went on to develop his artist-as-Nazi motif, painting gigantic versions of Nazi buildings and landscapes, often in ruins, featuring an overwhelming monumentality and a relentlessly imposed central perspective. (Central to this period was a series entitled *Tomb of the Unknown Painter.*) Here Kiefer was trying to manipulate his audience as he believed Hitler (remember, an unappreciated painter) had manipulated the German people, and trying, too, to capture the lure and seductiveness of fascist space, its power to transfigure ordinary life and make the oppressed and driven subject feel heroic and sublime. These paintings are both physically and conceptually strong, but also bombastic and overblown; it often looks as if the ruins could come crashing down on the artist's head as well as on our own. Kiefer's work of the 1970s skirts dangerously close to the kitsch he was fighting to transcend.

In the 1980s Kiefer has overcome this danger, and created (and endlessly recreated) an authentic modern primal scene. The scene is a barren field or heath, rendered in varied tonalities of black and grey, sometimes furrowed like a field, moving diagonally toward a high horizon, seen from below, as a soldier in a World War might see the battlefield from a trench. These 1980s works have incorporated layers of straw, tar, ashes and dust, oil and emulsions. No daylight breaks in on these brooding landscapes. Occasionally there are traces of a city on the horizon, but usually there is nothing. The overwhelming feeling is one of waste, of infinite nuances and gradations of wasteland.

In Kiefer's iconography, over the last decade, straw and ashes have come to symbolize the life destroyed in the Nazi Holocaust: 'Your golden hair Margarete, your ashen hair Shulamith.' The twin symbolic victims, Margarete and Shulamith, are drawn from 'Todesfugue' (Death Fugue), by Paul Celan, a heartbreaking poem written in a Nazi concentration camp by a Romanian Jew, one of the great poets of his generation, who killed himself in 1970. Shulamith stands for all the Jewish victims of Nazism; Margarete, possibly derived from Gretchen in Goethe's *Faust*, stands for all the German victims. Celan, writing in the language of the mass murderers, was telling them that they were murdering not only his people (Celan was the sole survivor in his family), but their own. Kiefer, born into a generation of murderers, embraces Celan's symbolism from the other side, and gives it new life after the poet's death. Painting the victims of the Holocaust again and again, with a searing intensity – and, moreover, painting them in the only form that remained after their murder and cremation, as burnt, bashed, gnarled, oozing, decomposing *material* – he forces Germans to face what has been done and done and done in their name. At the same time, making his people see and making them think, he is enabling them to be collectively alive in ways they may never have been fully alive before.

Writers about Kiefer tend to share his own obsessions with German (and Jewish) history. Considering what that history has been, it is easy to see why. But if Kiefer's painting were about Germany alone, it would grip us with far less power than it does. In all his art, but in his work of the 1980s more than ever, Kiefer has been addressing the question that T. S. Eliot asked in *The Waste Land*: 'What are the roots that clutch, what branches grow / out of this stony rubble?' After twenty years of excavating the mass graves of German history, Kiefer shows no signs of letting himself or his country walk away. He is more determined than ever to force the issues, to bring death to life, to work it through.[13] A talent like this matters not only in Germany, but all through a world where Shulamiths and Margaretes decompose together, in a century that has created more ruins and more victims than all earlier centuries combined. In art, at least, the anguish of destruction can be a force that unifies the world.

The most ambitious modernist work of the 1980s, and one of the most remarkable works to appear in any medium since World War II, is Salman Rushdie's novel *The Satanic Verses*. The storms that have broken over Rushdie's head since his book appeared in Britain late in 1988 – the book burnings, the death threats, the menacing

demonstrations (along with many inevitably less dramatic demonstrations of support), the commercial and governmental vacillations –
have magnified his notoriety, but obscured his real achievement,
which will take many years to unfold.

The Satanic Verses is actually not one but several books, each
brilliant and original in its own right: a *Bildungsroman*, a novel of
personal growth and development, with stress on the dynamics of
exile and return, and a deathbed reconciliation; a novel about London today, focusing on racist and anti-racist politics, exploring in-
terracial sex and love, and climaxing with a race riot; a similar novel,
fascinating but less fully realized, about Bombay; a fable about
Muhammad and his contemporaries, offering a revisionist account
of the genesis and early history of Islam; a short study of a crazed
Imam in exile, who rejoices in the martyrdom of his followers at
home, and dreams of smashing all the clocks in his country, so as to
stop time; a vision of a fundamentalist Hindu cult that marches into
the Arabian Sea, confident that the waters will part. So it goes.

So much has been said and written about *The Satanic Verses* as an
event, yet there is surprisingly little about what the book is actually
like. I want to take apart a brief early passage, just two sentences
long, in a way that will suggest the novel's richness and range.

The story begins high above the English Channel, where a hi-
jacked jet bound from Bombay to London is blown up. 'The aircraft
cracked in half'; two Indian actors, Saladin and Gibreel, who will
play central roles in the book, float and hurtle through the clouds,
and we follow them down: 'Above, behind, below them in the void
there hung reclining seats, stereophonic headsets, drinks, trolleys,
motion discomfort receptacles, disembarkation cards, duty-free
video games, braided caps, paper cups, blankets, oxygen masks.' The
genre in passages like this is comic realism, as Rushdie traces an
inventory of the paraphenalia of late twentieth-century air travel,
underscoring incongruities and absurd juxtapositions that most of
his readers, if not all, will have gone through. Here we can all laugh
together amiably, superficially, like gentlemen, and enjoy a sense of
fellowship without actually having to give anything of ourselves.

Suddenly, however, and without warning, Rushdie shoves us into
a very different atmosphere, and forces us to witness a scene of
painful intimacy and humiliation: 'Also – for there had been more
than a few migrants aboard, yes, quite a quantity of wives who had
been grilled by reasonable, doing-their-job officials about the length
of and distinguishing marks upon their husbands' genitalia, a suf-
ficiency of children upon whose legitimacy the British Government
had cast its ever-reasonable doubts – ...' It is very unlikely that

many of us, Rushdie's First World readers, have ever been taken off an airport customs line and transformed into something like prisoners. Our embarrassment proves our complicity, for the people who do get taken off the line are routinely humiliated and violated in our name. The narrator, our fellow-traveller a moment ago, has suddenly become caustic and angry at a life that has suddenly been polarized into a duel between the First World and the Third.

But now, in an imperceptible instant, the narrator changes again. He crosses the gulf he pointed out a moment ago, and once more asserts fellowship between us. Only now the solidarity is darker and more tragic: 'mingling with the remnants of the plane, equally fragmented, equally absurd, there floated the debris of the soul, broken memories, sloughed-off selves, severed mother-tongues, violated privacies, untranslatable jokes, extinguished futures, lost loves, the forgotten meaning of hollow booming words, *land, belonging, home*' (Rushdie 1988/1989: 4). Rushdie's narrator began with a pseudo-fellowship that granted members of the Third World all the modern conveniences of the First, without any of the rights. Then, by pointing to the people who always get taken off the airport customs lines, he unmasked the lie and exposed the polarities at the heart of modern life. In the end, however, he affirmed that modern life is universal after all, and that First World and Third World people really are kindred souls, not (as humanists and liberals have always said) because 'they' of the Third World are as civilized as 'we' of the First, but because we are as tragically uprooted and fragmented and twisted as they. And he reaches this dialectic and dives into it and shoots and twists through it with lightning speed, all in jump cuts, without skipping a beat.

One of the things that makes *The Satanic Verses* so agreeable to read is Rushdie's love of ordinary life, of facticity and detail. But although he loves all sorts of things, he has no respect for persons. He presents ironic and irreverent readings of Islamic tradition and history – this was his crime in Ayatollah Khomeni's eyes – but he is no less critical and iconoclastic in confronting Western culture and society. (Indeed, he may be even bitterer toward the West, precisely because for most of his life the West has been his promised land.) The first entry on Rushdie's bill of rights seems to be everybody's right to culture. This means, not only a right to the culture that he or she is born into, but to everybody else's culture as well; and not only the right to love, honour and cherish culture, but the right to hate it, caricature it, misread it, rip it off, use it as raw material to create something new. Rushdie is aware that many readers will not like his readings; if they don't, he would say, let them come up with better readings of their own. One of the best standards for assessing the real value of The Satanic Verses will be the range and fruitfulness of readings it can inspire.

But in what sense will they be *modernist* readings? And in what sense, finally, are the works of art that I have been discussing truly modernist, rather than postmodernist, works? One possible criterion for modernism today, suggested by some contemporary philosophers, is a conscious attempt to arrive at some sort of universal values – for instance, 'humanity as the hero of liberty'. Postmoderns, on the contrary, repudiate any sort of universal quest, and proclaim their will to live according to less ambitious ideas that are rooted in particular experiences, local interests, and 'the heterogeneity of language games' (Lyotard 1977/1984: xxiv–xxv, 31, 37–41). Salman Rushdie, and the other modernists of the 1980s, have learned to see through universal claims that have turned out to be mere con games. But they are not willing to infer from this that all great claims are con games; they go on struggling to break through to visions of truth and freedom that all modern men and women can embrace. This struggle animates their work, gives it an inner dynamism and a principle of hope.

In 1984, in an essay entitled 'Outside the whale', Rushdie proclaimed 'a genuine need for political fiction, for books that draw new and better maps of reality, and make languages with which we can understand the world'. Writers needed to throw themselves into 'the unceasing storm, the continual quarrel, the dialectic of history... If writers leave the business of making pictures of the world to politicians, it will be one of history's great and most abject abdications.' This meant participation in a political universe that is 'by turns farce and tragedy', and 'sometimes both at once' (Rushdie 1984: 136–8). In the five years since he wrote that, the farce and tragedy have played on, the plots have grown even more twisted, and Rushdie himself, condemned by a mad Imam who wanted to smash the clocks, has been a victim of both. But it is crucial to remember that he has also been a participant and a protagonist in both. He has struggled consciously and courageously, at tremendous cost, to assert his rights as a subject, to make himself felt, to make a difference. His enemies are right about one thing: he really is a symbol of what is possible in the modern world.

Rushdie's example brings this essay back to where it began: 'modernism in the streets'. All over the world, from Gdansk to Manila, from Soweto to Seoul, modernism has been stirring in the streets again. As I write (Spring 1989), the USSR has just experienced its first free election, amid an atmosphere of delirious excitement; at long last, Soviet citizens are talking freely, and saying out loud what they think and what they want. With amazing speed and headlong momentum, *glasnost* has created an atmosphere in which Marx's prophecy of modernity is coming true: all that was solid is melting into air, all that was holy is being profaned, and men and women at last are forced to face the real conditions of their lives and their relations with their fellow men. No one can say how far it will go, or where it will lead. But it is an exciting time to be alive.

POSTSCRIPT, JANUARY 1991

1989 was not only a great year, but a great *modernist* year. First, because millions of people learned that history was not over, that they had the capacity to make their own history – though not, alas, in circumstances chosen by themselves. Second, because in the midst of their motions, those men and women identified with each other: even in different languages and idioms, even thousands of miles apart, they saw how their stories were one story, how they all were trying to make the modern world their own. I fear that vision has faded from our public life. Maybe it will return, in ways we can't foresee. Meantime, I want to fight to keep the memory and the hope alive.

NOTES

1 'Behold, I am doing a new thing', and 'I create new heavens and a new earth' (Isaiah 43: 19 and 65: 17). Adapted in Revelation 21: 1: 'Then I saw a new heaven and a new earth'; and 21: 5: 'Behold, I make all things new.'

2 Cf. the more contemporary translation by A. V. Miller (Oxford: Oxford University Press, 1977), 18–19, which in this case sounds more archaic. The *Phenomenology*, completed just after Napoleon's defeat of Prussia, could be understood as one of the first modernist manifestos.

3 This image comes from Part I of the *Communist Manifesto*, in Tucker 1978: 476.

4 Material from the 1960s and 1970s is discussed and cited in *All that Is Solid*, Introduction. Here is a brief sampling of the immense and ever-growing body of literature from the late 1970s and 1980s: Lyotard 1977; *New German Critique*, 2 (Winter 1981) and 33 (Fall 1984), special issues, with essays by Jürgen Habermas, Peter Bürger, Andreas Huyssen, et al.; Foster 1983; Wallis 1984; Huyssen 1986; Kariel 1988.

5   In fact, a sophisticated discussion of nihilism can be found in one of the soberest accounts of everyday life in the modern world: Alexis de Tocqueville's *Democracy in America* (1835). Tocqueville described a pattern of incessant movement everywhere, and marvelled at the immense expenditures of human energy dedicated to the pursuit of happiness. But he grew increasingly agitated about where all these people were going. What was their perpetual motion for? What did their activities mean? What frightened him, when he thought about the human prospect ahead, was the possibility that it didn't mean anything at all. (See the later chapters in vol. 2, esp. 'Why great revolutions will become more rare'.)

6   Cf. Kaufmann 1954: 505–9 for a slightly later piece, 'What the Germans lack', from *The Twilight of the Idols* (1888).

7   Cited in Fussell 1975: 13. Both this book and Kern (1983) locate the war experience within the development of modernism.

8   See Marcus 1989 for a spirited and fascinating essay that traces Dada's radical sources (in various gnostic heresies) and outgrowths (in the punk rock subcultures of the 1970s).

9   For discussion of the sixties vis-à-vis the fifties, see Berman 1982, Introduction and ch. 5; also Dickstein 1977: esp. Part I.

10 A marvellous illustrated book (Anderson 1984) gives some sense of the intelligence and sensitivity behind *United States*. There is also an hour-long video presentation made in the early 1980s for PBS.

11 Because of these modernist virtues – and maybe also because of Lin's race and sex – the design almost didn't get built. A chauvinist crusade was mounted against it, led by the billionaire Ross Perot, President Reagan's Secretary of the Interior James Watt, the writer Tom Wolfe, the *National Review*, and a legion of White House intimates. For a narrative of this controversy, see Scruggs and Swerdlow 1985. Lin's enemies failed to stop the memorial, but did manage to compromise its design, by adding a sculpture of three soldiers by Frederick Hart. (Hart's work is executed in a socialist-realist style that would have been perfectly at home in Stalin's Moscow.) Considering the bitterness of this affair, it is remarkable – and, it must be said, a tribute to American political culture – that Lin's essential idea was realized in the end.

12 See the exhibition catalogue (Levine 1985), which includes an essay by Levine and an interview with him, photos of the billboards on the streets, and angry letters and editorials.

13 My sense of Kiefer's development derives largely from the 1987–8 retrospective show, organized by the Chicago Art Institute and the Philadelphia Museum of Art, which I saw at New York's Museum of Modern Art in November and December 1988. The exhibition catalogue, by Mark Rosenthal, provides extensive documentation: the 'Occupations' series is at 14–15; Margarete–Shulamith, including Celan's poem in German and English, at 95–104. A brilliant reading of Kiefer's career, which stresses his roots in the 1960s New Left culture of protest and confrontation, was given in October 1988 by Andreas Huyssen, in a lecture at the Museum of Modern Art, 'Anselm Kiefer: the terror of history and the temptation of

myth'; Huyssen's essay was published in the Spring 1989 issue of *October*, and also appeared in Huyssen's *After the Great Divide*.

REFERENCES

Anderson, Laurie 1984: *United States*. New York: Harper & Row.
Baudrillard, Jean 1983: 'The procession of simulacra', in *Simulations*, tr. Paul Foss and Paul Patton. New York: Semiotext(e). Also repr. in B. Wallis (ed.) 1984: *Art after Modernism*. New York: Godine/New Museum of Contemporary Art.
Berman, Marshall 1982: *All that Is Solid Melts into Air: The Experience of Modernity*. New York: Simon & Schuster; 1983: London: Verso; 1988 (2nd edn): Harmondsworth: Penguin.
Brown, Norman O. 1959: *Life against Death: The Psychoanalytical Meaning of History*. Middletown, Conn.: Wesleyan University Press.
Dickstein, Morris 1977: *Gates of Eden: American Culture in the Sixties*; 1989 (2nd edn): Harmondsworth: Penguin.
Dostoevsky, F. 1864: *Notes from Underground*; 1960 edn ed. and tr. R. Mattaw, New York: Dulton.
Foster, Hal (ed.) 1983: *The Anti-Aesthetic: Essays on the Post-modern Condition* Bay Press. Port Townsend Wash.: Bay Press.
Freud, Sigmund 1915: 'Thoughts for the times on war and death', tr. E. Colburn Mayne, in Freud, *Collected Papers*, vol. 4. New York: Basic Books. Also in Rieff 1962: 107–33.
Freud, Sigmund 1930, 1931: *Civilization and Its Discontents*; 1961: (new tr. by John Strachey) New York: Norton.
Fussell, Paul 1975: *The Great War and Modern Memory*. Oxford: Oxford University Press.
Hegel, G. W. F. 1910: *The Phenomenology of the Spirit* tr. J. B. Baillie. London: Allen & Unwin; 1955 repr. London: Macmillan, Preface.
Hemingway, Ernest 1929: *A Farewell to Arms*. New York: Scribner.
Huyssen, Andreas 1986: *After the Great Divide: Modernism, Mass Culture and Post-modernism*. Bloomington Ind.: Indiana University Press.
Huyssen, Andreas 1989: 'Anselm Kiefer: the terror of history and the temptation of myth', *October*, Spring.
Kariel, Henry 1988: *The Desperate Politics of Post-modernism*. Amherst, Mass.: University of Massachusetts Press.
Kaufmann, Walter (ed.) 1954: *The Portable Nietzsche*. New York: Viking.
Kern, Stephen 1983: 'The cubist war', in *The Culture of Time and Space, 1880–1918*. Cambridge, Mass.: Harvard University Press, 287–312.
Kupferberg, Tuli 1965: 'Nothing', on *The Fugs' First Album*, ESP 1018.
Levine, Les 1985: *Blame God: The Billboard Projects*. London: Institute of Contemporary Arts.
Lose, B. 1981: 'Nothing', on *Generic Flipper*, Subterranean Records, SUB 25.

Lowell, Robert 1962: *Imitations*. New York: Noonday.

Lyotard, Jean-François 1977: *La Condition postmoderne*; 1984 (Eng. tr. Geoff Bennington and Brian Massumi; Intro. Fredric Jameson) Minneapolis: University of Minnesota Press, as *The Postmodern Condition: A Report on Knowledge* (UK edn: Manchester University Press, 1986).

Marcus, Greil 1989: *Lipstick Traces: A Secret History of the Twentieth Century*. Cambridge, Mass.: Havard University Press.

Marx, K., and Engels, F. 1848: *The Communist Manifesto*, in Marx and Engels 1959: *Basic Writings on Politics and Philosophy*, ed. L. Feuer. New York: Anchor, 1–14.

Mill, J. S. 1859: *On Liberty*, ch. 3: 'Of individuality, as one of the elements of well-being', in Marshall Cohen (ed.) 1961: *The Philosophy of John Stuart Mill*. New York: Modern Library.

Nietzsche, F. 1883: *Thus Spoke Zarathustra*, Part I, in Kaufmann 1954.

Nietzsche, F. 1888; Eng. tr. 1968: *The Will to Power*, tr. Walter Kaufmann and R. J. Hollingdale, ed. Kaufmann. London: Weidenfeld & Nicolson; New York: Vintage, Bk I, 'European nihilism', esp. sections 13 and 23.

Oldenburg, Claes 1970: 'Store days', rpr. in Barbara Rose, *Claes Oldenburg*. New York: Museum of Modern Art.

Rieff, Philip (ed.) 1962: *Character and Culture*. New York: Collier.

Rotten, Johnny; Cook, Paul; Jones, Steve; Matlock, Glen, and Vicious, Sid 1977: 'No future', on *Never Mind the Bollocks Here's the Sex Pistols*, Warner Bros BSK 3147.

Rushdie, Salman 1984: 'Outside the whale', *Granta*, 11.

Rushdie, Salman 1988/1989: *The Satanic Verses*. London: Cape/New York: Viking.

Scruggs, Jan, and Swerdlow, Joel 1985: *To Heal a Nation: The Vietnam Veterans Memorial*. New York: Harper & Row.

Tocqueville, Alexis de 1835; Eng. tr. 1838: *Democracy in America*. Many edns.

Tucker, Richard C. (ed.) 1978: *Marx–Engels Reader*, 2nd edn. New York: Norton.

Wallis, Brian (ed.) 1984: *Art after Modernism*, intro. Marcia Tucker. New York: Godine/New Museum of Contemporary Art.

Watt, Kira, and Watt, Mike 1985: 'No one', on Minutemen, *3-Way Tie for Last*, SST 058.

2

Cosmopolitanism without emancipation: a response to Lyotard

Richard Rorty

In the form John Dewey gave it, pragmatism is a philosophy tailored to the needs of political liberalism, a way of making political liberalism look good to persons with philosophical tastes. It provides a rationale for non-ideological, compromising, reformist muddling-through (what Dewey called 'experimentalism'), urging that categorical distinctions of the sort philosophers typically invoke are useful only so long as they facilitate conversation about what we should do next. Such distinctions, Dewey says, should be blurred or erased as soon as they begin to hinder such conversation – to block the road of enquiry.

Dewey thinks that muddle, compromise and blurry syntheses are usually less perilous, politically, than Cartesian clarity. That is one reason why his books are so often thought bland and boring. For he neither erects an exciting new binary opposition in terms of which to praise the good and damn the bad, nor even distinguishes bad binary oppositions and some other form of discourse which somehow avoids using such oppositions. He just urges us to be on our guard against using intellectual tools which were useful in a certain socio-cultural environment after that environment has changed, to be aware that we may have to invent new tools to cope with new situations.

Dewey spent half his time debunking the very idea of 'human nature' and of 'philosophical foundations' for social thought. But he spent the other half spinning a story about universal history – a story of progress according to which contemporary movements for social reform within the liberal democracies are parts of the same over-all movement as the overthrow of feudalism and the abolition of slavery. He offered a historical narrative in which American democracy is the embodiment of all the best features of the West, while at the same time making fun of what Jean-François Lyotard, in his *Postmodern Condition*, has called 'metanarratives'.

Dewey thought that we could have a morally uplifting historical narrative without bothering to erect a metaphysical backdrop against which this narrative is played out, and without getting very specific about the goal for which it strives. Followers of Dewey like myself would like to praise parliamentary democracy and the welfare state as very good things, but only on the basis of invidious comparisons with suggested concrete alternatives, not on the basis of claims that these institutions are truer to human nature, or more rational, or in better accord with the universal moral law, than feudalism or totalitarianism. Like Lyotard, we want to drop *meta*narratives, but keep on recounting edifying first-order narratives.

In his 'Universal history and cultural differences' Lyotard raises the question: 'can we continue to organize the events which crowd in upon us from the human and non-human worlds with the help of the Idea of a universal history of humanity?' (Lyotard 1985: 559). The pragmatist answer is that we can and should, as long as the point of doing so is to lift our spirits through utopian fantasy, rather than to gird our loins with metaphysical weapons.[1] We Deweyans have a story to tell about the progress of our species, a story whose later episodes emphasize how things have been getting better in the West during the last few centuries, and which concludes with some suggestions about how they might become better still in the next few. But when asked about cultural differences, about what our story has to do with the Chinese or the Cashinahua, we can only reply that, for all we know, intercourse with these people may help modify our Western ideas about what institutions can best embody the spirit of Western social democracy.

We look forward, in a vague way, to a time when the Cashinahua, the Chinese, and (if such there be) the planets which form the Galactic Empire will all be part of the same cosmopolitan social democratic community. This community will doubtless have different institutions from those to which we are at present accustomed, but we assume that these future institutions will incorporate and enlarge the sorts of reforms which we applaud our ancestors for having made. The Chinese, the Cashinahua, and the Galactics will doubtless have suggestions about what further reforms are needed, but we shall not be inclined to adopt these suggestions until we have managed to fit them in with our distinctively Western social democratic aspirations, through some sort of judicious give-and-take.

This sort of ethnocentrism is, we pragmatists think, inevitable and unobjectionable. It amounts to little more than the claim that people can rationally change their beliefs and desires only by holding most of those beliefs and desires constant – even though we can never say in advance just which are to be changed and which retained intact. ('Rationally' here means being able to give a retrospective account of why one changed – what old beliefs or desires one invoked in justification of the new ones – rather than having to say, helplessly, 'it just happened; somehow I got converted'.) We cannot leap outside our Western social democratic skins when we encounter another culture, and we should not try. All we should try to do is to get inside the inhabitants of that culture long enough to get some idea of how we look to them, and whether they have any ideas we can use. That is also all they can be expected to do on encountering us. If members of the other culture protest that this expectation of tolerant reciprocity is a provincially Western one, we can only shrug our shoulders and reply that we have to work by our own lights, even as they do, for there is no super-cultural observation platform to which we might repair. The only common ground on which we can get together is that defined by the overlap between their communal beliefs and desires and our own.

The pragmatist utopia is thus not one in which human nature has been unshackled, but one in which everybody has had a chance to suggest ways in which we might clap together a world (or Galactic) society, and in which all such suggestions have been thrashed out in free and open encounters. We pragmatists do not think that there is a natural 'moral kind' coextensive with our biological species, one which binds together the French, the Americans and the Cashinahua. But we nevertheless feel free to use slogans like Tennyson's 'The Parliament of Man, the Federation of the World!' For we want narratives of increasing cosmopolitanism, but not narratives of emancipation. We think that there was nothing to emancipate, just as there was nothing which biological evolution emancipated as it moved along from the trilobites to the anthropoids. There is no human nature which was once, or still is, in chains.[2] Rather, our species has – ever since it developed language – been making up a nature for itself. This nature has been developed through ever larger, richer, more muddled, and more painful syntheses of opposing values.

Lately our species has been making up a particularly good nature for itself – that produced by the institutions of the liberal West. When we praise this development, we pragmatists drop the revolutionary rhetoric of emancipation and unmasking in favour of a reformist rhetoric about increased tolerance and decreased suffering. If we have an Idea (in the capitalized, Kantian sense) in mind, it is that of Tolerance rather than that of Emancipation. We see no reason why either recent social and political developments or recent philosophical thought should deter us from our attempt to build a cosmopolitan world society – one which embodies the same sort of utopia with which the Christian, Enlightenment and Marxist metanarratives of emancipation ended.

Consider, in this light, Lyotard's claim that his question 'Can we continue to organize the crowd of human events into a universal history of humanity?' presupposes that there 'persists' a 'we', and his doubt that we can preserve a sense for 'we' once we give up the Kantian idea of emancipation (Lyotard 1985: 560–1). My first reaction to such doubts is that we need not presuppose a *persistent* 'we', a trans-historical metaphysical subject, in order to tell stories of progress. The only 'we' we need is a local and temporary one: 'we' means something like 'us twentieth-century Western social democrats'. So we pragmatists are content to embrace the alternative which Lyotard calls 'secondary narcissism' (1985: 561). We think that, once we give up metaphysical attempts to find a 'true self' for man, we can only speak as the contingent historical selves we find ourselves to be.

Lyotard warns that adopting this alternative will land us pragmatic liberals in the same position as the Nazis were in: in renouncing unanimity we shall fall back on terror, on a kind of terror 'whose rationale is not in principle accessible to everybody and whose benefits are not sharable by everybody' (1985: 562). Against this assimilation of the pragmatist's inevitable ethnocentrism to Nazism, I would insist that there is an important difference between saying, 'We admit that we cannot justify our beliefs or our actions to all human beings as they are at present, but we hope to create a community of free human beings who will freely share many of our beliefs and hopes' and saying, with the Nazis, 'We have no concern for legitimizing ourselves in the eyes of others.' There is a difference between the Nazi who says, 'We are good because we are the particular group we are' and the reformist liberal who says, 'We are good because, by persuasion rather than force, we shall eventually convince everybody else that we are.'

Whether such a 'narcissistic' self-justification can avoid terrorism depends on whether the notion of 'persuasion rather than force' still makes sense after we renounce the idea of human nature and the search for trans-cultural and ahistorical criteria of justification. If I have correctly understood Lyotard's line of thought, he would argue that the existence of incommensurable, untranslatable discourses throws doubt on this contrast between force and persuasion. He has suggested that the collapse of metaphysics diagnosed by Adorno can be seen as a recognition of the 'multiplicity of worlds of names, the insurmountable diversity of cultures' (1985: 564). I take him to be saying that, because of this insurmountability, one culture cannot convert another by persuasion, but only by some form of 'imperialist' force. When, for example, he says that 'Nothing in a savage community disposes it to argue itself into a society of citizens [of Kant's cosmopolitan world-state]' (1985: 566), I interpret him to mean that when people from pre-literate cultures go to mission schools and European universities they are not freely arguing themselves into cosmopolitanism but rather being 'forcibly' changed, terrorized. I assume that he would also say that, when an anthropologist is so charmed by the tribe he studies that he abandons Europe and 'goes native', he too would not have been persuaded but, equally, 'terrorized'.

Lyotard would be justified in these distressing claims if it were the case, as he says it is, that the anthropologist describes 'the savage narrations and their rules according to cognitive rules, without pretending to establish any continuity between the latter and his own mode of discourse'. But surely this is overstated. The anthropologist and the native agree, after all, on an enormous number of platitudes. They usually share beliefs about, for example, the desirability of finding waterholes, the danger of fondling poisonous snakes, the need for shelter in bad weather, the tragedy of the death of loved ones, the value of courage and endurance, and so on. If they did not, as Donald Davidson has remarked, it is hard to see how the two would ever have been able to learn enough of each other's languages to recognize the other as a language-user, and thus as a person.

This Davidsonian point amounts to saying that the notion of a language untranslatable into ours makes no sense, if 'untranslatable' means 'unlearnable'. If I can learn a native language, then even if I cannot neatly pair off sentences in that language with sentences in English, I can certainly offer plausible explanations in English of why the natives are saying each of the funny-sounding things they say. I can provide the same sort of gloss on their utterances which a literary critic offers of poems written in a new idiom or an historian of the 'barbarism' of our ancestors. Cultural differences are not different in kind from differences between old and ('revolutionary') new theories propounded within a single culture. The attempt to give a respectful hearing to Cashinahua views is not different in kind from the attempt to give a respectful hearing to some radically new scientific or political or philosophical suggestion offered by one of our fellow Westerners.

So I think it is misleading to say, as Lyotard does in an essay on Wittgenstein, that Wittgenstein has shown that 'there is no unity of language, but rather islets of language, each governed by a system of rules untranslatable into those of the others' (Lyotard 1984: 61). We need to distinguish between the following two theses: (1) there is no single commensurating language, known in advance, which will provide an idiom into which to translate any new theory, poetic idiom, or native culture; (2) there are unlearnable languages. The first of these theses is common to Kuhn, Wittgenstein, and the common sense of the anthropological profession. It is a corollary of the general pragmatist claim that there is no permanent ahistorical metaphysical framework into which everything can be fitted. The second thesis seems to me incoherent. I do not see how we could tell when we had come up against a human practice which we knew to be linguistic and also knew to be so foreign that we must give up hope of knowing what it would be like to engage in it.

Whereas Lyotard takes Wittgenstein to be pointing out unbridgeable divisions between linguistic islets, I see him as recommending the construction of causeways which will, in time, make the archipelago in question continuous with the mainland. These causeways do not take the form of translation manuals, but rather of the sort of cosmopolitan know-how whose acquisition enables us to move back and forth between sectors of our own culture and our own history – for example, between Aristotle and Freud, between the language-game of worship and that of commerce, between the idioms of Holbein and of Matisse. On my reading, Wittgenstein was not warning us against attempts to translate the untranslatable but rather against the unfortunate philosophical habit of seeing different languages as embodying incompatible systems of rules. If one does see them in this way, then the lack of an overarching system of metarules for pairing off sentences – the sort of system which meta-narratives were once supposed to help us get – will strike one as a disaster. But if one sees language-learning as the acquisition of a skill, one will not be tempted to ask what metaskill permits such acquisition. One will assume that curiosity, tolerance, patience and hard work are all that is needed.

This difference between thinking of linguistic mastery as a grasping of rules and as an inarticulable technique may seem a long way from the question of the possibility of universal history. So let me now try to connect the two topics. I have been suggesting that

Lyotard sees languages as divided from one another by incompatible systems of linguistic rules, and is thereby committed to what Davidson (1984: 189) has called 'the third, and perhaps last, dogma of empiricism: the distinction between scheme and content'. He is committed, in particular, to the claim that we can usefully distinguish questions of fact from questions of language, a claim attacked by Dewey and Quine. It seems to me that only with the help of that distinction can Lyotard cast doubt on the pragmatist attempt to see the history of humanity as the history of the gradual replacement of force by persuasion, the gradual spread of certain virtues typical of the democratic West. For only the claim that commensuration is impossible will provide philosophical grounds for ruling out this suggestion, and only the language – fact distinction will make sense of the claim that incommensurability is something more than a temporary inconvenience.

I can try to put this point in Lyotard's own vocabulary by taking up his distinctions between *litige* and *différend*, and between *dommage* and *tort*. He defines a *différend* as a case in which 'a plaintiff is deprived of means of arguing, and so becomes a victim', one in which the rules of conflict resolution which apply to a case are stated in the idiom of one of the parties, in such a way that the other party cannot explain how he has been injured (Lyotard 1983: 24–5). By contrast, in the case of *litige*, where it is a question of *dommage* rather than *tort*, both sides agree on how to state the issues, and on what criteria are to be applied to resolve them. In a very interesting and enlightening synthesis of philosophical and political problems, Lyotard suggests that we can see everything from the semantic paradoxes of self-reference to anti-colonialist struggles in terms of these contrasts. Using this vocabulary, Lyotard's doubts about universal history can be put by saying that the liberal-pragmatist attempt to see history as the triumph of persuasion over force tries to treat history as a long process of litigation, rather than a sequence of *différends*.

My general reply to these doubts is to say that political liberalism amounts to the suggestion that we try to substitute litigation for *différends* as far as we can, and that there is no a priori philosophical reason why this attempt must fail, just as (*pace* Christianity, Kant and Marx) there is no a priori reason why it must succeed. But I also want to raise doubts about Lyotard's choice of terminology. It seems a bad idea – and indeed a suspiciously Kantian idea – to think of enquiry on the model of judicial proceedings. The philosophical tradition has pictured institutions or theories as being brought before the tribunal of pure reason, and if this were the only model available then Lyotard would have a point when he asks: 'What language do the judges speak?' But Dewey wanted to get rid of the idea that new ideas or practices could be judged by antecedently existing criteria. He wanted everything to be as much up for grabs as fensible as much of the time as feasible. He suggested that we think of rationality not as the application of criteria (as in a tribunal) but as the achievement of consensus (as in a town meeting.)

This suggestion chimes with Wittgenstein's suggestion that we think of linguistic competence not as the mastery of rules but as the ability to get along with other players of the language-game, a game played without referees. Both Dewey and Wittgenstein made the point which Stanley Fish has recently restated: that any attempt to erect 'rules' or 'criteria' will be an attempt to hypostatize and eternalize some past or present practice, thereby making it more difficult for that practice to be reformed, or gradually replaced with a different practice (Fish 1989).[3] The Deweyan idea that rationality is not the application of criteria goes together with holism in the philosophy of language, and in particular with the claim that there are no 'linguistic islets', no such things as 'conceptual schemes' but only slightly different sets of beliefs and desires. *Pace* Lyotard's interpretation of Wittgenstein, it seems to me profoundly un-Wittgensteinian to say, as he does, that 'there is no unity of language', or that 'there is an irredeemable opacity at the heart of language' (Lyotard 1984: 84). For language no more has a nature than humanity does; both have only a history. There is just as much unity or transparency of language as there is willingness to converse rather than fight. So there is as much of either as we shall make in the course of history. The history of humanity will be a universal history just in proportion to the amount of free consensus among human beings which is attained – that is, in proportion to the replacement of force by persuasion, of *différends* by litigation.

On the holistic view of language elaborated by Quine and Davidson, distinctions between cultures, theories or discourses are just ways of dividing up the corpus of sentences asserted so far into clusters, sorting out the sentences which have been held in the course of human history. These clusters are not divided from one another by incompatible linguistic rules, nor by reciprocally unlearnable grammars. They represent no more than differences of opinion – the sorts of differences which can get resolved by hashing things out. So when we say that Aristotle and Galileo, or the Greeks and the Cashinhua, or Holbein and Matisse, did not 'speak the same language', we should not mean that they carried around different Kantian categories, or different 'semantic rules', with which to organize their experience. Rather, we should mean merely that they held such disparate beliefs that there would have been no simple, easy, quick way for either to convince the other to engage in a common project. This phenomenon of disagreement cannot be explained by saying that they speak different languages, for that would be a *virtus dormitiva* sort of explanation – like explaining the fact that people do different things in different countries by pointing to the existence of different national customs.

I can put the disagreement between Lyotard and myself in another way by saying that what he calls the *défaillance* of modernity strikes me as no more than the loss of belief in the first of the two theses I distinguished earlier – a loss of faith in our ability to come up with a single set of criteria which everybody in all times and places can accept, to invent a single language-game which somehow can take over all the jobs previously done by all the language-games ever played. But the loss of this theoretical goal merely shows that one of the less important sideshows of Western civilization – metaphysics – is the process of closing down. This failure to find a single grand commensurating discourse in which to write a universal translation-manual (thereby doing away with the need to constantly learn new languages) does nothing to cast doubt on the possibility (as opposed to the difficulty) of peaceful social progress. In particular, the failure of metaphysics does not hinder us from making a useful distinction between persuasion and force. We can see the pre-literate native as being persuaded rather than forced to become cosmopolitan just insofar as, having learned to play the language-games of Europe, he decides to abandon the ones he played earlier – without being threatened with loss of food, shelter, or *Lebensraum* if he makes the opposite decision.

It is, of course, rare for a native to have been granted this sort of free choice. Western liberals typically *have* used force rather than persuasion to convince natives of our own goodness. It is useful to be reminded, as Lyotard reminds us, of Westerners' customary imperialist hypocrisy. But it is also the case that Western liberals have raised up generations of historian of colonialism, anthropologists, sociologists, specialists in the economics of development, etc., who have explained to us in detail just how violent and critical we have been. The anthropologists have, in addition, shown us that the pre-literate natives have some ideas and practices that we can usefully weave together with our own. These reformist arguments, of a sort familiar to the tradition of Western liberalism, are examples of the ability of that tradition to alter its direction from the inside, and thus to convert *différends* into processes of litigation. One does not have to be particularly cheerful or optimistic about the prospects for such internal reform, nor about the likelihood of a final victory of persuasion over force, to think that such a victory is the only plausible political goal we have managed to envisage – or to see ever more inclusive universal histories as useful instruments for the achievement of that goal.

By 'ever more inclusive' I mean such that one's conception of the goal of history – of the nature of the future cosmopolitan society – constantly changes to accommodate the lessons learned from new experiences (for example, the sort of ghastly experiences provided by Attila, Hitler and Stalin, the sort reported by anthropologists, and the sort provided by artists). This Deweyan programme of constant, experimental, reformulation means that (in Lyotard's phrase) 'the place of the first person' is constantly changing. Deweyan pragmatists urge us to think of ourselves as part of a pageant of historical progress which will gradually encompass all of the human race, and are willing to argue that the vocabulary which twentieth-century Western social democrats use is the best vocabulary the race has come up with so far (for example, by arguing that the vocabulary of the Casinahua can't be combined with modern technology, and that abandoning that technology is too high a price to pay for the benefits the Casinahua enjoy). But pragmatists are quite sure that their own vocabulary will be superseded – and, from their point of view, the sooner the better. They expect their descendants to be as condescending about the vocabulary of twentieth-century liberals as they are about the vocabulary of Aristotle or of Rousseau. What links them to the inhabitants of the utopia they foresee is not the belief that the future will still speak as they speak, but rather the hope that future human beings will think of Dewey as 'one of us', just as we speak of Rousseau as 'one of us'. Pragmatists hope, but have no metaphysical justification for believing, that future universal histories of humanity will describe twentieth-century Western social democrats in favourable terms. But they admit that we have no very clear idea what those terms will be. They only insist that, if these new terms have been adopted as a result of persuasion rather than force, they will be better than the ones we are using at present – for that is analytic of their meaning of 'better'.

Let me close by making a general remark about the relations between French and American philosophy, taking off from a remark of Lyotard's. He has written that contemporary German and American philosophers think of current French thought as 'neo-irrationalist', instancing Habermas's recent lectures in Paris, lectures which he describes as 'giving lessons in how to be progressive to Derrida and Foucault' (Lyotard 1984: 81). The Deweyan line I have been taking in these remarks is reminiscent of Habermas's 'consensus theory of truth', and it may seem that I too have been offering 'lessons in progressivism'. But I think that Lyotard mis-states the criticism which Habermasians and pragmatists are inclined to make of recent French thought. Given our non-criterial conception of rationality, we are not inclined to diagnose 'irrationalism'; since for us 'rational' merely means 'persuasive', 'irrational' can only mean 'invoking force', and we are not claiming that French thinkers resort to the lash and knout. But we *are* inclined to worry about their anti-utopianism, their apparent loss of faith in liberal democracy. Even those who, like myself, think of France as the source of the most original philosophical thought currently being produced, cannot figure out why French thinkers are so willing to say things like 'May 1968 refutes the doctrine of parliamentary liberalism' (Lyotard 1985: 563). From our standpoint, nothing could refute that doctrine except some better idea about how to organize society. No event – not even Auschwitz – can show that we should cease to work for a given utopia. Only another, more persuasive, utopia can do that.

More generally, we cannot figure out why philosophers like Lyotard are so inclined to take particular historical events as demonstrating the 'bankruptcy' of long-term efforts at social reform. This willingness – which is, perhaps, an after-effect of a long attempt to salvage something from Marxism, an attempt which has resulted in the adoption of certain characteristically Marxist habits of thought – sets contemporary French philosophy apart from philosophy in Britain, the United States and Germany. Such a willingness to interpret very specific political as well as economic and technological developments as indications of decisive shifts in the course of history will, to be sure, make the idea of 'the universal history of humanity' very dubious. Conversely, a willingness to see these as probably just more of the same old familiar vicissitudes is required to take the Dewey–Habermas line, to persist in using notions like 'persuasion rather than force' and 'consensus' to state one's political goals.

I find it strange, for example, that Lyotard should both drop the project of universal history and yet be willing to discover world-historical significance in, for example, new technologies of information-processing and new developments in the physical and biological sciences. The standard Anglo-Saxon assumption is that the determination of world-historical significance – deciding whether May 1968, or the development of the microchip, was a decisive turning-point or just more of the same – should be postponed until a century or so after the event in question has taken place. This hunch dictates a philosophical style which is very different from Lyotard's, one which does not try to make philosophical hay out of current events. The difference between that style and current French styles is, I think, the main reason for the frequent breakdowns of communication between American philosophers and their French colleagues.

Another way of formulating the difference between these two styles is to say that French philosophers specialize in trying to establish what Lyotard calls *maîtrise de la parole et du sens* by engaging in 'radical critique' – that is, by inventing a new vocabulary which makes all the old political and philosophical issues obsolete. Anglo-Saxon philosophers, by contrast, often try to pretend that everybody always has spoken the same language, that questions of vocabulary are 'merely verbal' and that what matters is *argument* – argument which appeals to 'intuitions' statable in the universal vocabulary which everybody has always used. As long as we Anglo-Saxons affect this implausible view, we shall continue to tend to resort to the clumsy and inapt epithet 'irrationalist'.

It is certainly the case that Anglo-Saxon philosophers would do better to renounce this epithet, to become a bit more 'French', and to realize that a universal vocabulary has to be worked for rather than taken for granted. But we Anglo-Saxons suspect that French philosophy could profit from realizing that adopting a new vocabulary only makes sense if you can say something about the debilities of the old vocabulary from the inside, and can move back and forth, dialectically, between the old and the new vocabulary. It seems to us as if our French colleagues are too willing to find, or make, a linguistic islet and then invite people to move onto it, and not interested enough in building causeways between such islets and the mainland.

This difference between wanting new vocabularies and wanting new arguments is closely connected with the difference between revolutionary and reformist politics. Anglo-Saxon intellectuals take for granted that (in countries, like France and the USA, where the press and the elections remain free) 'serious' politics is reformist. From this point of view, revolutionary politics in such countries can be no more than intellectual exhibitionism. By contrast, it seems to be taken for granted among French intellectuals that 'serious' political thought is revolutionary thought, and that offering concrete suggestions, phrased in the current political idiom of the day, to the electorate or to elected leaders is beneath the intellectual's dignity – or, at best, something one does only in one's spare time. I suspect that the differences between what Lyotard gets out of Wittgenstein and what I get out of him, and also between his interpretation of 'postmodernity' as a decisive shift which cuts right across culture and my view of it as merely the gradual encapsulation and forgetting of a certain philosophical tradition, reflect our different notions of how politically conscious intellectuals should spend their time.

NOTES

1 The May 1985 issue of *Critique* also includes a French translation of the original version of my response to Lyotard, as well as a paper by Vincent Descombes ('Les mots de la tribu') which comments on the exchange between us, as well as on my earlier paper 'Habermas, Lyotard, and postmodernity', reprinted in vol. 2 of these papers (R. Rorty, *Essays on Heidegger and Others*). It also includes the transcript of a brief conversational exchange between Lyotard and me.

2 See Yack 1986. Yack describes a tradition to which, as I see it, Foucault and Lyotard belong, but Dewey does not. It never occurred to Dewey that there was something inherently 'repressive' about society as such, or something wrong with using bio-power to create subjects. He took over from Hegel the idea that you have to be socialized to be human, and that the important question is how you can maximize both richness of socialization and tolerance for individual eccentricity and deviance. That is a question which can be answered only by designing and performing a lot of painful and difficult social experiments, a lot more than we have so far envisaged.

3 See 'Consequences', in Fish 1989. This essay was delivered as a contribution to the same symposium for which Lyotard's and my papers were written, and was published as 'La théorie est sans conséquences', in the same issue of *Critique* in which ours appeared.

REFERENCES

Davidson, Donald 1984: 'On the very idea of a conceptual scheme', in *Inquiries into Truth and Interpretation*. Oxford: Clarendon Press.

Fish, Stanley 1989: 'Consequences', in Idem, *Doing what Comes Naturally: Change, Rhetoric, and the Practice of Theory in Literary and Legal Studies*. Durham, NC: Duke University Press.

Lyotard, Jean-François 1985: 'Histoire universelle et différences culturelles', *Critique*, 41 (May).

Lyotard, Jean-François 1983: *Le Différend*. Paris: Minuit.

Lyotard, Jean-François 1984: *Le Tombeau de l'intellectuel et autres papiers*. Paris: Galilée.

Rorty, Richard 1991: *Essays on Heidegger and Others: Philosophical Papers*, vol. 1. Cambridge: Cambridge University Press.

Yack, Bernard 1986: *The Longing for Total Revolution: Philosophical Sources of Social Discontent from Rousseau to Marx and Nietzsche*. Princeton: Princeton University Press.

3

Modernity as postmodernity: Jean-François Lyotard

Christa Bürger

ON LYOTARD'S 'AFFIRMATIVE' AESTHETICS

For all that he inveighs against nostalgia and seeks to consign the word to oblivion, the writing of Jean-François Lyotard draws its inspiration from the memory of May 1968, from that time when theory and action were one, that privileged historical moment of boundless intensity which seemed to herald the sudden transformation of political into libidinal economy; his writing is 'an effort to raise theory to the same degree of intensity as had been attained by practice in May 68' (Lyotard 1973a: 10). In his texts of this period, which are reminiscent of Breton's surrealist manifestos, Lyotard announces a desire-revolution, in which the hybrid combination of key terms indicates the imaginary position of the writer, whose thinking follows 'pagan' byways, which unexpectedly converge into a trail where one finds the tracks of both Marx and Freud. For this reason it is no easy matter to discuss Lyotard's work and to 'reconstruct' his thinking is impossible, since he engages in a type of discourse which he himself describes as theory-fiction. His aim is to throw off the deceptive authority of meaning and, with his texts, to attain nothing other than states of excitation which will give rise to new texts, political actions, acts of protest, artistic productions, economic initiatives etc.:

> What is important in a text is not its meaning, what it is trying to say, but what it does and causes to be done. What it does: the affective charge it contains and communicates; what it causes to be done: the transformation of these potential energies into something else – other texts, but also paintings, photos,

film sequences, political actions, decisions, inspirations to love, refusals to obey, economic initiatives. (*Lyotard 1973a: 6*)

None the less, I shall attempt to identify certain of the leitmotifs of his thinking from his writings. This can, however, only be done with certain reservations, since Lyotard himself opposes the postulate of consistency, both in theory and in action; to subordinate oneself to it would mean handing a victory to reason which has to be combated precisely because it is so closely allied with power. 'Reason is already in power in capital. And it is not because it is not rational that we want to destroy capital, but because it is. Reason and power are one and the same' (1973a: 12–13).

Lyotard belongs to those intellectuals of our age who, even when they have from time to time found a niche within the movements of contemporary thought, have none the less always held to a basic position. In the case of Lyotard, this is a genuine anarchistic impulse. The texts which arise out of the élan of the May movement are written from the perspective of the *désirrévolution*. In the younger generation's attitude of refusal and protest, which does not arise out of deprivation, but precisely out of a phase of prosperous capitalism, Lyotard had been happy to welcome the signs of a spontaneous, directionless redistribution of libidinal energies: 'le désir ne s'investit plus dans le dispositif kapitaliste' (1973a: 16).

Even at that stage, however, a displacement in his thinking was becoming apparent, one which may cast light upon his shift from the pathos of critique to the pathos of forgetting (see Wellmer 1985: 53). As early as his *Dispositifs pulsionnels*, Lyotard was advancing the thesis that Marx had directed all his political energies to what was ultimately a morally based project, in terms of which Revolution presented itself as a type of gigantic reparation. The forces in this *dispositif* are the suffering proletariat as the accuser and capital as the accused party of exploiters. A book like Deleuze and Guattari's *Anti-Oedipus* (1977) had liberated Marxism from this compulsive scheme of thought.[1] Behind this argumentation one recognizes Nietzsche's polemic against 'pessimism of indignation' [*Entrüstungspessimismus*], against 'the claim to judge history, to divest it of its fatality, to discover responsibility behind it, *guilty men* in it' and its promise of 'redemption from all guilt' (Nietzsche 1973: vol. 3, 820–1).[2]

Lyotard thus wishes to rid the *dispositif* of modernity – in an ironic side-swipe against Habermas, he puts the word modernity in inverted commas – of the 'therapeutic attitude' (Lyotard 1977: 132) and, in so doing, he wishes to take his leave of one of the left-wing intelligentsia's key concepts, critique. For him, critique is merely a negative activity. Insofar as it is rational, it is basically dependent upon the system it is criticizing. It is necessarily either opposition (and thus merely reformist) or it itself goes over to the side of power. And it erects hierarchies. The critic (the educator) sets himself above what he is criticizing.

> The critic remains within the sphere of what is criticized...
> And [this activity is] profoundly hierarchic: from where does
> the critic derive his power over the object of his criticism? Does
> he *know* better? Is he the teacher, the educator? Is he then
> universality, the university, the State, the city reaching down to
> examine childhood, nature, singularity and the disreputable to
> raise them up to its level? The confessor and God helping the
> sinner to save himself? This staying-within-the-same-sphere re-
> formism sits very well with the maintenance of authoritarian
> structures ... one must drift beyond criticism. But more than
> this, *drifting is itself the end of criticism. (Lyotard 1977: 14–15)*

When Lyotard rejects critique *because* it is rational and, being rational, subject to the same principle which also sustains capitalism, namely the principle of efficiency, this reveals that his conception of critique – contrary to his own assertions – is precisely not that of 'Marxist tradition' (1977: 118), but rather of the rationalist tradition. Within that tradition, critics are in possession of firm yardsticks which ensure their superiority over the object of criticism. The strict methodology of science stands over against the capriciousness and arbitrariness of opinion and, to that extent, rationalist critique is geared to effectiveness and efficiency. By contrast, within the dialectical tradition a concept of immanent critique has developed which does not dogmatically conclude that because it is true the other is necessarily untrue, but gets inside the theory that is being criticized and derives an impetus to thinking from its lacunae and contradictions. Lyotard – and this is what is problematic about his polemic – not only identifies left-wing critique with a type of moralizing criticism such as one might encounter in dogmatic Marxist circles, but with a set of hierarchical social institutions, and this is absolutely absurd.

In a move which seems to be characteristic of periods of lost hope, Lyotard has, since the seventies, turned his attention to aesthetics. The age of manifestos is now past. In a philosophy of art, Lyotard is looking for an answer to the question of how we can offer resistance 'when we have no horizon of emancipation' (Lyotard 1984–5).[3] He characterizes this philosophy as 'affirmative'. In the footsteps of

Nietzsche, he is himself pursuing a 'new way to "yes" ' (Nietzsche 1973: 834) and professes allegiance to Nietzsche's pagan faith, the affirmation of existence. Lyotard develops the concept of affirmation in two directions: a concrete political one and a theoretical one which, with logical coherence, is constantly seeking to get around the frontiers between science and art. This at least suggests that Lyotard removes the theme from the traditional biological context in which it is caught up in Nietzsche's writings.

Politically he is concerned with the reinforcement of what he calls 'minority affirmations', which may perhaps be translated as counter-cultural movements. These have in common with art that they occur, unheeded by theory, as barely perceptible microscopic changes in everyday life – like the *tropismes* which Nathalie Sarraute described. 'They are refined and delicate, long before their expression or appearance on the public stage: thousands of muffled grumblings among housewives long before the Women's Liberation Movement; thousands of jokes told and re-told in Prague before the "Spring" ' (Lyotard 1977: 117). Lyotard's original, anarchistic impetus is recognizable when, using the example of the black economy, he also describes minority affirmations in economic categories. In so doing, he comes to similar conclusions to those of André Gorz:

> within the body of capital, there exists another form of socio-economic life, another non-centred 'domain' made up from a host of individual or anarchic acts of exchange, which have nothing to do with the 'rationality' of production. And it cannot be said that that form of life is a contestation or critique of capitalism (it is not even certain that it bears a relation to the *décadent* idea of work). But it reveals the following paradox: even in a society chiefly centred upon production and consumption, *working may become a minority activity* in the sense of being unrelated to the centre, i.e. neither stimulated nor controlled by it. (*Lyotard 1977: 137*)

Lyotard fights vehemently against such phenomena being interpreted, since interpretation, like critique, remains caught in the dichotomous categories of the dominant rationality and thus robs the patchwork of these numerous little affirmations of its specific power (1977: 116–17). He himself, however, provides a virtually classical interpretation: in the minority affirmations he sees a reversal of the 'ruse of reason' which no longer reveals itself in the course of world-history, but in 'la petite vie', gradually transforming it into 'a sort of "civil society" which has little to do with Hegel's, but is simultaneously informal and active, and continually eludes the instances of power' 1977: 138).

The switching of register, the nomadic wandering (to use Deleuze and Guattari's concept) between art and philosophy is, in Lyotard's fragmentary texts, thoroughly systematic. *Narrative* has been a key concept in his work since the late seventies, and with it in keeping with his conception of theory-fiction, he has purposely sown confusion. Marxist philosophy is as much regarded as narrative – though negatively connoted as metanarrative – as the affirmations which occur in 'la petite vie' or the 'minor literature' which Deleuze and Guattari, taking Kafka as their example, describe. His essays are also, because of such register shifts, difficult to follow; the fields of meaning of the concepts are ceaselessly shifting and running into one another.

There is a certain objective irony in seeing how Lyotard, who wishes to liberate the left from morality, comes forth in his *Instructions païennes* with the pointing finger of the prophet, to tell us a story of Fall and Redemption. And, as is typical with such stories, he supports his tale with a canonical text.[4] As an effect of his reading of Solzhenitsyn's *Gulag Archipelago*, Lyotard claims to have had a kind of 'awakening', which renders his whole previous intellectual existence invalid. It is from this experience that he claims to have gained the insight that intellectuals are but virtuosos of various types of metanarrative; theory is merely a subset of these. The emergence of such narratives appears in Lyotard's story as the Fall; it is accompanied by the destruction of narration. The canonical narrative, the evil in history, appears in two almost equally sinister guises: in Marxist and capitalist variants. Both are totalitarian; both demand belief. The first is based on the fiction that 'the people' occupies all narrative positions, that it is simultaneously narrator, narratee and narrated, the second on the cult of the narrator-genius. Lyotard describes the pragmatics of these narratives in the following way:

> If you are a citizen of one of these regimes, you are regarded as both the co-author of its narrative and a privileged listener, and ... you have to be word-perfect when you are told to act out an episode. You are officially assigned to three positions in the master-narrative, and in every aspect of your own life...
>
> The money-narrative is its [i.e. capitalism's] canonical story because it ... tells us that we can tell any stories we like, but it also tells us that authors must reap the profits on their

narratives... The money-narrative presupposes a first narrator, an author, an entrepreneur and a subject ... it precludes the possibility of moving from narratee–narrated to that of narrator... So there is an element of religion in capitalism: the exclusive worship of the narrative entrepreneur. (*Lyotard 1989: 131, 149–50*).

The establishment of metanarratives imposes silence upon those dependent upon them. Their last recourse is to narrate that there is nothing more to narrate, that there are no more listeners 'and that there is no more reality to invent' (1989: 132). Lyotard's narrative of the destruction of narration seems to me a rather convenient return to the doctrine of the deceitfulness of priests which is found in the early French Enlightenment and which draws a line through a whole swathe of the history of theory, the development of the concept of ideology. For – so runs Lyotard's argument – since totalitarian narrative pragmatics is a matter of power, it cannot be dealt with by theory, which is just another form of master-narrative.

Lyotard actually puts much more hope in the gradual erosion of master-narratives by the spread of 'unbelief', to which his *Instructions païennes* are intended to serve as an incitement. They have as their objective not truth, which seems to him, as to Nietzsche, only a 'form of the will to power' (on this point, see Nietzsche 1973: 764), but the destruction of the narrative monopolies by a politics of 'little narratives', which also treat metanarratives, theories and doctrines as narratives (Lyotard 1989: 153). Lyotard dates an erosion of master-narratives by 'thousands of uncomfortable little stories' (1989: 127) from events like May 1968 or the *Gulag Archipelago*, which he describes as a 'narrative explosion' in which 'the dignity of narration' was saved. This is, at the same time, the point at which he has aesthetics and politics converge: his admission that his own work is not theory, but 'only a work of art in itself, a product of the pure will of the imagination' is not only an impudent abbreviation of Kant's well-known definition (which he cites) of 'finality without ends' (1989: 133), but also Lyotard's farewell to history and the subject. The Gulag 'awakening' brings him the insight 'that history consists of a swarm of narratives ...; the people does not exist as a subject, it is a mass of thousands of little stories that are at once futile and serious... This succession of serial stories is admirably commonplace, and it implies no recurrence and no return' (1989: 134–5).

Strangely, Lyotard adds no practice of remembrance to this insight. His pagan prophet is, rather, a zealous advocate of forgetting.

He exorcizes theory on account of its piety of remembering and because of its need to struggle against oblivion (1989: 145). He prefers 'those who have no names, and peoples and children' who like stories, because they are 'a language form in which it is possible to love time for its power to forget... That is why they do not set themselves up as subjects and retain almost nothing of the so-called lessons of history: cultures are made up of stories that are assembled in series' (1989: 145). From this there follows the condemnation of theory on account of its piety of remembering, its struggle against all forgetfulness. As with everything in Lyotard's work, the polemic against memory also has its political point: because capitalism is a system which makes use of anything, it also pulls memory into its circle of operations, setting in train an endless movement of museification of culture. Only the radical destruction of memory can stop this movement. Thus in Lyotard's thinking, the battle against memory, forgetting – and ultimately even destruction – appear as the complement of libidinal economy. The pathos of forgetting turns into hatred of the past. This hatred is directed indiscriminately against the material institutions of bourgeois art (the museums) and its works, but also against everything which has not yet assumed the form of a work, which is still preserved formlessly in memory: 'Détruire l'œuvre, mais détruire aussi l'œuvre des œuvres *et des non-œuvres*, le kapitalisme comme musée, mémoire de tout ce qui est possible. Démémoriser comme l'inconscient' (Lyotard 1973b: 303: Destroy the work, but destroy also the work of works and non-works, kapitalism as museum, as the memory of everything possible. De-memorize, as in the unconscious). There is a striking parallel between this programme of destruction of the past and the futurists' attack upon cultural institutions – and morality. In the futurist manifesto which Marinetti published in 1909, we find the following provocative call: 'So let them come, the gay incendiaries with charred fingers!... Come on, set fire to the library shelves! Turn aside the canals to flood the museums!... Take up your pickaxes, your axes and hammers and wreck, wreck the venerable cities pitilessly!' (Marinetti 1973). The modernolatry of the futurists, who see the artist as representative of inhumanity, ended, as is well known, in their advocating war.

The futurism-postmodern constellation may cast light upon the fundamental ambivalence of an attitude of thought whose dynamic is directed against an abstract concept of power without adopting – in keeping with the teachings of Nietzsche – a 'standpoint of *desirability*' (Nietzsche 1973: 864). It is therefore no surprise that Lyotard subjects aesthetic modernity to a trial which is supposed to prove its complicity with power. Those in the dock alongside Adorno are Artaud and Brecht. These three, whose positions are dissimilar from other perspectives, have in common that they hold to the principle of 'representation'. According to Lyotard's critique, Artaud's theatre of cruelty does not allow free play to intensities, but merely creates a new grammar of gestures (1973b: 99–100). Lyotard criticizes Brecht's epic theatre as 'religious' insofar as it rests on a series of Marxist theorems, including particularly the conception of the proletariat as the subject of history. Brecht's theory of 'distantiation' seems to him a manifestation of nihilism, the demonstrative character of dramatic figures and action as a procedure which negates objects (1973b: 100–2). Lastly, he understands Adorno's aesthetic as negative theology (one of the essays is entitled 'Adorno comme diavolo') in which the destruction of the subject is bemoaned as a loss. Its 'dispositif libidinal' is sacrifice, not affirmation, and hence Adorno is ultimately a Romantic après la lettre, who has lost his hope of reconciliation (1973b: 115ff).

By the concept of representation, Lyotard understands what is, in his conception, the inevitably hierarchical referring back of a sign to its meaning. For Lyotard, all designation is a metaphysical (he uses the word 'theological') procedure, for it negates what is present in favour of a level which lies above or beneath it and is, therefore, pessimism or nihilism in the sense of Nietzsche's critique of a 'philosophy of desirability' (Nietzsche 1973: 865). In fact, if one accepts Lyotard's assumptions, both the theatre of cruelty and the theory of *Verfremdung* (distancing) have a hierarchical relation at their base: whether drive impulses or expressions of drives are concerned, or appearance and essence, in each case the vehicles of expression (or meaning) are negated for the sake of the content they are expressing. Lyotard's intention, which can be seen from these analyses, is to replace a two-stage schema of the appropriation of reality, which is characteristic both of the Hegel–Marx tradition and that of previous conservative cultural critique, by a one-dimensional schema, which accepts what is present as it is. 'It is,' writes Nietzsche, 'of cardinal importance that one should abolish the *true world* [that is, the distinction between true and apparent world, and thus a two-dimensional thinking]. It is the great inspirer of doubt and devaluator in respect of the world *we are*: it has been our most dangerous attempt yet to assassinate life' (1988: 314).

This is, however, also the common factor in Lyotard's other theoretical pieces on the tabooing of morality and the renunciation of the concept of critique. Both morality and critique presuppose two distinct levels, one being the level of what is present-at-hand and the other a level with which the existent can be confronted. Thus for Lyotard affirmation means precisely that renunciation of a second level from which the present-at-hand can be criticized as imperfect, as not corresponding with its concept. This becomes particularly clear in Lyotard's suggestion that we should think the 'pious' (Marxist) concept of alienation positively/affirmatively, that is, without the idea of a lost nature:

> We must stop conceiving [alienation] as the *loss* of something. We must rather conceive it positively: it leads to libidinal economy, to political economy being directly plugged in to libidinal economy, without representation. The law of value places us *potentially* in a non-hierarchical circulation, where tooth and palm are no longer in a relation of truth and illusion, cause and effect, signifier and signified (or vice-versa), but co-exist independently as transitory investments ... the tooth and the palm do not *mean* anything any more ... they are forces, intensities, present affects. (*Lyotard 1973b: 102*)

Lyotard is referring here to an example suggested by the painter Bellmer in which, when suffering from toothache, one presses one's nails into the palm of one's clenched hand.

Lyotard's affirmation of alienation shows itself in exemplary form in his essay on American photorealism ('Esquisse d'une économie de l'hyperréalisme') in which, beginning from a statement by Andy Warhol that he paints the way he does because he wants to be a machine (Lyotard 1973b: 108–9), he sees the photorealists' manner of proceeding as one in which the painter no longer makes use of a technical instrument (here photography) to produce an image, but rather, conversely, puts his skill as a painter to work to produce a photograph. He sees this subordination of the artist to the machine, precisely because of the alienation of the subject expressed in it (Lyotard speaks of a 'hysterical posture'), as an adequate example of an affirmative painting (1973b: 112–13).

Instead of bemoaning the destruction of the subject by capitalism as a loss, Lyotard pleads for our accepting it as a fact and indeed even goes a stage further and, in the dynamics of today's developed capitalism, discovers a force which eliminates all hierarchies at the same time as it eliminates the subject. In his conception, in present-day capitalism, money no longer functions as a sign for something else, but rather everything can stand as a sign for everything else; thus, for example, work can be posited as a simple sign for something else; with this, the principle of hierarchy is fundamentally thrown into question. His affirmative position toward social reality is based on this conception. One may certainly have some difficulties going along with this thought, for the fact that the actual relations of people in our society are subject to hierarchies and constellations of power is so obvious that Lyotard's reflections may strike one initially as mere intellectual games in which one cannot recognize the position of the critical intellectuals of the May movement. And yet the fact of Lyotard's being decisively marked by May 1968 suggests a possible explanation: at that point he had the extraordinarily pleasing experience of merging as an intellectual into an active collective. After the collapse of the May movement, he staked his all on reproducing just such a constellation with the means of thought. He could, however, only succeed in that if he rediscovered his anarchistic impulse directly in capitalism itself, short-circuiting economic forces with the libido. The fact that capitalist society develops anarchically is certainly well enough known by now (and has indeed been the constant object of Marxist criticism), but simultaneously this anarchy of the social totality still has as its counterpart a rationally and hierarchically ordered world of production and administration. The overall constitution of society is anarchic, but Lyotard looks for anarchy on precisely that level at which capitalism does not permit it, the level of individual development. At best, the intellectual can, with impunity, allow himself anarchic impulses on this level.

If we now attempt to relate what we shall call Lyotard's reflections on the philosophy of art to an aesthetic practice, we encounter difficulties, for these refer us to various practices at one and the same time:

(1) From Lyotard's concept of 'minor literature' we can draw a connection to the historical avant-garde movements and their reception in May '68 in Paris,[5] which once again brought to the surface the political dimension of the movement that had been to some degree concealed since the Second World War by the self-interpretation of the surrealists. 'Minor literature' is for Deleuze and Guattari and Lyotard what *écriture automatique* was for the surrealists:

> the rediscovery of a productivity which does not bow to the omnipresent pressure to perform, but is free productivity, an instrument of liberation from a reality lived as compulsion – a liberation which is no longer bound up with talent and genius, but which is attainable by everyone. The egalitarian element inherent in the conception of *écriture automatique* and the

production of a literary text freed both from the knowledge of a cultural tradition and the nimbus of genius

aims at overcoming the division of labour and ending the division of culture into high and low. 'Here poetry becomes practical at least to the extent that, for the writer, it coincides with the experience of liberation' (P. Bürger 1971: 156–7).

(2) From his critique of Adorno (an advocate of high modernism in counterposition to the avant-gardes of the 1920s), however, Lyotard derives a set of guidelines for aesthetic production which preserve the avant-gardist impulse to equality only for the act of production, but, by contrast, are wholly consonant with Adorno's aesthetic canon. Adorno's thesis that the autonomous status of works provides a guarantee of their critical content is rejected, but he takes over the dogma of the self-referentiality of art, which is conceived in Adorno's work as a prohibition on taking social material (*Gesellschaftliches*) as a theme. For Adorno, only when mediated through the aesthetic material might history enter the work of art. Admittedly, Lyotard invests the taboo on realism with other conceptions than Adorno. In the work of art, he is interested not in form as a condition of critique, but tone (or colour) as intensity (cf. for example Lyotard 1973b: 315). Non-representational painting is not for him the result of a process of abstraction, in which the loss of totality is reflected, but the eruption of libidinal energies, which pour forth in colours. Lyotard speaks of a 'libido chromatisée' (1973b: 246) and for his descriptions of pictures he chooses works by Yves Klein and Robert Delaunay. The release of chromatic libido – and here he is nearer to Adorno than to the surrealists – has as a consequence the total autonomy of painting (1973b: 273 and *passim*).

(3) Lyotard's readiness to accept a commission from France's socialist government to organize an exhibition (which means conforming to its line in cultural policy) throws light on the ambivalence of his aesthetic anarchism. His affirmative aesthetics can at any point go over into a 'saying-yes to the world just as it is, without deviation, exception and selection' (Nietzsche 1973: 834) and at the same time saying yes to power, which he is supposed to be combating. For Lyotard today, this means being totally in accord with technological development. The exhibition, to which he gave the title *Les Immatériaux*, documents a virtually ecstatic approval of the new technical revolution,[6] which is angled expressly against the Greens' 'apocalyptic' visions of the future. This includes the disappearance

of the concept of 'man', a concept which Lyotard, like Foucault, puts in inverted commas as a short-lived product of the process of evolution.

> The 'human', as substantivized adjective, refers to an old domain of knowledges and interventions which is today shared by the techno-sciences that have broken into that domain... One 'reads' the human cerebral cortex as one reads an electronic field; one 'influences' human affectivity through the neuro-vegetative system like a complex chemical organization of information... On the strength of these facts, the ideas associated with the concept of 'material', which fuel the immediate sense that the human being possesses a particular identity, have become weaker. These ideas are experience, memory, work, autonomy (or freedom), and even 'creation', and generally the radical distinction of the human from the non-human. The idea of general interaction has, by contrast, grown stronger. (*Lyotard 1984–5*)[7]

Clearly Lyotard is concerned to counterpose modernity, which he associates with the concepts of material, subject and project, to postmodernity, in which *les immatériaux*, the disappearance of the subject and interaction are the corresponding terms.

Although, in the passage cited, he seems to hold back from value judgement, such a judgement can clearly be deduced from the context insofar as Lyotard characterizes the modernist project of an appropriation of the world by humanity as arrogance and the postmodernist renunciation of such a project as wise melancholy. (Again, the fact that he fantasizes about advances in medicine leading to the production of an artificial third sex or the possibility of making death 'curable' as objectives for postmodernity can scarcely be said to fit in with such conceptions.)

(4) These changes in the sphere of production, which are also transforming our ideas of human beings and work and our forms of perception, are confirmation for Lyotard that the present is indeed a postmodern period of rupture, of transition. Thus he takes up the concept of the postmodern, but he does so in a peculiarly contradictory way. In his more recent book, *Le Différend*, he announces an epoch of philosophizing, which is to supersede that of the grand metanarratives (1984–5).[8] When transposed into the area of art, that epoch's entry into the postmodern signifies, correspondingly, its *becoming reflexive*. In an interview on *Le Différend*, Lyotard declares, 'What has been happening in painting or in music for a

century to some degree anticipates the postmodern I am speaking of. All attempts at definition of the "avant-garde" have been directed by a single question: what is painting? . . . painting has become essentially reflexive' (Lyotard 1984).

Irrespective of whether one can pin the whole avant-garde in painting down to a single question (the surrealists, for example, did not concern themselves with the question of what painting was) and irrespective of whether it would be advisable to separate the concepts of modernity and avant-garde (and to define the latter, focusing upon Dadaism and surrealism, as a historical movement that was sustained by the attack on the art institution), it is quite evident that in the aesthetic field Lyotard is clearly concerned precisely not to define the postmodern in opposition to the modern, but to connect it to it. It is only thus that he can bring his *own* aesthetic position into play.

Interestingly, he makes the French painter Albert Ayme, who can most easily be regarded as being in the tradition of the Bauhaus or *De Stijl* movements, into the representative of a postmodern painting. Like Mondrian – if one accepts Lyotard's commentaries – Ayme understands painting as *'the exact representation of relations alone'* (Mondrian 1919). The spectator is not so much expected to see as to think. What he or she sees are areas of paint which are built up out of monochrome rectangles and coloured borders set against these and contrasting with them. It is, however, expected of the spectators that they discover the hidden, underlying abstract principle of the series of overlaid layers of paint and that they grasp the rhythm in which the application of paint is carried out (Lyotard 1980: para. 7).

According to Lyotard, this shift in the reception of art from sense perception to reflection characterizes the postmodern. In a manner that is difficult to follow and, as ever, rather forced, he repeats a part of Friedrich Schlegel's artistic programme when he proclaims that painting becomes reflection and philosophy painting.[9] It is all the more irritating then that he himself cuts out of his commentaries the philosophical dimension which gave the *De Stijl* movement its modernity: universality and 'the will to the collective' (See van Eesteren 1927: 225). The tendency to abstraction is interpreted by Mondrian (1919: *passim*) chiefly as *'liberation from the individual'* and as a pathway to the universal and the collective.

Lyotard's definition of the postmodern also seems to me strategic insofar as it allows him to dissociate himself from a specific interpretation which he rejects (1985: 100) as 'consumer eclecticism' and which he closely associates with the activities of the Italian art theorist and manager Achille Bonito Oliva.[10] He is of course clearly aware that this involves him in definitional problems. The way he construes these matters blurs the dividing lines between the modern and the postmodern and between modernity and the avant-garde. The dynamic of Lyotard's thinking led him initially to take his leave of central categories of left-wing thought (critique, morality etc.) and to find a new – positive – point of reference in libidinal economy. The logical outcome of this dynamic should have been his attachment to the aesthetic postmodernism of the Americans (or Feyerabend's blithe 'anything goes'). Or to the Italian trans-avantgarde, which sees 'the practice of painting as an affirmative practice' (Oliva 1980).[11] If he has not done so, this is perhaps because he received his formative aesthetic experience from classical modernism. It may be this that prevents him from extending his approval of postmodern society into the aesthetic field. He thus prefers to accept inconsistency in his thinking rather than strive to outdo the postmodernism of the trans-avantgarde for radicalism. As a counter-move, he develops an astonishing radicalism in the defence of neo-expressionism (*Neue Wilden*) in the German Federal Republic, of the young Italians and of American postmodernism. 'This "trans-avantgarde", on the pretext of preserving the heritage of the avant-garde, is clearly a good means of getting rid of it.' Not only does the concept of heritage sit uneasily within the kind of anarchist thinking Lyotard represents, but so too does the peculiarly elitist and moralizing tone, which he criticizes so vehemently elsewhere. (He thus reproaches postmodernism for its successes as a market strategy and denounces it as an attempt to make art fit in with 'the given state of "culture"'; cf. 'The sublime and the avant-garde' and Lyotard's conversation with G. Daghini in *Change International* (1984)).

A DIGRESSION ON OLIVA'S TRANS-AVANTGARDE PROGRAMME

It seems to me far from accidental that Lyotard does not engage with the Italian trans-avantgarde either politically or in terms of artistic theory. His polemic confines itself to the level of a competent practitioner of 'art-appreciation'. This very omission, however, points once again to the contradictoriness of his own position. Admittedly, the propositions emanating from Oliva's pen do not have the status of aesthetic theory, but of prescriptions for production; they are of the order of an artist's programmatic statements. They are, however, statements of a kind which at least allow us to identify a line of attack and an enemy; aesthetically, what is being called for is the rejection of the modern and, politically, for a rejection of the sixties. The pattern of thinking underlying this programme is purely dichotomous: the art of the sixties was dominated by the primacy of the political (Oliva 1980/1982: 61, 96 and *passim*).[12] The trans-avantgarde movement releases artists from the thrall of dogmas and ideologies (Oliva 1980/1982: 83 and *passim*). To the 'aestheticism of politics' it opposes the 'biology of art'. The sixties are said to have been stamped by an aesthetic Darwinism, which can be seen in the compulsion always to produce something new. (This particular sally is perhaps directed against the concept of development of material or the logic of the material which is central to Adorno's aesthetic theory.) By contrast the trans-avantgardists are said to have liberated art from the 'tyranny of innovation', so that, after a period of petrification and 'depersonalization', a climate can now be created in which the expressivity and subjectivity of artists may freely unfold (Oliva 1980/1982: 61, 68–9). Art's commitment to morality, which is said to have led necessarily, with its 'self-tormenting and masochistic attitude', to the 'self-expropriation of the creative urge', is now said to be ended and supplanted by a readiness to surrender to the 'drifting' of spontaneity. In short, the negativity of the modern has been left behind; it has been succeeded by a position which Oliva does not shrink from describing in terms of health (Oliva 1980/1982: 96–7, 98, 99). 'The opposition operates with the perspective of a possible reconciliation with the world' (p. 86). 'In art, the *deep gaze* rules; and it is, in a positive way, short-sighted where the contingencies of the real are concerned' (p. 89).

The prescriptions for production which Oliva derives from his declaration of war on the art of the sixties, are all, without exception, directed towards the total emancipation of art from all rules, styles, taboos and all moral, social and political commitments, including the commitment to logical coherence. 'Trans-avantgarde means the assumption of a nomadic position which respects no ultimate commitment, which possesses no privileged ethic whatever, but simply follows the inspirations of a spiritual temperament and a material which is synchronous with the here and now of the work' (Oliva 1980/1982: 63; cf. also 74, 83, 89). This is a profession of a *pragmatism* uninterrupted by any reflection (p. 63). Interestingly, this 'mutation' of art, which Oliva calls a 'minor emotion', is in reality a return to pre-avantgardist positions. Trans-avantgardism presents itself very emphatically in the name of the particular and the fragmentary, yet triggers off a genuine rage against the historical avant-gardes. The latter rightly sought to promote subjectivity, the particular, expression and free creativity in quite another way. That is, the historical avant-gardes opposed the conceptions laid down by the art institution. The political provenance of this emotion is betrayed in Oliva's equation of the avant-garde with the May movement. 'The intoxication of '68 had created the myth of a crossing of boundaries, the myth of a loss of the specific... Art seemed to have conquered incomparable territories, while deliberately practising the loss of its own identity, in the hope of a limitless expansion' (p. 84). What is involved in trans-avantgardism is the reversal of the avant-gardist project of a dissolving of art into the practice of life (pp. 58–9). The restoration of the work and its aura, its contemplative reception and the concept of genius all run in to one here (p. 60). 'The art of the seventies [i.e. the trans-avantgarde] is endeavouring to return the art work to a place where it can be agreeably contemplated, where the mythic distance, the distance of contemplation, becomes charged with eroticism and all the energy which flows from the intensity of the work and its inner metaphysics' (pp. 64–5). This restoration has, admittedly, nothing of the ascetic severity about it which distinguished the metaphysics of early modern art, but it is biologically inflected in an extremely problematic way.

PETER BÜRGER: AN AESTHETICS OF THE SUBLIME

Lyotard has emphatically claimed the concept of the postmodern as a concept of social theory (see esp. Lyotard 1986b).[13] However, since such theorists of architecture and art as Jencks or Oliva have, as we have seen, turned the term into the battle-cry of a thoroughly aggressive anti-modernism, he has at the same time had to distance himself from the aesthetic postmodern. He seeks to resolve the difficulties which he brings upon himself in so doing by differentiating between a 'true' and a 'false' postmodernism and indeed deeming aesthetic modernism to belong quite unproblematically to the (true) postmodern. 'Postmodernism thus understood is not modernism at its end, but in the nascent state, and that state is constant' (Lyotard 1986a).

More interesting than this merry confusion of concepts is Lyotard's suggestion that modern art should be explicated with the help of Kant's analytic of the sublime. Behind this suggestion lies the legitimate question whether modern art can still be conceived in the concepts which are ultimately derived from Kant's analytic of the beautiful (a delight apart from any interest, a finality that is devoid of any end). Modern art is not a reconciliation, one might go on to argue, but rupture and contradiction; it therefore cannot be conceived on the basis of a concept of form in which sensibility and spirit, the particular and the general are posited as a unity. Within the tradition of idealist aesthetics (and this could be said to be difficult to separate from what we call art, since it constitutes the normative core of the art institution), there are only two categories which bring together the sensible and meaning in any way, which is not guilty of 'identity-thinking': these are allegory and the sublime. By contrast with the concept of symbol in which the sensible and meaning are posited as a unity, these two categories allow the two to be maintained as distinct.[14] This explains both Benjamin's efforts to give enhanced status to allegory and Lyotard's turn to the category of the sublime.

We must, however, immediately add that Lyotard interprets the concept of the sublime in a thoroughly unconventional way. And this is true even of the reference point of his analysis. He does not, as one might have expected, focus on the disfigured bodies in the pictures of Francis Bacon, which in fact awaken in the spectator what Kant calls 'negative pleasure', an attraction shot through with horror; he is thinking rather of the objectless painting of a Malevich and he correspondingly takes the non-representable as the real object of the aesthetics of the sublime. It is only possible to do this, however, insofar as he draws less on Kant's argumentation and more on individual concepts like formlessness and non-representability (Kant 1952/1978: 90–1). To put it another way, Lyotard makes a series of essential changes to Kant's analytic of the sublime, but he does not make these explicit (1985: 98):

1   For Kant the experience of the sublime comes mainly from natural objects, because only in contact with these can the 'point at which our faculty of imagination breaks down' be experienced; Lyotard, by contrast, concerns himself with art works.
2   Kant's theory is formulated wholly from the perspective of the experiencing subject. He seeks to explain how it is possible for a phenomenon characterized by magnitude and fearfulness to give us pleasure; Lyotard, by contrast, discusses the problem of non-representability from the perspective of the producer. Whereas Kant begins from an experience which he seeks to explain, Lyotard is describing an artistic project.
3   For Kant, the experience of the sublime is connected with rational ideas (such as infinity or immortality) which show their strength and superiority when we see a phenomenon which exceeds our powers of imagination; this is how we come to find

pleasure in the midst of horror. For Lyotard, however, it is a question of the representation of the unrepresentable: 'Thus one cannot represent the absolute. One can, however, represent that an absolute exists'.

Lyotard is not to be criticized for reformulating the Kantian theory, but for omitting to account for having done so. Since he does not do this, he also does not see what he loses in recasting the question in this way. For eighteenth-century theorists from Burke to Kant the sublime was first and foremost a disturbing experience demanding elucidation. How could 'something forbidding to sensibility' have 'an attraction for us' (Kant 1952/1978: 90–1; see also P. Bürger 1983: 144ff)? This dimension is lost in Lyotard's version. Neither Malevich's white square nor the painting of Albert Ayme is forbidding to our sensibility. When Karl Heinz Bohrer (1981: 84–5) strives to develop an aesthetics of horror, he is presumably nearer to what Kant calls the sublime than Lyotard.

Any attempt to use the theory of the sublime for an understanding of the art of modernity would also have to make explicit what it means to exchange the perspective of the recipient of art for that of the producer: insofar as objects are produced which precisely provoke those disturbing experiences which the eighteenth-century writers sought to explain, the entire situation changes. The 'formlessness' and 'ugliness' of the object now turn out to be its particular form. The break with a definite form already contains elements of a new unity (not visible for most contemporaries). The sublime is overtaken by the aesthetics of beautiful illusion against which it rebelled. In other words, one will have to ask oneself whether, with the displacement of the gaze on to (art-) objects, which are supposed to have in them the quality of the sublime, precisely the particular mode of experience that is supposed to be involved is not itself excluded. Whilst no producing subject and thus also no meaning can be ascribed to a natural event which exceeds our powers of comprehension, that is not the case with a work of art. To what can be perceived by the senses, however repellent, deviant and formless it may be, a meaning (however indistinct) will always tend to be attributed. The metaphysical concept of form, which idealist aesthetics has explicated, still leaves its mark on the concept of a sublime art sketched out in opposition to it. If we were to look at the works of Joseph Beuys, we would see that things are no different where the allegorical is concerned. However, it is precisely out of the tension between an intention directed toward the sublime or the allegorical and its symbolic interpretation by the recipient that the art of the present might be said to derive its peculiar force.

With his recourse to the analytic of the sublime, Lyotard was doubtless taking a step which is particularly suggested by the practice of the avant-garde (one need only think of the *faits-précipices*, which Breton writes of at the beginning of *Nadja*, or Artaud's theatre of cruelty); but the reference to non-figurative painting, which is dominant in Lyotard's considerations, seems to us to lack the crucial element of an art of the sublime, namely horror.

NOTES

1 'Marxism will be then that enterprise of reparation and remonstrance ... where all political energy will be put into the project of putting right a wrong ... the living wrong that is the proletariat, the wrong of alienation ... This *dispositif* of negativity and culpabilization is the one of which *Anti-Oedipus* rids Marxism' (Lyotard 1973b: 25).
2 The translation is from W. Kaufmann and R. J. Hollingdale (trs), *The Will to Power* (Nietzsche 1888/1968), 400. Subsequent references to quotations from *Aus dem Nachlass der Achtzigerjahre* made in the text will be marked Nietzsche 1973 – or Nietzsche 1988 when translated in *The Will to Power*.
3 Translated from Lyotard 1985: 69.
4 Lyotard uses several terms for such legitimating narratives: meta-, master- or canonical narrative.
5 Here too he is conscious of his opposition to Adorno's idiosyncratic disapproval of 'repressive desublimation', to use Marcuse's term, and altogether opposed to his concealed anti-avantgardism: 'Adorno a vu dans le mouvement dit étudiant des années 60 un stravinskisme politique' (Lyotard 1973b: 133).
6 On the futurists' similar enthusiasm for technology, compare Umberto Boccioni's lecture on futurist painting from 1911: 'The day will come when a picture will no longer be enough. Its immobility will seem to us a ridiculous anachronism amidst the dizzying and constantly accelerating movement of life. The human eye will perceive colour as feeling. The multiplying colours will need no forms for us to perceive and grasp them. We shall lay aside canvas and brushes. Instead of paintings, we shall offer the world giant, ephemeral pictures from the radiant colours created by electrical floodlights and coloured glass. As their beams, spirals and webs harmonize in the firmament, they will fill the complex soul of the human masses of the future with inspiration.' (Quoted in Baumgarth 1966: 71.)
7 Translated from Lyotard 1985: 80. Compare once again a passage from Marinetti's first futurist manifesto, in which the vision of an inhumane human being is anticipated: 'We believe in the possibility of an incalculable number of human transformations and declare with total seriousness that within man's flesh wings lie buried. On the day it becomes possible for man

to direct his will outwards in such a way that it stretches out before him like an invisible arm, dream and desire, which today are empty words, will reign supreme over vanquished space and time. The mechanical, non-human type, who is built for speed in all aspects of life, will naturally be cruel, omniscient and aggressive.' (Quoted in Baumgarth 1966: 135.)

8 Translated from Lyotard 1985: 36 and *passim*.

9 'Dans la postmodernité, la couleur étant prise comme la conscience et la conscience comme la couleur, la peinture se fait reflexion et la philosophie peinture' (Lyotard 1980: para. 9).

10 The text in question, 'The sublime and the avant-garde', has appeared in two different versions in English; the first, translated by Lisa Liebmann, in *Artforum*, 22/8 (April 1984), 36–43; the second, with additional material, translated by G. Bennington and M. Hobson, in Benjamin 1989: 196–211.

11 Oliva is quoted here (as throughout) from the German translation, *Im Labyrinth der Kunst*, 55.

12 Oliva speaks also of 'art as guerrilla warfare' (1980/1982: 96).

13 See also the critique of this work by Honneth (1982) and Benhabib (1986).

14 In the concept of symbol in the idealist aesthetic of the beautiful, the sensuous sign (form) and content are posited as a unity. This principle of necessary form also constitutes the basis of immanent interpretation. The allegorical sign, by contrast, is not a necessary one and, for that reason, classical aesthetics has treated it as being of lesser value. In the sublime, a relationship between the sensuous and meaning can be identified which is comparable to that in allegory. It is not the spectacle of nature in its particular essence (*Sosein*) which enables the Kantian observer to experience the power of human reason, but its superior might.

REFERENCES

Baumgarth, C. 1966: *Geschichte des Futurismus*. Reinbek bei Hamburg: Rowohlt.

Benhabib, S. 1986: 'Kritik des postmodernen Wissens – eine Auseinandersetzung mit Jean-François Lyotard', in A. Huyssen and K. Scherpe (eds), *Postmoderne: Zeichen eines kulturellen Wandels*. Reinbek bei Hamburg: Rowohlt, 103–27.

Benjamin, A. 1989: *The Lyotard Reader*. Oxford: Blackwell.

Bohrer, K. H. 1981: *Plötzlichkeit: Zum Augenblick des ästhetischen Scheins*. Frankfurt a.M.: Suhrkamp.

Bürger, Peter 1971: *Der französische Surrealismus*. Frankfurt a.M.: Athenäum.

Bürger, Peter 1983: *Zur Kritik der idealistischen Ästhetik*. Frankfurt a.M.: Suhrkamp.

Chupp, H. P. 1968: *Theories of Modern Art*. Berkeley: University of California Press.

Deleuze, G., and Guattari, F. 1977: *Anti-Oedipus*. New York: Viking.

Eesteren, C. van 1927: 'Zehn Jahre "Stijl"', in H. Bächler and H. Letsch (eds), *De Stijl. Schriften und Manifeste*. Leipzig and Weimar: Kiepenheuer.

Honneth, A. 1982: 'Der Affekt gegen das Allgemein', *Merkur*, 8 (1984), 131–42.

Kant 1952: *Critique of Judgement*, tr. J. C. Meredith. Oxford: Clarendon Press.

Lyotard, Jean-François 1973a: *Dérive à partir de Marx et Freud*. Paris: UGE.

Lyotard, Jean-François 1973b: *Des dispositifs pulsionnels*. Paris: UGE.

Lyotard, Jean-François 1977: *Rudiments païens*. Paris: UGE.

Lyotard, Jean-François 1980: *Sur la constitution du temps par la couleur dans les œuvres récentes d'Albert Ayme*. Paris: Editions Traversière.

Lyotard, Jean-François 1984: 'Conversation with G. Daghini', *Change internationale* (Paris), 2 (May).

Lyotard, Jean-François 1984–5: 'Interview with Bernard Blistène', *Flash Art*, 6 (Winter); repr. in Lyotard 1985: *Immaterialität und Postmoderne*. Berlin: Merve.

Lyotard, Jean-François 1986a (1977): 'Answering the question: what is postmodernism?', tr. Régis Durand, in Lyotard 1986b, 71–82.

Lyotard, Jean-François 1986b: *The Postmodern Condition: A Report on Knowledge*, tr. G. Bennington and B. Massumi. Manchester: Manchester University Press.

Lyotard, Jean-François 1989: 'Lessons in paganism', in A. Benjamin 1989.

Marinetti, F. T. 1973: 'The founding and manifesto of futurism 1909', in Umbro Apollonio (ed.), *Futurist Manifestos*. New York: Viking.

Mondrian, P. 1919: 'De nieuwe beelding in de schilderkunst', *De Stijl*, 1.

Nietzsche, F. 1888; Eng. tr. 1968: *The Will to Power*, tr. Walter Kaufmann and R. J. Hollingdale. London: Weidenfeld & Nicolson.

Nietzsche, F. : *Aus dem Nachlass der Achtzigerjahre*, in *Werke*, ed. K. Schlachta 1973. Munich: Hanser.

Oliva, A. B. 1980: *La transvanguardia italiana*. Milan: Jean-Carlo Politi; German tr. 1982: *Im Labyrinth der Kunst*. Berlin: Merve.

Wellmer, A. 1985: *Zur Dialektik von Modern und Postmoderne*. Frankfurt a.M.: Suhrkamp.

4

The disappearance of meaning: essay at a postmodern reading of Michel Tournier, Botho Strauss and Peter Handke

Peter Bürger

The question whether postmodern works exist – and in particular postmodern literary works – can in no sense be regarded as settled. I am reminded here of the despair (certainly not feigned) of a colleague who, as editor of a volume on the postmodern, was confronted by readers with what is after all the understandable request that he name five postmodern authors. Ihab Hassan, an American theorist of the postmodern (if his loosely assembled reflections can be called theory), characterizes writers like Kafka, Beckett, Genet and the authors of the *nouveau roman* as postmodern, without thereby fundamentally questioning their conventional classification as modern (see Hassan 1984: 82–95).[1] What is gained by this redesignation? If we move away from what is to some extent the sure ground of architecture, where the concept denotes a turning away from the functionalist architectural thinking of modernity, we run up against obscurities, differences of opinion and open questions at every turn.

Is it reasonable to describe the neo-expressionist painting of the *Neue Wilden* as postmodern, when the expressionism with which these painters are associated is generally regarded as a movement within artistic modernity? Is one to call an author like Michel Tournier postmodern because he resorts to the traditional forms of narration of the novel with an omniscient author? The criterion seems inadmissible given the fact that there is in France an unbroken tradition, acknowledged by literary criticism, of realist narrative fiction in the twentieth century. And are Peter Handke's invocation of Stifter's 'gentle law' and the concomitant expressions of annoyance at Kafka sufficient to have us hail him – or denounce him – as postmodern?[2] Is it enough for someone, as Umberto Eco has done, to combine an illusionist fresco of medieval monastic culture with a thrilling detective story and to present the whole thing with a sly wink, using the tiredest of illusionist's techniques, for us to speak of a postmodern novel – or even of a masterpiece of postmodernism?

There are, of course, more complex definitions of the postmodern, but significantly these mostly relate to theoretical assumptions, not to literary procedures and techniques of representation. It is a central thesis of postmodern thought that in our society signs no longer refer to a designatum, but always only to other signs, and that we thus in our discourse no longer arrive at anything resembling meaning, but merely move around within an infinite chain of signifiers. On this view, the sign, which was for Saussure still a solid unity of signifier and signified, lies shattered. That this thought is at least familiar to Italian painters is attested in a programmatic drawing by Francesco Clemente. It shows two figures running in opposite directions, each holding half of a broken ring in which we can read the word 'symbolon'. And in fact, by comparison with the non-constructivist, abstract painting of the fifties and sixties, it has been possible in painting since the seventies to observe a return of signs hinting at meaning, though it has also been a peculiar feature of these signs that meaning cannot in actual fact be assigned to them. In many of the paintings of the new Italian school and also of the German *Neue Wilden*, the autonomous sign is merely a trap the painter sets for observers so that they will lose themselves in the maelstrom of possible interpretations.

Here too, however, we must be careful about asserting that this is a new phenomenon, which we may term postmodern. After all, the surrealists already used the technique of signs suggesting profundity which were in fact quite empty. In Magritte's picture 'The Museum of a Night', a hand, an apple and a shapeless form are arranged alongside each other in boxes, whilst a fourth box has a pattern over it. The spectator feels challenged to offer an interpretation, but his or her attempt to do so finds nothing to clutch on to. The signs yield no meaning; the open boxes with their symbols are just as closed to us as the fourth box into which we cannot see. Postmodernism is not then the first movement to sabotage meaning: surrealism has already done so.

If, at a first attempt, we are unable to make out whether there are any works of art corresponding to the discourse on the postmodern, then the thought occurs that the concept may be serving only to breathe new life into an old strategy of culturally conservative writers, who on many occasions in the past have pronounced the death of modernity. One has only to recall Arnold Gehlen's argument that cultural modernity had already arrived at the stage of 'crystallization' before World War I, meaning that it was no longer capable of further renewal (see Gehlen 1964: 212). In short, the debate might not be about a knowledge of phenomena (in this case, developments in the field of art since the 1970s), but about intellectual power positions. If we start out from this assumption, then the question is not 'what can we know of the object and what is to be learnt from the debate?', but 'what are the strategies deployed in this battle for intellectual hegemony?'

At least since the analyses of Pierre Bourdieu and his school we have been aware that questions of power play an essential role in intellectual disputes, but such disputes are not merely power struggles (see e.g. Bourdieu 1984). Those who are unable to see anything in postmodernism but a conservative strategy of cultural 'roll-back' are surrendering the opportunity of deciphering the signs of the times within it. They are forgoing the possibility of understanding the changes in aesthetic sensibility which show through in the debate as the expression of a modified attitude towards social reality on the part of the intellectual.

Even if it should turn out that it is not possible to identify a postmodern art as an autonomous entity, independent from modernism, this does not mean that discussion of the postmodern has no object. Its object would not then be a new art, but an altered attitude both to art and to society. The changes which the postmodernism debate seeks to come to grips with would then lie not so much at the level of works as at the level of institutions, that is, of the normative discourses, which initially make works of art into works of art.

That in the last fifteen years a not inconsiderable change has indeed taken place in the aesthetic sensibility of that part of the educated elite interested in art is attested by the changed attitude to the historical architecture of the nineteenth century. What in the fifties and sixties seemed contemptible in such architecture – the arbitrary recourse to past styles and the fondness for ornament – are now re-valorized and recognized as an understandable striving for a human style of building.[3] The painting of previously whitewashed façades and the setting off of ornament through the choice of a darker colour of paint attest to this changed attitude, which goes with an increasing rejection of modern glass and concrete architecture. It might be argued that something comparable can be observed in the field of painting. Many of the abstract works of the 1950s and early 1960s seem decorative and pleasing to the present-day observer. There is something conformist about them, which was not perceptible at the time. At the same time interest is growing in painters like Bonnard who did not fully participate in the turbulent developments of twentieth-century art, and even the realistic painting of the *Neue Sachlichkeit* movement is undergoing re-evaluation. Since, in the field of literature, modernism has never achieved an uncontested position of hegemony, the changes here are a little less easy to grasp. But if even a leading figure in the *nouveau roman* like Robbe-Grillet is returning to autobiography (though he is doing so with a bad aesthetic conscience), this points to a changed attitude towards traditional genres of fiction.

If one understands the postmodernism debate as a thoroughly open endeavour to conceptualize the changes in aesthetic sensibility alluded to here, then the question arises as to where the starting-points for such an undertaking lie.

If we try to identify what connects together the artistic modernism of the fifties and early sixties, to determine what functionalist architecture, abstract painting and the *nouveau roman* have in common, we find that it is a peculiar pathos of purity. In the same way as architecture divested itself of ornamental elements, painting freed itself from the primacy of the representational, and the *nouveau roman* liberated itself from the categories of traditional fiction (plot and character). If painting saw its task as being to free the gaze of the spectator from the compulsion of an object-orientated and goal-directed perception, Robbe-Grillet's novel sought to present the mere existence of things, rather than a universe of subjectively produced meanings. The purity of the artistic medium appeared to be if not exactly an ultimate objective then at least a crucial precondition for success, and success was closely bound up with the thorough elaboration of the individual work of art. Two further characteristics emerge from this: an emphatic conception of the work of art and the marking off of artistic production both from everyday life and also from art that is designed simply to entertain.

This work-centred modernism could, however, only become culturally dominant at the cost of repressing that other modernism which stood in an awkward relation to it: the historical avant-garde movements. These movements had raised the impurity of the artistic medium to a central principle, in the form of its intermixing with the abysses of psychology (in *écriture automatique*) and the play of the intellect (in Magritte's painting). They had sought not to pin down the aesthetic in the work of art , but to free it from the boundaries of such work and to release it as life-changing potential into the everyday sphere. Even the boundary with lowbrow art, rigidly preserved by art work-orientated modernism, had long been broken down by the avant-garde movements through audacious borrowings and provocative vulgarizations (one only need think of the use of advertising material by the Dadaists). They even brought into question the concept of necessary form, which had prevailed since the institutionalization of art's autonomy, by having recourse to allegory, which is a non-necessary and pre-set form.

In short, an artistic modernism, which sought to produce not a closed art work, but none the less one which had its own integrity, and which had everyday life as its exterior and trivial and lowbrow art as its enemy, was only possible on the basis of an anti-avantgardism, and it is of no consequence here whether the producers were aware of this or not (see P. Bürger 1983).

This would, however, mean that central themes of the postmodernism debate – the questioning of the emphatic conception of the work, the levelling of previously opposed notions of 'high' and 'low' art and, lastly, the preference for allegory – go back to the historical avant-garde movements. What we are trying to grasp today in the rather unhelpful concept of the postmodern might therefore turn out to be the irruption into the art of modernity of the avant-gardist problematic. The taboos which art work-orientated modernity has built up are once again being questioned. If the modernism of the fifties and early sixties was marked by a striving after purity in the artistic medium, today it is precisely the impure which seems to gain the kudos. This can be seen in a variety of areas, from the unreflecting return to the object in painting and the ease with which anecdotal narrative is now accepted, via pleasure in 'quotation', through to the ironically exhibited renunciation of aesthetic 'finish'. Though modernity did discover everyday life as a subject at an early stage (Flaubert), it none the less accorded the frontier between the work of art and real life the significance of a metaphysical principle, and one which was on no account to be infringed. Today it seems permissible once again to cross this frontier, and not only in the return to autobiography. Pop art had already questioned the frontier with the everyday in a cryptically playful way and in so doing again confronted art with its abyssal nature (Warhol's Brillo packets are like ... Brillo packets). Lastly, if austere modernism had evacuated the semantic as something alien to the purity of the aesthetic and trusted to form alone as a residual meaning element, we are today seeing an almost excessive return of meaning-laden signs, though, in a perverse way, these actually leave unfulfilled the promise of meaning which they seem to bear.

Clearly the vantage-point from which one chooses to view the postmodern makes a difference. If one chooses the historical avant-garde movements as one's point of reference, then common features come into view. If, on the other hand, one chooses the modernism described in Adorno's aesthetic theory, then differences come starkly to the fore. Since, however, literary modernism can no longer be restricted to Adorno's canon, but now takes in the avant-garde movements, defining the relationship between the modern and the postmodern remains a peculiarly enigmatic task.

II

Let us attempt to get a more precise idea of this relationship by turning to the programmatic statements of Michel Tournier, whom we can with some justification describe as a postmodern author.

A central tenet of aesthetic modernism is the principle of formal innovation. This connects together such different writers as Flaubert, Kafka and the *nouveau roman* authors. If Michel Tournier admits then that he wants to write like Bourget or Bazin – names which in France stand for a traditional form of the novel – he has clearly dropped the modern writer's claim to innovate within the novel form. But Tournier goes further. He elevates this renunciation of formal innovation into a programme: 'It is not my aim to be formally innovative, but, on the contrary, to communicate, in a form which is as traditional, safe and reassuring as possible, a content which possesses none of these qualities' (1983: 195).

In modernism, form is a category of the particular; it aims at a specific shaping of the work in each individual case and, as such, it is not separable from content. Tournier puts in question this notion of a semantically rich form, constitutive of our aesthetic experience. Traditional form is here meant only to lend an appearance of the familiar to an unsettling content; it does not stand in any relation of correspondence to it. There can be no doubt that in this Tournier is distancing himself from the aesthetic which has dominated the modern novel since the canonization of Flaubert. It is more difficult to determine whether this distancing is simply a softening of his own claim or whether there is not concealed behind it a claim to a radical innovation. The fact that he compares his own project with that of the surrealist painters, who had sought to revolutionize the real through the most precise reproduction of it, speaks in favour of the second assumption. 'In order to break things open, they put their trust more in the infallible certainty of the stroke [*trait*] than in the atmospheric quaverings of dreams. The more flatly one copies the real, the more one will enter its innermost recesses to overturn it. This seems to me to be the nature of their wager' (Tournier 1983: 115).

In referring back to the painting of the surrealists, Tournier lends his formal traditionalism an anti-traditionalist aim: objectivistic re-production is to veer over into the hallucinatory. Just as the surrealist painters broke ranks with the tradition of modern painting to connect up again with the salon painting of the nineteenth century, Tournier turns away from the methods of modernist fiction writing and back to writing psychological novels of the Paul Bourget type. Insofar as he is giving up the principle of formal innovation, Tournier is setting himself against aesthetic modernism. However, to the extent that he makes a claim to innovation with such a renunciation, he is continuing the tradition of modernism. The result might be seen as characteristic of the ambiguity of postmodernism.

When Robbe-Grillet – one of the leading figures in the experimental novel in France since the 1950s – begins an autobiographical text in 1977 with the words 'I have never spoken about anything else but myself', he is also reintroducing those categories of narration against which the *nouveau roman* rebelled: the authorial 'I' as the origin of the narration, inwardness as an object of expression and the reproduction of something pre-given as a principle of representation. And Robbe-Grillet too bases his action on its value as provocation. In view of the canonization of the *nouveau roman* and the conceptions that go with it, the traditional categories receive a potential for innovation which the methods of the *nouveau roman* have themselves lost in the intervening period. However, Robbe-Grillet is not simply returning to the traditional supposition that autobiography tells the truth about the writer. He knows that the experienced past, as it presents itself in the book, first arises in the process of writing.[4]

Not only does the renunciation of modern techniques of narration function as innovation, that renunciation is further disrupted by the awareness that the truth of autobiographical narration is narration. To summarize, then, the renunciation of formal innovation and the return to traditional narrative techniques, which at first sight seem to mark a clear break with aesthetic modernity, turn out on closer examination to be ambiguous. On the one hand, the return to traditional techniques itself conforms to a thoroughly modernist logic of innovation, only now canonized modernism itself occupies the position from which the modification deviates. On the other hand, such different writers as Tournier and Robbe-Grillet are both pursuing a project of subversion. If Tournier is staking his all on objectivistic representation veering round into hallucination, Robbe-Grillet is seeking to expose autobiography as fiction by precisely fulfilling the expectations raised by the traditional genre.

If we were to ask what is the target of this subversion, the answer would be the category of meaning. Modern literature had confronted a situation characterized by the absence of meaningful experience in life. It did not, however, despair of the possibility of producing meaning. From Proust's *A la recherche du temps perdu* to Sartre's *La Nausée*, it was regarded as the function of the work of art to produce meaning. Perhaps, by contrast, we might define as postmodern that body of literature which has altogether given up the attempt to produce meaning.

Admittedly, this was already the case with the work of Beckett, who is none the less generally regarded as a modernist writer. Not only does he renounce the production of a positive meaning, but in his texts he systematically destroys the possibility of conveying meaning through speech. Beckett repeatedly has his narrators doubt whether they are connecting sounds and meanings together correctly. The eponymous hero of the novel *Watt* discovers a disturbing non-correspondence between word and meaning; he is unable to call pots 'pots' any more. Molloy, the protagonist and narrator of another novel, admits that he often perceives even his own words only as the buzzing of an insect and not as bearers of meaning. With signifier and signified falling apart in this way, the other levels of the constitution of meaning also disintegrate. The relation between one linguistic sign and another becomes fragile, the relation to fictional reality doubtful. Molloy constantly contradicts himself.

However, Adorno's interpretation of Beckett does show that it is possible all the same to relate his texts to social reality and interpret them as a cipher of our age. He understands the linguistic impotence of Beckett's characters as an 'unprotesting representation of omnipresent regression' (Adorno 1961: 198). A postmodern literature would, however, be one which closed off the possibility of any such interpretation, one which could no longer be referred back to any reality whatever. One can show that this is precisely the case with Michel Tournier's *Erl-king*. Unlike Beckett, Tournier neither puts into question the form of the traditional novel, nor the capacity of language to convey meaning. But he creates such a tight mesh of cross-references between fictional reality and the figure of his perverse hero, the French garage-owner Abel Tiffauges, that the reader becomes, as it were, entangled in it. To Tiffauges the world seems a huge accumulation of signs which demand to be interpreted. One of his first journal entries reads: 'All is sign. But only a piercing light or shriek will penetrate our blunted sight and hearing' (Tournier 1972: 12).

An event in his childhood already provides Tournier's protagonist with such a light: having run away from school because he had been punished, but having then been sent by his father, he finds the school on fire. In this occurrence Tiffauges discovers the connection between his individual destiny and events in the world. In the course of his captivity as a prisoner of war in Germany, which brings him to Rominten in East Prussia, Goering's hunting ground, and the Kaltenborn Napola, another relationship is revealed to him: the common ground between his attraction to children and National Socialism's youth cult. In a manner consistent with this discovery, in the last days of the Napola, shortly before the end of the war, he is given the task of recruiting new blood for the Nazi elite-school. Tiffauges, who is passionately fond of carrying children, is simultaneously the children's friend and the man-eater of the fairy-tale, the ogre who steals children from their parents. The novel ends with the destruction of the Kaltenborn Napola, which the fanatical commandant defends to the last with the children against the advancing Russian army. With a Jewish boy who has escaped from a concentration camp, Tiffauges flees from the deadly battle; however, in the attempt to avoid a street that is under fire, he gets – willingly/unwillingly – into a bog: he is thus at one and the same time both St Christopher who saves the child and the Erl-king who steals and murders him.

Insofar as the battle for Kaltenborn reveals the man-eating essence of National Socialism, one might read the novel precisely as the counter-project to the modern or postmodern evacuation of meaning, that is, as a consistent effort to reintroduce the dimension of meaning into literature. And yet we should not allow ourselves to be misled by the frequency with which concepts like *signe, symbole* and their synonyms occur in the novel. It is first and foremost merely the case that reality is considered here as signs. What attracts Tiffauges to Nazi Germany is the fact that what he continually encounters there is a 'significant reality': 'here I'm always face to face with a *significant-reality* which is almost always clear and distinct; or, when it does become difficult to read, that's because it's growing more profound and losing in obviousness what it gains in richness' (Tournier 1972: 225).

Reality has a significant character for Abel Tiffauges for the reason that it seems to refer to his own psychic deformations. Tournier intermingles the story of his (perverse) protagonist and that of National Socialist Germany to such an extent that the two reflect each other and are at the same time also paralleled in Goethe's ballad of the child-stealing Erl-king. Abel Tiffauges's love of children is at the same time ogreishness, just as the orientation of National Socialism towards youth ultimately proves to be a programme for the annihilation of youth. The two things mirror each other reciprocally and run together in the paranoid *folie d'interprétation* of the protagonist.

The decisive question for the interpretation of the novel is as follows: can this connection be regarded as a serious attempt at a mythical interpretation of German history during the Nazi period? In other words, can the book legitimately be compared with a work like Thomas Mann's *Doctor Faustus*? Answering this question is made more difficult by the fact that Tournier is clearly of the opinion that he has, with his book, made a contribution to the understanding of National Socialism. In an essay which mixes autobiography and commentary on his works, he himself speaks of the 'cannibalistic vocation' of the Nazi regime', to which, moreover, he ascribes a certain childlike aspect. 'One has indeed to admit that fascist political life has something childlike about it, by which I mean that it manifests itself at a level that puts it within the grasp of the young through its perpetual parades, festivals, bonfires, hikes and youth organizations' (Tournier 1983: 105–6).

Obviously National Socialism is not going to be explained by depicting Goering and Hitler as child-eating fairy-tale monsters (they are called 'the ogre of Rominten' and 'the ogre of Rastenburg' in the novel). The reference to the fairy-tale figure of the ogre or the Goethean Erl-king does not explain the history of National Socialism; instead, it draws this history into a literary game of reciprocal references. Similarly, the historical reality is woven into a network of relationships in which everything refers to everything else. In the process, however – whether or not it is Tournier's intention to do this – the assignment of meaning is bypassed.

Beckett shows the absence of meaning through the destruction of the principles of coherence, which form the basis of linguistic communication; he cannot, however, prevent his texts from being interpreted as an expression of a historical situation. The work of Tournier, by contrast, who does not for one moment cast doubt upon the possibility of coherent linguistic communication and whose texts are full of references pregnant with meaning, cannot, paradoxically, be interpreted as an expression of the age. His novel places before us a closed chain of signifiers, referring to nothing else, not even to the author's present. However, perhaps there is a last link in the chain of signs, though admittedly this remains carefully concealed in Tournier's work: this is the French schoolbook, whose picture of Germany with Erl-king and German forest, hugely magnified, Tournier's novel shows to the reader. Culture is culture. After all, Tournier comes from a family of Germanists.

This interpretation does, however, require some modification. The assertion that Tournier's *Erl-king* can no longer be related to social reality is, if strictly understood, impossible to establish. It would be quite conceivable for a critic to see the reflection of the history of National Socialist Germany in the private perversion of the protagonist, the misbegotten myth (St Christopher/the ogre) and the endless play of references which never touch ground as the expression of the period after the collapse of the May 1968 movement (the novel appeared in 1975). The plunge into myth would then be a sign of the loss of a social perspective which is today by no means confined to the French intelligentsia. Such an interpretation is all the more legitimate in that it would be capable of explaining Tournier's success. It follows from this that the interpretation of the *Erl-king* sketched out above is a postmodern reading of the novel. Such a reading might also be made of Beckett (against Adorno's interpretation) and the reader could call on the author's own understanding of what he is doing in support of his interpretation. If this is correct, then it becomes questionable whether such a strict opposition exists between Beckett's modern text (which still refers to reality) and Tournier's postmodern text (which excludes such a relation to reality). The postmodern taboo on the relation between text and reality would then above all be a mode of operating with texts, or, more precisely, a mode of speaking about them, but not a set of indications which can be drawn out of the text itself. The result shows us clearly once again how much the things we speak of are shaped by the way in which we speak of them. Although it is part of the self-understanding of any serious critic that one must engage with the specificity of one's object, one's approach is none the less determined by assumptions which cannot be avoided but which can at least be controlled by an effort of thought. When related to the object under consideration here, this means that what is talked of as postmodern literature might actually prove to be a change in the institutionalized discourse on literature. To formulate this in an exaggerated fashion, one might say that there is a postmodern treatment of literature, but no postmodern literature.

III

Let us test out this conclusion on Botho Strauss's short story 'Theorie der Drohung', which we might very properly regard as a postmodern work and not merely a work which permits of a post-modern reading. The title 'Theorie der Drohung', which might be translated as 'Theory of Threat', leads the reader to expect an essay, were it not for the fact that the text is published in a volume bearing the generic title 'Short Stories'. Is theory, then, to be the subject of a short story? It is, in fact, rather to be a means of confusing the reader. Botho Strauss neither employs the theoretical languages of science to comment on the action he represents, as Musil did, nor does the short story coincide with a fictive theory as it does on occasion in Borges; rather he uses theoretical language as one type of discourse among others, that is, as artistic material. The confusion which this produces is only one form among many within the story. Indeed it is in no way easy to say what the story is about, because it narrates two events, which in fact come down in the end to only one. On the one hand, there is the meeting of the first-person narrator, a writer, with Lea, a mentally disturbed woman whom he does not know and who claims to have lived with him in the past, providing evidence for this assertion in a way that astonishes the narrator. On the other, there is the account of the narrator's various literary projects, the last of which coincides with the story of Lea. This would seem, then, to be nothing but an allegory of writing. And indeed, on his very first meeting with Lea, the narrator interprets her contorted gestures as a striving for expression.

> Did it not rather seem as though these over-specific gestures, which overstepped the law and shattered the standard forms of a moderate participation by our bodies in social communication, were striving to come close to an extreme perfection and identity in their own expression?... Without doubt I immediately read in Lea's madness the nightmarish version of my own agonizing attempts to express myself in my writing.
> (*Strauss 1980: 53–4*)

Each time the reader gains the impression that he or she is dealing with a 'real' figure (for example in the account of their journey to England together), the figure slides over into the allegorical: 'Now I was quite sure I would write about Lea ... because the feeling of loving Lea was nothing other than the feeling of beginning a book' (1980: 96–7).

After entering into reading the story as allegory, the reader finds himself or herself induced to recognize the allegorical transposition of prevalent literary-theoretical topoi in the disparate fragments from which it is made up. Two examples here: the narrator hits upon a 'theoretical conjecture' in his notebook which he finds astonishing.

Whatever I write, it writes about me. I am continually writing
this alien thing which threatens me. What I am writing knows
who I am, knows also how I will end and everyone can read
about me in my writing, the way old women read tea leaves –
except me. I can't do it; I can't read it; the meaning is sealed
off; I miss the warnings which are there in every line. *(1980: 75)*

This rather mysterious note discloses its meaning when one understands it as an allegorical transposition of the hermeneutic principle
formulated by Schleiermacher, that the interpreter can understand a
text better than its author.

While Botho Strauss projects this reception-related principle into
the production situation, writing appears as a monstrous act of
self-alienation, which delivers up the self to the Other and at the
same time eludes the reflexive grasp of the ego. At the end of the
story, writing appears as just such a total self-alienation. On a
journey, the narrator discovers that he has turned into Lea: 'Yes, it
was her hairstyle, her way of pinning up her hair over her temples,
it was also her make-up ... I was Lea. Or at least, I had made
everything which remained of Lea my own' (1980: 108–9). Here too
Strauss is staging a well-known literary-historical topos, namely
Flaubert's dictum 'Madame Bovary, c'est moi'. The fantastic scene
proves to be the allegorization of a quotation.

The components of which the story is made up already belong to
literature. Though he is striving for self-expression, the narrator
is unable to produce anything but a string of plagiarisms: 'I, this
non-person, this way-station of all possible literature' (1980: 85).
And if the story refers to anything, then, once again, it is to literature. As with Tournier's *Erl-king*, the 'Theorie der Drohung' seems
to set in place an endless chain of signifiers, which never come to rest
in a signification that has not already appeared in literature. This
reading is confirmed by the theory of writing which the story
expounds. According to that theory, writing is not (as the realists
assumed) an act of communication of reality, nor is it (as modernist
authors from Proust to Nathalie Sarraute have believed) a process of
classification of experience, but a primary drive event, which produces a de-realization of reality. The act of writing has no outside,
neither object which it represents nor addressee to whom it is
directed. It is pure self-referentiality. This is not, however, conceived
on the model of a consciousness transparent to itself; it rather
appears as an event whose mechanisms remain hidden to the ego and
thus is more like autistic compulsive action than the free activity of a
self-conscious subject.

That the ego precisely does not possess the autonomous mastery which classic subject theory imputed to it has, from the beginning, been one of literary modernity's central themes. In this regard, it might be difficult to make out anything that could be termed specifically postmodern in 'Theorie der Drohung'. Even allegory is, as we have been aware since Benjamin's Baudelaire studies, a modern form. The question remains whether Strauss's handling of this form departs from the modern in such a way as to make the designation 'postmodern' appear meaningful.

Botho Strauss is not principally concerned to put into question the autonomous mastery of the subject; that was done by modernist authors many years ago (for example by Gottfried Benn in his 'Rönne' stories). He is concerned with the consequences of the powerlessness of the subject for the project of writing. An authorial 'I' which is merely a way-station for other texts, which it reproduces without being clearly aware of this, can no longer make the claim to interpret the world; yet this has been the claim of modern literature right up to Beckett.

However, does Strauss not become entangled in a contradiction here? The text says that it is impossible for the author, the non-person, to produce a coherent textual meaning. And he demonstrates this, by putting together in the text a variety of discourse types without any connection between them: quasi-realistic narration, diary entries, psychological treatises and an essay in literary theory. There is indeed no relation between the types of discourse, but this heterogeneous multifariousness corresponds precisely to the thesis that the author is a non-person. The text is, therefore, coherent and also has an interpretable meaning; it thus contradicts the thesis that it is impossible for the author to produce meaning.

Perhaps Botho Strauss is pursuing no other goal than to lure the reader into this contradiction. It is really not so easy to write a text which has no meaning, since a context only has to be added for it to appear to have one (we have indeed seen this in the example of Adorno's reading of Beckett). If, however, one writes a text which contradicts itself as completely as 'Theorie der Drohung', then one comes very close to the meaningless text.

Even the way in which Strauss deploys allegory corresponds to such a reading. The modern allegory refers to reality; it is interpreting a bit of the world. When, for example, Kafka's Gregor Samsa wakes up one morning as a gigantic beetle, this is telling us something about the consciousness of the lowly office-worker. In 'Theorie der Drohung', by contrast, the allegory refers only to itself. It does not designate something in the world, but merely the act of writing. When Botho Strauss gradually allows Lea to disappear, he is staging the destruction of the material sign by meaning, a destruction which constitutes the essence of allegory. The meaning which is involved in this process is not, however, any particular meaning, but the entirely abstract category of meaning itself.

Even if one accepts this interpretation, it might still be possible to interpret the withdrawal from meaning as an expression of despair at a world which is so single-mindedly engaged upon its own destruction as our own. This would be the view of Adorno, who, in spite of his historical pessimism, was ultimately an incurable optimist, as are all dialectical thinkers. But it is just this optimism which is lacking in those who have made the postmodern mentality their own.

IV

In discussions of the postmodern, alongside the name of Botho Strauss, that of Peter Handke is repeatedly cited. However, if we compare Handke's short story, 'The long way around' with Botho Strauss's 'Theorie der Drohung', we see more differences between the two than similarities. Whereas, in Strauss's work, the writing 'I' is opaque to itself, Handke's narrator has an unproblematic access to the experiences of Sorger, the geologist, whom he also addresses as 'You' at the end of the story. By contrast with the opaque 'I' whose story is told by Strauss, Handke's work contains a figure who, even in the life-threatening crisis, never loses his own self from sight.

This ability of Handke's figure to see into himself might well turn out to be an illusion, to which even the narrator (if not indeed the author) succumbs. Sorger is at first unsuccessful in his attempt to leave Alaska; the mail plane has to turn back on account of a snowstorm; back on the airfield, he is violently attacked by a drunkard. The peaceable and peace-loving Sorger reacts with an outburst of misanthropy. This connection seems unambiguous and is unambiguously reflected in Sorger's consciousness. He does not acknowledge that the aggression, which comes to him from outside, might be his own (immediately before, Sorger has learnt that the Indian woman he had lived with had already begun a new relationship with his colleague). The self-transparency of the ego is illusion.

Another difference between the two stories is even more striking. Botho Strauss does everything in his power to make clear that it is not the author who produces the meaning of a text. It is different with Handke. His character is permanently employed in ascribing meaning to anything and everything. No matter whether he is in Alaska, by the sea on the American West Coast or in a coffee shop in New York, what he perceives is meaningful to him.

Not only the bruised tabletop but also the floor of the coffee shop imitated the surface of the earth. Near the cash desk it formed a slight hollow, and for a terrifying moment Sorger felt that the ground was gone from under his feet, as though the floorboards had been laid on the bare, unleveled earth; and through this irregularity of the room the city became, in its very depths, a living and powerful natural organism. (*Handke 1985b: 116*)

Sorger establishes connections (here between the hollow in the floor of the café and the shape of the earth in Manhattan) and delightedly sees himself as the person forging these relationships. In a comparable way, the surrealists in their day sought out – and affectively cathected – 'correspondences' of this type within everyday life. Admittedly, they still believed that, in so doing, they were dependent on chance. Handke – or his character – has, however, developed the production of meaningful experience into a technique which, almost unfailingly, gives the subject the experience of a fulfilled existence. Are we now also to characterize this exuberance of meaning as postmodern?

There are good reasons for doing so. Handke's procedure can be very easily described without recourse to the concept of meaning. Sorger reads the world as a universe of signs, in which each sign refers to another (the scratches on the table-top or the dip in the floor of the café referring to Manhattan as a 'natural body'). We also seem to be dealing with a chain of signifiers here; no signified would seem to be in view. Against this one might admittedly adduce that Sorger certainly experiences something which he calls 'peace', 'harmony', 'harmonic wholeness' or 'bliss'. Right at the beginning of the story, mention is made of the 'need for salvation' and, at the end, of 'an eternally wild need for redemption'. Surely these are quite emphatic signifieds.

Against this, let us return once again to a strong postmodern reading. First, it is striking that the concepts 'peace', 'harmony', 'bliss' and 'salvation' are all more or less applied as synonyms. They denote a kind of heightened sense of being alive which appears as soon as Sorger sets about transforming the world into a chain of signs, whose links are all interrelated. Insofar as this feeling – if we leave aside the rare moments of forlornness – always remains the same, at least in its basic tone, then the association of emphatic signifieds with the individual links in the sign chain is very loose. If all signs have more or less the same meaning, then indeed the individual sign has no definite meaning. Drawing on Lacan, one might say that meaning or, rather, what remains a vague meaning-complex slips beneath the chain of signifiers. What at first appeared as plenitude of meaning turns out to be its opposite. We came to a similar conclusion in regard to the work of Tournier.

Clearly, Handke's story also permits of two quite different readings: a traditional one, which follows the states of consciousness that are represented, and another which focuses its attention on the relationship between sign and meaning and which one might properly term postmodern. It is quite odd how, on this latter reading, the affirmation of life, which Handke lays on very thick, evaporates into the mere gesturing towards something which is snatching at a meaning that is always slipping away from it. Admittedly, I find it difficult to avoid the suspicion that the postmodern interpretation of Handke is protecting a terribly affirmative text from necessary criticism. The disappearance of meaning in this way assumes the character of a substitutive meaning. Whereas, for Adorno, it was still unquestionably the case that even the works of modernity which cast off all representational intentions still expressed something about social reality, precisely this interpretive assumption has begun to falter. With the fading of a future dimension to society, the capacity to relate works of art to reality as bearers of meaning seems also to be waning. Its place is taken either by a curious inclination to content oneself with a literal reading of what is narrated (the story says what it says) or what might perhaps be termed a metaphysical enthusiasm for the meaningless sign. By comparison, the catastrophic world-view of an Adorno still has a great utopian content, since for it signs still have something definite to say.

NOTES

1 Hassan evades a possible critique of his arbitrary classification of authors as modern or postmodern by challenging the reader to 'Make your own list' (1984: 88). On the postmodernism debate in the USA, see Huyssen 1986; Jameson 1984; C. Bürger 1987.

2 On Handke's reference to Stifter, see Handke 1985a: 141, 176. On Kafka, he writes: 'I hate Franz Kafka, the Eternal Son' (1983: 94); see also 1983: 49 and 89ff.

3 On the criticism of postmodern architecture, see Müller 1987.

4 Robbe-Grillet (1984: 13) expressly refers to his autobiography as fiction: 'Et c'est encore dans une fiction que je me hasarde ici.'

REFERENCES

Adorno, T. W. 1961: 'Versuch, das Endspiel zu verstehen', in *Noten zur Literatur*, vol. 1. Frankfurt a.M.: Suhrkamp.

Bourdieu, P. 1984: *Distinction*, tr. R. Nice. London: Routledge & Kegan Paul.

Bürger, C. 1987: 'Das Verschwinden der Kunst: Die Postmoderne-Debatte in den USA', in C. Bürger and P. Bürger (eds), *Postmoderne: Alltag, Allegorie und Avantgarde*. Frankfurt a.M.: Suhrkamp, 34–55.

Bürger, P. 1983: 'Zum Anti-Avantgardismus Adornos', in *Zur Kritik der idealistischen Asthetik*. Frankfurt a.M.: Suhrkamp.

Gehlen, A. 1964: 'Über kulturelle Evolutionen', in H. Kuhn and F. Wiedemann, *Die Philosophie und die Frage nach dem Fortschritt*. Munich: Anton Pustet.

Handke, P. 1983: *Phantasien der Wiederholung*. Frankfurt a.M.: Suhrkamp.

Handke, P. 1985a: 'The lesson of Mont Saint-Victoire', in *Slow Homecoming*. London: Methuen.

Handke, P. 1985b: 'The long way around', in *Slow Homecoming*. London: Methuen.

Hassan, I. 1984: 'POSTmodernISM: a paracritical bibliography', in M. Pütz and P. Frese (eds), *Postmodernism in American Literature*. Darmstadt: Thesen Verlag.

Huyssen, A. 1986: 'Postmoderne – eine amerikanische Internationale?', in A. Huyssen and K. R. Scherpe (eds), *Postmoderne: Zeichen eines kulturellen Wandels*. Reinbek bei Hamburg: Rowohlt, 13–44.

Jameson, F. 1984: 'Postmodernism, or the logic of late capitalism', *New Left Review*, 146, 53–92.

Müller, M. 1987: *Schöner Schein: Eine Architekturkritik*. Frankfurt a.M.: Athenäum.

Robbe-Grillet, A. 1984: *Le Miroir que revient*. Paris: Minuit.

Strauss, Botho 1980: 'Theorie der Drohung', in *Marlenes Schwester: Zwei Erzählungen*. Munich: Dentscher Taschenbuch Verlag.

Tournier, M. 1972: *The Erl-king*, tr. Barbara Bray. London: Methuen.

Tournier, M. 1983: *Le Vent paraclet*. Paris: Gallimard.

Part II

Representation and the transformation of identity

5

Popular representation: recasting realism

Nicholas Abercrombie, Scott Lash and Brian Longhurst

The avalanche of discussion of modernism and postmodernism in past years has placed the question of 'realism' as a cultural paradigm in a decidedly new light. Realism, post-postmodernism, as it were, has unfortunately not been investigated with the tenacity that it deserves. One main reason for this is that today's debates are largely cast, not in the descriptive and explanatory statements of the social sciences, but instead in the prescriptive utterances of aesthetic and political discourse. In these latter, normative discourses, there are plenty of analysts with a host of good reasons who take the side either of modernism or of postmodernism. But who, with the exception of a few atavistic followers of Lukács, would dare publicly to be identified with the aesthetic and political discourse of realism? This is even more the pity because, as we shall illustrate below, realism is still probably the most pervasive regime of 'signification' in popular culture today, and indeed makes a lot of the running in high culture as well. In this essay, then, we wish rather dispassionately to separate fact from value (though indeed we do hold political and aesthetic values) and operate primarily in the realm of fact. Thus we are permitted more or less coldly to begin to analyse realism in the face of both modernism and postmodernism.

The advantage that the analyst of realism has in the late 1980s, after a good half-decade of widespread debate on postmodernism, is that realism is now much more clearly set into relief as a socially and historically delimited cultural paradigm. This was surely not the case in the controversies surrounding realism in the 1970s. At this point debates were largely dominated by Colin MacCabe (e.g. MacCabe

1981: 216–35). These analyses, from our point of view – and with the hindsight granted to us in the 1990s – had significant shortcomings. MacCabe's notion of realism was both ahistorical and neglected the dimension of the social. That is it first, somehow rather simplistically identified realist culture with 'closed texts' and non-realist cultural products with 'open texts' regardless of the historicity of the former and the latter. Second, MacCabe's virtually singular focus on cultural texts themselves tended to ignore their conditions of production and conditions of reception, and in particular their social conditions of production and reception. Finally, on MacCabe's account the spatio-temporal pervasion of realist cultural forms was almost unlimited. *Le réalisme*, on this view, *était partout*, or at least almost everywhere.

In part the ahistorical and unsociological nature of such analyses was not surprising. MacCabe and his colleagues at *Screen*, like their traditionalist predecessors and counterparts in English departments in the UK, not to mention both avant-garde and traditional figures in both the US and France in modern languages and culture studies more generally, have been primarily involved in *aesthetic* discourse. There is nothing wrong with this, because that is their business. The business of aesthetic discourse is to make evaluative statements, though as Habermas notes, in a subjective mode, and back such statements up with arguments pertaining to aesthetic value. Cultural debates in Germany, to the contrary – and here a lineage extends from Hegel through Simmel and Weber, through Benjamin and Lukács, and from Marcuse and Adorno through contemporaries like Jauss and Peter Bürger – have significantly been located in historical, institutional and sociological context. The advantage of such analyses is that both aesthetic and sociological dimensions have been taken seriously. In the Anglo-American and French theoretical worlds, if aesthetic discourse did not take the social dimension seriously, then sociological analysis had paid scant attention to the aesthetic dimension. The very best of such sociological work – for example from the Birmingham Centre for Contemporary Culture Studies and that of Pierre Bourdieu and his colleagues – has not centrally engaged with the problem of realism or with the historicity of cultural forms.

What we propose to do in this essay is to begin to make some inroads into such a sociological analysis of realism. In this pursuit we should like first to attempt a re-definition of realism. This re-definition will historically rather radically delimit the types of cultural object that are realist. In this connection we will then argue that a realist aesthetic discourse is used to justify cultural forms which are in important ways non-realist, and in particular to argue for the validity of modernist and postmodernist cultural forms. The second part of this essay is addressed to demonstrating just how widespread realism is in today's popular culture. In this we contend that realism must be understood as an ideal-type, and is never in popular culture found in anything like its pristine form. The final section then begins to construct around this realist ideal-type – in a vein inspired by the work of Raymond Williams – a periodization, or a historical sociology of popular culture. Here we focus, not so much on cultural products themselves, but on their socio-historical conditions of reception.

REALISM AS A CULTURAL PARADIGM

Realism is a specific and historical cultural configuration. It must be understood in juxtaposition with cultural 'paradigms' which are not realist. The latter include not just modernism and postmodernism, but pre-realist Western cultural configurations, such as medieval art, Western peasant folk culture, and literature and the fine arts in classical antiquity. Non-Western culture – African, Arab, Japanese, Indian, Chinese – is also on most important counts non-realist. Realism is most commonly viewed as having origins in fifteenth- and sixteenth-century Renaissance painting and in the nineteenth-century novel. The third of the art forms, music, is not referential in the sense that the visual arts and literature can be. Yet measured and ordered harmonic structure, bearing similarities on important counts with pictorial and narrative realism, do characterize Western classical music – as they characterize equally non-referential neo-classical architecture – from the seventeenth through to the nineteenth centuries. Aspects of such visual, literary and aural realism continue to play a pervasive role in twentieth-century popular culture.

What is it that unites all of these, as well as the popular culture forms we shall discuss below, under the banner of realism? The answer could well be that all are rooted in a particular cosmology, in fact in a particular 'ontology', or theory of the nature of reality. Such ontologies are not any sort of natural preserve of elites, but are just as importantly found in the popular classes. Christian ontology, for example, began as an elite theory of priest–intellectuals before it became an ontology of the masses. The same is true of the ontology in which realism is anchored, which had origins arguably at about the time of the Renaissance as an elite world-view before it became widespread as a 'popular ontology' in the twentieth century.

To define realism is evidently to say that cultural forms must be plausible and significantly conform with visions of reality in everyday life. But to make sociological sense, realism must be substantially more spatio-temporally delimited than this. Realism must include only cultural forms which conform with a particular vision of everyday reality, with a particular 'high' or 'popular' ontology. Christian ontology, for example, as high or popular ontology, presupposes that time and space in everyday life are largely constructed and structured through a sort of deity-driven teleology. And Christian narratives in the sphere of culture are typically teleological. Christian narratives have thus been plausible in their very conforming with high and popular ontology, but it makes little sociological sense to call them 'realist'. To be realist a cultural form must be compatible with an ontology rooted in secular and scientific cosmology. And more specifically in a scientific cosmology (based on Galilean and Newtonian concepts) that is primarily mechanistic.

The belief in a specific ontology by elites ('high ontology') or by the masses ('popular ontology') conditions an audience in the reception of particular cultural forms. But the cultural forms (or a cultural paradigm such as realism) is *not* the same thing as high or popular ontology. A cultural paradigm is instead a *regime of signification*. A 'regime of signification' is a particular mode of signifying. Modernism, for example, as a regime of signification, devalues the 'referent' to emphasize the formal qualities of signifiers. Postmodernism as a regime of signification once again puts important value on the referent, but then problematizes the referent itself, so that the place of the signifier is often taken by the referent and that of the referent by the signifier. The corresponding postmodernist popular ontology features the pervasion of reality itself by representations. In a corresponding vein, pre-realist (and many non-Western) modes of signification, in their characteristic weighting of symbolism, tend to privilege the signi*fied*. Signifiers here point thus not to the referent (that is, to reality) but to signifieds or meanings of a higher order, such as deities or ideal forms as in some varieties of classicism. The realist mode of signification privileges the referent, as does postmodernism. But referent and signifier in realism, unlike postmodernism, are clearly differentiated, each in its proper place. Realism, modernism and postmodernism are all regimes of signification which are situated in the culture of Western modernity. Realism's origins were in early modernity, and modernism's and postmodernism's are in 'late' modernity. Unlike pre-modern or non-Western modes of signification, all three of these modes in Western modernity devalue symbolism and the role of the signified. Finally, unlike pre-modern and non-Western aesthetic *dis*courses, whose main legitimation arguments relate to cultural forms corresponding to an ideal world of some sort, all three of modernity's modes of signification are backed by aesthetic *discourses* of realism, in which correspondence to reality (and not to an ideal world) is an important criterion of validity.

By 'aesthetic *discourse*' we mean, straightforwardly, a set of arguments for the validity or value of particular high- or popular-culture representations. Our argument is that realist arguments or assumptions are used in regard to the merit of very *non*-realist (modernist or postmodernist) art. For example, the modernist novel, as Peter Bürger suggests in chapter 4 above, is situated not in an objective reality, but in experience. Yet aesthetic discourse or arguments for the value of these novels could understand such experience as part of the very grain of reality. Or correspondingly 'punk' in popular music, which has commonly been seen as postmodern, foregrounds cacophony, disharmony and an aesthetic of the ugly. Yet arguments for the value of punk would stress how all of this is in fact quite consistent with a brutal, highly contingent if not chaotic reality. Thus realist arguments are used to legitimate classic realist, modernist and postmodernist culture. It is true that such arguments presuppose varying notions of the real. But that said, each does have recourse to the real. And this suggests that realism, modernism and postmodernism have more in common with one another than with non-Western or premodern art. Which further implies that all three are situated in the broad framework of Western modernity. More on this below.

There seem to be three main parameters of realism: (1) realism offers a window on the world; (2) realism employs a narrative which has rationally ordered connections between events and characters; (3) realism conceals authorship and disguises the production process of a text. Let us consider these in sequence.

(1) Realism offers a window on the world. Our first and second parameters largely correspond to on the one hand pictorial, and on the other, narrative realism. Pictorial realism, indeed the pictorial qualities of any cultural paradigm, is a matter of the organization of *space*. Narrative realism, and the narrative qualities of all cultural paradigms, have to do with the organization of time. All cultural paradigms – realist, modernist, postmodernist, Christian, Chinese and Indian – can be characterized in terms of their specific mode of organization of time and space. They can be characterized in terms of (a) *how* time and space are organized and (b) in terms of *what* imparts organization to time and space. On the first of these counts realist time and space are organized along lines of order and stability

rather than of contingency and instability. This sort of spatio-temporal organization is found also in non-realist, for example Christian and classical Greek, cultural paradigms, though it definitively is *not* present in modernist and postmodernist cultural paradigms.

Regarding the spatial organization of representations, paradigmatic for realism is of course quattrocento perspective (see Martin Jay in chapter 7, below) and its assumptions of a single viewing eye. On this account the painting mediates between the eye and the reality (say, the landscape depicted). It is true that *all* culture mediates, but in quattrocento perspective – and pictorial realism – such mediation takes a very specific form. There are three particular assumptions at work here which regard producer, text and audience or correspondingly speaker, utterance and addressee:

(a)   In the position of producer or speaker is, not the author, but the referent or reality itself. Note that previous to realism, the position of producer or speaker was occupied by a higher-order signified or meaning.

(b)   In the position of the audience or addressee is the perceptual, rather than the cognitive, apparatus. And within perception, not the ear, not even 'feeling', but the eye is hegemonic. Finally this is, not binocular vision, but the single eye.

(c)   In the position of the text or utterance (or media) is a window, literally stationed between the eye and the referent, along geometric sight lines which connect the eye to the referent.

(2) We don't want to make too hard and fast a distinction between the just-discussed window-on-the-world, or pictorial, realism and narrative realism. For example, both pictorial and narrative realism partake of the same mechanistic cosmology. Yet it makes good analytical sense to hold to such a distinction.

Western and non-Western cultural paradigms differ from one another, not just in terms of their spatio-temporal organization of representations, but also on the count of *what* imparts spatio-temporal organization. Here narrative realism speaks first and foremost the language of scientific causation. This means that causes must be immanent either to everyday life or the cultural object under question, and the cause be prior to effect. This contrasts with Ancient Greek or Christian models of explanation in which causes are transcendent and not necessarily prior to the explanans. Because modernism and especially postmodernism speak the language of contingency rather than that of order, they are less concerned with causation altogether.

Narratives, discourses and myths, for example, signify over a temporal dimension – unlike, say, the word or the statement. The rationality of cause and effect is manifested in realist narrative. Realist cultural forms consist of a caused, logical flow of events, often structured into a beginning, a middle and a closed conclusion. Classical novels have such a format, even if a 'slice of life' from the continuous flow of history is presented. The typical Hollywood film, to take another example, consists of three elements: initial stability, interruption, and movement to new stability and closure (Kuhn 1982: 29). The important point is that for realist texts the narrative is the central organizing principle. In this respect realist forms may be contrasted with those texts that are essentially 'spectacular'. The pleasure of texts involving 'spectacle' lies in the images themselves; it is a visual, not a narrative, pleasure.

Such rationality also applies to what might be thought to be non-narrative cultural forms. Realist photographs and paintings often have a 'before' and 'after' outside the specific moment captured in the frame. They are episodes in a story and imply the rest of the narrative in the nature of their images and the meanings that these construct. The meaning of the picture is given by its place in an implied narrative. Non-realist forms do not imply such a narrative. They do not imply a story so much as invite contemplation, disrupting the flow of everyday life and its 'rational' construction of cause and effect.

(3) The third aspect of realism is the concealment of the production of the cultural form. Realist cultural forms present themselves as already constructed or as a report upon external events. Many realist texts encourage the audience to think that there is no author. That is, as just mentioned, the referent so to speak takes the place of the author. The form conspires to convince us that we are not reading or viewing something that has been constructed in a particular fashion by a determinate producer or set of producers. Even nineteenth-century novels which have an author 'speaking' directly to the readers and which might, hence, imply that the narrative had been constructed in a particular pattern, maintain that events are being *reported upon*. A classic example of this is *Jane Eyre*, with its famous 'Reader: I married him' statement. Even in such novels the author's hand is concealed: the work of the production of the text is simplified or omitted. Reality (as everyday life) is seen to be simply reproduced on the page, film or television screen. Realist forms, in other words, are fictions but do not present themselves as fictions. For many analysts, this characteristic of realism makes the audience

into passive observers. They are not invited into the text, as active participants, because they can see how it is made, but are made to sit back and simply observe an apparently seamless whole; audiences do not do any work on the texts.

Modernism is 'a regime of signification' which, in its privileging of the signifier, does show the author's hand. Modernism in this sense valuates the formal properties of the aesthetic material. Its focus is on the producer's systematic working through of the possibilities in the aesthetic material, such as Schoenberg's twelve-tone system, or Picasso's facet-planes, or Proust's experiments with time. Thus modernist cultural forms pre-eminently show the author's hand. Postmodernism, on the contrary, is not concerned particularly with the qualities of the aesthetic material. A postmodernist film like Beneix's *Diva* does not reveal the production process like modernist films directed by, for example, Godard. Like realism, a film such as *Diva* brings the viewer right in and 'glues' him or her to the referent; only the referent or the real then turns out to be a chimerical world of simulations.[1] It seems in fact that it is only modernism as a mode of signification which shows the author's hand. Pre-realist and non-Western cultural paradigms also typically conceal the production process.

REALIST AND NON-REALIST CULTURAL FORMS

Realism has been the dominant cultural form for the past 200 years (MacCabe 1981). The initial development of realist conventions in the English novel have been traced by Ian Watt (1963) and the dominant tradition through the nineteenth century was realist. A late example of this form is the work of Trollope, who offers us a view of a particular and complicated world. The narrative is made up of events, often individual occurrences, which are connected in chains of cause and effect and the author's role in the construction of the text is concealed from the reader. Such a tradition has been carried through to the popular fiction of the present day and most thrillers and many science-fiction novels, for example, have such a structure.

   Much contemporary television output also follows realist conventions. On our definition dramas such as *Dallas* are clearly realist. *Dallas* presents us a view of a plausible world, even if, as some viewers relate, very unlikely things happen and unusual domestic arrangements are taken for granted (Ang 1985: 34–7). Narrative realism, while dispensing with final causality, must be true to the

Aristotelian tenets of plausibility and predictability. Thus *Dallas* presents a believable world and the narrative links events causally; JR makes things happen to other people, who are often powerless. The construction of *Dallas* is seamless; it is not interrupted by moments of disclosure of the 'artificiality' of the production. It may well be that *Dallas* is a particular type of realism and following Ang's useful study this can be labelled 'emotional realism' (1985: 45), as the aspect of being a 'window on the world' of external events is not as prominent as the other aspects of realism. The world presented may therefore be less plausible than that constructed in documentary-influenced drama such as the British working-class soap opera *Coronation Street* (Longhurst 1987: 633–49). However, *Dallas* is still realist, albeit at the melodramatic end of the realist spectrum: a position corresponding to that of writers like the Brontës or Dickens in nineteenth-century realist fiction.

Certain forms of television which might be thought to be 'fantastic' or 'fantasy' are in our terms realist. For example, by our definition, the British science-fiction series *Dr Who* (Fiske 1983: 14–15; Tulloch and Alvorado 1983) and the space-travel drama *Star Trek* are realist. Despite not being directly concerned with 'our' world (though in both cases the action often takes place on Earth at some time in the past or the future), the worlds that are a setting for the action and which are constructed through the narrative are plausible in the terms of everyday life. Even the irrational or the strange is still explicable in quasi-scientific or everyday terms. Indeed, the science in such forms is often closer to our imagined view of the nature of science than its reality. This parallels the use made of science and technology in James Bond films and books (Zorzoli 1966). Realism, then, cuts across the genres of TV, cinema and literature: soap operas, police series, thrillers, adventure stories and science fiction are all realist.

Modernism can be defined by contrasting it with realism. Modernism does not depict a plausible everyday world in the manner of realism; the world is often strange or fragmented. There is a break with mechanistic, scientific discourse. The narrative is less concerned with a beginning, a middle and an end; it often becomes episodic and 'difficult'. The consequence is that the production and authorship of the text are foregrounded rather than concealed. There is a preoccupation with the role of the artist and form; authorship becomes artistically important in its own right rather than simply a means of representing 'reality'. Postmodernism, developing out of the critique of modernism begun by the 1920s and 1930s avant-garde, criticizes modernism's concern with high culture (see e.g.

Bürger 1984). It seeks to break the barriers between high and popular culture, taking the objects of everyday life as the subject for art. Its subjects are different from modernism's, however, as is its critique of society. Such forms of culture break with the conventions of realism, often in an explicit fashion. This does not necessarily mean that they break with the idea that there is a real world; rather they often maintain that the real world is more complex than has been assumed in realist culture.

Drawing upon Jameson's stimulating analysis of poststructuralism and postmodernism's abandonment of 'depth models' (1984: 53–92), it is possible to distinguish between modernism's and postmodernism's relation to the real. Much modernist writing and drama, despite being non-realist, still seeks to expose what it would call the real world. Often, the visible is the *unreal*: it confuses and conceals and the function of art is to lay bare the essential workings of the system. Such a view is found in certain versions of Marxist aesthetics. Brecht's aim, for example, is to make the nature of the world clear, to reach a deeper truth and 'expose' reality. The method chosen for this purpose is a modernist one. The drama does not present a view of everyday life or a world that is plausible in everyday terms. The narrative is not one of a story with rational connections between discrete events. In contrast to realism, the author's hand and the production process are revealed, encouraging speculation on the construction of the drama. The audience is not led into the seamless structure of realism but is made to participate.[2] Postmodernism often adopts a similar procedure: the link with an external, real world has become more tenuous. There is less explicit critique of the world, which continues to exist in many postmodernist products even if they do not adopt Marxist positions.

It should not be thought that the critique of realism is a characteristic of 'high culture' alone, for such positions can also be found in popular culture. Some television programmes attempt to break from dominant realist conventions. Two popular dramatic examples of this are the BBC series *Gangsters* (Kerr 1981: 73–8; Paterson 1981: 79–82) and *Boys from the Blackstuff* (Millington and Nelson 1986). The initial play and first series of *Gangsters*, shown in 1975 and 1976, and the play *The Blackstuff*, shown in 1980, can both be seen as falling within the realist conventions of British TV drama. The second series of *Gangsters*, shown in 1978, and the series *Boys from the Blackstuff*, first transmitted in 1982, were increasingly non-realist. The plausibility of the world depicted became increasingly strained. For example in *Gangsters* 'strange', non-realist characters appeared and *Boys from the Blackstuff* contained a surreal redundancy party. The connections between events became increasingly tenuous as the logic and flow of the narrative was disrupted by fantasy and dream sequences. Authorship and production were revealed, especially in *Gangsters* (Kerr 1981: 77).

Other popular dramatic fictions often involve a break with the conventions of realism. In the cinema the 'spaghetti westerns' of Sergio Leone contain certain modernist and postmodernist elements. The world that such films construct may be linked to our world or the recognizable world of the western, but it is such a world made strange: commonplace expectations of what should or would happen are disrupted. The hero has become an anti-hero and familiar or conventional roles are reversed (Frayling 1981). For example, in *Once upon a Time in the West*, we are shocked when Henry Fonda the actor turns out to be a ruthless killer. In an early scene we half-expect him to spare the lone child who has survived the massacre of the rest of his family by Fonda's gang; Fonda shoots him in cold blood.

Spaghetti westerns often somewhat disrupt the progression of the narrative. The long holds on faces that are characteristic of Leone's style potentially interrupt the flow. This stylistic feature demonstrates the films' interest in spectacle as much as narrative. With realist films the narrative is the organizing feature. In spaghetti westerns the narrative is fairly minimal and the 'look' is of equal importance. Likewise, the overt symbolization used in these films with their attention to Catholic imagery has the effect of disrupting the narrative of cause and effect. The utilization of such devices also makes the fact that these are fictions relatively plain. In addition, spaghetti westerns, in common with other contemporary popular fictions, often quote stories and scenes from other films. This carries the audience's attention outside the text itself and further disturbs the realism.

For other genres of popular television and film it can be intrinsically difficult to adopt realist conventions. One important example here is the musical. The classical Hollywood musical (Altman 1981) interrupts the narrative with song and spectacle which in their own ways break the depiction of a plausible world with a highly structured narrative. The sheer 'staged' nature of such interruptions also shows the element of construction that is involved in many such dramas. Such disruptive effects of song and music have been used deliberately in attempts to move away from realist convention. Potter's *Pennies from Heaven* – initially shown on British television and subsequently remade as a Hollywood film – is one of the best-known examples, and Julian Temple's controversial box-office flop

Absolute Beginners would be another illustration. In the latter the world is stylized; the narrative episodic, being broken with song and dance; and the construction and manipulation are plain. Some of these techniques were previously employed in a more experimental and direct form in Temple's collaboration with David Bowie on the video of *Jazzin' for Blue Jean*. Other genres also do not fit realist canons. Situation comedy on television, for instance, often involves an audience and does show authorship. The same is true, at the other extreme, of forms of art which depend on performance – in pristine high modernism.

It is clear, then, that it is possible to distinguish realist and non-realist cultural forms. However, it should not be thought that such divisions are always clear-cut, as not every cultural form can always be easily placed into one or other of the types. For example, in many contemporary realist dramas, such as the films of Steven Spielberg, the narrative flow is interrupted by moments of almost pure spectacle. Special effects become a form of art almost by themselves and many modern films are organized as much round these as round a strong story-line. These tend to disengage the spectator from the plot of the film and, to some degree, break the dominant realist drive. Likewise in James Bond films, the jokes and 'knowing' remarks which have become more common as the series has developed play on the audience's previous knowledge of the series and to some degree expose the artificiality of the narrative (Woolacott 1983). The same is true of *Dr Who*, where at points much of the dialogue consists of in-jokes for science-fiction buffs and the adult audience. The net effect of these devices will be to remove the audience from the text, to produce a sense of distance, and to emphasize the fictional character of the narrative.

The more melodramatic forms of realism as manifested in the cinema and in some forms of contemporary television drama also go some way toward breaking realist conventions (Feuer 1984; Kuhn 1984; Ang 1985). We have already mentioned that such narratives may seem less 'plausible' than other realist forms. For example, the number of events that happen to one family may seem 'unreal' in the empirical sense, as may the cosiness of the Rovers Return in *Coronation Street* (Geraghty 1983). The use of highly 'typed' characters as in *Dynasty* and *Return to Eden* may also, to some degree, break from realism. In addition, the narrative, while maintaining the relationship between cause and effect, never ends (Geraghty 1981). There may be moments of 'temporary resolution' but final closure never arrives. Furthermore, the linking devices, use of caricature and jokiness of some of these dramas can lead to an awareness that they have been constructed (Jordan 1981: 37–8).

In the first section of this essay we defined realism according to three criteria. In this second section we have tried to show how criteria might apply by describing cultural forms that do not fit them that are non-realist. Our argument is that the dominant form of popular culture, especially in film and television, is realist. However, we should not get carried away by this claim. If one takes popular television as a whole, many programmes are not realist in any sense: quiz shows, sports programmes or musicals, for example. However, much more important is the realization that in even the most realist of texts there is a persistent slippage from realism in a number of respects; spectacle becomes increasingly important as a means of organization, the author's hand is shown, and fictional worlds are not as plausible as they might first seem to be. There is not, in other words, a sharp distinction between realism and non-realism in the same cultural object.

We also have spoken about a number of different types of realism – melodramatic, documentary, emotional, naturalistic, science-fiction, fantasy etc. Realism as a cultural paradigm, as a mode or regime of signification, is an ideal-type. In its pure form it is found almost nowhere. Perhaps Balzac's novels come closest, but even there the characters take on too much the shape of icons. George Eliot's *Middlemarch*, often cited as a paradigm case, departs from realism in the romanticist direction, which as in the case of Marx comes from the influence on Eliot of Ludwig Feuerbach. Realism, as we argued above, privileges the referent. The signified is devalued, as symbolisms are ruled out of court; what this means is that there is only one referent, only one real world; any 'shadow world' of signifieds, of a *deus ex machina* in narratives, is precluded. Finally, signifier and signified are firmly rooted in their respective and proper places. And mechanistic assumptions of pictorial and narrative order, in a seamless world of cause and effect, with no space for contingency, are the rule.

Thus horror films, unlike science fiction, depart significantly from realist canons to the extent that a number of narrative events are only explicable by recourse to other than scientific explanation; causes are often from an evil shadow-world. Horror films are in this sense literally 'gothic', as (spatially) symbolisms abound and (temporally) non-natural causes are common. While perhaps David Cronenberg's horror films like *The Fly* and *Videodrome* are postmodern in their concern with the body and implosions of the mediascape, truly gothic horror films are importantly pre-realist and pre-modern (to the extent that realism, modernism and postmodernism are all located in cultural modernity). Melodrama and 'emotional' realism also depart from realist canons in their portrayal of stereotyped and 'larger-than-life' characters. There is thus a departure from privileging the referent and instead portraying a world of idealized characters or 'signifieds'.

Similarly, the neoclassical painting of David for example, would be non-realist to the extent that it portrays a shadow and ideal world, though a rather different shadow and ideal world than that portrayed in monumentalist and poly-centred (as distinct from being determined by a single principle) baroque productions. Romanticism departs from realist canons in both pre-realist and modernist directions. Romanticism, insofar as it hypostasizes 'nature' as a shadow world, is pre-realist, as is the idealization in, for example, Richard Strauss of the nation or 'the hero'. On the other hand, romanticism partakes in the Kantian revolution's problematization of the subject, and in its development of the subjective mode; this is particularly apparent in, for example, El Greco and Wagner. It is a precursor, to this extent, of modernist movements like expressionism or the work of Kafka.

If the melodrama and emotionalism of, for example, *Dallas* and mainstream Hollywood cinema of, say, the 1950s, while being realist, depart from realist canons in a pre-realist direction through their privileging of the signified, then naturalism and documentary realism tend to depart from realism in a post-realist or modernist direction. Naturalism, rather differently from the realist ideal-type, refers to the simple reproduction of what we perceive. Realism *can* involve naturalistic images but it does not have to, if only because the construction of a plausible world must involve selection from the array of perceived images. Indeed naturalism can be pushed so far that it becomes positively unrealistic; for example, some documentary-influenced films break with realism due to the sheer weight of everyday life that they attempt to portray. To show too much of the everyday, too much detail, paradoxically tends to disrupt realist convention. An example of this genre is Chantal Akerman's film *Jean Dielman, 23 Quai du Commerce, 1080 Bruxelles* (see Kuhn 1982).

The realist view of causation and rationality is connected to the rise of the mechanistic scientific outlook in contemporary Western societies. In the familiar conception of science, events are observable and connected through cause and effect. This view of science has become pervasive in Western society and its connection with realism in culture is of fundamental importance (Williams 1977a, b). The connection is further illustrated by the way in which the growth of *non*-realist artistic forms in Western culture, such as modernism, have coincided with the breakdown of 'mechanistic' accounts of nature, as exemplified by the non-Newtonian physics of the early part of this century (Forman 1971). Naturalism is most often associated with the paintings of Courbet and Zola's novels. But the documentary style of British film makers of the 1950s and 1960s also was naturalistic, as has been much of British soap opera. Where naturalism is the most realist of realisms (according to our ideal-type) is in the portrayal of characters. Ordinary working-class types are portrayed in everyday life situations ('kitchen sinks') in a break with the idealization (privilege of the signified) in, say, Hollywood melodrama. But in naturalism lies the contradiction inherent in realism itself. This contradiction is that the pursuit of the real to its furthest and logical extent breaks with realist canons themselves and slides over into modernism. What naturalism begins not to do is to portray life as a seamless web of cause and effect. Instead a lot of room is made for *contingency*. This contingency is both temporal and spatial. Temporally, for example Chantal Akerman explicitly refuses to make her narratives move along. Spatially Robert Altman, in some of his films such as *Nashville*, refuses to give the spectator a single viewpoint from which he or she can see the screen as a coherent whole. Instead several conversations will be taking place at the same time. In this sense some critics have referred to Joyce's supremely modernist *Ulysses* as 'naturalist', in its stream-of-consciousness writing; stream of consciousness here is not a matter of causes and effects in some sort of logical sequence, but, like free association, is much more contingent. Or critics have referred to the famous market scene in Flaubert's *Madame Bovary* as naturalist. Here Flaubert builds in contingency by refusing to give the reader a single viewpoint as a group of scenes are going on in a sort of senseless babble in the market at the same time.

This leads to our point above about cultural conflict. The point is that non-realist cultural paradigms will make use of a realist aesthetic discourse to argue for the validity of these paradigms. To make an argument via realist aesthetic discourse is to argue that a given cultural form corresponds better to reality, or to 'the referent' than does another cultural form. This would be an argument for the justification of, say, classic realist nineteenth-century novels or of twentieth-century films or TV shows. But, as suggested above, realist aesthetic discourse has been used to legitimate supremely modernist (thus non-realist) cultural texts such as Joyce's *Ulysses*. The argument here would be that stream of consciousness corresponds better to reality as we perceive it than the ordered classic realist text. Other cultural forms such as punk music and clothing styles with their break with harmony and an ordered aesthetic of beauty for an aesthetic of contingency, rawness and ugliness are clearly miles away from classic realism. Yet proponents of punk argue that their cultural objects are a lot truer to lived reality than, say, the more harmonically ordered rock music – or, say, classic popular culture realist narratives. The same is true of surrealism. Surrealist paintings and films typically manifest the displacement and condensation that characterize Freudian primary process. Yet surrealists have argued that indeed the Freudian primary process is at the very basis of reality.

Marxists too have a particularly realist aesthetic discourse. Analysts such as Derrida and his followers have often implied that orthodox Marxism, much like Christianity, is only a reconstructed neo-Platonism in its privileging of a sort of 'transcendental signified'. The critics of Marxism have made a fundamental mistake in this claim. When Marxists argue that there is more basic reality behind the often ideologically tinged surface reality, this more basic reality has nothing to do with the ideal conceptions of forms, that is, of signifieds, of Christianity and of Platonism. Marxism's claims have little to do with signifieds. Instead Marxist aesthetic (and theoretical) discourse is about *referents*. Its claims are that the true referent lies beneath the apparent referent. And it favours aesthetic forms which somehow show this true referent. Hence the social realism that orthodox Marxism endorses differs in its conception of the referent from classic realist texts, which are seen to be bourgeois to the extent that the social ordering they portray is only a surface social ordering. The same sort of realist aesthetic discourse (only the connections are more highly mediated) has been used to justify Marxist modernist cultural objects, such as Brecht's plays and Godard's films. The Brechtian and Godardian strategies of distancing point, as we noted above, to a different reality than the superficially perceived one, and in particular the superficial reality portrayed in classic realist texts.

TOWARDS A HISTORICAL SOCIOLOGY OF CULTURAL PARADIGMS

In the first two sections of this chapter we have worked, largely via illustrations, towards a definition of realism. We have argued that realist cultural forms are characterized by a specific organization of space, by specific organization of time, in realist narrative; and by the concealment of the production process of cultural objects. We have delineated an ideal type of cultural realism, which in addition to the just-mentioned characteristics is also a specific 'regime of signification'. All regimes of signification involve specific relationships between signifier, signified and referent. We have argued that realism privileges the referent and – unlike postmodernism – assumes that referent and signifier are in their proper places. We have shown how realism in its ideal-typical form almost never exists, and how realist cultural objects almost always have some modernist, postmodernist, or even more importantly pre-modern and pre-realist characteristics. We have finally argued that even the non-realist cultural forms are often backed up by a realist aesthetic discourse. This type of aesthetic discourse is only prevalent in modernity. Prior to modernity aesthetic discourses attributed validity to cultural objects, not insofar as they corresponded to the real world but insofar as they corresponded to an ideal world.

In the third section of the chapter we shall begin to outline a historical sociology of culture, which largely derives its structure from the 'ontologies' that producer and receiver groups hold. Very often the ontologies that producer groups hold are 'ahead' of those that receiver groups hold. In such cases it makes sense to speak of 'avant-gardes'. And among reception groups the ontologies of elites is often ahead of those of the masses. What we propose is a sort of 'trickle-down' theory of both cultural forms and ontologies from producers to elites to the masses.

In outline it goes like this. Prior to the full development of industrial capitalism, high and folk cultures were almost completely separated. Folk culture was associated with the rural life of lower-class groupings. The stories that were repeated orally in such cultures are predominantly non-realist. In folk cultures that continue to exist in the contemporary world such tales still often take the supernatural or otherworldly as their subject-matter. Events here do not take place in a recognizable, everyday world, and the narratives are not structured by cause and effect. A strong moral message may also be present. These folk cultures are also 'celebratory' rather than 'serious' and are removed from realist high culture, associated with the dominant classes of the early nineteenth century.

In many ways this realist high culture should be seen as the popular culture of the literate population. It is exemplified by the classical European tradition of oil-painting and the realist novel. Such novels often describe a particular sector of society and the interactions that take place within it; that is within the confines of a knowable community in Williams's terms (1970; 1975). The relationships between the characters (who are often of one social class) are knowable (even though there may be hidden depths that are revealed in the course of the narrative) and the outcomes of actions are predictable. The treatment of non-bourgeois characters is less socially grounded and the depictions of Adam Bede and Felix Holt illustrate later difficulties.

In many respects, what we have called folk and high culture are, at this point, examples of what Jameson calls 'popular' or 'folk art'. This was 'in fact the "organic" expression of so many distinct social communities or castes, such as the peasant village, the court, the medieval town, the polis and even the classical bourgeoisie when it was still a unified social group with its own cultural specificity' (Jameson 1979: 134). Jameson's point is particularly important as it shows how, while being different in form, both high and folk cultures are produced in relative isolation. There is little of the tension or antagonism between these different cultural forms that is manifested in the twentieth century.

As the nineteenth century progressed several cultural changes took place, within both high and folk culture. Folk culture was transformed by a variety of forces into a mass-produced popular culture. For example, 'performance' gradually became less important to this popular culture, though still present in forms such as music hall and vaudeville, which acted as a link between the older, oral tradition of folk culture and the new mechanically reproduced and realist forms of radio, cinema, phonograph and popular song.

This reception of realist cultural forms was conditioned by changes in both high and popular ontologies. Key here was acceptance of secularization and the acceptance of the assumptions of Galilean and Newtonian physics. This of course conditioned the existence of an audience among elites for Renaissance painting and the nineteenth-century novel. The 'masses', however, continued to consume pre-realist cultural forms until a much later date. This is partly because of their much later acceptance of a secularized ontology. Thus the consumption of realist forms by the masses is at the same time the birth of popular (as distinct from folk) culture.

Further, it is about the same time (late nineteenth century) that popular culture was born, and realist cultural forms consumed on a large scale. And of course this coincided with the rapid development of the working class. At the same time high culture, split as it were into two. It split into, on the one hand, a continuing but backward-looking realist high culture, as manifested in the continuing popularity of non-experimental forms of 'classical music' and representational art; and, on the other hand, modernism, which is non-realist. Not only was modernism anti-realist in form, but, in addition, many of its practitioners deliberately and consciously criticized the previous modes of artistic expression. This phase arguably became progressively stabilized between the late nineteenth and mid-twentieth centuries.

There are two levels to the explanation of these shifts: 'internal' cultural change and wider social processes. As we have noted, popular culture appears with the relative decline of oral transmission of culture and of performance. As popular culture develops this process becomes clearer, with the establishment of cultural reproduction by mechanical means. This makes cultural transmission from one group to another more likely. It facilitates a process in which popular culture effectively borrows from the realism of high culture. The transformation and divergence in high culture can be related initially to the creation of an artistic avant-garde which separates itself from the rest of the elite social classes. In the competition for resources and prestige, these groups begin to challenge the dominance of realism. Realism is the dominant cultural form and hence is the site for struggle over scarce artistic resources. The avant-garde differentiates itself from the other producers of high culture at this point, through the attack on conventional, dominant forms of realism. In later periods the 'innovative' edge of dominant culture will similarly attack the convention of modernist culture.

As far as the movement in working-class culture from folk to popular forms is concerned, some theorists would explain the change by the *imposition* of commodification and massification. This suggests that the working-class group is passive, their culture changed by manipulation to which they accede in a relatively straightforward fashion. Although there may be something in such an explanation, it is necessary, in addition, to consider how the culture expressed by working-class groups relates to the situation in which they find themselves. Culture is not simply imposed on dominated groups from above, but is always, at least partly, a response to dominant cultural forms and to such groups' social locations (see e.g. Clarke et al. 1981). Such responses need not always be 'resistances', but can be seen as having various political dimensions and consequences, some of which will often be contradictory. Bourgeois groups also respond to their changed social location. The new developments in capitalism will impinge on culturally and economically dominant groups, creating social divisions of various kinds. It is important that such divisions in dominant groups be recognized, and the work of Bourdieu (1984) is suggestive in this respect. It is clear, for example, that upper-class writers respond to economic and political change in different ways (see e.g. Williams 1963).

In the widest terms the explanations of these cultural changes lie in the movements of industrial and urban capitalism. In the period 1840–1940 a new industrial working class is established. In addition, cultural commodification penetrates all sections of society (Jameson 1979). As the working class moves into the new cities, there is a gradual loss of the established forms of a collective and folk culture. The working class were previously relatively separated from other social classes and the possibility of cultural communication was slight. Their social position was familiar, and particular patterns of work and behaviour were established. Of course, these did not change immediately with the coming of industrialization and population migration, and in this respect it is important to consider the mediating effect of the continuing development of the capitalist/ bourgeois city.

From the 1980s work in cultural studies has addressed the vitally important question of the effect of city redevelopment and change upon cultural life (see e.g. Berman 1982). Such work is important, as it provides evidence about a linking mechanism between the structural processes involved in the development of industrial capitalism (and patriarchy) and specific forms of cultural expression. Thus T. J. Clark (1985) relates impressionism to change in the nature of the city, alterations in class relations and hence to the development of the capitalist economic system. Clark's argument can be summarized as follows. The changing nature of Paris and its development by Haussmann were the product of class struggle, itself related to the movement of capitalism. Haussmannization was not a unified, one-way process, but was itself subject to struggle. The texts of impressionism were a product of these movements, ushering in modern life in Paris. They often contain a contradictory critique of modernity, and the changing nature of the city and class relations. Such a critique is often implicit and a good number of the paintings depict the outskirts of Paris and the areas of (especially) petty bourgeois leisure, thus relating to the changing nature of class relations and the development of urbanism.

The general framework and the fine detail contained in Clark's book are stimulating. He suggests that realism in popular culture can provide a base for the criticism of the existing social order. The depiction of what exists in the creation of a rational narrative accords a degree of objectivity to the world. Once the nature of a world is clarified its criticism becomes possible. Realism does not simply accommodate to the existing order, as events will be depicted which might otherwise have been concealed.

Realism in popular culture can also play a compensatory role, acting as a guide to the nature of the social structure and describing the relatively new situation that working-class people found them-selves in. This is not a static situation and culture obviously under-goes changes in the course of a long-run development. The changes in the industrial process and consequently in the structure of the city may lead to a breakdown of the relative certainty and rhythms of previous existence. For example, Clark describes how the trans-formation of Paris broke up the established working-class life (1985: 30–78). One of the ways of compensating for this is to develop a cultural form depicting a relatively solid and predictable world. Such a world would not be chaotic but rational. It would in a sense be a 'knowable community' compensating for the confusion and un-knowability of everyday life.

Much modernism in art relates to the development of the city. The increased pace of change produces a need to explain and criticize the nature of society. For those working within high culture the only way of doing this was with new artistic forms. The old ways could not cope. Modernism has a critical edge which is represented in an attempt to go beyond realism to depict the 'true' reality beneath the surface appearance. Realism is criticized as an inadequate instrument and much modernist work seeks to pass beyond the depiction of an everyday or plausible world, to produce deeper insights, expose the true meaning or irrationality of life and sometimes to show how life should be ordered. Modernism can also act as compensation. As the clarity of life is disrupted, modernism attempts to produce a new order or new certainty. If this is not possible, it may shift its focus away from the centres of dislocation, or show the places where change is taking place in a particular light.

In the period between the two World Wars the relationships between realist high culture and the non-realist modernism of avant-gardes became especially antagonistic, as did those between the latter and realist popular culture. These different forms of culture became increasingly addressed to one another and critical of each other's mode of expression. Now cultural forms were no longer separated and non-antagonistic. These cultural struggles and conflicts were, of course, related to actual political and economic conflicts.

So far we have speculated that culture in the early part of the nineteenth century consisted of realist high and non-realist folk forms, which were not antagonistic. These were transformed during a transition period driven by changes in the nature of capitalism manifested in the alteration of the city. Another phase is then reached where there is a realist high culture, a modernist avant-garde and realist popular culture which are relatively antagonistic to one another. This formation is relatively stabilized between 1880 and

1945. Developments since World War II have ushered in a new phase and it is to this that we now turn.

In the post-war period realist high culture continues to exist, even though it has been affected by modernism to a limited extent. Modernism itself has been challenged by a new, postmodernist, avant-garde. Postmodernism is non-realist and often less directly critical than modernism. Realism, as manifested in best-selling novels and 'soap opera', for example, is still dominant in popular culture. However, perhaps the most significant development in this period is the degree of fusion that has taken place between the postmodernist avant-garde operating within the framework of high culture and the avant-garde of popular culture, which is also essentially postmodernist. This fusion between high and popular culture is most noticeable in pop music.

Pop music contains elements of realism, modernism and postmodernism. Like other forms, it is a site of cultural struggle and antagonism. At different points groups in struggle will draw upon different resources and political positions. In mid-1970s Britain, for example, the decay of critical, 'modernist' rock music (initiated by the popular culture avant-garde of the 1960s) into an over-concern with form was criticized from realist and postmodernist directions in punk.

In some respects this development entailed a return to realism. A plausible world was addressed, the songs were narratives, and they sought to be transparent and simple. Construction and complexity were disguised. The early work of The Ramones is realist in many of these ways. The songs were short, realist stories performed at manic speed; contrivance was ostensibly covered up. The early work of the major British punk bands, such as The Sex Pistols, The Clash and The Jam, was similar.

The fusion between high and popular culture in rock music has happened at various times. Examples of this are the association of The Grateful Dead with Ken Kesey in the mid-sixties on the West Coast of the US; the cooperation of The Velvet Underground (which itself fused high and popular culture elements) with Andy Warhol; David Bowie's connections with the same circle on the US East Coast; and latterly the work of The Clash with Allen Ginsburg in the 1980s.

A few concluding speculations. Realism still dominates high culture despite the influence of modernism. Most popular culture also continues to be realist. Between these forms there is a certain merging of the avant-garde of high culture which, in a process of struggle, has moved away from modernist to postmodernist forms, and the cutting edge of popular culture, which is itself experimenting with non-realist forms akin to modernism and postmodernism in high culture. The relationships between these forms are less antagonistic than in previous periods. While there are still criticisms of popular culture and its 'mass' effects, their vehemence has decreased. For example, there is less concern about the Americanization of British culture which worried commentators in the 1950s (see e.g. Hoggart 1957/1969). The distinction between high and popular culture has become less salient. Popular culture is respectable. It is important to consider the social determinants of these developments and the current situation.

Again, these developments can be related to changes in the structure of society. We may arguably be now living in a period of 'late' or 'disorganized' capitalism (Lash and Urry 1987). Age, gender and race have become increasingly important as nodes of social and cultural struggle, and class relations have become more complex. These developments have intensified since the 1960s. Youth, for example, is important in the confluence of high and popular culture in pop music that we have described above. The construction of a period of adolescence and the 'teenager' are important characteristics of this period. As Martin (1981) has argued, these can provide a period of 'liminality', where the structured routines of everyday social and cultural life are broken down. It is in this period that the concern with style and spectacle that we have identified as non-realist moments within popular culture become particularly important. Such a period or form of life was common among the avant-garde bourgeois groups engaging in artistic experiment, and it is here that cultural fusion occurs. The emphasis on youth and youth culture has therefore produced a degree of cultural homogenization, although its extent must not be overstressed.

We have now come full circle back to the issue of popular and high ontology, through which these changes can be understood. The reception of modernist cultural forms among elites has largely been conditioned by changes in ontology and in particular changes in perceptions, in the experience of time and space. Two important changes of such space–time ontology were the influence of post-Newtonian physics and urbanization. Post-Newtonian physics fosters an ontology of a less ordered and more contingent view of time and space, as does the experience of the city. Time is here disordered because of experiences with travel. Space takes on an extraordinary plurality and intensity of succession of impressions in comparison with the stability of earlier village life. Thus an audience is created for the reception of cultural forms (modernist forms) which are disordered, made more contingent or at least differently structured. The development of television stands in a similar relationship to the reception of postmodernist forms. Now popular ontology is characterized by a surfeit of images, in which large chunks of everyday life are comprised of images. A new ontology in which reality and image are so intertwined and often even confused predisposes an audience to the reception of cultural forms which problematize the relationship between signifier and referent. The difference is that this creation of an audience for postmodern culture develops among elites and masses at about the same time. This may be partly because there are similar shifts in both high and popular ontology.

Thus, *après le postmoderne*, realism continues to be of the utmost significance. First, because a great portion of high and popular culture texts continue to exemplify classic realism. But perhaps even more importantly because realist ontologies condition the reception even of modernist and postmodernist cultural forms. To be sure, these popular ontologies presuppose a different, and far more contingent, even cynical, vision of what is real than did their nineteenth-century counterparts. And to be sure, much of turn-of-the-twenty-first-century realist culture will be of a qualitatively more 'brute', disharmonic nature than its predecessors. The new realist culture may indeed be cast in a mould that is neither semiotic, nor mimetic, but starkly *indexical* in coloration. Yet, this said, realist cultural forms will persist. And those who will increasingly consume modernist and postmodernist culture will do so for realist reasons. Critics of the twenty-first century, then, will be well advised once again to take realism seriously.

NOTES

Celia Lury and John Urry are to be thanked for comments on a previous draft of this paper.
1   See Peter Bürger in ch. 4 of this book.
2   See parallel discussion by Peter Bürger in ch. 4 of this book.

REFERENCES

Altman, R. (ed.) 1981: *Genre: The Musical*. London: Routledge & Kegan Paul/British Film Institute.

Ang, I. 1985: *Watching Dallas*. London: Methuen.

Berman, M. 1982: *All that Is Solid Melts into Air: The Experience of Modernity*. New York: Simon & Schuster; 1983: London: Verso; 1988 (2nd edn): Harmondsworth: Penguin.

Bourdieu, P. 1984: *Distinction*, tr. R. Nice. London: Routledge & Kegan Paul.

Bürger, P. 1984: *Theory of the Avant Garde*. Manchester: Manchester University Press.

Clark, T. J. 1985: *The Painting of Modern Life*. London: Thames & Hudson.

Clarke, J., et al. 1981: 'Sub-cultures, cultures and class', in T. Bennett et al. (eds), *Culture, Ideology and Social Process*. London: Batsford/Open University Press, 53–80.

Dyer, R. et al. 1981: *Coronation Street*. London: British Film Institute.

Feuer, J. 1984: 'Melodrama, serial form and television today', *Screen*, 25, 18–28.

Fiske, J. 1983: '*Doctor Who*: ideology and the reading of a popular narrative text', *Australian Journal of Screen Theory*, 14/15.

Forman, P. 1971: 'Weimar culture, causality and quantum theory, 1918–1927: adaptation by German physicists and mathematicians to a hostile intellectual environment', *Historical Studies in the Physical Sciences*, 3, 1–115.

Frayling, C. 1981: *Spaghetti Westerns*. London: Routledge & Kegan Paul.

Geraghty, C. 1981: 'The continuous serial – a definition', in Dyer et al. 1981: 9–26.

Geraghty, C. 1983: '*Brookside* – no common ground', *Screen*, 24, 137–41.

Hoggart, R. 1957/1969: *The Uses of Literacy*. Harmondsworth: Penguin.

Jameson, F. 1979: 'Reification and utopia in mass culture', *Social Text*, 1, 130–48.

Jameson, F. 1984: 'Postmodernism, or the cultural logic of late capitalism', *New Left Review*, 146, 53–92.

Jordan, M. 1981: 'Realism and convention', in Dyer et al. 1981.

Kerr, Paul 1981: '*Gangsters*: conventions and contraventions', in T. Bennett et al. (eds), *Popular Television and Film*. London: British Film Institute/Open University Press.

Kuhn, A. 1984: 'Women's genres', *Screen*, 25, 18–28.

Lash, S. and Urry, J. 1987: *The End of Organized Capitalism*. Cambridge: Polity Press.

Longhurst, B. 1987: 'Realism, naturalism and television soap opera', *Theory, Culture and Society*, 4, 633–49.

MacCabe, Colin 1981: 'Realism and the cinema: notes on some Brechtian theses', in T. Bennett et al. (eds). *Popular Television and Film*. London: British Film Institute/Open University Press.

Martin, B. 1981: *A Sociology of Contemporary Cultural Change*. Oxford: Blackwell.

Millington, B., and Nelson, R. 1986: *The Boys from the Blackstuff: The Making of TV Drama*. London: Comedia.

Paterson, R. 1981: '*Gangsters*: the pleasure and pain in the text', in T. Bennett et al. (eds), *Popular Television and Film*. London: British Film Institute/Open University Press.

Tulloch, J. and Alvarado, M. 1983: *Dr Who: The Unfolding Text*. London: Macmillan.

Watt, I. 1963: *The Rise of the Novel*. Harmondsworth: Penguin.

Williams, Raymond 1963: *Culture and Society, 1780–1950*. Harmondsworth: Penguin.

Williams, Raymond 1970: *The English Novel*. London: Chatto & Windus.

Williams, Raymond 1975: *The Country and the City*. St Albans: Paladin.

Williams, Raymond 1977a: *Marxism and Literature*. Oxford: Oxford University Press.

Williams, Raymond 1977b: 'Realism and non-naturalism', Edinburgh International Film Festival Official Programme.

Woolacott, J. 1983: 'The James Bond films: conditions of production', in J. Curran and V. Porter (eds), *British Cinema History*. London: Weidenfeld & Nicolson.

Zorzoli, G. B. 1966: 'Technology in the world of James Bond', in O. Del Bueno and U. Eco (eds), *The Bond Affair*. London: Macdonald.

6

Popular culture and the construction of postmodern identities

Douglas Kellner

According to anthropological folklore, in traditional societies, one's identity was fixed, solid, and stable. Identity was a function of predefined social roles and a traditional system of myths which provided orientation and religious sanctions to one's place in the world, while rigorously circumscribing the realm of thought and behaviour. One was born and died a member of one's clan, a member of a fixed kinship system, and a member of one's tribe or group with one's life trajectory fixed in advance. In pre-modern societies, identity was unproblematical and not subject to reflection or discussion. Individuals did not undergo identity crises, or radically modify their identity. One was a hunter and a member of the tribe and that was that.

In modernity, identity becomes more mobile, multiple, personal, self-reflexive, and subject to change and innovation. Yet identity in modernity is also social and Other-related. Theorists of identity in modernity, from Hegel through G. H. Mead, have often characterized identity in terms of mutual recognition, as if one's identity depended on recognition from others combined with self-validation of this recognition. Yet the forms of identity in modernity are also relatively substantial and fixed; identity still comes from a circumscribed set of roles and norms: one is a mother, a son, a Texan, a Scot, a professor, a socialist, a Catholic, a lesbian – or rather a combination of these social roles and possibilities. Identities are thus still relatively circumscribed, fixed, and limited, though the boundaries of possible identities, of new identities, are continually expanding.

Indeed, in modernity, self-consciousness comes into its own; one engages in reflection on available social roles and possibilities and gains a distance from tradition (Kolb 1986). One can choose and make – and then remake – one's identity as fashion and life-possibilities change and expand. Modernity also increases Other-directedness, however, for as the number of possible identities increases, one must gain recognition to assume a stable, recognized identity. In modernity, there is still a structure of interaction with socially defined and available roles, norms, customs, and expectations, among which one must choose, appropriate, and reproduce in order to gain identity in a complex process of mutual recognition. In this way, the Other is a constituent of identity in modernity and, consequently, the Other-directed character is a familiar type in late modernity, dependent upon others for recognition and thus for the establishment of personal identity (Riesman et al. 1950).

In modernity, identity therefore becomes both a personal and a theoretical problem. Certain tensions appear within and between theories of identity, as well as within the modern individual. On one hand, some theorists of identity define personal identity in terms of a substantial self, an innate and self-identical essence which constitutes the person. From Descartes's *cogito*, to Kant's and Husserl's transcendental ego, to the Enlightenment concept of reason, identity is conceived as something essential, substantial, unitary, fixed, and fundamentally unchanging. Yet other modern theorists of identity postulate a non-substantiality of the self (Hume), or conceive of the self and identity as an existential project, as the creation of the authentic individual (Nietzsche, Heidegger, Sartre).

Anxiety also becomes a constituent experience for the modern self. For one is never certain that one has made the right choice, that one has chosen one's 'true' identity, or even constituted an identity at all. The modern self is aware of the constructed nature of identity and that one can always change and modify one's identity at will. One is also anxious concerning recognition and validation of one's identity by others. Further, modernity also involves a process of innovation, of constant turnover and novelty. Modernity signifies the destruction of past forms of life, values, and identities, combined with the production of ever new ones (Berman 1982). The experience of *modernité* is one of novelty, of the ever-changing new, of innovation and transitoriness (Frisby 1985). One's identity may become out of date, or superfluous, or no longer socially validated. One may thus experience anomie, a condition of extreme alienation in which one is no longer at home in the world.

By contrast, one's identity may crystallize and harden such that ennui and boredom may ensue. One is tired of one's life, of who one has become. One is trapped in a web of social roles, expectations, and relations. There appears to be no exit and no possibility of change. Or, one is caught up in so many different, sometimes conflicting, roles that one no longer knows who one is. In these ways, identity in modernity becomes increasingly problematical and the issue of identity itself becomes a problem. Indeed, only in a society anxious about identity could the problems of personal identity, or self-identity, or identity crises, arise and be subject to worry and debate. Theorists of self-identity (Kierkegaard, Nietzsche, Heidegger, Sartre) are often anxious concerning the fragility of identity and analyse in detail those experiences and social forces which undermine and threaten personal identity.

Thus, in modernity, the problem of identity consisted in how we constitute, perceive, interpret, and present our self to ourselves and to others. As noted, for some theorists, identity is a discovery and affirmation of an innate essence which determines what I am, while for others identity is a construct and a creation from available social roles and material. Contemporary postmodern thought has by and large rejected the essentialist and rationalist notion of identity and builds on the constructivist notion which it in turn problematizes. Consequently, one of the goals of this essay will be to explicate how identity is formulated in postmodern theory and is present in contemporary cultural forms. At stake is whether identity is fundamentally different in so-called postmodern society and whether a distinction between modernity and postmodernity can be sustained.

IDENTITY IN POSTMODERN THEORY

From the postmodern perspective, as the pace, extension, and complexity of modern societies accelerate, identity becomes more and more unstable, more and more fragile. Within this situation, the recent discourses of postmodernity problematize the very notion of identity, claiming that it is a myth and an illusion. One reads in the Frankfurt School, in Baudrillard, and in other postmodern theorists that the autonomous, self-constituting subject that was the achievement of modern individuals, of a culture of individualism, is fragmenting and disappearing, owing to the social processes and the levelling of individuality in a rationalized, bureaucratized, mediatized, and consumerized mass society (Jameson 1983 and 1984; Kellner 1989a). Poststructuralists in turn have launched an attack on the very notions of the subject and identity, claiming that subjective identity is itself a myth, a construct of language and society, an overdetermined illusion that one is really a substantial subject, that one really has a fixed identity (Coward and Ellis 1977; Jameson 1983 and 1984).

It is thus claimed that in postmodern culture, the subject has disintegrated into a flux of euphoric intensities, fragmented and disconnected, and that the decentred postmodern self no longer experiences anxiety (with hysteria becoming the typical postmodern psychic malady) and no longer possesses the depth, substantiality, and coherence that was the ideal and occasional achievement of the modern self (Jameson 1983 and 1984). Postmodern theorists claim that subjects have imploded into masses, that a fragmented, disjointed, and discontinuous mode of experience is a fundamental characteristic of postmodern culture, of both its subjective experiences and texts. It is argued that in postmodern media and information society one is at most a 'term in the terminal' (Baudrillard 1983) or a cyberneticized effect of 'fantastic systems of control' (Kroker and Cook 1986). Deleuze and Guattari (1977) even celebrate schizoid, nomadic dispersions of desire and subjectivity, valorizing precisely the breaking up and dispersion of the subject of modernity. In these theories, identity is highly unstable and has in some postmodern theories disappeared altogether in the 'postmodern scene' where: 'The TV self is the electronic individual *par excellence* who gets everything there is to get from the simulacrum of the media: a market-identity as a consumer in the society of the spectacle; a galaxy of hyperfibrillated moods ... traumatized serial being' (Kroker and Cook 1986: 274).

Many of the postmodern theories privilege popular culture as the site of the implosion of identity and fragmentation of the subject, yet there have been few systematic studies of popular culture from this perspective. With the exception of the work of Jameson (see Kellner 1989c), few of the major postmodern theorists have carried out systematic and sustained examination of the actual texts and practices of popular culture. For instance, Baudrillard's few references to the actual artifacts of popular culture are extremely sketchy and fragmentary, as are those of Deleuze and Guattari (while Deleuze has written extensively on film, he does not theorize it as postmodern). Foucault and Lyotard have ignored popular culture almost completely. And while Kroker and Cook carry out detailed readings of contemporary painting, they too neglect to carry out concrete studies of mass-mediated culture in their explorations of the postmodern scene (though, à la Baudrillard, they ascribe tremendous power to the media in the constitution of postmodernity).[1]

In this essay, then, I shall examine in somewhat more detail than is usual in rapid postmodern raids into popular culture some mass-mediated artifacts to see what they tell us about identity in contemporary societies. My selections are hardly innocent, though they are symptomatic of what is generally taken to be salient features of postmodern culture: proliferation and dissemination of images; glitzy, high-tech produced intensities; pastische and implosion of forms; and quotation and repetition of past images and forms. My focus will be on images of identity in a popular television series *Miami Vice*, which is often taken as a symptomatic postmodern popular text, and cigarette ads which so far have been relatively unexplored by postmodern theory, but which reveal some interesting changes in contemporary image production. Some 1980s cigarette ads provide examples of the dramatic shift in the nature and substance of personal identity in contemporary society. Together these studies should illuminate some of the dynamics of postmodernity and identity in contemporary techno-capitalist societies. After an examination of these artifacts, I shall draw some provisional conclusions concerning identity and postmodernity.

My take on identity in so-called postmodern culture will, however, be critical of several central claims of postmodern theory. I shall criticize what I consider to be one-sided and inadequate positions on contemporary culture and what I take to be the limitations of excessively formalistic postmodern analysis. I shall also put in question several central claims concerning postmodern culture and conclude with some critical reflections on the very concept of postmodernity and the concept of postmodernism as a cultural dominant.

TELEVISION AND POSTMODERNITY

While the postmodern intervention in the arts is often interpreted as a reaction against modernism, against the stifling elitist canonization of the works of high modernism, the postmodern intervention within television is a reaction against realism, against precisely that aesthetic which modernism itself had earlier attacked. Modernism never took hold in television, especially in the commercial variety produced in the United States – which is culturally hegemonic in many places throughout the world. Instead, commercial television is predominantly governed by the aesthetic of representational realism, of images and stories which fabricate the real and attempt to produce a reality effect.[2] Television's relentless representational realism has also been subordinate to narrative codes, to story-telling. Commercial television has been constituted as an entertainment medium and it appears that its producers believe that audiences are most entertained by stories, by narratives with familiar and recognizable characters, plot lines, conventions, and messages. This aesthetic poverty of the medium has probably been responsible for the contempt in which it is held by high cultural theorists and its designation as a 'vast wasteland' by those who have other aesthetic tastes and values.

If for most of the history of television, narrative has been the name of the game, for postmodern television *image* often decentres the importance of narrative. In those programmes usually designated 'postmodern' – MTV, *Miami Vice*, *Max Headroom*, high-tech ads, etc. – there is a new look and feel: the signifier has been liberated and image takes precedence over narrative, as compelling and highly expressive and non-realist aesthetic images detach themselves from the television diegesis and become the centre of fascination, of a seductive pleasure, of an intense but highly transitory aesthetic experience.

While there is some truth in this conventional postmodern position, such descriptions are also in some ways misleading. In particular, in this study I shall reject the familiar account that postmodern image culture is fundamentally flat and one-dimensional. For Jameson, postmodernism manifests 'the emergence of a new kind of flatness or depthlessness, a new kind of superficiality in the most literal sense – perhaps the supreme formal feature of all the postmodernisms' (1984: 60). According to him, the 'waning of affect' in postmodern image culture is replicated in postmodern selves who are allegedly devoid of the expressive energies and individualities characteristic of modernism. Both postmodern texts and selves are said to be without depth and to be flat, superficial, and lost in the intensities and vacuities of the moment, without substance and meaning. Such one-dimensional postmodern texts and selves put in question the continued relevance of hermeneutic depth models such as the Marxian model of essence and appearance, true and false consciousness, and ideology and truth; the Freudian model of latent and manifest meanings; the existentialist model of authentic and inauthentic existence; and the semiotic model of signifier and signified. Cumulatively, postmodernism thus signifies the death of hermeneutics; in place of what Ricoeur (1970) has termed a 'hermeneutics of suspicion' and the polysemic reading of cultural symbols and texts there emerges the postmodern view that there is nothing behind the surface of texts, no depth or multiplicity of meanings for critical enquiry to discover and explicate.

Elsewhere, Steve Best and I (1987) have polemicized against the formalist, anti-hermeneutical postmodern type of analysis connected with the postulation of a flat, postmodern image culture, and we have delineated an alternative model of a 'political hermeneutic' which draws on both postmodern and other critical theories. Building on this work, I shall argue here that interpretive analysis of both image and narrative continues to be of importance in analysing even those texts taken to be paradigmatic of postmodern culture. I shall also argue that both the images and the narratives are saturated with ideology and polysemic meanings, and that therefore – against certain postmodern positions – ideology critique continues to be an important and indispensable weapon in our critical arsenal.

In addition, there is another familiar postmodern position from which I would equally like to distance myself: the view, associated with Baudrillard, that television is pure noise in the postmodern ecstasy, a pure implosion, a black hole where all meaning and messages are absorbed in the whirlpool and kaleidoscope of radical semiurgy, of the incessant dissemination of images and information to the point of total saturation, of inertia and apathy where meaning is dissolved, where only discrete images glow and flicker in a fascinating mediascape within which no image any longer has any discernible effects, where the proliferating velocity and quantity of images produces a postmodern mindscreen where images fly by with such rapidity that they lose any signifying function, referring only to other images *ad infinitum*, and where eventually the multiplication of images produces such saturation, apathy, and indifference that the tele-spectator is lost forever in a fragmentary fun house of mirrors in the infinite play of superfluous, meaningless images.

Now, no doubt, television can be experienced as a flat, one-dimensional wasteland of superficial images, and can function as well as pure noise without referent and meaning. One can also become overwhelmed by the number, velocity, and intensity of images, so that television's signifying function can be decentred and can collapse altogether. Yet there is something wrong with this account. People regularly watch certain shows and events; there are fans for various series and stars who possess an often incredible expertise and knowledge of the subjects of their fascination; people do model their behaviour, style, and attitudes on television images; television ads do play a role in managing consumer demand; and, most recently, many analysts have concluded that television is playing the central role in political elections, that elections have become a battle of images played out on the television screen, and that television is playing an essential role in the new art of governing (Kellner 1990).

Against the postmodern notion of culture disintegrating into pure image without referent or content or effects – becoming at its limit pure noise – I would argue that television and other forms of mass-mediated culture play key roles in the structuring of contemporary identity. I have argued elsewhere that television today assumes some of the functions traditionally ascribed to myth and ritual (that is, by integrating individuals into the social order, celebrating dominant values, offering models of thought, behaviour, and gender for imitation, and so on). I also argued that TV myth resolved social contradictions in the way that Lévi-Strauss described the function of traditional myth and provided mythologies of the sort described by Barthes which idealize contemporary values and institutions and thus exalt the established way of life (Kellner 1982). I shall illustrate these points in the next two sections where I discuss how certain television shows and advertising function to provide models of identity in the contemporary world. Consequently, I would argue that much postmodern cultural analysis is too one-sided and limited in either restricting its focus on form, on image alone, or in abandoning popular culture analysis altogether in favour of grandiose totalizing metaphors (black holes, implosion, excremental culture, etc.). Instead, it is preferable to analyse both form and content, image and narrative, and postmodern surface and ideological problematic in specific exercises which explicate the polysemic nature of images and texts and which endorse the possibility of multiple encodings and decodings. With these qualifications in mind, let us, first, examine *Miami Vice*, to discover what we might learn concerning television, postmodernity, and identity.

MIAMI VICE AND THE POLITICS OF IMAGE AND IDENTITY

Miami Vice, along with MTV, is many critics' favourite example of postmodern television (Gitlin 1987; Fiske 1987; Grossberg 1987). In *Miami Vice* images are detached from the narrative and seem to take on a life of their own. Its producers have rejected familiar earth tones and offer instead a wealth of artificial images, emphasizing South Florida colours of flamingo pink, lime green, Caribbean blue, subdued pastels, and flashing neon. In addition, the use of lighting, camera angles, cutting, musical background, and the exotic terrain of Miami's high-tech, high-rise, high-crime, and multiracial culture make for a wealth of resonant images which its producers sometimes successfully weave into the production of aesthetic spectacles that are intense, fascinating, and seductive. The sometimes meandering narratives replicate experiences of fragmentation and of slow ennui, punctuated with images of hallucinogenic intensity. Image frequently takes precedence over narrative and the look and feel become primary, often relegating story-line and messages to the background. No doubt, this arguably postmodern style is a fundamental aspect of *Miami Vice* and yet I would submit that most postmodern analyses get it wrong. Privileging Jameson's category of the waning of affect, Gitlin (1987), for example, claims that *Miami Vice* is the ultimate in postmodern blankness, emptiness, and world-weariness. Yet, against this reading, one could argue that it pulsates as well with intense emotion, a clash of values, and highly specific political messages and positions (see Best and Kellner 1987, and the following analysis).

Another reading which argues that *Miami Vice*, like other postmodern culture, obliterates meaning and depth is found in Grossberg (1987: 28), who claims: '*Miami Vice* is, as its critics have said, all on the surface. And the surface is nothing but a collection of quotations from our own collective historical debris, a mobile game of Trivia. It is, in some ways, the perfect televisual image, minimalist (the sparse scenes, the constant long shots, etc.) yet concrete.' Grossberg goes on to agree that 'indifference' (to meanings, ideology, politics, etc.) is the key distinguishing feature of *Miami Vice* and other postmodern texts, which he suggests are akin to billboards to be scanned for what they tell us about our cultural terrain rather than texts to be read and interrogated. Against Grossberg, I would argue that *Miami Vice* is highly polysemic and is saturated with ideologies, messages, and quite specific meanings and values. Behind the high-tech glitz are multiple sites of meaning, multiple subject positions, and highly contradictory ideological problematics. I shall also argue that *reading* the text hermeneutically and critically provides access to this polysemic wealth and that therefore it is a mistake to speed by such artifacts, however their audiences may relate to them.

Thus, for a one-dimensional postmodern reading, an artifact like *Miami Vice* is all surface without any depth or layered meanings. For a political hermeneutic, by contrast, the form, narrative, and images constitute a polysemic text with a multiplicity of possible meanings which require multivalent readings that probe the various layers of meaning. For a political hermeneutic, the artifact is a social text which tells us some things about contemporary society. In particular, I wish to suggest that *Miami Vice* provides many insights into the fragmentation, reconstruction, and fragility of identity in contemporary culture and that it also provides insight into how identities are constructed through the incorporation of subject positions offered for emulation by popular culture. Against the Althusserian position, taken over at one time by *Screen*, which claims that ideological texts interpellate subjects into subject positions that are homogeneous, unified, and untroubled, I shall suggest that on the contrary the subject positions of popular culture are highly specific, contradictory, fragile, and subject to rapid reconstruction and transformation.

To begin, popular culture provides images and figures which its audiences can identify with and emulate. It thus possesses important socializing and enculturating effects via its role models, gender models, and variety of subject positions which valorize certain forms of behaviour and style while denigrating and villainizing other types. For example, it is well documented that *Miami Vice*'s detectives Crockett (Don Johnson) and Tubbs (Paul Michael Thomas) have become fashion icons, arbiters of taste. Crockett's unconstructed Italian jackets, his tennis shoes without socks, his T-shirts and loose trousers, his frequently stubbled beard, his changing hair-style, and so on have produced a model for a new male look, a new, hip alternative to straight fashion, a legitimation for 'loose and casual'. Tubbs, by contrast, provides an icon of the hip and meticulously fashionable with his Vern Uomo double-breasted suits and narrow Italian ties, fashionable shoes, trendy ear-ring, and nouveau-cool demeanour. Their male associates, Zito and Switek, with their Hawaiian shirts, loose, colourful trousers, and very lack of high fashion provide models of more informal clothing and looks, while the women detectives Gina and Trudy are constantly changing their clothes, hair-styles, and looks, validating a constant turnover and reconstruction of image and look.

Crockett and Tubbs and their colleagues are arguably role models for macho white males, blacks, hispanics, women, and teenagers, while the criminal underclass portrayed no doubt identifies with its villains. As I shall argue, quite specific gender and role models and subject positions are projected, as are quite different images of sex, race, and class than are usual in the typical mediascapes of the television world. In general, *Miami Vice* positions its viewers to identify with and desire an affluent, up-scale lifestyle via its projection of images of a high-tech, high-consumption affluent society. Its iconic images of high-rise buildings, luxury houses, fast and expensive cars and women, and, of course, the pricey and ambiguous commodities of drugs and prostitution produce images of affluence and high-level consumption which position viewers to envy the wealth and power of the villains while identifying as well with the lifestyles, personality traits, and behaviour of the heroes. The challenge of *Miami Vice* is to present the 'good' cops as more appropriate and desirable role models than the 'bad' drug dealers and affluent criminal underworld who in a sense live out the fantasy of unbridled capitalism.

The programme also invites viewers to identify with a fast, mobile lifestyle focusing on exciting consumerist leisure. The opening iconic images of the show present a speedboat racing across the ocean with blue waves and white foam pulsating to an intense musical beat; the images cut to exotic birds, sensual women, sports competition, horse- and dog-racing, and other leisure images with affluent Miami as the backdrop. These opening images are packed together with quick editing to provide a sensation of speed and mobility, iconic invitations to get into the fast lane and join the high life. The show itself will then demonstrate how individuals enter into this leisure utopia and find the good life within its spectacles and enticements.

As its narratives unfold, *Miami Vice* presents some revealing insights into the problematics of identity in contemporary techno-capitalist societies. The chief characters (Crockett, Tubbs, and their boss Castillo) all have multiple identities and multiple pasts which intersect in unstable ways with the present. In each case, their identity is fragmented and unstable, different and distinctive in each character, yet always subject to dramatic change. Crockett is presented as an ex-football star, a Vietnam veteran, and a young man familiar with the criminal underworld, with the players in the drug and crime scene. His nickname 'Sonny' codes him as an icon of youth while his last name 'Crockett' evokes the hero image derived from the name of one of the heroes of the Alamo, Davey Crockett, who was the subject of a successful Disney TV mini-series in the 1950s. Unlike the stolid bourgeois Davey, however, Sonny is presented as having been married and divorced, with several episodes depicting him with his former wife and son; yet these encounters are infrequent and he gains no real lasting identity as a father or husband in the series.

Instead, Crockett is portrayed in multiple relationships, relatively unstructured and subject to quick change. In early seasons, he is shown involved with his colleague Gina and is also involved with a fashionable architect, a stewardess who dies of a drug overdose, and a woman doctor who is also a drug addict. These relationships were featured in single episodes within which the relationship disintegrated, never to reappear (his two lovers involved with drugs died). In the 1987–8 season, Crockett marries a successful rock singer whom he was assigned to protect (played by Scottish rock star Sheena Easton), yet she soon disappears on a seemingly interminable rock tour and when he is shot and almost dies ('A bullet for Crockett', 1988), she cannot be reached and only his colleagues are there for the death watch – a substitute family of a type increasingly familiar in the TV world as the divorce rate soars in the real world.

Tubbs, by contrast, is presented as a streetwise black cop who leaves New York after his brother is shot and comes to Miami to seek his brother's killer; he decides to stay and teams up with Crockett. His name, Ricardo Tubbs, his nickname Rico, and his dark, multiple-hued skin code him as of mixed racial descent. Tubbs rarely talks about his past and lives a perpetual present, closely connected only to his partner Crockett. Their boss Castillo (played by Edward James Olmos) was also a Vietnam veteran who worked as well for the Drug Enforcement Agency in Thailand, where he married and lost his wife in a battle with a drug lord. Presumed dead, she and the drug lord arrive in Miami ('Golden Triangle', 1985); Castillo learns that she is now happily married and is in effect the hostage of the drug lord. After he rescues her, in a *Casablanca*-inspired ending, he bids her and her husband farewell at the end of the episode.

Castillo appears as the brooding patriarch, the self-contained and self-enclosed autonomous subject who defines himself by his morality and actions. He is the most stable identity in *Miami Vice* and is a figure with an autonomous self and a strongly fixed personal identity. Yet Castillo too is presented as a man of great passion and intensity, which he constantly suppresses, producing the image of a smouldering figure who could explode any moment into violence and chaos, whose carefully constructed moral boundaries might at any moment dissolve – a quiet, tragic figure who could easily fall into the more chaotic world of violence and nihilism which threatens all boundaries and identities in the fragile and unstable world of *Miami Vice*.

Crockett and Tubbs, in contrast to Castillo, are constantly changing their looks, styles, and behaviour. At the beginning of the 1988–9 season, Crockett appeared with extremely long, shoulder-length hair, sometimes bound together in a ponytail, while Tubbs appeared with a thick beard – which disappeared later in the season. The instability of the cops' identity in *Miami Vice* is exploited in a plot device which utilizes their multiple identities as cops and undercover players in the underworld. Both assume undercover roles, with Crockett living on an expensive boat, masquerading as a drug runner Sonny Burnett, while Tubbs assumes the role of a buyer/dealer Ricardo Cooper, who sometimes assumes a Jamaican, Caribbean persona, while at other times he appears as a hip, black urban hood. One would think that the word would soon get around that 'Burnett' is 'really' the vice cop Crockett and that the various criminals 'played' by Tubbs are 'really' masks for the vice cop Tubbs. Yet in show after show, Crockett and Tubbs assume their criminal identities and slide from good guy to bad guy as easily as one would change one's undershirt. Such double-coded identities signals the artificiality of identity, that identity is constructed not given, that it is a matter of choice, style, and behaviour rather than intrinsic moral or psychological qualities. It also suggests that identity is a game that one plays, that one can easily shift from one identity to another.

Postmodern identity, then, is constituted theatrically through role-playing and image construction. While the locus of modern identity revolved around one's occupation, one's function in the public sphere (or family), postmodern identity revolves around leisure, centred on looks, images, and consumption. Modern identity was a serious affair involving fundamental choices that defined who one was (profession, family, political identifications, etc.), while postmodern identity is a function of leisure and is grounded in play, in gamesmanship. The notion of a 'player' central to identity construction in *Miami Vice* provides clues to the nature of postmodern identity. A 'player' knows the rules and the score and acts accordingly. Players play with and often flout social conventions and attempt to distinguish themselves through ritualized activities, through gambling, sports, drug-dealing and drug use, sexual activity, or other leisure and social concerns. The players 'become someone' if they succeed and gain identity through admiration and respect of other players.

One of the structuring principles of *Miami Vice* points to a schizoid dichotomy within the identity construction of the two main characters which I believe points to tensions within contemporary identity construction. As noted, Crockett and Tubbs are both cops and players in many episodes, acting as criminals to entrap the 'real' players. In the 1988–9 season, the plot lines played on this double identity, as Crockett schizophrenically slid from Burnette back to Crockett. The story suggests that it is easy to fall into, to become, the roles that one plays and that identity construction today is highly tenuous and fragile. Suspense was built around whether 'Crockett' could continue to be 'Crockett' or whether he would suddenly become 'Burnett'. The moral seems to be that when one radically shifts identity at will, one might lose control, one might become pathologically conflicted and divided, disabled from autonomous thought and action.

Thus it appears that postmodern identity tends more to be constructed from the images of leisure and consumption and tends to be more unstable and subject to change. Both modern and postmodern identity contain a level of reflexivity, an awareness that identity is chosen and constructed. In contemporary society, however, it may be more 'natural' to change identities, to switch with the changing winds of fashion. While this produces an erosion of individuality and increased social conformity, there are some positive potentials of this postmodern portrayal of identity as an artificial construct. For such a notion of identity suggests that one can always change one's life, that identity can always be reconstructed, that one is free to change and produce oneself as one chooses. This notion of multiple, freely chosen, and easily disposed of postmodern identities can be interestingly contrasted to more traditional images where the police had quite different 'modern' identities and offered quite different subject positions. In *Dragnet* (1951–9 and 1967–70) Jack Webb's Sgt. Friday was the model of the tight, moralistic, and ascetic authoritarian personality, while Robert Stack's Elliot Ness on *The Untouchables* (1959–63) was literally untouchable and incorruptible by women or criminals. Both were extremely rigid, authoritarian figures without personal lives or without any individuality or complex personality traits. The chief cop in *The FBI* (1965–74) was also highly impersonal, without distinctive personal identity, as were the cops in 1950s police dramas like *Highway Patrol, M Squad*, and *The Naked City*.

In the 1960s and 1970s more 'personable' cops began to appear with *Columbo, Kojak, Baretta, Starsky and Hutch*, etc. Yet these TV cops too had relatively fixed identities which were readily identifiable by their personality quirks, by their marks of individuality. Columbo's shuffling, modest and sly method of interrogation, Kojak's bully-boy masculist tactics, Baretta's identification with the little guy and rage at criminals who hurt 'his' people, and Starsky and Hutch's explosions of moral rage provided these TV cops with stable, familiar identities – more highly individualized than previous ones, but equally substantial and fixed. Such stability is no longer visible in *Miami Vice*, where Crockett and Tubbs assume different hair-styles, looks, roles, and behaviour, from show to show, season to season.

Yet, although identity in *Miami Vice* in the figures of Crockett and Tubbs is unstable, fluid, fragmentary, disconnected, multiple, open, and subject to dramatic transformation, it privileges certain male subject positions. In particular, macho male identity is positively valorized throughout; Crockett, Tubbs, and Castillo are all highly macho figures and their male and female subordinates emulate their behaviour. The viewer is thus positioned to view highly aggressive, highly masculist, and, fairly often, highly sexist behaviour as desirable, and a macho male subject is thus privileged as the most desirable role model. The two women vice cops – Trudy and Gina – are often assigned to play prostitutes or to seduce criminals and are thus presented in negative stereotypes of sluts and seducers; they often fall into situations of danger and must be rescued by the male cops. When they are allowed subjectivity of their own, they fall for criminals, as when Gina falls in love with an unscrupulous IRA thug in 'When Irish eyes are shining' (1985). The women cops are presented most positively when they engage in aggressive male behaviour, as when Gina shoots the IRA gunmen or Trudy shoots an especially sleazy criminal whom she was forced to sleep with in her undercover work. Such macho behaviour replicates the images of women warriors which became an increasingly central image in the late 1970s and 1980s (*Alien, Aliens, Superwoman, Sheena*, etc.). Equality in this ideological scenario thus become equal opportunities to kill, to become women warriors equal to the macho males in the realm of primal aggressivity.

The show is also arguably racist, privileging the white male Crockett as the subject of power and desire, as the centre around which most of the narratives revolve. In January of 1989, NBC devoted its Friday night prime-time schedule to 'Three for Crockett', broadcasting three straight episodes that centred on the white male figure. In terms of image construction, white is also the privileged colour: Crockett often wears white jackets, drives a white car, carouses on white sand beaches, and pursues beautiful white women. Black – as in the traditional melodrama genre – is coded as the site of danger, mystery, uncertainty, and evil. Few shows have used as many and as menacing black, night-time backdrops, in which the light forms and figures are privileged as the positive index against the negatively valorized black background.

And yet the black/white friendship of Crockett and Tubbs – described by some critics as blatantly homoerotic (e.g. Butler 1985) – presents one of the most striking images of inter-racial friendship in the history of television, and Tubbs and Castillo are two of the most positive images of people of colour yet to appear. On the other hand, while Tubbs arguably provides a positive role model for young black males and while Castillo provides a model for Hispanic men, most of the images of blacks, Hispanics and Third World people of colour are strongly negative. Two informers featured on many episodes – the Cuban Izzie and the black Noogie – are stereotypes of Hispanic and black street hustlers, the improper role models against which Tubbs and Castillo are defined. Two black policemen have been featured in supporting roles – an obnoxious New York officer and an overly aggressive and incompetent federal drug enforcer – who also present the negative antithesis of the ideal black professional. The criminals are also stereotyped people of colour who play the stereotyped roles: drug dealers, war lords, prostitutes, gun runners, etc. They are predominantly vicious, unprincipled, dangerous, and violent.

Third World scenes are likewise presented negatively as places of corruption, violence, and multiple forms of evil; and these negative emanations from the site of otherness, the hearts of darkness, are shown as threatening the utopia of Miami with its easy affluence and up-scale lifestyles. The underclass of the United States by contrast is rarely portrayed, though some episodes have shown quite striking images of ghetto life and one 1986 episode realistically depicts the problems of ghetto blacks in a story of a young black athlete, unable to escape from the violence and degradation of the ghetto.

In fact, there are some socially critical and progressive aspects to the series. In a sense, the 'vice' portrayed is as much capitalism's vice as Miami's. While Miami is the site of unbridled crime, it is also the site of unbridled 'free enterprise', and drug dealing is the ultimate in high-profit capital acccumulation, while drugs are the ultimate fantasy of an ultra-capitalist commodity that is cheap to produce and that can provide tremendous profits in its selling. A Thai drug lord in a 1985 episode, 'The Golden Triangle', states that drugs are 'no different from tapioca or tin ore from Malaysia. It is simply a commodity for which there is a demand.' Indeed, the series is one of the few to present critical images of capitalism. One episode, 'The Prodigal Son' (1985), featured the *Living Theater* impresario Julien Beck as a New York banker who stated that the financial establishment favoured continued drug trade to help them recoup their loans to Third World countries, for whom drugs was one of the few high-yield exports.[3]

Like Balzac and Brecht, then, *Miami Vice* associates wealth with crime, capitalist enterprise with criminality. On the other hand, the very glamorizing of crime also glamorizes high-powered capitalism, so the equation of crime and business is highly ambiguous – an ambiguity that runs through the series and which constitutes postmodern identity as ambiguous as well. For identity is often constructed in contemporary society *against* dominant conventions and morality; thus there is something amoral or morally threatening about postmodern selves which are fluid, multiple, and subject to rapid change. From this perspective, Crockett is a highly ambiguous hero for American culture: he is frequently unshaved, never wears a tie, and often goes without socks, is sexually promiscuous, and often reverts into his undercover 'Burnett' role in which he plays with gusto the hip 'player', ready to do anything for some bucks.

Yet *Miami Vice* is really neither nihilistic nor celebratory of crime.

Like the traditional gangster genre in Hollywood film (see Warshow 1962), the series can be read as a cautionary morality tale which shows that those who go beyond acceptable boundaries in the pursuit of wealth and power are bound to fall. Like the gangster genre, *Miami Vice* is deeply attracted to its criminal underworld and plays out the primal passion play of capitalist free enterprise: devotion at all costs to maximizing capital accumulation. *Miami Vice* thus identifies the ultra-capitalist subject position as one of greed, uncontrolled appetite, and violent aggression which inevitably leads to death and destruction.

And yet the images of the affluent lifestyles of the criminals are so attractive and appealing that the series itself is morally ambiguous, charging both the professional identity of the cops and the outlaw identity of the criminals with positive value – an ambiguity intensified by the dual identities of Crockett and Tubbs, who play out both affluent criminal roles and professional cop roles, within the same episode. Such ambiguity perhaps intensifies the sort of relativism that certain postmodern theorists claim is symptomatic of the contemporary condition. The series also puts on display and reinforces tendencies in contemporary society to adopt multiple identities, to change one's identity and look as one changes one's clothes, job, or habitat. This analysis of *Miami Vice* suggests, in fact, that *image* and *look* are key constituents of a postmodern image culture and key constituents of postmodern identity.

Consequently, *Miami Vice* puts on display the way that identity is constituted in contemporary society through images and suggests that such a mode of identity is highly fluid, multiple, mobile, and transitory. Yet I have attempted to show that images are connected to content and values, to specific modes and forms of identity, and that the images of popular culture are also saturated with ideology, so that identity in contemporary societies can (still) be interpreted as an ideological construct, as a means whereby enculturation produces subject positions which reproduce dominant capitalist and masculist values and modes of life. Through such analysis, I have attempted to redeem Marxist and feminist modes of ideology critique against postmodern formalism which abstracts ideological content from image and spectacle and which affirms theses concerning the collapse of meaning and identity in a postmodern mediascape. Against this operation, I have suggested that far from identity disappearing in contemporary society, it is rather reconstructed and redefined; and I have attempted to show the relevance and importance of theories which focus on specific ideological subject positions and modes of identity formation to help illuminate these processes. Thus, whereas the modern self often assumed multiple identities, the necessity of choice and instability of a constructed identity often produced anxiety. Moreover, a stable, substantial identity – albeit self-reflexive and freely chosen – was at least a normative goal for the modern self: a type of stable identity clearly observable in television heroes from the 1950s to the 1970s. The rapid shifts of identity in *Miami Vice*, by contrast, suggest that the postmodern self accepts and affirms multiple and shifting identities. Identity today thus becomes a freely chosen game, a theatrical presentation of the self, in which one is able to present oneself in a variety of roles, images, and activities, relatively unconcerned about shifts, transformations, and dramatic changes.

This analysis would suggest that what might be called postmodern identity is an extension of the freely chosen and multiple identities of the modern self that accepts and affirms an unstable and rapidly mutating condition, which was a problem for the modern self, producing anxiety and identity crisis. I would not, however, want to go as far as Jameson (1984: 62f), who claims that anxiety disappears in postmodern culture; nor would I want to deny that identity crises still occur and are often acute. (A psychiatrist friend told me recently that gender confusion is especially acute today among teenagers, who are deeply attracted to androgynous figures like Boy George and Michael Jackson, as well as to feminine males like Prince or macho women like Madonna.) Yet one surmises that there is a shift in identity formation and that postmodern selves are becoming more multiple, transitory, and open. For Jameson (1984: 76) the figure of David Bowie gazing in fascination at a stack of television sets was a privileged figure of the postmodern self – an image to which we might add figures of the TV channel switcher, rapidly changing channels and mediascapes, or the modem-connected computer freak, rapidly switching from computer games to bulletin boards, to word-processing systems and personal files, which figure the new postmodern self.

ADVERTISING AND IMAGES

Like television narratives, advertising can be seen as providing some functional equivalents of myth. Like myths, ads frequently resolve social contradictions, provide models of identity, and celebrate the existing social order. Barthes (1957/1972) saw that advertising provided a repertoire of contemporary mythology, and in the following discussion I shall suggest how cigarette ads contribute to identity formation within contemporary society. The following analysis is intended to show that even the static images of advertising contain subject positions and models for identification that are heavily coded ideologically. As in the previous discussion, I shall argue here – against a certain type of postmodern formal analysis – that the images of mass culture are important in the mode of their formal image construction and surface, as well as in terms of the meanings and values which they communicate. Accordingly, I shall discuss some print ads which are familiar, are readily available for scrutiny, and lend themselves to critical analysis.

Print ads are an important sector of the advertising world with about 50 per cent of advertising revenues going to various print media, while 22 per cent is expended on television advertising. Let us look first, then, at two cigarette ads: a 1981 Marlboro ad aimed primarily at male smokers and a 1983 Virginia Slims ad which tries to convince women that it is cool to smoke and that the product being advertised is perfect for the 'modern' woman (see Figures 6.1 and 6.2).[4] In the tobacco industry as in other industries, corporations undertake campaigns to associate their product with positive and desirable images and gender models. Thus in the 1950s, Marlboro undertook a campaign to associate its cigarette with masculinity, associating smoking its product with being a 'real man'. Marlboro had been previously packaged as a milder women's cigarette, and the 'Marlboro man' campaign was an attempt to capture the male cigarette market with images of archetypally masculine characters. Since the cowboy, Western image provided a familiar icon of masculinity, independence, and ruggedness, it was the preferred symbol for the campaign. Subsequently, the 'Marlboro man' became a part of American folklore and a readily identifiable cultural symbol.

Such symbolic images in advertising attempt to create an association between the products offered and socially desirable and meaningful traits in order to produce the impression that if one wants to be a certain type of person – for instance, to be a 'real man' – then one should buy Marlboro cigarettes. Consequently, for decades, Marlboro used the cowboy figure as the symbol of masculinity and the centre of their ads. In a postmodern image culture, individuals get their very identity from these figures; thus advertising becomes an important and overlooked mechanism of socialization, as well as manager of consumer demand.

Ads form textual systems with basic components which are interrelated in ways that positively position the product. The main components of the classical Marlboro ad is its conjunction of nature, the cowboy, horses, and the cigarette. This system associates the

Figure 6.1 Marlboro ad

Figure 6.2 1983 Virginia Slims ad

Marlboro cigarette with masculinity, power, and nature. Note, however, in Figure 6.1 how the cowboy is a relatively small figure, dwarfed by the images of snow, trees, and sky. Whereas in earlier Marlboro ads, the 'Marlboro man' loomed largely in the centre of the frame, now images of nature are highlighted. Why this shift?

All ads are social texts which respond to key developments during the period in which they appear. During the 1980s, media reports concerning the health hazard of cigarettes became widespread – a message highlighted in the mandatory box at the bottom of the ad that 'The Surgeon General Has Determined That Cigarette Smoking Is Dangerous to Your Health.' As a response to this attack, the Marlboro ads now feature images of clean, pure, wholesome nature, as if it were 'natural' to smoke cigarettes, as if cigarettes were a healthy, 'natural' product, an emanation of benign and healthy nature. The ad, in fact, hawks Marlboro Lights, and one of the captions describes it as a 'low tar cigarette'. The imagery is itself 'light', white, green, snowy, and airy. Through the process of metonymy, or contiguous association, the ad tries to associate the cigarettes with 'light', 'natural', healthy snow, horses, the cowboy, trees, and sky, as if they were all related, 'natural' artifacts, sharing the traits of 'nature', thus covering over the fact that cigarettes are an artificial, synthetic product, full of dangerous pesticides, preservatives, and other chemicals.[5]

Thus, the images of healthy nature are a Barthesian mythology which attempt to cover over the image of the dangers to health from cigarette smoking. The Marlboro ad also draws on images of tradition (the cowboy), hard work (note how deeply in the snow the horse is immersed; this cowboy is doing some serious working!), caring for animals, and other desirable traits, as if smoking were a noble activity, metonymically equivalent to these other positive social activities. The images, texts, and product shown in the ad thus provide a symbolic construct which tries to cover over and camouflage contradictions between the 'heavy' work and the 'light' cigarette, between the 'natural' scene and the 'artificial' product, between the cool and healthy outdoors scene and the hot and unhealthy activity of smoking, and between the rugged masculinity of the 'Marlboro man' and the Light cigarette, originally targeted at women. In fact, this latter contradiction can be explained by the marketing ploy of suggesting to men that they can both be highly masculine, like the 'Marlboro man', and smoke a (supposedly) 'healthier' cigarette, while also appealing to macho women who might enjoy smoking a 'man's' cigarette which is also 'lighter' and 'healthier', as women's cigarettes are supposed to be.

The 1983 Virginia Slims ad (Figure 6.2) attempts in a similar fashion to associate its product with socially desired traits and offers subject positions with which women can identify. The Virginia Slims textual system classically includes a vignette at the top of the ad with a picture underneath of the 'Virginia Slims woman' next to the prominently displayed package of cigarettes. In the example pictured, the top of the ad features a framed box that contains the narrative images and message, which is linked to the changes in the situation of women portrayed through a contrast with the 'modern' woman below. The caption under the boxed image of segregated male and female exercise classes in 1903 contains the familiar Virginia Slims slogan, 'You've come a long way, baby.' The caption, linked to the 'Virginia Slims woman', next to the package of cigarettes, connotes a message of progress, metonymically linking Virginia Slims to the 'progressive woman' and 'modern' living. In this ad, it is the linkages and connections between the parts that establish the message which associates Virginia Slims with progress. The ad tells women that it is progressive and socially acceptable to smoke, and it associates Virginia Slims with modernity, social progress, and the socially desirable trait of slimness.

In fact, Lucky Strike carried out a successful advertising campaign in the 1930s which associated smoking with weight reduction ('Reach for a *Lucky* instead of a sweet!'), and Virginia Slims plays on this tradition, encapsulated in the very brand name of the product. Note too that the cigarette is a 'Lights' variety and that, as in the Marlboro ad, the intention is to associate the product with health and well-being. The pronounced smile on the woman's face also tries to associate the product with happiness and self-contentment, struggling against the association of smoking with guilt and dangers to one's health. The image of the slender, light woman not only associates the product with socially desirable traits, but in turn promotes the ideal of slimness as the ideal type of femininity.

Later in the 1980s, Capri cigarettes were advertised as 'the slimmest slim!', building on the continued and intensified association of slimness with femininity. The promotion of smoking and slimness is far from innocent, however, and has contributed to eating disorders, faddish diets and exercise programmes, and a dramatic increase in anorexia among young women, as well as rising cancer rates. As Judith Williamson points out (1978), advertising 'addresses' individuals and invites them to identify with certain products, images, and behaviour. Advertising provides a utopian image of a new, more attractive, more successful, more prestigious 'you' through purchase of certain goods. Advertising magically offers self-transformation and a new identity, associating changes in consumer behaviour, fashion, and appearance with metamorphosis into a new person. Consequently, individuals are taught to identify with values, role models, and social behaviour through advertising which is thus an important instrument of socialization as well as a manager of consumer demand.

Advertising sells its products and view of the world through images, rhetoric, slogans, and their juxtaposition in ads to which tremendous artistic resources, psychological research, and marketing strategies are devoted. These ads express and reinforce dominant images of gender and position men and women to assume highly specific subject positions. Two 1988 and 1989 Virginia Slims ads, in fact, reveal a considerable transformation in its image of women during the 1980s and a new strategy to persuade women that it is all right and even 'progressive' and ultra-modern to smoke. This move points to shifts in the relative power between men and women and discloses new subject positions for women validated by the culture industries.

Once again the sepia-coloured framed box at the top of the ad (Figure 6.3) contains an image of a woman serving her man in 1902; the comic pose and irritated look of the woman suggests that such servitude is highly undesirable and its contrast with the 'Virginia Slims woman' (who herself now wears the leather boots and leather gloves and jacket as well) suggests that women have come a long way while the ever-present cigarette associates woman's right to smoke in public with social progress. This time the familiar 'You've come a long way, baby' is absent, perhaps because the woman pictured would hardly tolerate being described as 'baby' and because women's groups had been protesting over the sexist and demeaning label in the slogan. Note, too, the transformation of the image of the woman in the Virginia Slims ad. No longer the smiling, cute, and wholesome potential wife of the earlier ad, she is now more threatening, more sexual, less wifely, and more masculine. The sunglasses connote the distance from the male gaze which she wants to preserve and the leather jacket with the military insignia connotes that she is equal to men, able to carry on a masculine role, and is stronger and more autonomous than women of the past.

The 1988 ad is highly anti-patriarchal and even expresses hostility toward men, with the overweight man with glasses and handlebar moustache looking slightly absurd, while it is clear that the woman is being held back by ridiculous fashion and intolerable social roles. The 'new' 'Virginia Slims woman', however, who completely dominates the scene, is the epitome of style and power. This strong woman

Figure 6.3 1988 Virginia Slims ad

can easily take in hand and enjoy the phallus (that is, the cigarette as the sign of male power accompanied by the male dress and military insignia) and serve as an icon of female glamour as well. This ad links power, glamour, and sexuality and offers a model of female power, associated with the cigarette and smoking. Ads work in part by generating dissatisfaction and by offering images of transformation, of a new personal identity. This particular ad promotes dissatisfaction with traditional images and presents a new image of a more powerful woman, a new lifestyle and identity for the Virginia Slims smoker. In these ways, the images associate the products advertised with certain socially desirable traits and convey messages concerning the symbolic benefits accruing to those who consume the product.

Although 'Lights' and 'Ultra Lights' continue to be the dominant Virginia Slims types, the phrase no longer appears as a highlighted caption in the 1988 ad and the package does not appear either. No doubt this 'heavy' woman contradicts the 'light' image and the ad connotes instead power and (a dubious) progress for women rather than slimness or lightness. Yet the woman's teased and flowing blonde hair, her perfect teeth which form an obliging smile, and especially her crotch, positioned in the ad in a highly suggestive and inviting fashion, code her as a symbol of beauty and sexuality, albeit more autonomous and powerful.

The 1989 Virginia Slims ad (not reproduced here) by contrast, depicts a more conventional image of woman, but one that is significantly different from the earlier, more traditional images of women in the ads. At the top of the 1989 ad, there are, once again, two vignettes in black and white which connote the bad old days for women. On the left, a working woman lights up a cigarette and angers her boss. Below, however, the beautiful 'Virginia Slims woman' confidently and happily holds the cigarette in her hand. The ad as a whole connotes the standard message of progress, linking Virginia Slims to the 'modern woman' who has progressed from oppressed servant of men to independent subject of her own life.

Note how the appearance of the 1989 'Virginia Slims woman' contributes to this message. Her hair is teased, her make-up is perfect, her smile is dazzling, and her clothes are flamboyant. Indeed, the woman could easily be a model for a fashion ad: she wears long, phallic ear-rings to connote her (quasi-masculine) power; the ear-rings are also mismatched, connoting her independence, style, and non-conformity. The 'loud' red hat, carelessly slung over her shoulder also connotes her individuality, while the bright red shirt, which exposes both her shoulders and part of her stomach, connotes daring and sexuality. The gold bracelet on her wrist connotes luxury and high fashion style, while the belt with the silver buckle and the exotic short shirt connotes colourfulness and creative individual fashion. Thus the Virginia Slims cigarette is not only associated with modernity and progress, but also with individuality, sexuality, fashion, and style.

The point I am trying to make is that it is precisely the images which are the vehicles of the subject positions and that therefore critical literacy in a postmodern image culture requires learning how to read images critically and to unpack the relations between images, texts, social trends, and products in commercial culture (Kellner 1989c). My reading of these ads suggests that advertising is as concerned with selling lifestyles and selling socially desirable subject positions associated with their products as with selling the products themselves – or rather, that advertisers use the symbolic constructs with which the consumer is invited to identify to try to induce her to use their product. Thus the 'Marlboro man' (that is, the consumer who smokes the cigarette) is smoking masculinity or natural vigour as much as a cigarette, while the 'Virginia Slims woman' is exhibiting modernity, thinness, or female power when she lights up her Slim.

This sort of reading of advertising not only helps individuals to resist manipulation but it also depicts how something as seemingly innocuous as advertising can depict significant shifts in subject positions, in modes of identity. For example, the two Virginia Slims ads suggest that at least a certain class of women (white, upper-middle and upper-class) were gaining more power in society and that women were being attracted by stronger, more autonomous, and more masculine images.

A comparison of two 1988 and 1989 Marlboro ads (the 1988 ad is reproduced here: Figure 6.4) with their earlier ads also yields some interesting results. While the Marlboro ads once centred on the 'Marlboro man', and in the early 1980s continue to feature this figure, curiously, by the late 1980s, human beings disappeared altogether from some Marlboro ads, which projected pure images of wholesome nature associated with the product (Figure 6.4). The caption 'Made especially for menthol smokers', the green menthol insignia on the cigarette package, and the blue and green backdrops of the trees, grass, and water in the ad all attempt to incorporate icons of health and nature into the ads, as if these menthol Lights would protect the buyer from cigarette health hazards. Undoubtedly this transformation in the Marlboro ads points to growing concern about the health hazards of cigarettes which required even purer emphasis on nature. Yet the absence of the Marlboro cowboy might also point to the obsolescence of the manual worker in a postmodern

Figure 6.4 1988 Marlboro ad

information and service society where significant sectors of the so-called 'new middle class' work in the industries of symbol and image production and manipulation.

The prominent images of the powerful horses in the ad, however, point to a continued desire for power, for identification with figures of power. The actual powerlessness of workers in contemporary capitalist society make it in turn difficult to present concrete contemporary images of male power that would appeal to a variety of male (and female) smokers. Eliminating the male figure also allows appeal over a wider range of social classes and occupational types, including both men and women who could perhaps respond more positively to images of nature and power than to the rather obsolete cowboy figure. Further – and these images are clearly polysemic, subject to multiple readings, – the new emphasis on 'Great refreshment in the Flip-Top box' not only harmonizes with the 'refreshing' images of green and nature but points to the new hedonist, leisure culture in postmodern society with its emphasis on the pleasures of consumption, spectacle, and refreshment. The refreshment tag also provides a new legitimation for cigarette smoking as a refreshing activity (building on the famous Pepsi 'pause that refreshes'?), which codes an obviously dangerous activity as 'refreshing' and thus as health-promoting.

Finally, the absence of human figures in the recent Marlboro ads could be read as signs of the erasure of the human in postmodern society, giving credence to Foucault's claim that in a new episteme the human itself could be washed away like a face drawn on sand at the edge of the sea (1970: 387). Yet the human cannot so easily be wished away and, lo and behold, in 1989 not only human figures but the 'Marlboro man' himself returned in a new ad campaign. One ad (not reproduced here) provides an example of a new advertising strategy which requires consumers to produce the meaning themselves, much like a modernist text. This fully two-page ad portrays giant hands (presumably those of the 'Marlboro man' himself) holding a pair of gloves, with a cigarette held between two gnarled and weather-beaten fingers. The only caption – besides the federally mandated list of ingredients and warnings to one's health – says: 'Come to where the flavor is.' There is no Marlboro cigarette box portrayed, nor any caption stating the brand name. Instead one has to look quite closely at the small brand name inscribed on the cigarette itself to discern precisely what brand is being advertised.

Half of the two-page ad is buried in darkness with only the caption and difficult-to-decipher fragments of images emerging. The other half of the ad centres on the gnarled hands, perhaps projecting the subliminal message to those concerned with the health risks of smoking that it is possible to smoke and survive. For the heavily lined hands are obviously those of someone who has lived life to the full, whose vicissitudes and experience are etched into the very skin of his hands, whose deeply textured skin attests to a long-lived life. In this way, the cigarette is associated with survival and a full life, thus assuaging worries that smoking constitutes a serious risk of cancer and other dread diseases and providing subliminal functions of anxiety reduction – a typical task of contemporary advertising.

This Marlboro ad is one of a genre of contemporary ads which forces the consumer to work at discerning the brand being sold and at deciphering the text to construct meaning. The minimalism of product-signifiers appeals to readers jaded with traditional advertising, tired of the same old stale images, and bored with and cynical toward advertising manipulation. To the cool postmodern reader, the association of masculinity with smoking Marlboros might be laughable, yet even such minimalist ads utilize product differentiation and use new images while building on old cues. In addition to appealing to a survivalist urge in contemporary smokers, the ad invites them to 'Come to where the flavor is.' The emphasis on flavour appeals to hedonist tastes: to enjoy the flavour, to light up for pleasure. Such appeals encourage contemporary individualist-hedonist impulses to have fun, to do what one wants and pleases at all costs – even the destruction of one's health.

The textual system of this ad as a whole thus addresses its readers as individuals able to read the complex ad and to choose their own pleasures as they will. There is thus a subliminal appeal to the individual's freedom and creativity which invites one to interpret the ad as one chooses and to light up the cigarette when one pleases in disregard of the obligatory government warnings linking cigarettes to health risks. The gnarled hands as well are those of an individual who is in charge of his life and who makes his own decisions, so the text as a whole is structured to associate smoking Marlboro with individuality. Interestingly, this ad and the other Marlboro ads which erase human subjects play down gender identity and one might read this as a de-centring of gender identity in contemporary society, as a disassociation between the product and gender, as a bracketing of the centrality of gender in the constitution of identity. In addition, the appeal here is directly to use-value, to the pleasure and flavour that the cigarette produces rather than the sign value of masculinity, or the appeal to power.

In addition, this text works to get the reader to identify with the product and to produce a pleasurable feeling from the feat of producing meaning, from reading the ambiguous text, that is presumably then transferred to and associated with the product, so that the image of Marlboro is associated with free choice and creativity. And yet the highly paid cultural interpreters who work for advertising agencies are hedging their bets concerning the Marlboro ads of recent years. For 1989 and 1990 saw a return of the previous realist ads which centre on the old Marlboro cowboy, along with production of a new type of ad just analysed, as well as a new series of pure nature imagery such as was discussed in the analysis of Figure 6.4. Such a multiplicity of strategies show that the advertising agencies of contemporary capitalism are not at all sure as to what will attract consumers to their products or with what images consumers identify. For, as I have been arguing, one of the features of contemporary culture is precisely the fragmentation, transitoriness, and multiplicity of images, which refuse to crystallize into a stable image culture.

In a sense, it is undecidable whether contemporary image culture and forms of identity should be described as modern or postmodern. This multiplicity of types of Marlboro ads currently circulating helps put into question claims concerning a radical postmodern rupture with modernity and concerning the alleged cultural dominance of postmodern image culture. For the Marlboro ads currently circulating draw on traditional, modernist, and postmodern image production and aesthetic strategies and use a variety of traditional, modern, and contemporary ideological appeals as well. Rather than taking postmodernity as a new cultural totality, I would thus argue that it makes more sense to interpret the many facets of the postmodern as an emergent cultural trend in opposition to residual traditional and modern values and practices.

On the other hand, one could describe precisely this coexistence of styles, this mixture of traditional, modern, and postmodern cultural forms, as 'postmodern'. Perhaps the lack of a cultural dominant is postmodern. Yet contemporary Marlboro advertising campaigns suggest that the highly paid and often acute interpreters of the contemporary scene in the employment of corporate capital see the continuing existence of traditional identities, where masculinity is still important, combined with a modern concern for power and enjoyment as a continuing social force and matrix. At the same time such ads show that this culture coexists with a postmodern culture in which new forms of image are needed to catch the attention of a jaded and cynical consumer. If postmodernity were the cultural totality that some of its celebrants claim, one imagines that the most highly paid and sophisticated image producers would inundate its denizens with postmodern imagery. But no: contemporary advertising suggests that instead the contemporary culture is highly fragmented into different taste cultures that respond to quite different images and values. A megacorporation like Marlboro goes after all of these audiences. Thus one sees a certain heterogeneity to its image productions, with different appeals sent out to different audiences according to market segmentation: the old 'Marlboro man' for readers of *TV Guide*; horses and nature for the health- and vitality-conscious readers of fashion magazines like *Elle* and *M*; and more complex aesthetic spectacles for the gourmet hedonists who read *Vanity Fair* and the like.

The multiplicity of advertising strategies pursued by Marlboro also points to the immanent contradictions of commodity culture. For advertising attempts to produce identities by offering products associated with certain traits and values. And yet the inexorable trends of fashion and the new advertising campaigns undermine previously forged identities and associations to circulate new products, new images, new values. And so it is that advertising, fashion, consumption, television, and popular culture constantly destabilize identity and contribute to producing more unstable, fluid, shifting, and changing identities in the contemporary scene. And yet one also sees the inexorable processes of commodification at work in this process. The market segmentation of multiple ad campaigns and appeals reproduces and intensifies fragmentation and destabilizes identity which new products and identifications are attempting to restabilize. Thus, it seems that it is capital itself which is the demiurge of allegedly postmodern fragmentation, dispersal of identity, change, and mobility. Rather than postmodernity constituting a break with capital and political economy, as Baudrillard and others would have it, wherever one observes phenomena of postmodern culture one can detect the logic of capital behind them.

This argument suggests that much postmodern theory is excessively abstract in detaching political economy and capitalism from the phenomena which it describes and thus occluding their economic underpinnings. Furthermore, such theory tends to overgeneralize, taking examples from new emergent trends which it conflates into a new cultural dominant. Some postmodern cultural theory also ignores ideological content and effects, focusing merely on formal structures or image construction. Against such positions, I have argued that rather than advertising and the other images of mass culture being flat, one-dimensional and without ideological coding, as some postmodern theory would have it, many ads are multi-dimensional, polysemic, ideologically coded, open to a variety of readings, and expressive of the commodification of culture and attempts of capital to colonize the totality of life, from desire to satisfaction.

Although identity is problematized in a postmodern image and commodity culture, it is neither volatilized, imploded, nor obliterated to the extent that it is by extreme postmodern theorists like Baudrillard or in the cyberpunk fiction of a William Gibson or Bruce Sterling. Advertising, television, and pop iconography depict figures in ads, TV shows, and films, as well as entertainers like Michael Jackson and Madonna, changing their identities at will, shedding old looks and images for new ones as one gets rid of last year's fashions to be 'in' and 'up to date'. And yet there is a certain continuity in the looks, gendering, and behaviour celebrated in the cultural industries.

Identity becomes much more problematical in Baudrillard and the visions of the future in Gibson and Sterling. In Gibson's 'sprawl' stories and novels (i.e. *Neuromancer, Count Zero, Mona Lisa, Overdrive*, and some of the stories in *Burning Crome*) prostheses, implants, programming of brain electrons, interfacing with computer-generated cyberspace, and control of individuals by computer programs and corporate mind-altering techniques imperil the very survival of the individual and the human. Yet Gibson hangs onto a version of romantic, hard-boiled individualism and his heroes struggle valiantly to maintain their identity in the high-tech world of the future.

Bruce Sterling's *Schismatrix* and other writings, by contrast, portray a situation of 'posthumanity' that delineates a far more radical rupture than the romantic humanism of a Gibson. In Sterling's posthuman 'clades', new species of genetically and cybernetically altered beings appear that are human in shape and appearance but with chemical implants, the transformation of 'human' life knows no limits. Here identity is the construct of science and genetic engineering and diversity overwhelms all commonalities. Identity is so radically unstable that it in effect disappears in a postmodern, posthuman, postidentitarian world. In contrast with this vision, the mutations of identity in contemporary society are rather 'modern' in nature and scope.

CONCLUSIONS

My analyses have suggested that in a postmodern image culture, the images, scenes, stories, and cultural texts of so-called popular culture offer a wealth of subject positions which in turn help structure individual identity. These images project role and gender models, appropriate and inappropriate forms of behaviour, style, and fashion, and subtle enticements to emulate and identify with certain subject positions while avoiding others. Rather than identity disappearing in a postmodern society, it is merely subject to new determinations and new forces while offering as well new possibilities, styles, models, and forms. Yet the overwhelming variety of subject positions, of possibilities for identity, in an affluent image culture no doubt create highly unstable identities while constantly providing new openings to restructure one's identity.

It is difficult to say whether on the whole this is a 'good' or 'bad' thing and it is probably safer to conclude with Jameson that the phenomena associated with postmodernity are highly ambiguous and exhibit both progressive and regressive features. There does seem to be more of an acceptance of multiple and unstable identities in the contemporary cultural milieux than was the case previously. Modern identities – however multiple and subject to change – appeared to be more stable, whereas there currently seems to be more acceptance of change, fragmentation, and theatrical play with identity than was the case in the earlier, heavier, and more serious epoch of modernity.

On one hand, this increases one's freedom to play with one's identity and to change one's life dramatically (which may be good for some individuals) while, on the other hand, it can lead to a totally fragmented, disjointed life, subject to the whims of fashion and the subtle indoctrinations of advertising and popular culture. Against a totally dispersed, fragmented, and disconnected subject, one might want to valorize certain features central to modern identity, like autonomy, rationality, commitment, responsibility, and so on; or one might want to disregard or reconstruct these concepts, as, for instance, Habermas has attempted to do with rationality. In any case, identity continues to be the problem it was throughout modernity, though it has been problematized anew in the contemporary orgy of commodification, fragmentation, image production, and societal, political, and cultural transformation that is the work of contemporary capitalism.

So does postmodernity exist? Have we left modernity behind and entered a 'new postmodern scene? Is the current construction of identity distinctly postmodern, and has a fundamental shift in the construction of identity taken place? I would argue that it is equally arbitrary and open to debate as to whether one posits that we are in a situation of late modernity or a new postmodernity. Either could be argued. The features that I have ascribed to postmodern identity could be read as an intensification of features already present in modernity, or as a new configuration with new emphases that one could describe as 'postmodern'. In fact, concepts and terms, like identity itself, are social constructs, arbitrary constructs which serve to mark and call attention to certain phenomena and which fulfil certain analytical or classifactory tasks. So the debate over postmodernity is largely a debate over what terminology we should use to describe the contemporary socio-cultural matrix.

NOTES

For helpful comments on an earlier draft of this paper I am grateful to Steve Best, Bob Goldman, and Scott Lash.

1 On Baudrillard, see Kellner 1989b. On postmodernism and popular culture, see the articles in *Screen*, 28/2 (1987); *Journal of Communication Inquiry*, 10/1 (1986) and 10/2 (1986); and Ross 1989.

2 See Kellner (1980) and Abercrombie et al. in ch. 5 of this book.

3 For further examples of progressive political messages in the series, see Best and Kellner 1987.

4 The method of reading ads and the interpretation of advertising that follows is indebted to the work of Robert Goldman.

5 The tobacco leaf is (for insects) one of the most sweet and tasty of all plants – so that a large amount of pesticides is required to keep insects from devouring it. Cigarette makers use chemicals to produce a distinctive smell and taste to the product and use preservatives to keep it from spoiling. Other chemicals are used to regulate the burning process and to filter out tars and nicotine. While these latter products are the most publicized dangers in cigarette-smoking, actually the pesticides, chemicals and preservatives may well be more deadly. Scandalously, cigarettes are one of the most unregulated products in the US consumer economy. (European countries, for example, carefully regulate the pesticides used in tobacco-growing and the synthetics used in cigarette production.) Government-sponsored experiments on the effects of cigarette-smoking also use generic cigarettes, which may not have the chemicals and preservatives of named brands; thus no really scientifically accurate major survey on the dangers of cigarette-smoking has ever been done by the US government. The major media, many of which are part of conglomerates with heavy interests in the tobacco industry or depend on cigarette-advertising for revenue, have never really undertaken to expose to the public the true dangers attached to cigarette-smoking and the scandalous neglect of this issue by government and media in the United States. Cigarette addiction is thus a useful object lesson in the unperceived dangers and destructive elements of the consumer society and the ways these dangers are covered over. (My own information on the cigarette industry derives from an *Alternative Views* television interview which Frank Morrow that I did with

Bill Drake on the research which will constitute his forthcoming book on the dangers of tobacco.)

REFERENCES

Barthes, R. 1957/1972: *Mythologies*. New York: Hill & Wang.

Baudrillard, J. 1983: *Simulations*. New York: Semiotext(e).

Berman, M. 1982: *All that Is Solid Melts into Air: The Experience of Modernity*. New York: Simon & Schuster; 1983: London: Verso; 1988 (2nd edn): Harmondsworth: Penguin.

Best, S., and Kellner, D. 1987: '(Re)watching television: notes towards a political criticism', *Diacritics* (Summer), 97–113.

Butler, J. B. 1985: *Miami Vice* and the legacy of film noir', *Journal of Popular Film and Television*, 13/3, 132–43.

Coward, R. and Ellis, J. 1977: *Language and Materialism*. London: Routledge.

Deleuze, G., and Guattari, F. 1977: *Anti-Oedipus*. New York: Viking.

Fiske, J. 1987: 'Miami vice, Miami pleasure', *Cultural Studies*, 1/1, 113–19.

Foucault, M. 1970: *The Order of Things*. New York: Pantheon.

Frisby, D. 1985: *Fragments of Modernity*. Cambridge: Polity Press.

Gitlin, T. (ed.) 1987: *Watching Television*. New York: Pantheon.

Grossberg, L. 1987: 'The in-difference of television', *Journal of Communication Inquiry*, 10/2, 28–46.

Jameson, F. 1983: 'Postmodernism and the consumer society', in N. Foster (ed.), *Postmodern Culture*, Seattle: Bay View.

Jameson, F. 1984: 'Postmodernism, or the cultural logic of late capitalism', *New Left Review*, 146, 53–92.

Kellner, D. 1982: 'Television, mythology and ritual', *Praxis*, 6, 133–55.

Kellner, D. 1989a: *Critical Theory, Marxism and Modernity*. Cambridge: Polity Press.

Kellner, D. 1989b: *From Marxism to Postmodernism and Beyond: Critical Studies of Jean Baudrillard*. Cambridge: Polity Press.

Kellner, D. 1989c: 'Reading images critically: towards a postmodern pedagogy', *Journal of Education*, 170/3, 31–52.

Kellner, D. 1990: *Television and the Crisis of Democracy*. Boulder, Colo.: Westview Press.

Kolb, D. 1986: *The Critique of Pure Modernity*. Chicago: University of Chicago Press.

Kroker, A., and Cook, D. 1986: *The Postmodern Scene*. New York: St Martin's Press.

Ricoeur, P. 1970: *Freud and Philosophy*. New Haven, Conn.: Yale University Press.

Riesman, D. et al. 1950: *The Lonely Crowd*. Garden City, NY: Anchor Books.

Ross, A. 1989: *Universal Abandon?* Minneapolis: University of Minnesota Press.

Warshow, R. 1962: *The Immediate Experience.* Garden City, NY: Anchor Books.

Williamson, J. 1978: *Decoding Advertisements.* London: Marion Boyars.

7

Scopic regimes of modernity

Martin Jay

The modern era, it is often alleged, has been dominated by the sense of sight in a way that sets it apart from its pre-modern predecessors and possibly its postmodern successor (see e.g. Febvre 1982; Mandrou 1975). Beginning with the Renaissance and the scientific revolution, modernity has been normally considered resolutely ocularcentric. The invention of printing, according to the familiar argument of McLuhan (1964) and Ong (1967), reinforced the privileging of the visual abetted by such inventions as the telescope and the microscope (see also Eisenstein 1979). 'The perceptual field thus constituted,' concludes a typical account, 'was fundamentally nonreflexive, visual and quantitative' (Lowe 1982: 26).

Although the implied characterization of different eras in this generalization as more favourably inclined to other senses should not be taken at face value,[1] it is difficult to deny that the visual has been dominant in modern Western culture in a wide variety of ways. Whether we focus on 'the mirror of nature' metaphor in philosophy with Richard Rorty (1979) or emphasize the prevalence of surveillance with Michel Foucault (1979) or bemoan the society of the spectacle with Guy Debord (1983), we confront again and again the ubiquity of vision as the master sense of the modern era.

But what precisely constitutes the visual culture of this era is not so readily apparent. Indeed, we might well ask, borrowing Christian Metz's term (1982: 61), is there one unified 'scopic regime' of the modern or are there several, perhaps competing ones? For, as Jacqueline Rose has recently reminded us, 'our previous history is not the petrified block of a single visual space since, looked at obliquely, it can always be seen to contain its moment of unease (1986: 232–3). In fact, may there possibly be several such moments, which can be discerned, if often in repressed form, in the modern era? If so, the scopic regime of modernity may best be understood as a contested terrain, rather than a harmoniously integrated complex of visual theories and practices. It may, in fact, be characterized by a differentiation of visual subcultures, whose separation has allowed us to understand the multiple implications of sight in ways that are now only beginning to be appreciated. That new understanding, I want to suggest, may well be the product of a radical reversal in the hierarchy of visual subcultures in the modern scopic regime.

Before spelling out the competing ocular fields in the modern era as I understand them, I want to make clear that I am presenting only very crude ideal-typical characterizations, which can easily be faulted for their obvious distance from the complex realities they seek to approximate. I am also not suggesting that the three main visual subcultures I single out for special attention exhaust all those that might be discerned in the lengthy and loosely defined epoch we call modernity. But, as will soon become apparent, it will be challenging enough to try to do justice in the limited space I have to those I do want to highlight as most significant.

Let me begin by turning to what is normally claimed to be the dominant, even totally hegemonic, visual model of the modern era, that which we can identify with Renaissance notions of perspective in the visual arts and Cartesian ideas of subjective rationality in philosophy. For convenience, it can be called Cartesian perspectivalism. That it is often assumed to be equivalent to the modern scopic regime *per se* is illustrated by two remarks from prominent commentators. The first is the claim made by the art historian William Ivins Jr., in his *Art and Geometry* (1946: 81) that 'the history of art during the five hundred years that have elapsed since Alberti wrote has been little more than the story of the slow diffusion of his ideas through the artists and peoples of Europe'. The second is from Richard Rorty's widely discussed *Philosophy and the Mirror of Nature*, published in 1979: 'in the Cartesian model the intellect *inspects* entities modeled on retinal images... In Descartes' conception – the one that became the basis for "modern" epistemology – it is *representations* which are in the "mind"' (1979: 45). The assumption expressed in these citations that Cartesian perspectivalism is *the* reigning visual model of modernity is often tied to the further contention that it succeeded in becoming so because it best expressed the 'natural' experience of sight valorized by the scientific world-view. When the assumed equivalence between scientific observation and the natural world was disputed, so too was the domination of this visual subculture, a salient instance being Erwin Panofsky's celebrated critique of perspective as merely a conventional symbolic form (Panofsky 1924/5).

But for a very long time, Cartesian perspectivalism was identified with the modern scopic regime *tout court*. With full awareness of the schematic nature of what follows, let me try to establish its most important characteristics. There is, of course, an immense literature on the discovery, rediscovery or invention of perspective – all three terms are used depending on the writer's interpretation of ancient visual knowledge – in the Italian quattrocento. Brunelleschi is traditionally accorded the honour of being its practical inventor or discoverer, while Alberti is almost universally acknowledged as its first theoretical interpreter. From Ivins (1938), Panofsky and Krautheimer to Edgerton, White and Kubovy, scholars have investigated virtually every aspect of the perspectivalist revolution, technical, aesthetic, psychological, religious, even economic and political.

Despite many still disputed points, a rough consensus seems to have emerged around the following points. Growing out of the late medieval fascination with the metaphysical implications of light, light as divine *Lux* rather than perceived *Lumen*, linear perspective came to symbolize a harmony between the mathematical regularities in optics and God's will. Even after the religious underpinnings of this equation were eroded, the favourable connotations surrounding the allegedly objective optical order remained powerfully in place. These positive associations had been displaced from the objects, often religious in content, depicted in earlier painting to the spatial relations of the perspectival canvas themselves. This new concept of space was geometrically isotropic, rectilinear, abstract and uniform. The *velo* or veil of threads Alberti used to depict it conventionalized that space in a way that anticipated the grids so characteristic of twentieth-century art, although as Rosalind Krauss has reminded us (1985: 10), Alberti's veil was assumed to correspond to external reality in a way that its modernist successor did not.

The three-dimensional, rationalized space of perspectival vision could be rendered on a two-dimensional surface by following all of the transformational rules spelled out in Alberti's *De Pittura* and later treatises by Viator, Dürer and others. The basic device was the idea of symmetrical visual pyramids or cones with one of their apexes the receding vanishing or centric point in the painting, the other the eye of the painter or the beholder. The transparent window that was the canvas, in Alberti's famous metaphor, could also be understood as a flat mirror reflecting the geometricalized space of the scene depicted back onto the no less geometricalized space radiating out from the viewing eye.

Significantly, that eye was singular, rather than the two eyes of normal binocular vision. It was conceived in the manner of a lone eye looking through a peephole at the scene in front of it. Such an eye was, moreover, understood to be static, unblinking and fixated, rather than dynamic, moving with what later scientists would call 'saccadic' jumps from one focal point to another. In Norman Bryson's terms, it followed the logic of the Gaze rather than the Glance, thus producing a visual take that was eternalized, reduced to one 'point of view' and disembodied. In what Bryson calls the 'Founding Perception' of the Cartesian perspectivalist tradition,

> the gaze of the painter arrests the flux of phenomena, contemplates the visual field from a vantage-point outside the mobility of duration, in an eternal moment of disclosed presence; while in the moment of viewing, the viewing subject unites his gaze with the Founding Perception, in a moment of perfect recreation of that first epiphany. (*Bryson 1983: 94*)

A number of implications followed from the adoption of this visual order. The abstract coldness of the perspectival gaze meant the withdrawal of the painter's emotional entanglement with the objects depicted in geometricalized space. The participatory involvement of more absorptive visual modes was diminished, if not entirely suppressed, as the gap between spectator and spectacle widened. The moment or erotic projection in vision – what St Augustine had anxiously condemned as 'ocular desire'[2] – was lost as the bodies of the painter and viewer were forgotten in the name of an allegedly disincarnated, absolute eye. Although such a gaze could, of course, still fall on objects of desire – think, for example, of the female nude in Dürer's famous print of a draftsman drawing her through a screen of perspectival threads – it did so largely in the service of a reifying male look that turned its targets into stone.[3] The marmoreal nude drained of its capacity to arouse desire was at least tendentially the outcome of this development. Despite the occasional exception, such as Caravaggio's seductive boys, the nudes themselves fail to look out at the viewer, radiating no erotic energy in the other direction. Only much later in the history of Western art, with the brazenly shocking nudes in Manet's *Déjeuner sur l'herbe* and *Olympia*, did the crossing of the viewer's gaze with that of the subject finally occur. By then the rationalized visual order of Cartesian perspectivalism was already coming under attack in other ways as well.

In addition to its de-eroticizing of the visual order, it had also fostered what might be called de-narrativization or de-textualization. That is, as abstract, quantitatively conceptualized space became more interesting to the artist than the qualitatively differentiated subjects painted within it, the rendering of the scene became an end in itself. Alberti, to be sure, had emphasized the use of perspective to depict *istoria*, ennobling stories, but in time, they seemed less important than the visual skill shown in depicting them. Thus, the abstraction of artistic form from any substantive content, which is part of the clichéd history of twentieth-century modernism, was already prepared by the perspectival revolution five centuries earlier. What Bryson in another of his books, *Word and Image* (1981: ch.1), calls the diminution of the discursive function of painting (its telling a story to the unlettered masses, in favour of its figural function) meant the increasing autonomy of the image from any extrinsic purpose, religious or otherwise. The effect of realism was consequently enhanced as canvases were filled with more and more information that seemed unrelated to any narrative or textual function. Cartesian perspectivalism was thus in league with a scientific worldview that no longer hermeneutically read the world as a divine text, but rather saw it as situated in a mathematically regular spatio-temporal order filled with natural objects that could only be observed from without by the dispassionate eye of the neutral researcher.

It was also complicitous, so many commentators have claimed, with the fundamentally bourgeois ethic of the modern world. According to Edgerton (1975: 39), Florentine businessmen with their newly invented technique of double-entry book-keeping may have been 'more and more disposed to a visual order that would accord with the tidy principles of mathematical order that they applied to their bank ledgers'. John Berger (1972: 109) goes so far as to claim that more appropriate than the Albertian metaphor of the window on the world is that of 'a safe let into a wall, a safe in which the visible has been deposited'. It was, he contends, no accident that the invention (or rediscovery) of perspective virtually coincided with the emergence of the oil-painting detached from its context and available for buying and selling. Separate from the painter and the viewer, the visual field depicted on the other side of the canvas could become a portable commodity able to enter the circulation of capitalist exchange. At the same time, if philosophers like Martin Heidegger (1977: 17) are correct, the natural world was transformed through the technological world-view into a 'standing reserve' for the surveillance and manipulation of a dominating subject.[4]

Cartesian perspectivalism has, in fact, been the target of a widespread philosophical critique, which has denounced its privileging of an ahistorical, disinterested, disembodied subject entirely outside of the world it claims to know only from afar. The questionable assumption of a transcendental subjectivity characteristic of universalist humanism, which ignores our embeddedness in what Maurice Merleau-Ponty liked to call the flesh of the world, is thus tied to the 'high-altitude' thinking characteristic of this scopic regime. In many accounts, this entire tradition has thus been subjected to wholesale condemnation as both false and pernicious.

Looked at more closely, however, it is possible to discern internal tensions in Cartesian perspectivalism itself that suggest it was not quite as uniformly coercive as is sometimes assumed. Thus, for example, John White distinguishes between what he terms 'artificial perspective', in which the mirror held up to nature is flat, and 'synthetic perspective', in which that mirror is presumed to be concave, thus producing a curved rather than planar space on the canvas. Here, according to White (1987: 208), Paolo Uccello and Leonardo da Vinci were the major innovators, offering a 'spherical space which is homogeneous, but by no means simple, and which possesses some of the qualities of Einstein's finite infinity'. Although artificial perspective was the dominant model, its competitor was never entirely forgotten.

Michael Kubovy has recently added the observation that what he calls the 'robustness of perspective' (1986: ch. 4) meant that Renaissance canvases could be successfully viewed from more than the imagined apex of the beholder's visual pyramid. He criticizes those who naively identify the rules of perspective established by its theoretical champions with the actual practice of the artists themselves. Rather than acting as a procrustean bed, it was practically subordinated to the exigencies of perception, which means that denunciations of its failings are often directed at a straw man (or at least his straw eye).

Equally problematic is the subject position in the Cartesian perspectivalist epistemology. For the monocular eye at the apex of the beholder's pyramid could be construed as transcendental and universal – that is, exactly the same for any human viewer occupying the same point in time and space – or contingent – solely dependent on the particular, individual vision of distinct beholders, with their own concrete relations to the scene in front of them. When the former was explicitly transformed into the latter, the relativistic implications of perspectivalism could be easily drawn. Even in the seventeenth century, this potential was apparent to thinkers like Leibniz, although he generally sought to escape its more troubling implications. These were not explicitly stressed and then praised until the late nineteenth century by such thinkers as Nietzsche. If everyone had his or her own camera obscura with a distinctly different peephole, Nietzsche gleefully concluded, then no transcendental worldview was possible (Kofman 1973).

Finally, the Cartesian perspectivalist tradition contained a potential for internal contestation in the possible uncoupling of the painter's view of the scene from that of the presumed beholder. Interestingly, Bryson identifies this development with Vermeer, who represents for him a second state of perspectivalism even more disincarnated than that of Alberti. 'The bond with the viewer's physique is broken and the viewing subject,' he writes, 'is now proposed and assumed as a notional point, a non-empirical Gaze' (Bryson 1983: 112).

What makes this last observation so suggestive is the opening it provides for a consideration of an alternative scopic regime that may be understood as more than a subvariant of Cartesian perspectivalism. Although I cannot pretend to be a serious student of Vermeer able to quarrel with Bryson's interpretation of his work, it might be useful to situate the painter in a different context from the one we have been discussing. That is, we might include him and the Dutch seventeenth-century art of which he was so great an exemplar in a visual culture very different from that we associate with Renaissance perspective, one which Svetlana Alpers (1983) has called *The Art of Describing*.

According to Alpers, the hegemonic role of Italian painting in art history has occluded an appreciation of a second tradition, which flourished in the seventeenth-century Low Countries. Borrowing Georg Luckács's distinction between narration and description, which he used to contrast realist and naturalist fiction, she argues that Italian Renaissance art, for all its fascination with the techniques of perspective, still held fast to the story-telling function for which they were used. In the Renaissance, the world on the other side of Alberti's window, she writes, 'was a stage in which human figures performed significant actions based on the texts of the poets. It is a narrative art' (1983: xix). Northern art, in contrast, suppresses narrative and textual reference in favour of description and visual surface. Rejecting the privileged, constitutive role of the monocular subject, it emphasizes instead the prior existence of a world of objects depicted on the flat canvas, a world indifferent to the beholder's position in front of it. This world, moreover, is not contained entirely within the frame of the Albertian window, but seems instead to extend beyond it. Frames do exist around Dutch pictures, but they are arbitrary and without the totalizing function they serve in Southern art. If there is a model for Dutch art, it is the map with its unapologetically flat surface and its willingness to include words as well as objects in its visual space. Summarizing the difference between the art of describing and Cartesian perspectivalism, Alpers posits the following oppositions:

> attention to many small things versus a few large ones, light reflected off objects versus objects modeled by light and shadow; the surface of objects, their colors and textures, dealt with rather than their placement in a legible space; an unframed image versus one that is clearly framed; one with no clearly situated viewer compared to one with such a viewer. The distinction follows a hierarchical model of distinguishing between phenomena commonly referred to as primary and secondary; objects and space versus the surfaces, forms versus the textures of the world. (*Alpers 1983: 44*)

If there is a philosophical correlate to Northern art, it is not Cartesianism with its faith in a geometricalized, rationalized, essentially intellectual concept of space but rather the more empirical visual experience of observationally orientated Baconian empiricism. In the Dutch context Alpers identifies it with Constantin Huygens. The non-mathematical impulse of this tradition accords well with the indifference to hierarchy, proportion and analogical resemblances characteristic of Cartesian perspectivalism. Instead, it casts its attentive eye on the fragmentary, detailed and richly articulated surface of a world it is content to describe rather than explain. Like the microscopist of the seventeenth century – Leeuwenhoeck is her prime example – Dutch art savours the discrete particularity of visual experience and resists the temptation to allegorize or typologize what it sees, a temptation to which she claims Southern art readily succumbed.

In two significant ways, the art of describing can be said to have anticipated later visual models, however much it was subordinated to its Cartesian perspectivalist rival. As we have already noted, a direct filiation between Alberti's *velo* and the grids of modernist art is problematic because, as Rosalind Krauss has argued, the former assumed a three-dimensional world out there in nature, whereas the latter did not. A more likely predecessor can thus be located in the Dutch art based on the mapping impulse. As Alpers notes,

> Although the grid that Ptolemy proposed, and those that Mercator later imposed, share the mathematical uniformity of the Renaissance perspective grid, they do not share the positioned

viewer, the frame, and the definition of the picture as a window through which an external viewer looks. On these accounts the Ptolemaic grid, indeed cartographic grids in general, must be distinguished from, not confused with, the perspectival grid. The projection is, one might say, viewed from nowhere. Nor is it to be looked through. It assumes a flat working surface. (*Alpers 1983: 138*)

Secondly, the art of describing also anticipates the visual experience produced by the nineteenth-century invention of photography. Both share a number of salient features: 'fragmentariness, arbitrary frames, the immediacy that the first practitioners expressed by claiming that the photograph gave Nature the power to reproduce herself directly unaided by man' (Alpers 1983: 43). The parallel frequently drawn between photography and the anti-perspectivalism of impressionist art, made for example by Aaron Scharf (1986: ch. 8) in his discussion of Degas, should thus be extended to include the Dutch art of the seventeenth century. And if Peter Galassi is correct in *Before Photography* (1981), there was also a tradition of topographical painting – landscape sketches of a fragment of reality – that resisted Cartesian perspectivalism and thus prepared the way both for photography and the impressionist return to two-dimensional canvases. How widespread or self-consciously oppositional such a tradition was I will leave to experts in art history to decide. What is important for our purposes is simply to register the existence of an alternative scopic regime even during the heyday of the dominant tradition.

Alpers's attempt to characterize it is, of course, open to possible criticisms. The strong opposition between narration and description she posits may seem less firm if we recall the de-narrativizing impulse in perspective art itself mentioned above. And if we can detect a certain fit between the exchange principle of capitalism and the abstract relational space of perspective, we might also discern a complementary fit between the valorization of material surfaces in Dutch art and the fetishism of commodities no less characteristic of a market economy. In this sense, both scopic regimes can be said to reveal different aspects of a complex, but unified phenomenon, just as Cartesian and Baconian philosophies can be said to be consonant, if in different ways, with the scientific world-view.

If, however, we turn to a third model of vision, or what can be called the second moment of unease in the dominant model, the possibilities for an even more radical alternative can be discerned.

This third model is perhaps best identified with the baroque. At least as early as 1888 and Heinrich Wölfflin's epochal study, *Renaissance and Baroque* (1964), art historians have been tempted to postulate a perennial oscillation between two styles in both painting and architecture.[5] In opposition to the lucid, linear, solid, fixed, planimetric, closed form of the Renaissance, or as Wölfflin later called it, the classical style, the baroque was painterly, recessional, soft-focused, multiple and open. Derived, at least according to one standard etymology, from the Portuguese word for an irregular, oddly shaped pearl, the baroque connoted the bizarre and peculiar, traits which were normally disdained by champions of clarity and transparency of form.

Although it may be prudent to confine the baroque solely to the seventeenth century and link it with the Catholic Counter-Reformation or the manipulation of popular culture by the newly ascendant absolutist state – as has, for example, the Spanish historian José Antonio Maravall (1986) – it may also be possible to see it as a permanent, if often repressed, visual possibility throughout the entire modern era. In the recent work of the French philosopher Christine Buci-Glucksmann, *La Raison baroque* (1984) and *La Folie du voir* (1986), it is precisely the explosive power of baroque vision that is seen as the most significant alternative to the hegemonic visual style we have called Cartesian perspectivalism. Celebrating the dazzling, disorientating, ecstatic surplus of images in baroque visual experience, she emphasizes its rejection of the monocular geometricalization of the Cartesian tradition, with its illusion of homogeneous three-dimensional space seen with a God's eye view from afar. She also tacitly contrasts the Dutch art of describing, with its belief in legible surfaces and faith in the material solidity of the world its paintings map, with the baroque fascination for opacity, unreadability and the undecipherability of the reality it depicts.

For Buci-Glucksmann, the baroque self-consciously revels in the contradictions between surface and depth, disparaging as a result any attempt to reduce the multiplicity of visual spaces into any one coherent essence. Significantly, the mirror that it holds up to nature is not the flat reflecting glass that commentators like Edgerton and White see as vital in the development of rationalized or 'analytic' perspective, but rather the anamorphosistic mirror, either concave or convex, that distorts the visual image – or more precisely, reveals the conventional, rather than natural quality of 'normal' specularity by showing its dependence on the materiality of the medium of reflection. In fact, because of its greater awareness of that materiality – what a recent commentator, Rodolphe Gasché (1986) has drawn attention to as the 'tain of the mirror' (its silver backing) – baroque visual experience has a strongly tactile or haptic quality, which prevents it from turning into the absolute ocularcentrism of its Cartesian perspectivalist rival.

In philosophical terms, although no one system can be seen as its correlate, Leibniz's pluralism of monadic viewpoints,[6] Pascal's meditations on paradox, and the Counter-Reformation mystics' submission to vertiginous experiences of rapture might all be seen as related to baroque vision. Moreover, the philosophy it favoured self-consciously eschewed the model of intellectual clarity expressed in a literal language purified of ambiguity. Instead, it recognized the inextricability of rhetoric and vision, which meant that images were signs and that concepts always contained an irreducibly imagistic component.

Baroque vision, Buci-Glucksmann also suggests, sought to represent the unrepresentable and necessarily failing, produced the melancholy that Walter Benjamin in particular saw as characteristic of the baroque sensibility. As such, it was closer to what a long tradition of aesthetics called the sublime, in contrast to the beautiful, because of its yearning for a presence that can never be fulfilled. Indeed, desire, in its erotic as well as metaphysical forms, courses through the baroque scopic regime. The body returns to dethrone the disinterested gaze of the disincarnated Cartesian spectator. But unlike the return of the body celebrated in such twentieth-century philosophies of vision as Merleau-Ponty's, with its dream of a meaning-laden imbrication of the viewer and the viewed in the flesh of the world, here it generates only allegories of obscurity and opacity. Thus, it truly produces one of those 'moments of unease' which Jacqueline Rose sees challenging the petrification of the dominant visual order (the art of describing seeming in fact far more at ease in the world).

A great deal more might be said about these three ideal-typical visual cultures, but let me conclude by offering a few speculations, if I can use so visual a term, on their current status. First, it seems undeniable that we have witnessed in the twentieth century a remarkable challenge to the hierarchical order of three regimes. Although it would be foolish to claim that Cartesian perspectivalism has been driven from the field, the extent to which it has been denaturalized and vigorously contested, in philosophy as well as in the visual arts, is truly remarkable. The rise of hermeneutics, the return of pragmatism, the profusion of linguistically orientated structuralist and poststructuralist modes of thought have all put the epistemological tradition derived largely from Descartes very much on the defensive. And, of course, the alternative of Baconian observation, which periodically resurfaces in variants of positivist thought, has been no less vulnerable to attack, although one might argue that the visual practice with which it had an elective affinity has shown remarkable resilience with the growing status of photography as a non-perspectival art form (or if you prefer, counter-art form). There are as well contemporary artists like the German Jewish, now Israeli painter Joshua Neustein, whose fascination with the flat materiality of maps has recently earned a comparison with Alpers's seventeenth-century Dutchmen (see Rogoff 1987).

Still, if one had to single out the scopic regime that has finally come into its own in our time, it would be the 'madness of vision' Buci-Glucksmann identifies with the baroque. Even photography, if Rosalind Krauss's recent work on the surrealists is any indication, can lend itself to purposes more in line with this visual impulse than the art of mere describing (Krauss 1985b; Krauss and Livingstone 1985). In the postmodern discourse that elevates the sublime to a position of superiority over the beautiful, it is surely the 'palimpsests of the unseeable', as Buci-Glucksmann calls baroque vision (1986: ch. 6), that seem most compelling. And if we add the current imperative to restore rhetoric to its rightful place and accept the irreducible linguistic moment in vision and the equally insistent visual moment in language, the timeliness of the baroque alternative once again seems obvious.

In fact, if I may conclude on a somewhat perverse note, the radical dethroning of Cartesian perspectivalism may have gone a bit too far. In our haste to denaturalize it and debunk its claims to represent vision *per se*, we may be tempted to forget that the other scopic regimes I have quickly sketched are themselves no more natural or closer to a 'true' vision. Glancing is not somehow innately superior to gazing; vision hostage to desire is not necessarily always better than casting a cold eye; a sight from the situated context of a body in the world may not always see things that are visible to a 'high-altitude' or 'God's eye' view. However we may regret the excesses of scientism, the Western scientific tradition may have only been made possible by Cartesian perspectivalism or its complement, the Baconian art of describing. There may well have been some link between the absence of such scopic regimes in Eastern cultures, especially the former, and their general lack of indigenous scientific revolutions. In our scramble to scrap the rationalization of sight as a pernicious reification of visual fluidity, we need to ask what the costs of too uncritical an embrace of its alternatives may be. In the case of the art of describing, we might see another reification at work, that which makes a fetish of the material surface instead of the three-dimensional depths. Lukács's critique of naturalist description in literature, unmentioned by Alpers, might be applied to painting as well. In that of baroque vision, we might wonder about the celebration of ocular madness, which may produce ecstacy in some, but bewilderment and confusion in others. As historians like Maravall have darkly warned, the phantasmagoria of baroque spectacle was easily used to manipulate those who were subjected to it. The current version of 'the culture industry', to use the term Maravall borrows from Horkheimer and Adorno in his account of the seventeenth century, does not seem very threatened by postmodernist visual experiments in 'la folie du voir'. In fact, the opposite may well be the case.

Rather than erect another hierarchy, it may therefore be more useful to acknowledge the plurality of scopic regimes now available to us. Rather than demonize one or another, it may be less dangerous to explore the implications, both positive and negative, of each. In so doing, we won't lose entirely the sense of unease that has so long haunted the visual culture of the West, but we may learn to see the virtues of differentiated ocular experiences. We may learn to wean ourselves from the fiction of a 'true' vision and revel instead in the possibilities opened up by the scopic regimes we have already invented and the ones, now so hard to envision, that are doubtless to come.

After the initial presentation of this paper,[7] I became increasingly aware of the more practical ways in which the three scopic regimes it discusses have been realized. In particular, an invitation to refashion it for a conference on the modern city at the Institute of Contemporary Arts in London led me to speculate on the possible correlations between each regime and different styles of urban life. Georg Simmel's contention that visual experience is paramount in the modern metropolis has been widely repeated, but precisely what that experience has been is often unduly homogenized. Applying the three scopic regimes to different urban visual cultures may provide a useful way to discriminate among the varieties that are often conflated into one version of 'the modern city'.[8]

Cartesian perspectivalism best corresponds to the model of the rationally planned city, whose origins go as far back as Rome. Here the ideal of a geometric, isotropic, rectilinear, abstract and uniform space meant the imposition of regular patterns, usually grids or radial concentric circles, on the more casual meanderings of earlier human settlements. The rationalization of urban space was generally suspended during the Middle Ages, but was revived during the Renaissance. Popes like Sixtus V (1585–90) sought to rebuild Rome along radial lines and recapture its earlier glory. During the reign of Louis XIV, the town of Richelieu, built as a double rectangle alongside the chateau of the cardinal, demonstrated the link between the mono-cular, perspectivalist subject and the power of the sovereign's gaze (Boudon 1978). Later palace-cities like Versailles, Karlsruhe, Mann-heim, even L'Enfant's Washington showed the fit between state power and urban space built according to the visual principles of the dominant scopic regime of the modern era.

During the Enlightenment, utopian architects like Jean-Jacques Lequeu, Étienne-Louis Bouillée and Claude-Nicolas Ledeux pro-duced even more grandiose plans for rigorously geometric cities in the service of Reason, plans that were never directly realized. Only in the nineteenth century with Baron Haussmann's Paris, the grids of American cities like New York and Philadelphia, and Ildefonso Cerdà's 'Extension' of Barcelona was urban space remade in Car-tesian perspectivalist terms. The twentieth-century dreams of Le Corbusier and other technologically inspired International Style architects represent perhaps the purest expressions of the dominant visual order of modernity. The much maligned Brasilia planned by Lucio Costa in the 1950s was the culmination of their project.

For those who do the maligning, an appealing alternative has often appeared in the urban space more closely approximating our second scopic regime, that associated with the Dutch art of describing. Delft, Haarlem and of course Amsterdam itself represent cities spared the imposition of geometricalized grids or intimidating monumental vistas. Perspectivalist effects are self-consciously absent, as streets and canals provide informal, curved views that defy a central vanishing point. The textures of building materials and the interplay of stone, brick and water create as much a haptic as purely visual experience; clear form is less important than atmosphere. As a result, such cities seem less like visual incarnations of the disciplining state bent on controlling its citizenry through surveillance and more like comfortable sites of an active civil society.

The celebrated interiors so often painted by Vermeer, De Hooch and other masters of the art of describing suggest an urban life spent with great gratification in the private space created by bourgeois prosperity. Dutch cities rarely contain the monumental squares or rectilinear boulevards that create the backdrop for a more public life, either political or cultural. And as Alpers notes (1983: 152), the views of their cities by Ruisdael, Cuyp and Vermeer reveal a close continuity between urban and rural life very different from the rupture between 'culture' and 'nature' evident in Cartesian perspectivalist urban space. Although rarely duplicated by design and destined to be surpassed by other urban models, such cities remain as reminders of highly attractive alternatives to the dominant scopic/urban regime.

A third possibility, of course, is the more frequently realized baroque city, which came into its own in the seventeenth century with such planners as Bernini in Rome. Abandoning the rectilinear perspectivalism of Pope Sixtus, he sought to subvert the rational neoclassicism of the Renaissance. As Germain Bazin has noted:

> spectacular surprise effects are the very essence of the baroque ... Baroque planning ... was addressed not to reason but to the senses. The baroque architect endeavoured to turn the meanest spaces to advantage by the fragmentation of planes, by the elasticity of curves. He had no desire to bring uniformity to the facades of different houses and buildings; these should charm the spectator by their variety. *(Bazin 1968: 311)*

Baroque cities had large public squares but, unlike their Cartesian perspectivalist counterparts, they were secret enclaves (like the Plaza Major in Madrid or the Piazza Navona in Rome) unconnected to the arteries of commercial traffic. Such spaces were often the theatrical arenas for everything from religious festivals to autos-da-fé.

More could obviously be said to flesh out the linkages between the scopic regimes of modernity and its urban styles. But as earlier, I want to conclude with a plea for the creative nurturing of all of them rather than the erection of a new hierarchy. In fact, each has tended to a certain extent to generate the others, at least as a minor accompaniment. Thus, for example, the geometricalized regularities of French classicism at the height of the *ancien régime* were sometimes softened by baroque effects. Haussmann's monumental boulevards with their houses of equal height and vistas culminating in monuments became the locus for that evanescent phantasmagoria of modern Parisian street life celebrated by Baudelaire and many since. Cerdà's grids were soon enlivened by brilliantly decorated *art nouveau* façades on the chamfered corners where his streets intersected.

Similarly, the Dutch cityscape has been interpreted as covertly baroque because of the individuality of the houses lining its canals (Bazin 1968: 312). And, of course, for all its giddy disorientation of the senses, the baroque itself could not do away entirely with the classical underpinnings of the buildings in which it placed its *trompe l'œil* interiors and on which it hung its extravagant façades. If postmodernism can be said to have resurrected the baroque impulses celebrated by Buci-Glucksmann, it too has retained the modernist shells of Cartesian perspectivalism. In short, just as there is no 'natural' vision prior to cultural mediation and therefore no intrinsically superior scopic regime, there is no one urban style which can satisfy by itself the human yearning for ocular stimulation and visual delight.

NOTES

1 For an account of the positive attitude towards vision in the medieval church, see Miles 1985. Contrary to the argument of Febvre and Mandrou, which has been very influential, she shows the extent to which sight was by no means widely demeaned in the Middle Ages.
2 Augustine discusses ocular desire in ch. 35 of the *Confessions*.
3 For a discussion of the gender implications of this work, see Alpers 1982: 187.
4 Heidegger's most extensive critique of Cartesian perspectivalism can be found in his essay 'The age of the world picture', in Heidegger 1977.
5 See also the systematic development of the contrast in Wölfflin 1932.
6 As Buci-Glucksmann recognizes, Leibnizian pluralism retains a faith in the harmonizing of perspectives that is absent from the more radically Nietzschean impulse in the Baroque. See Buci-Glucksmann 1986: 80, where she identifies that impulse with Gracián and Pascal.
7 It was first given at the Dia Art Foundation in New York in April 1988, and was published in Foster 1988.
8 Another potentially interesting application would be to varieties of landscape architecture, the interface between 'nature' and 'culture', which might get beyond the time-honoured dichotomies of the garden versus the wilderness, or the French and English gardens.

REFERENCES

Alpers, Svetlana 1982: 'Art history and its exclusions', in Norman Broude and Mary D. Garrard (eds), *Feminism and Art History*. New York: Harper & Row.
Alpers, Svetlana 1983: *The Art of Describing: Dutch Art in the Seventeenth Century*. Chicago: University of Chicago Press.
Bazin, Germain 1968: *The Baroque: Principles, Styles, Modes, Themes*. London: Thames & Hudson.
Berger, John 1972: *Ways of Seeing*. London: BBC.

Boudon, Philippe 1978: *Richelieu, ville nouvelle*. Paris: Dunod.

Bryson, Norman 1981: *Word and Image: French Painting of the Ancien Régime*. Cambridge: Cambridge University Press.

Bryson, Norman 1983: *Vision and Painting: The Logic of the Gaze*. New Haven, Conn.: Yale University Press.

Buci-Glucksmann, Christine 1984: *La Raison baroque: de Baudelaire à Benjamin*. Paris: Editions Galilée.

Buci-Glucksmann, Christine 1986: *La Folie du voir*. Paris: Editions Galilée.

Debord, Guy 1983: *The Society of the Spectacle*. Detroit: Wayne State University Press.

Edgerton, Samuel Y., Jr. 1975: *The Renaissance Rediscovery of Linear Perspective*. New York: Basic Books.

Eisenstein, Elizabeth 1979: *The Printing Press as an Agent of Change*. Cambridge: Cambridge University Press.

Febvre, Lucien 1982: *The Problem of Unbelief in the Sixteenth Century: The Religion of Rabelais*, tr. Beatrice Gottlieb. Cambridge, Mass.: Harvard University Press.

Foster, Hal 1988: *Visions and Visuality*. Seattle: Bay View Press.

Foucault, Michel 1979: *Discipline and Punish: The Birth of the Prison*, tr. Alan Sheridan. New York: Pantheon.

Galassi, Peter 1981: *Before Photography: Painting and the Invention of Photography*. New York: Museum of Modern Art.

Gasché, Rodolphe 1986: *The Tain of the Mirror: Derrida and the Philosophy of Reflection*. Cambridge, Mass.: Harvard University Press.

Heidegger, Martin 1977: 'The question concerning technology', in *The Question Concerning Technology and Other Essays*, tr. William Lovitt. New York: Harper & Row.

Ivins, William M., Jr. 1938: *On the Rationalization of Sight*. New York: Metropolitan Museum of Art.

Ivins, William N., Jr. 1946: *Art and Geometry: A Study in Space Intuitions*. Cambridge, Mass.: Harvard University Press.

Kofman, Sarah 1973: *Camera obscura: de l'idéologie*. Paris: Editions Galilée.

Krauss, Rosalind E. 1985a: *The Originality of the Avant-Garde and Other Modernist Myths*. Cambridge, Mass.: The MIT Press.

Krauss, Rosalind E. 1985b: 'The photographic conditions of surrealism', in Krauss 1985a.

Krauss, Rosalind E., and Livingstone, Jane 1986: *L'Amour Fou: Photography and Surrealism*. New York: Abbeville Press.

Krautheimer, Richard 1974: 'Brunelleschi and linear perspective', in I. Hyman (ed.), *Brunelleschi in Perspective*. Englewood Cliffs, NJ: Prentice-Hall.

Kubovy, Michael 1986: *The Psychology of Perspective and Renaissance Art*. Cambridge: Cambridge University Press.

Lowe, Donald M. 1982: *History of Bourgeois Perception*. Chicago: University of Chicago Press.

McLuhan, Marshall 1964: *Understanding Media: The Extensions of Man*. New York: McGraw-Hill.

Mandrou, Robert 1976: *Introduction to Modern France, 1500–1640*, tr. R. B. Hallmark. New York: Holmes & Meier.

Maravall, José Antonio 1986: *Culture of the Baroque: Analysis of a Historical Structure*, tr. Terry Cochrane. Minneapolis: University of Minnesota Press.

Metz, Christian 1982: *The Imaginary Signifier: Psychoanalysis and Cinema*, tr. Celia Britton et al. Bloomington, Ind.: Indiana University Press.

Miles, Margaret R. 1985: *Image as Insight: Visual Understanding in Western Christianity and Secular Culture*. Boston: Beacon Press.

Ong, Walter J. 1967: *The Presence of the Word*. New Haven, Conn.: Yale University Press.

Panofsky, Erwin 1924/5: 'Die Perspektive als "symbolische Form"', *Vorträge der Bibliothek Warburg*, 4, 258–331.

Rogoff, Irit 1987: 'Mapping out strategies of dislocation', in the catalogue for the Neustein show at the Exit art gallery, New York, 24 October–26 November.

Rorty, Richard 1979: *Philosophy and the Mirror of Nature*. Princeton: Princeton University Press.

Rose, Jacqueline 1986: *Sexuality in the Field of Vision*. London: Verso.

Scharf, Aaron 1986: *Art and Photography*. New York: Penguin.

White, John 1987: *The Birth and Rebirth of Pictorial Space*. 3rd edn. Cambridge, Mass.: Belkuap Press.

Wölfflin, Heinrich 1932: *Principles of Art History: The Problem of the Development of Style in Later Art*, tr. M. D. Hottinger. New York: G. Bell & Sons.

Wölfflin, Heinrich 1964: *Renaissance and Baroque*, tr. K. Simon. Ithaca, NY: Cornell University Press.

8

Identity and reality: the end of the philosophical immigration officer

Dieter Hoffmann-Axthelm

(Translated from German by James Polk)

The paradigmatic scene, perhaps, of the modern era, and today therefore embarrassingly archaic, is that of the immigration officer examining a passport. This is a scene which is both obvious and fathomless. Obvious is the enforced obligation of having an identity as this or that person: fathomless, and therefore insidious, is the method of proving that – which? – identity.

In the matter of being forced to prove one's identity, public and private interests form an alliance. The possibility of non-identity would as much pose a threat to public security as it would entail madness for the individual. Although no type of direct transition is permitted between both identity interests and identity concepts, an alliance of fear permeates them in such a manner that the assumed concept of identity as the agreement of public and private statements about one and the same person cannot be questioned.

However, this is in direct contradiction to the methods (which are breaking that agreement) used to verify identity. For the practical purposes of control technique, it is essentially a private matter whether or not the controlled person 'really' is himself or herself, that is exhibits the sameness of person that can be substantiated by the person's experienced and asserted reality. An individual might possibly display a complete and incurable dissociation of personality without that at all influencing the work of the immigration officer examining the passport. He checks the identity of an individual unknown to him – an identity that, being assigned to the individual and contingent upon the possession of an external object, represents a methodic humiliation of the subjective certainty of selfhood. Regardless of how accurately the text, photo, face type and number might circumscribe the individual being checked, with respect to the identity document itself, he remains something suspicious that must repeatedly be verified. The identity of the person is called more radically into question the more exact the certified verification becomes.

Proof of identity is based on previous forms which are thousands of years old and has drawn legitimacy from the gaps present in those previous forms. The passport ritual is a form of initiation that has since acquired permanence: the *rite de passage* of the transition from sociability to the principle of the state appeared late in history, and it is one which painfully lacks the oblivion of other transitions in early human history. For that reason, it must constantly be repeated and technically perfected to the point of self-contradiction. The task that must be accomplished is in itself contradictory: on the one hand to foster individual mobility;[1] on the other hand, to maintain personal identifiability while abandoning the pre-modern aspect of identification on the familial, local, and personal level.

Passport identity is based on two practices. The first of these practices is the archaic measure of name giving; the second is the distinctly modern element of numbering and picturing. The modern preventive measure of police identification has its legitimacy in that it is largely a transmogrified form of archaic name-giving. Arbitrariness in innovation is thus avoided. The state's suspension and restatement of the person displaces the phenomenon into the archaic realm from which it then receives the materiality necessary to make the identification practicable.

The archaic foundation of name-giving or nomination is an extreme designation of the self: 'Your name is Jack.' But the designation was accomplished at a time when the designated was not conscious of himself, and hearing it has the quality of a statement about self: 'My name is Jack.' The social fact that people distinguish themselves from one another by means of names is above the naive suspicion of arbitrariness. Perhaps I may hate my name; I might even become accustomed to other names which I prefer. But I cannot withstand the social coercion imposed on me by a name as such. And moreover, for what reason should I resist this necessity? After all, a name does not enchain. It provides a general basis for designations, but not an inescapable identity. Completely different people may have the same name, and mix-ups based on the confusion of names are not infrequent.

Name, as a linguistic point of fixation, is distinguished from the actual body-picture in its possible detachment from the latter. However, names do reflect the difficulties which they were designed to combat. Linking names with physical appearances is a decisively innovative step in which levels of possible exchange are conjoined to the person. Even if every individual in a given society were named 'Jack', the individual connection of the name with the physical appearance ('big Jack', 'little Jack') would guarantee their distinction. Returning to a state without names would not imply that we could more readily distinguish individual differences, but rather would entail a complete loss of discernibility. From a social point of view, the corporally present human being does not prove anything at all. The coupling of name and form, however, produces the first step of identity.

That names do get confused is a fact that is valid only on a higher historical level. As long as mobility was an exception – a fact characteristic of antiquity including slave trade – the problems associated with the absence and proof of identity were dealt with in terms of genealogy, friends and acquaintances made abroad, distinctive features such as the scar of Odysseus, banners or ensigns, or even a notable reputation. It was the millenary accomplishment of the Middle Ages that delivered a foretaste of the radical mistrust that was being brought into that world of trustworthy signs and symbols. Prior to combat, the mere listing of social status, of titles, number of serfs, and familial relations, was sufficient to distinguish the name from the corporeal appearance. In instances of martial encounter, the person appearing was often not even visible, but rather veiled in an attire of heraldry which itself symbolized the name – but only as an assertion. Although the archaic foundation was thereby repressed, the assertion did accomplish its aim: it proved the identity of individuals in an era which no longer trusted its eyes.

It was only after capitalism had destroyed the semantic web of stable vassal and familial relations and had begun to break apart all reliable personal ties that the process of naming unfolded the ambiguity of actual physical appearances and their designations. The name then became replaceable and was subsequently reduced to the mere material of a system of order which concealed the order of names. The abstraction of the modern state is also the destruction of all concrete and competing social ties. The state nationalized those social bonds it was not able to destroy: the church and the family. From the state's point of view, all were equals: as subjects. That can, of course, be read in the opposite direction. But we know that nothing is thereby changed. In fact, the abstraction, and therefore controllability, only become more marked. The method employed by the state is derived from modern logic and is its *fundamentum in re*: all those within the boundaries of the state are its subjects. What makes them identical is the fact of their birth as native or alien. From the certificate of baptism to their tax registration. The immigration officer is also the figure that makes possible the formulation of identity. His work of distinguishing native from alien passports, not persons, also identifies persons who are identifiable by virtue of their mere existence, even if such persons should never cross a national border in their lifetime.

The passport is that object which contains the identity; without it, one is not allowed a change of place. Passports assert the identity of the individual as subject, first of all by their very form which lifts all suspicion. This is then supported by the seal of the issuing authority and the signature of the issuing official. The name of the passport bearer is not more than a shadow to which subsequent additions are made by way of descriptions, fingerprints, and photos. But all of that is secondary, illustrative proof for the purpose of checking the identity asserted in the document. The assertion does not read 'This is Jack', but rather the state has posited an identity, the name of which is Jack, male, 5ft 9in, green eyes, distinguishing features: none.

The passport unites all previous levels of cognizance under the dominant assertion of the form: the pre-societal moment of the distinguishability of bodies and the genuinely social, orderly array of names. In this century, two elements have decisively contributed to a fateful aggravation of that tension: the passport-photo and numeration, both of which are contrivances of police accuracy that has become *scientific* and therefore which in all practicality is far superior to the predecessors that employed only fingerprints and signatures. It was through the emergence of the passport-photo that control was finally attained over the entire spectrum of physical identifiability. It is the documented particularity of natural history which is valid and not the social image. The neutral number, on the other hand, produces a type of uniqueness which was never achieved by names. In contrast to names that were subject to mix-ups, repetition, and forgetfulness, neutral numbers produce a particular type of uniqueness. Through the replacement of names by numbers and photos, the unity that was originally held together by the name, that is the physical distinctness and purely social title, is split apart.

Those who do not believe in cycles are likely to interpret that as a sign of a crisis. The externality attributed to political identity is carried to an extreme which no longer concerns individuals. State and subjective identity become distinctly different entities, while at the same time, international frontiers become increasingly insignificant as such.

The concept of identity thereby loses its propelling tension.

In contrast, the state as a system of control excludes the mixture of social elements that once carried its power. Computer-read identity cards are as transparent to the central police computer as they are indecipherable for the real human. The characteristics that are read into the computer and then adjusted have transcended the separation of language and photos; the key situation disintegrates.

On the other hand, those subject to control are interested in picture and name as external proof of *their selves* and develop their own use. At the time that passports came into institutional existence, names and appearances belonged in terms of the Lutheran doctrine of two worlds to the secular side and described particular persons who owed respect to the sovereign in the light of the innermost identity of the subject before God. That which was once the realm of Caesar is now the line of personal self-imagery without recourse to the inner limits of an abstract identity. This hints of a perception of self which, though uncertain, is beyond both police and metaphysical control.

II

Identity was one of the grand promises of the modern. In the name of identity, laws of the species were to be abolished; traditions and corporate chains cast aside. It was hoped that dominion of collective suppression and prevailing linguistic patterns would end and that identity would be based in one's own person and one's own responsibility. Identity was the paradise of a secularized promise – in a world in which, as far as justice and truth were concerned, one need not be torn apart, or identify with any rival power – but could remain true to oneself. In its exhaustive effort, civil society's ideal of the mediation between the destructive contradictions within the subject has, in our time, been sufficiently unmasked. The ideal is indispensable for both the state and for culture at large; it has become no less transparent with respect to its political and economic prerequisites. It could also be perilous, implying that being crushed between interest groups was voluntary. But the desire itself for identity is not thereby eliminated. In fact, having become useless, it reconstitutes itself as pure desire. Identity as the agreement between public value and private self-assertion must be completely re-thought in terms that are contrary to historical forms. What, then, has been disposed of historically?

The changes which we are dealing with here cannot be grasped via political economy, nor as a 'great narrative' (Lyotard 1979). The opening references to passport rituals do not describe a *metaphor* of power. Police procedure is not a metaphor; it stands as official state procedure. Moreover, it casts light on other assertions of identity. That state procedures can be described in metaphysical categories might be explained by the fact that metaphysics can develop via metaphors in the state securement of frontiers. In addition, there is the political and economic interpretation of the philosophy of identity which was one of the most profound insights of the Frankfurt School as early as the 1920s. But it offers little with respect to the relationship of identity to the modern. In contrast to the dynamics of the state, the movement of capital is not particularly conducive to the formation of identity; although it does create subjects of capital en masse, it immediately obliterates each stepping stone as it is actually attained. Therefore, the true concern cannot be about a one-sided decoding. State, economic, and private identities each fulfil in a particular way, within an interchanging network, the one project of the modern era.

For that reason, the concept of identity must be analysed into both the competing and the concurrent constituents of a society that is built on the hopes of individuals.

The individual's capacity for experience is one of those components and not just a passive, powerless one. And contrary to all preconceptions of the power elite, it is a component embodied with power. Although the component of individual experience could and can only assert itself within the existing framework of the social project, in the midst of the labour of enlightenment and modernization, it has delivered via the concept of 'identity' not only losses and our experience of misuse, but also gains. It is encoded both in the exercise of each identity project, and as a part in the critical programme of further-reaching identity formation. The negative constituent of that programme is tangible only as the difference between those images of hope which are propagated under the title 'identity of society', and the insipid states of modernization that emerge from such ideal efforts.

The mutual adhesion between the modernization of society and the subjective emancipation of the identity-project constitutes the one-way character and the blind, driving, insistent force of the relentless modern era. The foundation of the subject has always been the foundation of the state, while all motion to escape nationalization in favour of free subjectivity could only manifest itself in an alliance with capital and the acceleration of its utilization. But the alliance between subjectivity and capital was no less ambiguous. The utilization of anything and everything did indeed serve to slash the chains of the subjective search for identity, but it severed the roots of that subjectivity at the same time. Why be identical, if in the machinery of utilization everything was equal in its property as mere raw material? Help was promised again by the conservative retreat to law and order as an attempt to rescue nature, origin, land, customs, and ties – without which the concept of identity would be void of any object – from their dissolution in capitalism.

It offers little help to make the concept of identity *per se* more transparent, whether within the history of metaphysics (Heidegger) or within the framework of a critique of ideology (Adorno, Sohn-Rethel). As Sohn-Rethel convincingly pointed out, the concept of identity is a product of commodity exchange. That shows more clearly the insoluble schism of identity: only through non-identity can identity be conceived and presented. According to modern understanding, identity is indeed stated as a proposition (and as a proposition thereof). This has a twofold meaning: Identity is ascribed, attributed, and it is a proposition of external origin. Identity cannot be asserted as a matter of fact; nor can it be described as an assertion of being-within-itself of the identical. And it most certainly cannot be seen as such. The assertion 'A is A' is only possible as a peculiarly empty linguistic feat, namely as an imageless statement. This characterizes the philosophical construction of identity as an offspring of commodity exchange and is a correlate to the concept of value in political economy. The short circuit between the monetarism of the Ionian States in the sixth century BC on the one hand and the construction of transcendental subjectivity in Kant's *Critique of Pure Reason* in 1781 on the other, omits the intermediate stages of learning and vocabulary that were constitutive of the modern era's central problem of consciousness. What is not resolved in the process is the sensual residue, the linguistic character of the statement of identity. The social distance of language is not identical with the mode and means of exchange; nor does the statement at its highest level of abstraction, namely that of the form of exchange ('A is A') converge with the economic condition based therein. Likewise, the latter does not converge with underlying social conditions. Instead, it verbalizes another type of identity that can only be remembered, not seen or demonstrated. The loss which is thereby touched on is not the natural state of exchange trade, but the objectivity (*Gegenständlichkeit*) that, though repressed, is inherent therein.

The subjective identity-desire remains dependent on that objectivity, without being allowed to revert to it. As long as socially authenticated identity was visible and tangible, there was no room for individualization. Concrete identity was that of a god-like figure attained through the sacrifice of individuals. In contrast, the philosophic concept of identity in each historical era is an attempt to mediate between a visible societal identity in the face of which individuals are nothing, and a dispersed individuality that is free of coercion, clarity, entirety, i.e. void of the necessity of selfhood.

At its outset in the elaborations of Parmenides – and again (at the point of its practical conquest in favour of the organized mass murder of individuals) at the end of metaphysics, with Heidegger – philosophy has been synonymous with the inability to return to visibility, but rather to remember it fearfully as enciphered. Philosophy has been concerned to remember that visibility through an even greater fear of future annihilation. The visible selfness of being, as a sphere which Parmenides spoke of (abstracting from the naked, worthless appearance even in written form), brings to mind the content of what has been conquered and lost in the assertion 'A is A'. The mere linguistic character and its formalism are the price which must be paid for the fact that we speak of the individual, and that being can be spoken of in an individualized form.

The history of the identity-wish of historical individuals is inseparable from the defeat of that wish through its consumption by the state and capital. However, at least in the history of philosophy that wish does have its own historiography and history of production. An attempt should be made to understand its development in that way, regardless of its entwinement with the historical development of social institutions and capital. What the ego desires is different from the mere proposition 'A is A'; it desires the spherical, tranquil selfness which Parmenides attributed to being that is the same as thinking (or as Heidegger mistakenly translated but correctly construed: that lives within the same). Selfness, however, is not an attribute of the modern ego (seen from Parmenides' perspective: Being like God). The step towards individuation at the lowest level of individual differentiation was too violent to be able to retain the trait of unbroken selfhood within itself. Quite the opposite became possible: the linguistic assurance in algebraic form which in the very same moment that it attributes selfness, qualifies that selfness as broken. This is so empty of intuition that it does not even mention the name of the ego, nor the wealth of unbroken introspective intuition that constitutes the dream of identity, of undisturbed selfness.

The net cost inherent in the substantial change in the concept of identity, from the predication of deities in antiquity to the modern statement of subject, is revealed in the problem of individuation in the Middle Ages. How can individuality be statable at all? The philosophical background is well known and only needs to be touched upon. It is the problem of establishing the individuality of the individual as *species infima* – a dignity that in scholasticism was attributed not only to God (as in the writings of Thomas Aquinas), but also to angels. But in proceeding to the simple human individual, it was argued that within the debate over universals, being could not be attributed to the human individual as essence (which had constituted the characteristic visibility of angels), but only as an externally assigned name.

Selfness that is only possible as a statement is simultaneously a list of the losses representing just as many breaks in the philosophical construction of the subject. If everything depended on the pledge of identity that is externally ascribed to the subject, then this confirmation had to be defended at all costs, in particular since a more secure, less accidental form did not exist. But at the same time, each measure of security intensified the crack in ascribed identity itself. This served to make even more apparent the fact that the identity of the modern self had indeed become more secure, but that in spite of that security, it could not finally achieve selfness. In other words, it became clear what the arrival of the subject would in fact herald; that the modern subject would be no more than that identity-wish that had ventured out from the protective maternal womb of genus and species.

The primary break of selfness was one of a transition necessary for the acquirement of subjectivity. Identity is only indubitable if and when it is antecedent to everything else. The prerequisite of this would be to establish itself as permanence in contradistinction to everything in existence, and thereby to establish the character of the latter as alien. The more identical the subject is, the more foreign it is to the world. The philosopher in the role of the immigration officer had nothing else to do but try out the conditions of identity in this dialectic. Of utmost importance was the separation from the body. The body had been, from Aristotle to Aquinas, the principle of individuation. Now, it became, both in philosophy and social practice, the price for emancipation which concerned not only the breakthrough of technology-orientated thought, but also of sacrificial rites. When Leibniz attacked the Cartesian separation of subject from the body machine, through challenging the Cartesian negation of animal souls, it was already too late. Leibniz was only able to integrate the body into the subject by assuming a transitory state in which both body and subject were established as an identity from time immemorial, in which body/soul was a monad of the angel brought down into the empirical uniqueness of human individuals. (Leibniz's concept of the monad refers directly to Thomas Aquinas's definition of angels, cf. *Discours de métaphysique*, paragraph 9). A is A. This remarkably empty *principium identitatis* of established scholastic philosophy prescribed unconditionally the necessity of naming and became identical with that necessity. This only intensified the designative function, that is, it amplified the designation 'This is Socrates' into the modern statement of identity 'I am I'. Fichte, Schelling, and Hegel showed quite clearly that social action as the asserted synthesis of freedom and necessity is hidden in the copula, that is, in the verb 'to be'. But this pledge to the subject of self-identity has shown philosophy to be inextricably entangled in the conflict described above.

For the individual trying to save his own skin, identity ('you shall be as Gods') in the post-Hegel era could no longer be established on the basis of the subject, that is, on faith and philosophy. That had become too expensive. The romantic, aesthetically inclined literate members of society that did insist on it – Kierkegaard, Baudelaire, Nietzsche – relinquished the concept of normality within civil society. Others were able to submit to a state, capital, or class-based destiny, with identity based on subordination to various forces such as patriarchal violence, modern virtuosity at endless consumption, or revolutionary movements.

Therefore, the modern object of desire, identity, proved to be empty. I, the self-identical individual, can only be 'I' by renouncing relationships and memberships including the relation I have to myself. As Kant puts it in his *Critique of Pure Reason*, identity is indubitable only as a withdrawn, borderline concept of myself without which I could not reflect upon myself; by virtue of which, however, I can never belong to myself, or have a perception of myself ('Der Satz der Identität meiner selbst': Kant. *Kritik der reinen Vernunft*. B 408), in order to allow me to repose in myself or to enjoy intuitive perception.

To change these conditions is to dismiss the metaphysical immigration officer who passed judgement on identity. Only intangible identity of which I cannot dispose is capable of conceptualization; it is also the only type that nourishes concepts and encourages labour with them. If in empirical individuals the desire to possess oneself should overcome the commandment of not being evident to oneself, then a rupture in the modern as institution will become apparent. What has been pursued as identity in the modern era disintegrates into nothingness in the moment that it becomes manageable. Then a change in position occurs. The necessary condition of the intuition of objects becomes an object of intuition, not just one object among many, but an identity-object as well. At the same time, a multitude of identities are possible, existing side by side. They are comparable and exchangeable. My personal identity exists next to me as a status object which can be shown to myself and others, and can be changed, modified and reproduced.

This does not imply being at peace with oneself, being-in-oneself, or the selfness of the illusory but archaic memory of desire. In contrast to the encoded messages of the philosophy of identity, the gaps have become clearer to sociologists. Today's subject and identity films are symbolic acts; they stage images of reconciliation, of being-in-oneself. The fact that their production is possible, that selfness is made available and presentable and for the first time in the history of humanity is actually received 'below', at the end of a long history of downward transformations that began with Parmenides – that is the unprecedented historical novelty of the situation. But it owes its relevance to reality, to the rupture of the established condition. Such cinematic representations are made possible by the fact that they are relieved of the trial of changing reality. They are reduced to the intention of representations, to symbolizing fulfilment, not its actual production.

Through this symbolically mediated dramatization of desire, peace and remaining-in-oneself are unthinkable. The images are valid and convincing only in the instant they are produced; inevitably they instantaneously become outdated and lose their power of conviction and consolation. They develop power, but only the power of desire that has experienced the total emancipation of self. They are manifestable, but only at the price of being unconditionally utilizable by the media, the culture industry and factories for the production of aesthetics. One way or other, they are subject to the dictates of permanent reproduction under the penalty of becoming antiquated, banal, or of being deleted from the list of candidates of possible and legitimate desires. This implies labour to the point of exhausting the subject and its identity-desire in a form of time that is mercilessly flattening and forgetful.

III

On a societal level, the establishment of personal identity is never an end in itself, but a passing historical prerequisite for making forms of activity clear. Modern navigation taught us to establish our own position and thereafter to determine direction, instead of using the traditional means of orientation in space by the relation of the earth and stars. The goal was to arrive at a conceived destination. In the same way the modern individual was required to hold good as the focal point of all activities in practical life from which all the social techniques at his or her disposal could be instituted. With respect to actions, personal identity constituted a surrogate point of central reference which had been lost since the Copernican theory was propounded. That substitute centre of reference was modelled in the Copernican theory in which there was no central individual upon whom all other individuals would have been dependent for identification. Instead, the theory posited stages of systems in which every conceivable hierarchical position was related to laws that held the entire system together. That also meant that in the final analysis all individuals were equal. Identity was the formation of relative operational centres, each with a specific locality within the entire system. These centres were not capable of standing on their own, as the provisions for their instrumentation depended solely on the system as a whole.

We can observe this institution today, not only because we view it as a completed historical achievement, but also because we have been able to witness at first hand the establishment of a new type of social potential for action. Automatized intelligence, perception, and motor sensitivity in object form have become a part of our daily experience, from the personal computer to automated assembly lines. The instrumentation of the modern individual worker occurred as an adventure in self-discovery, as belief, *cogito*, the eye of empirical reality. In this inner-New World, as with the outer, discovery and colonization go hand in hand.

In retrospect it seems clear that the modernized individual in this social programming procedure was given not only new instruments to use, but also that realms of achievement and performance that were originally open to him have now been removed in order to confine him to his own realm and to prevent his intrusion into areas where he is not permitted to enter.

This loss of original capacities is due to the intermediate phase of modernity. At that stage, we were not able to transfer the desired goal-orientated rationality to machines; instead, that first had to be performed on oneself in order to produce those machines. The set objective was clear: to become univocal. The result was a one-dimensional world. Just as the subject-desire could not be separated from modernization, so too both the acquisition and the destruction of the world were inseparable from one another. Univocality is only possible with closed eyes. A blind subject corresponds to a blind world.

Ego-identity is the decline of independent perception. And the power of perception in this emphatic sense is nothing other than the physiological corollary of the philosophical identity of being – of selfness. The god-images of the internal world are also brought crashing down by the pervasion of controlled perception. Here again, the Middle Ages carried out almost a thousand years of preliminary work, just as it had done with the problem of individuation. In both instances, the duration of time describes the monstrosity of social achievement. If signs were considered more important than things in the Middle Ages – and they frequently proved to be devastating in the struggle against science – then that use of symbols is much nearer to modernity than is antiquity's faculty of description in its subject-less expressivity. The standpoint of an internal nature independent of perception first had to be solidified so that it would not be endangered by the return to reality. The return to the sensual world discovers ubiquitous forms of subjectivity and is synonymous with the end of the laborious studies of the Middle Ages and an initial step into the modern world. What human eyes perceived as they opened again was a world full of colourful objects that had always been encased in the subjectively intuitive realm of associations of perception.

The task was then at hand of working through the technicalities of separation, dissecting and re-grouping; piece by piece, the world was to be made to fit into the mechanics of modernization. The univocal view decomposed the concrete things of the world into raw material which would be exploited, split up into its components, and which revealed chemical properties that were utilized in manufacture.

For over 300 years, after having entered the modern world with its founding fathers, this view had to be generalized and taught to the lower classes of the population in order for the labour-power of the Industrial Revolution to come into existence. It is noteworthy how each of these three centuries developed its own characteristic theme for that very purpose, each with its own theoretical and social spectrum. Each stage developed an unmistakable didacticism of non-perceptive vision, as pure functionality of the senses under the command of efficiency-orientated concepts: the topic of reading and writing in the sixteenth, the order of spatial perception in the seventeenth and that of lexical designations in the eighteenth century.

The school of reading and writing was the Reformation, and the translation of the Bible into the vernacular was appropriately called the Scriptures. In written form, the doctrine of salvation was easily accessible to everyone. The eyes of worshippers could finally be drawn away from the transubstantiations at the altar in order to read what was said and written. This brought about a twofold change.

One of these changes can be described as individualized perception. Each individual, because he could read, was not only able to be witness, he was also responsible. The faith depended on the individual capacity to hear or to read the true word. In this, reading, listening and writing were the school of the instrumental rationalization of the senses. This then was the second transformation: Whereas medieval science had sacrificed the visible, there was now liberty to look at all things. But only as a function of conceptual knowledge, of written theory and for the sake of organizing the world.

Numerous interrelated aspects demonstrate how the Reformation utilized the preliminary training of perception that occurred during the Middle Ages. The novelty of this, however, was the generalization which encompassed all of society and, correspondingly, the emergence of didacticism as the appropriate compendium of study in the modern school. The latter offered, when compared with similar institutions of antiquity or the Middle Ages, something completely novel and different. It was only on the basis of the achievements of the sixteenth century that the seventeenth century was able to devote its attention to the topic of vision and to establish a newly derived type of sensuality that was dependent on script and legibility. It was for that reason that the visual excess of the baroque coincided with the unchallenged leading role and profound importance of music that was unsurpassed prior to or after the era. Seeing and hearing were both reconceived in a scriptural mode which characterized both the access to their realization and the experience of them. Identity was by now displayed as sensual and, as a true hero and subject, presented by means of an arrangement of the delights of art and sound in a didactically moulded social context. In music, that was achieved by the basso continuo; in architecture by geometric urban design. In both instances, the extreme univocality of each single form coincided with totally unconstrained use.

Music and architecture were contemporaries of the baroque theatre. They too, were a theatre of fixed, average identities that could not be moulded into empirically perceivable individuals without prematurely interrupting the festival of sensuality. The eighteenth century then reacted critically to the anticipated relapse. Verbalization and visual perception characterized by modern spatiality were the prerequisites for the next phase: that of the object-identity of knowledge. Objects were no longer alliances of script and images, but evolved in the eyes of the person describing them. Didacticism – as represented in Diderot's *Encyclopedia* and in Salzmann's *Schnopfentaler Musterschule* – aimed at the unconditional empirical identification, classification, analysis and composition of a number of existing objects, with no tolerance of unsolved ponderosity. The grip on observation and classification was to function automatically and constituted the immediacy of each subject to each and everything in the context of global production. Script and phenomenal space disappeared as objects of fetishism and were replaced by the cold sameness of the utilizable object.

The attained aim of perception was to see what is; that was the goal that was to be envisaged as success in the Industrial Revolution. Here, where the sphere of adventure in nature and aesthetic experience was neatly separated from the objectives of trade and commerce, all the senses could evolve and develop without endangering the output of production. A division of this kind would not have been possible in the seventeenth century. The school of identity had by now finally arrived at its destination where vision inasmuch as it was concerned with culture, was no longer separable from work performance. This type of vision entailed all that had been of interest to society in the process of the subject's identity development, and not the Cartesian ego or the romantic artist. It was the machine-side of the world that was at issue. This could only be unleashed by a police-trained ego whose heart of stone reified all living relations in terms of technical usefulness.

From the perspective of the history of the subject, the modern ego was not able to become identical without devaluing the perceptual world. The functional view of the world underbids the actual performance of perception in its expectation of objects by dissecting them into molecules, performance ratings and production costs. What is not completely absorbed must be set in a segregated series of events – as experiences of beauty, nature and things. We are indebted to the music, lyric poetry and visual art of civil society for the laceration of reality into the forms of technical access and cultural experience. Without the capacity of the subject to experience the pain of this laceration (that is, to thematize the loss of perceivable reality in the realm of aesthetics and to designate that loss appropriately), beauty in such a society would no longer exist.

IV

Even if we perceive that exchange as a fair one, we have nothing more to gain. Pain has become outdated and has ceased to replace its loss with symphonies and poetry. Experienced historical narrowness

– even of bourgeois beauty – just describes once more the extent of modernity. In its final days, even the split of the subject in terms of functional and aesthetic behaviour becomes fully transparent. Both forms were subordinated under the same propelling force of identity that moved down and consumed everything at hand: the force of labour. After consuming its material on all levels, work-identity emerges in its excessive character. We have arrived at the end of the modern era. The instrumental rationality of the modern subject has moulted into automatons who can be observed at work – work that is so perfectly confined to the limits of instrumental rationality that the ludicrousness of the entire project is obvious.

Freed from labour-encrusted identity and perception, we again desire our own perception of reality itself even if it is only possible to express that desire by means of photographs, films and poetry. Simultaneously, we demand the inheritance of civil identity as something that has been paid for and for which there is no earthly reason to relinquish anything at all. The only question is *how*.

Perception now has become communicative. After a long ordeal it has been freed to attain identity but is incapable of constructing objects. Unlike identity-achievement in civil society, perception has not been made obsolete. It moves in a sovereign manner, both at work and in leisure. Perception's postindustrial achievement is its ability to abbreviate – a capacity acquired during the historical process of perception's own destruction. It is no longer necessary for the whole hierarchy of steps in a decision-making process to be carried out. The controlled grasp that perception has unexpectedly acquired, allows hierarchies of decisions to go on in a subordinate register somewhere else. It then comprehends these hierarchies (including the historical labour of the self-identical ego) almost simultaneously as a unit under a higher-ranked sign, and thereby anticipates them equally well as decisions. The decisive control is found at the level of higher signs (whereby it is assumed that the implied binary details are either present or can be appended).

Historically, perception is a conceptual counterpart to reason's logic of identity. In the German tradition, the concept of perception is indebted to Leibniz's opposition to radical Cartesianism. Early science was not able to acknowledge perception as a distinct continent of research. Civil society saw sensual activity only in its role as servant to the understanding, and believed it was escaping the confines of method by discovering ways in which perception might be deceived. To conceive perception as independent and autonomous assumes the devaluation of modernity's and of civil society's paradigm. Free discourse on this has only really become possible today, but it too needs the relevant historical context. Perception today is an interrelated thought process describing the losses that have occurred in history. The reacquisition of those losses requires a realm void of constraint – a realm that may concede the invalidity of modern identity.

Perception today is the form taken by the movement of subjectivity that has emigrated from the coercive confines of the identity-project without relinquishing the desire for identity as such. This movement permits neither the centrality of the identical subject, nor the diffusion characteristic of mere structures. At this level of now diluted signifying practices, the primary issue is still the mediation between demands that are essentially monopolistic in nature. One could describe this subject of perception that has escaped its historical armour-plating as an *identity subject*. Its most prized virtues (mobility, fluency in decision-making, virtuosity in organizing vast amounts of data etc.) are the immediate results of subjectivity in civil society. Sociologically, this corresponds to the new fascination we witness with managers, entrepreneurs and small independent manufacturers, or in general terms, with intelligent, economic independence as a basis of cultural and political expression.

The use of perception in economic life which supports the new subject-ideal is itself ambivalent. On the one hand it signifies one further step on the wrong path of social utilization of perception, but a step which does imply a historical turning point. The character of perception that was oppressed at all costs during the five centuries of the modern era in order to further the identity-project, is now being socially utilised, namely the gaze. The use of the gaze at the level of historically interdicted and dissipated perception is an expression of its superiority over logical operations in their unwieldy and slow-moving nature.

Operationality, by means of images, and the speed of immediate access are being utilized. In other words, the archaic layer of the perceptive faculty is being used at this new level. Not only is this retrospective review validated by the fact that perception does achieve this; descriptions of the faculty of perception as a substantial historical counterpart to identity formation are equally validated by the fact.

Perception is *un*-identical: an openness to an increasing number of scenes, strata and forces. Perception sees phantasms: without this ability, it would not be able to fulfil its obligation of relying on and expecting objectivity. Perception defies domestication and does not become univocal. What was factually possible and socially enforced was the reduction of perception to a meagre role as assistant in the labour process which transformed components of reality into controllable raw material. When this pressure is diminished, structure-orientated capacities, that is, faculties based on the objectivity of signs, are liberated. A dominant or super-sign is nothing more than the paradox of a sign that has been compressed into its opposite, namely a thing or object, at the level of signifying processes.

Because it is more useful than the fiction of a world that should be subjected to methodical order, the new leading function of perception encompasses its twin concept: reality. Until now, reality has been only a critical concept that stood for the limitations of the identity-project. By trusting in the finite extent to which the jungle known as 'the world' could not be cleared, it also represented the possibility of escaping. Kierkegaard used his apotropaic concept of reality to oppose Hegel's affirmation of reason as proof of infinite non-identity. Reality means that critical non-availability of the world that is disclosed in the ambiguity of perception. In traditional philosophy the concept was always somewhat dishevelled, not quite tangible or comprehensible, that is, non-identifiable. It signified that which could be annihilated by mathematics, but not taken alive. Like perception, the reality *contra* identity model was servant to many gods; it also had many doors, heavens and abysses. Now, the concept of reality, too, is changing its role and threatens to occupy a leading position. Reality that is not measurable, that is operationally tangible only in individual projects and that is inaccessible to a will united towards change has become a primary paradigm in our understanding of science. From there it directs our attention towards an increasing number of catastrophes based on safety precautions, technological and global economic practice.

In that respect, remaining critical and alert demands a twofold movement: On the one hand, the continued retreat from the identity-project into a safety zone must be promoted and encouraged. In political reality, that would mean the termination of bombastic technical adventures, from nuclear energy projects and weapons to gene technology. This positive development in perception does not signify defeat for its use in information society. On the other hand, it would mean questioning the genealogy first of identity (because the defeat of the identity-project is not the victory of intact subjectivity); and secondly, that of the political subject of the Enlightenment in toto, that is, of the historical spectre of the left. Now is the time, therefore, to intercept the subjective hopes and desires that were invested in the identity-project. No type of 'either – or' is of any further benefit here, but instead the coexistence of both historically driven figures. If perception can be constituted as a space of social resistance, then this is only possible in conjunction with the historically shattered identity-wish.

At issue here is the social use of perception. And the two projects of the divided subject have been integrated in this result: the projects of desire for identity and of perception. Historical results of this type can easily be turned against those integrated subjective desires and declared to be settled without anyone's readiness to listen to complaints about being exploited or being made redundant after use. This is due to the fact that we become a part of all that we strive for. The survival of socially critical subjectivity depends on the ability to disinvest energy from these outcomes and to reinvest it in opposition to the new configuration and its promises/threats of an 'end to history' and ban on movement (*Bewegungsverbot*). In the model of perception already sketched, a role-change is called for between identity and reality, and between the achieved subject and perception. This reversal of roles can be radicalized and can serve as an impetus. The contradictory social mandate of the identity-project was to unite mobility with univocality, and thereby to render the self transportable and reproducible. That is exactly what has been attained in the fundamental character of perception that is abstracted from its object. The motto here is to open up and listen to the beat of one's own drum, or at least to make it independent. That implies a counterpoint: identity with the ability to perceive. An entity of that type is unknown to history thus far. From Kant to Robespierre, the identity of enlightenment was one robbed of the faculty of perception. But identity now has, after defeat, lost its obsessive character. Identity now can develop – *not* as a continuation of the existing but unsuccessful lineage of enlightenment, but on the basis of the new level of perception. Ego itself must be recast in the subversion inherent in perception. The point of departure is where the space of perception comes face to face with social facts. Danger awaits there, and innovation is necessary to avoid defeat in the modernity of appearances.

V

If we compare the two sets of consequences that have been sketched here – of identity and of perception – then a possibility emerges: distance. This consists in the self-intuition of the subject which has become reality under the prerequisite that it relinquish reality. One can have and perceive oneself in the signs of subjectivity that are offered, but under a twofold restriction: First, self-possession and self-perception can only be attained outside the social production process on the level of signs. And these are continuously subject to decay, emptiness and the necessity of replacement. But it is also possible from another perspective in which the vision of the subject is maintained by distorting the reality of things. The reversal of perception here is still wanting, as is the reflexive reference to reality made accessible by the production process. Second, the outcome is also the activity of perception that has become dominant and, in a reversed role, an instrument of labour. The price has been its indispensable relation to concrete objects. It now becomes instead ingrained in the social context of a powerless, semantical reality of accelerated accomplishments in abstraction from historical objectivity. Identity and reality, the logic of identity, and perception, have ceased to be antithetical, because in its social use, perception, too, has lost its foundation. The faculty of perception in its entire spectrum is liberated – but void of body-weight, stability, security and contentment.

The exchange is surprising and beautifully symmetrical. There is reason to believe that the modern split in individuality is approaching its zenith, and therefore its point of no return. This corresponds with the scenario of gender conflict if we (admittedly in a somewhat unrefined manner) replace self with masculinity and reality with femininity. For quite some time, we have been moving in circles in which the classic lines of concept demarcation are no longer valid. The immemorial demands of identity (which once secured the outcome of the effect) are thawing out and revealing the entire family history. The concept itself shows that it has been released from the realm of philosophy (as philosophy has been released from the history of identity, and made altogether homeless). Today, psychology has become the competent authority in questions of identity. The desire for identity reads: I want to be identical, that is, distinguishable and publicly recognized as me, and to accomplish something here, and by means of this object. When it is expressed in this manner we cannot fail to recognise the infantile character of the mission. That it is meant for a boy is of course taken for granted. Female identity always entered into the work relations making masculine identity possible. In other words, to be real was to be so through a man, and even more so through children. A comparable expression of this would be in terms of the remnant desire for self: I (because and as long as I am pretty) (at least) want to be seen.

As far as individuality of leisure-time is concerned, we are in the very midst of exchange negotiations. What was once historically separated is now in a state of mutual permeation whereby both sides have been abolished in favour of a new unity of both: the egoism of self-realization in which identity and reality collapse. Each individual creates for himself as much reality as he can stand until he suffers a heart attack or a nervous breakdown in old age.

This corresponds to the functional, *productive* side of socially usable and socially produced perceptual intelligence. The latter, by means of a new, hitherto repressed feminine faculty of perception and reality, has been made faster and more aggressive than the prevailing masculine strategy of identity itself. In particular, the convergence of these opposites has determined the time-signal common to both lines of development, separated by only the short-circuited architecture of society.

The whole of this essay has held the playground of subject-desires to be the issue: desires for intuitive selfness, for residing in the world without being disavowed as an individual – the perceptive being-perceived. Suggestions are of little value – neither those in favour of acceleration, nor those that plead for slowing down (an option particularly popular these days). In relation to the status quo, both are necessary in order to avoid being crushed by the glacial masses of social reality. But both are only a means and, as therapeutic training, quite obviously a method. The quintessence of experienced disappointments is the fact that the survival mission can only be described privately – even if it concerns the earth in its entirety. But the latter, too, is only statable in private terms and depends, therefore, on the biographical thread that links me with the historically improbable green colour of a meadow which I know to be the product of market decrees within the European Community.

No longer extant is the classical figure of the immigration officer of real existing states who could protect individuals from their own rude particularity. Even where the wall of the essentially identifying state functioned up to now, namely in Eastern bloc nations, an east wind has thawed out icy formations and forced people to express identity in terms of the lowest common denominator – that of their own living realm. It will demand strength, love and patience to uphold that realm as the decisive one. In a world falling apart, it is the only way of being identical, or of being self, or of participating in the self-constitution of society.

NOTE

1 The invention of controlled frontiers was a matter of the opening up of closed societies instead of – as it is today – the closing of open societies.

REFERENCES

Heidegger, M. 1957: *Identität und Differenz*. Pfullingen: Neske.

Heinrich, K. 1964: *Versuch über die Schwierigkeit nein zu sagen*. Frankfurt a.M.: Suhrkamp.

Hoffmann-Axthelm, D. 1984: *Sinnesarbeit. Nachdenken über Wahrnehmung*. Frankfurt a.M.: Campus.

Lyotard, J.-F. 1979: *La Condition postmoderne*; 1984 (Eng. tr. G. Bennington and B. Massumi), Minneapolis: University of Minnesota Press, as *The Postmodern Condition: A Report on Knowledge* (UK edn Manchester: Manchester University Press, 1986).

Sohn-Rethel, A. 1970: *Geistige und körperliche Arbeit: Zur Theorie der gesellschaftlichen Synthesis*. Frankfurt a.M.: Suhrkamp.

Part III

Spaces of self and society

9

Postmodern urban landscapes: mapping culture and power

Sharon Zukin

The conjuncture of social, cultural, and spatial changes that has so excited those who write about cities in recent years is loosely gathered in the term 'postmodern urban landscape'. While no clear understanding separates modern from postmodern cities, we sense a difference in how we organize what we see: how the visual consumption of space and time is both speeded up and abstracted from the logic of industrial production, forcing a dissolution of traditional spatial identities and their reconstitution along new lines. Postmodernity in general exists as both a social process of dissolution and redifferentiation and a cultural metaphor of this experience. Consequently, the social process of constructing a postmodern landscape depends on an economic fragmentation of older urban solidarities and a reintegration that is heavily shaded by new modes of cultural appropriation. The genius of property investors, in this context, is to invert the narrative of the modern city into a fictive nexus, an image that a wide swathe of the population can buy, a dreamscape of visual consumption.

Elements of this vision shape the common vocabulary of cultural criticism, radical geography, and urban political economy. Thus Fredric Jameson and Ed Soja are captivated by the dominance of space over time in postmodernity, Phil Cooke ties urban and regional reorganization to the global economic restructuring associated with 'post-Fordism', and David Harvey emphasizes, under the rubric of 'flexible accumulation' and the influence of Debord and Baudrillard, how cultural appropriation has become a strategy of enhancing economic value. Pressed for examples they all point to the same illustrations. They understand a postmodern urban landscape, on the one hand, in terms of tall, sleek towers that turn away from the street (Jameson's 'hyperspace'), using their technical virtuosity to enclose a milling crowd of office workers, tourists, and consumers in a panorama of the bazaar of urban life. Aside from the notorious Bonaventure Hotel in Los Angeles and Detroit's Renaissance Center, such projects include the Broadgate office complex at London's Liverpool Street Station and, to some extent, the entire new construction of Docklands. But on the other hand, a postmodern urban landscape also refers to the restoration and redevelopment of older locales, their abstraction from a logic of mercantile or industrial capitalism, and their renewal as up-to-date consumption spaces behind the red-brick or cast-iron façade of the past. These places include Faneuil Hall and Fan Pier in Boston, Baltimore's Inner Harbor, South Street Seaport in New York City, London's Covent Garden, and Prince's Street in Glasgow (Jameson 1984; Soja 1989; Scott and Cooke 1988; Harvey 1989).

Space both initiates and imitates this ambiguity. The specific locales of the modern city are transformed into postmodern *liminal spaces*, both slipping and mediating between nature and artifice, public use and private value, global market and local place. Liminality here begins with Victor Turner's concept, as Jean-Christophe Agnew has turned it around from the original anthropological meaning of the transition of certain groups, notably age groups, from one social status to another, toward a new social and cultural meaning of transitional space.[1] Naming a liminal space, however, does not simplify the phenomenon. Mixing functions and histories, a liminal space situates users 'betwixt and between' institutions. Learned behaviour is always in question when liminality crosses profit-making with non-profit places, home with work space, (residential) neighbourhood with (commercial) centre. Liminal space may also stir an ontological confusion, as E. L. Doctorow describes it (1971), between individual introspection and the products of commercialized collective fantasy.

Liminality complicates the effort to construct a spatial identity. The very features that make liminal spaces so attractive, so competitive, in a market economy also represent the erosion of local distinctiveness. The sources of this erosion lie in three broad processes of change that run through the entire twentieth century: the increasing globalization of investment and production, the continuing abstraction of cultural value from material work, and the shift in derivation of social meaning from production to consumption. Yet liminal spaces situate these general changes in our life experience, shaping the expressiveness of daily routines and extending the limits of perspective. Thus a postmodern urban landscape not only maps culture and power; it also maps the opposition between *markets* – the economic forces that detach people from established social institutions – and *place* – the spatial forms that anchor them to the social world, providing the basis of a stable identity (see Zukin 1991).

The mapping process is important for understanding the current transformation of landscape, arguably the major example of cultural appropriation in our time. Far from a mere cognitive reorganization, as Jameson's docile reading of urban planner Kevin Lynch would have it, mapping the landscape is a *structural* process that resonates with both the built environment and collective representations of it. It demands a more dynamic reading of spatial structures than Pierre Bourdieu's habitus, an inscription of capital in spatial forms that none the less acknowledges the diminished influence of the logic of production. This requires a model that transcends the individual, an ensemble of spatial forms and cultural practices.

Postmodernity suggests, in fact, two contrasting archetypal urban landscapes. For older cities like New York, London, and Paris the transformations of postmodernity are modelled on gentrification. For newer cities, however, and mainly ex-urban development projects, especially those outside 'postmodern cities' like Los Angeles and Miami, postmodern landscape takes the form of Walt Disney's World in Florida (hereafter Disney World). These are certainly not representative of *all* spatial transformations. Nor do they equally affect the more affluent and less affluent parts of the population, all regions of a national economy, or all 'developed' countries of the world. But the ensemble of motifs they represent, their visible importance in a common, consumption-orientated global culture, and the sheer creative destruction of landscape they inspire under private (that is, market) auspices, make gentrification and Disney World the essential postmodern mappings of culture and power.

LANDSCAPE AS CULTURAL APPROPRIATION

Landscape is the key concept to grasp in spatial transformation. From the academic notion related to genre painting, landscape has broadened in meaning to include an appreciation of material culture, 'text', and social process (Rowntree 1986). It is also used to refer metaphorically to non-visual phenomena, for example, an institutional field ('the financial landscape'), a cognitive construct ('the landscape of modern poetry', 'abstraction as landscape') or, more broadly, an existing social order ('the historical landscape'). While landscape's new uses reflect, in part, a widespread awareness of the importance of spatiality (as in 'the landscape of the city'), they also respond to an effort to retrieve spatiality from the domain of geography and analyse it historically, making space the co-equal of time. Space is now considered a dynamic medium that both exerts an influence on history and is shaped by human action. As the confluence of individual biography and structural change, space is potentially an agent that structures society (Soja 1989; Gregory and Urry 1985).

From a structural as well as a historical view, however, landscape is clearly a spatial order that is imposed on the built or natural environment. Thus landscape is always socially constructed: it is built around dominant social institutions (the church, the major landowner, the factory, the corporate franchise), and ordered by their power. The doyen of landscape geographers, J. B. Jackson, contrasts this vision of majestic or stately order with the more humble, 'self-built' creations of local society that ordinary people develop over time. Though the political landscape and the inhabited landscape – as Jackson calls them – always develop side by side, the creators of the political landscape enjoy greater power. Their resources provide the stability that the inhabited landscape requires. In slightly different terms Jackson writes (1984): 'What gives the vernacular way of life its vitality and persistence is its ability to adjust to circumstances, to external factors beyond its control, *provided that somewhere in the environment there is some institution with permanence and long-range purpose.*'[2] Landscape thus gives material form to an asymmetry of economic and cultural power.

This asymmetry of power shapes the dual meaning of landscape. Even in Jackson's terms, landscape refers to both the special imprint of dominant institutions on the natural topography and social terrain, and the entire ensemble of the built, managed, or otherwise rearranged environment. While in the first sense the landscape of the powerful clearly opposes the imprint of the *powerless* – that is, the cultural construction we choose to call *vernacular* – landscape in the second sense combines these antithetical impulses in a single, broadly coherent view.

In the art-historical sense, landscape suggests asymmetrical power in terms of the ability to impose a view. Landscape painting traditionally refers to both a piece of countryside and the perspective from which it is viewed. But the act of taking a perspective has consequences for both cognitive perception and material appropriation. Innovations in charts and maps underlay the rise of Europe's great trading powers in the fifteenth and sixteenth centuries. And by the middle of the eighteenth century, landscape painting had become so successful that in Northern Europe rural scenery began to be viewed as if it were in a picture. Whether it was the seigneurial countryside of the English enclosures and corresponding village 'improvement' or the flatter landscape of the Netherlands that was less differentiated by social class, landscape was increasingly seen as mediated by means of form. The material landscape was mediated by a process of cultural appropriation, and the history of its creation was subsumed by visual consumption (see Barrell 1972; Alpers 1983: ch. 4; cf. Harvey 1989).

From the point of view of 'point of view', as well as resources, the upper class enjoy asymmetrical power in the landscape. Because the aristocracy and gentry were geographically mobile, even over small distances, they expanded their repertoire of landscapes for visual consumption.

> Their mobility ... meant that the aristocracy and gentry were not, unlike the majority of the rural population, irrevocably involved, so to speak, bound up in, any particular locality which they had no time, no money, and no reason ever to leave. It meant also that they had experience of more landscapes than one, in more geographical regions than one; and even if they did not travel much, they were accustomed, by their culture, to the *notion* of mobility, and could easily imagine other landscapes. (*Barrell 1972: 63*)

Similarly, 'capital flight' today ties change in the material landscape to the capacity to impose multiple perspectives from which this landscape can be viewed. While mobile capital can subject an otherwise stable landscape to disruption by 'market forces', the daily activities and social rituals that constitute the vernacular are ineluctably tied to 'place'. Thus capitalist interests play an essential role as agents in the dialectic between market and place. By implication, moreover, their revision of landscape instigates change in the vernacular.

Asymmetrical power in the visual sense suggests capitalists' great ability to draw from a potential repertoire of images, to develop a succession of real and symbolic landscapes that define every historical period, including postmodernity. This reverses Jameson's dictum that architecture is important to postmodernity because it is the symbol of capitalism. Rather, architecture is important because it is the capital of symbolism.

Older modern cities (built 1750–1900) and newer modern cities (built 1900–50) suggest two contrasting urban landscapes that paradigmatically express how the landscape of the powerful coexists with the vernacular of the powerless.

In older modern cities like New York, Chicago, London, or Paris, the political (and financial) landscape concentrated power in the centre; this power was viewed as the skyline – the landscape of the modern city itself. The vernacular meanwhile occupied wide swathes of the historical inner city, its tenements, manufacturing lofts, and publicly subsidized council flats nibbling at the knees of the high-rise buildings of dominant institutions. The changing economic value of urban land relative to other investments provides the context in which this material landscape was constructed over time. Yet the legitimation of using space for specific social groups was often derived from cultural patterns of historical occupancy or social entitlement.[3] From 1900 to the end of the 1960s, the 'modern' city seemed an unchanging tapestry that juxtaposed landscape and vernacular: the Gold Coast cheek by jowl with the Slum, the patrician hill next to the ghetto.[4]

Newer modern cities, on the other hand, lacked the spatial concentration that equated power with centrality. In Los Angeles, Miami, and Houston, the entire city was until quite recently decentralized on a 'suburban' model. Dominant institutions were dispersed throughout a large geographical area; those at the centre were relatively modest in architectural form, morphologically isolated, failing to produce the symbolic landscape, that is the skyline, which elsewhere identified modern urban form. Instead, the landscape of dominant institutions was diffused in the vernacular. Both landscape and vernacular were represented in freeways, shopping malls, and single-family houses, the whole a low-rise ensemble of auto-mobility (see Banham 1971; Bottles 1987; Feagin 1988).

Not until the return of private-sector capital investment to the city centre were these two paradigms altered. From the 1960s, a sizeable number of upper-middle-class people in New York and London moved into lower-class residential areas and manufacturing districts; they were attracted both by centrality and the aspirations to cultural power that centrality represents. From the 1970s, for somewhat different reasons, new capital, mainly from Latin America and the Pacific Rim, flowed into the centres of Los Angeles and Miami. At the lower end, this transnational migration of capital and labour was attracted to entrepreneurial opportunities that centrality offered in a number of related, low-technology industries. At the high end, however, it was drawn to opportunities for deal-making in global financial markets: on the one hand, banks, real estate, and financial services, and on the other, drugs, contraband weapons, and laundering cash (see Mohl 1983; Lernoux 1984; Didion 1987; Rieff 1987).

By the early 1980s, the urban landscape had expanded beyond the incremental house-buying of gentrification to massive projects of new construction; the 'urban pioneers' of New York and London were replaced, with governmental approval, by 'yuppies'. By the same token, the ex-urban growth poles outsides Los Angeles, San Francisco, and Miami continued to expand into denser concentrations of private housing, 'clean' industry, and financial offices. The generally diffuse realms of Orlando (Florida) and Orange County (California) appropriated the central forms of cultural power that modern cities used to monopolize; they built concert halls and civic centres beside the pedestrian malls.[5]

Postmodernity refers to the new reversal of socio-spatial identities between landscape and vernacular that these changes imply. With gentrification and new construction in the older city centres, the remaining vernacular, especially dilapidated, single-family housing, is re-viewed as landscape and invested with cultural power. But with simultaneous recentralization and continued decentralization in Los Angeles, Miami, Orlando, and Orange County, the vernacular, especially fairly comfortable low-rise housing, is incorporated into the landscape and projected back as an image invested with cultural power.

The predominance of image in the latter landscape accounts for the tendency to identify cities like Los Angeles and Miami – rather than New York and London – with postmodern urban forms. To some extent, this focus is justified by the timing of their development, from 1920 to 1970. Since the economic restructuring that began around 1973, however, the reversal of meaning in landscape and vernacular has created an experience of postmodernity in nearly all modern cities. In the material sense, this process articulates with a recentralization of global investment in major cities and capital accumulation in service-dominated economies. In the symbolic sense, however, it depends on capitalists' ability to impose multiple perspectives on the landscape and sell them for visual consumption.

The restructured urban landscape in New York and London provides a mirror image of postmodernity in Miami or Los Angeles. While gentrification redefines the social meaning of a historically specific *place* for a *market* segment, denser decentralization redefines a housing *market* in terms of a sense of *place*. Both processes carry significant implications for property values, employment, and other economic factors that promise to erode further both place and vernacular. But they depend less on strategies of capital accumulation than on processes of cultural appropriation.[6]

DIRECTED CULTURAL APPROPRIATION

Under the impact of Pierre Bourdieu's sociology of culture, most analyses of both postmodernism and gentrification focus on questions of taste. Changing tastes evoke a chain of 'structural' and contingent factors, from the demographics of the Baby Boom to the urban renewal critiques of Jane Jacobs and others, the rise in college graduates and investment bankers, the diminution of distinguishing or positional goods, and the power of art or the attraction of shopping as a social activity.[7] More important than new class/new tastes debates, however, is the larger structural issue of how new cultural products are formed, or how strategies of cultural appropriation articulate with patterns of consumption and production (see Sahlins 1976: 166–204).

In the new spatial identities we see in older urban areas like New York or London, artists play an important role as 'primary consumers'. They not only produce new cultural goods for their own consumption but also establish cultural categories. In newer urban areas like Los Angeles or Miami, landscape itself – ocean, mountains, freeway, shopping centre – takes the primary role in cultural mediation.

Although the exhaustion of utopia has led in both cases to a renewed concern with history, the way in which history is 'produced' for cultural consumption reflects the historical development of each urban landscape. History in New York, London, or most modern cities, is literally and visually in the streets. The parks and churches where famous meetings took place and battles were fought, the residential neighbourhoods of Georgian or Victorian building stock, the working-class and ethnic ghettos where grandparents sweated, the very shape of narrow streets and bulky towers: these constitute the material products of visual consumption.

Newer cities, on the other hand, lack the authentic historical monuments of a distant past. With the exception of small shabby Skid Rows in Los Angeles, Phoenix, or Fort Worth, for example, Sunbelt cities in the United States do not have the sense of a museum in the streets that older cities have. No one knows exactly where the *pueblo*, the historical centre, of Los Angeles was, and neither California nor Florida has preserved many architectural remains from the Spanish colonial past. In these newer regions, history has been mythologized since the end of the nineteenth century: it is fabricated in images of the past like California's Mission Revival or Florida's Mediterranean villas, and sold to avid visual consumers (see Weitze 1984; Curl 1984).

Both modes of consumption are primarily visual and mix motifs. But while the mode of consumption in older cities leans toward the didactic, in newer ones it tends toward entertainment.

Because of simultaneous disinvestment and new construction in the built environment, this has been the first period when consumers can view an entire 'living panorama' of modern history – including industrial architecture in derelict loft and warehouse districts, tenements in Brick Lane and Avenue D, and classical commercial ensembles for early mass consumption in Oxford Street or Broadway – and contrast it with their own environment. Just as tourists took the impression of historical sites in Rome in the nineteenth century, so today they marvel at historic landmark districts in London and New York. Such touristic consumption has elements of entertainment, as Henry James found in Rome's architecture and style of life, and the presence of art in the streets. But it also requires a guide for full appreciation of the museological array. If 'Italy was the *didactic* museum of the past' for nineteenth-century tourists (Novak 1980), the cultural value of modern cities must be explored, explained, and affirmed by contemporary artists and intellectuals. This group establishes the proper perspective for viewing the historical urban landscape. By their labour as well as their cultural products – especially cultural critique – they act as a critical infrastructure in the postmodern urban landscape.

GENTRIFICATION

The process of cultural appropriation in gentrification often begins in historic urban neighbourhoods with the walking tour. This tour is staffed by volunteers who individually become fascinated by the combination of archaism and beauty, or authenticity and design, that has languished for years under 'lower-class' uses. Their sensibility is appalled that the historic landscape of mercantile or industrial power has been encapsulated by a contemporary vernacular of garment shops, low-income housing, and cheap stores. New primary consumers, such as artists in lofts or the first few hardy souls to restore houses in Boerum Hill or Islington, assert an opposing claim to this space, a claim based not on occupancy or entitlement but on appreciation of the space (or its built form) as a product for cultural consumption. Used as a shelter for homeless men, Hawksmoor's Christ Church in Spitalfields is emptied and claimed for restoration as an architectural monument. Manufacturing lofts in New York's SoHo are converted behind their cast-iron façades (a legally protected landmark) into luxurious living lofts.

Even in the very early stages of gentrification, cultural appropriation is a two-step process. First, a social group that is not indigenously related to either landscape or vernacular takes a perspective on both. Second, the imposition of their view – transforming vernacular into landscape – leads to a material process of *spatial* appropriation.

So cultural appropriation leads to a dilemma. On the one hand, the aura of the ensemble will be ruined by continued economic disinvestment. But on the other, it will be submerged by an influx of capital with the resulting risk of nearby new construction. The change in central districts' population from lower class to 'gentry' is by this point well known, although the newcomers may eventually develop – within cultural limits – a variety of impoverished or trendy styles (that is, *echt* Downtown).

Clerkenwell, near London's Smithfield Market, provides a recent example. Tours of the area are led by the founder of the Clerkenwell Heritage Centre, who, as a teacher, moved into the working-class and commercial neighbourhood in 1980. Previously, Clerkenwell was unknowable, inaccessible as a spatial or cultural whole. Visitors, few as they were, viewed segments of the area from very narrow perspectives. 'People only came here as part of specialized groups and saw particular sites', the tour leader says, referring to the Marx Memorial Library and sixteenth-century St John's Gate. 'But you don't have to be Marxist or a member of the St John Ambulance Brigade to appreciate Clerkenwell. No other part of London has such a concentration of different [historic] things.' As a result of these walking tours, and the literature that accompanies them, Clerkenwell began to be seen, appreciated, consumed as an ensemble. Architects' and designers' offices located themselves there. From a rather nondescript vernacular known to a few, Clerkenwell was transformed into an urban landscape accessible to many (Mandel-Viney 1988).

New and expanding service careers make the critical infrastructure especially visible in this process of cultural valorization. These are not only artists and performers and leaders of local historical societies; they are also museum professionals, advisers to corporate art collectors, staffs of art galleries (both alternative and mainstream), and independent curators. They sell cheese at the local gourmet food store. They are restaurant waiters as well as chefs and owners; they are also the restaurant critics whose reviews are eagerly devoured. The critical infrastructures are not a new class, for they include both entrepreneurs and hourly labour. Their activity, however, constitutes a cultural category that in turn helps constitute the production system of a postmodern city (Sahlins 1976: 185).

On the one hand, the work of the critical infrastructure contributes to tourism, food, publishing, and art; on the other, their consumption practices become an accessory to property development. While their presence helps to establish a liminal 'scene' between market and place, the scene's success acts as a vehicle of economic valorization. The sense of *place* that is their material product succumbs in time to the higher rents of *market* forces.

Patrick Wright (1985: 228–9) has described the 'cultural oscillation' between past and present that this broadly middle-class social group lives off and lives for.[8] They pursue the authenticity of the past in newly fabricated replicas of eighteenth-century plumbing fixtures, faded armoires bought at auction sales, and the entire decorating genre associated with chintz.[9] But the cult of the handmade and the hand-me-down coexists with devotion to the manufactured, mainly the latest, state-of-the-art products of modern technology and design. By means of design, in any case, the critical infrastructure appropriates both the authenticity of the past and the uniqueness of the new. Their cultural and spatial appropriation maps centrality with power. This general motif reorganizes the postmodern cultural landscape in older modern cities regardless of specific urban forms (loft buildings or houses; Beaux Arts or Georgian style).

But cultural appropriation in Los Angeles and Miami pursues the security of the past and the continuity of the new. Here the dominant motif of the postmodern landscape – from vernacular architecture to Disney World – maps comfort with power.

DREAMSCAPE

History in Los Angeles and Miami has often been visualized in the form of fantasy architecture that acts as a literal stage set for consumption. Fast-food stands in the shape of frankfurters, family restaurants in huge Polynesian thatched-roof huts, or 'daydream houses' (Jencks 1978) of Hollywood movie stars exaggerate the common images of a mythical past – blending function and symbol – to appeal to a highly mobile society. Though Rayner Banham (1971:

124) described four ecologies and their related architectures as typical of Los Angeles, he thought the commercial fantasy of restaurants and drive-ins provided the city's only real public space.

This dreamscape, however, originates in resort architecture. At the turn of the century, when Henry James visited Palm Beach, he criticized the twin hotels that were frequented by rich North Americans because they dramatized the ahistorical, market-place consumption (without the moderating influence of an aristocracy) that he found so vulgar. For James, the artifice of their tearooms and boutiques, their imitation Borromean villas, and their grandiose decor recalled 'a Nile without the least little implication of a Sphinx'. As a space for public life, this was mediocre. Yet it was magnificent as a stage set, mediating between nature and artifice, 'on a strip of land between the sea and the jungle ... between the sea and the Lake' (James 1907: 443, 462).

James's paradigm of hotel civilization and Banham's description of fantasy architecture suggest three elements of an ex-urban postmodern landscape: it is a stage set, a shared private fantasy, and a liminal space that mediates between nature and artifice, market and place.

All three elements get full play in the landscape of Walt Disney's World. As a landscape of postmodernity, Disney World both incorporates a stage set into the 'real' tourist world and sets it apart from the everyday concerns of work, home and family, traffic jams, and household budgets. Further, Disney World develops on the basis of commercializing a shared private fantasy (originating in fairy tales, dreams of adventure and frontier, and Disney Studio products), and expands by continually mediating that fantasy by means of new adventures, theme parks, and product spin-offs. Consequently, the huge consumption complexes of Disney World – including the original Disneyland in Orange County, California, Disney World in Orlando, Florida, Japanese Disney World, and European Disney World in France – are not only real spaces but also fantasy sites. People pay quite a bit of money to enter Disney's markets – but they also pay for the singular experience of visiting a specific place. This dreamscape is a paying venture.

Like its antecedent, the Disneyland that Walt Disney created in Orange County, California, in the early 1950s, Disney World was built for visual consumption. It offers both a panorama and a collage of postmodernity. The variety of playground ensembles or theme parks allows the simultaneous viewing of real and fictional landscapes, some of which are imaginative historical re-creations and others purely imaginary. While the façades on Disney's Main Street abstract an image of security from North America's historical vernacular, the pasteboard stage prop of his Magic Kingdom evokes a continuity between childhood fantasies and new construction. This is a landscape for the eye of the child in the mind of an adult.

Disney's urban planning by 'imagineering', moreover, purifies the material landscape: 'This is what the real Main Street should have been like,' says an imagineer who works for Disney World. 'What we create,' another planner says, 'is a "Disney realism", sort of Utopian in nature, where we carefully program out all the negative, unwanted elements and program in the positive elements' (Wallace 1985: 35–6). By the same token, a Disney landscape replaces the narrative of a socially constructed place with a fictive nexus derived from the market products of the Disney Studio, the whole representing 'the jealous cultivation of the common mean' that James found in south Florida long ago (James 1907: 442).

Disney World features the selective consumption of time as entertainment. It abstracts an image of desire and childhood pleasure from the vernacular, and projects it through the landscape of an amusement park. The abstraction of desire becomes the 'wienie' (frankfurter), the commercial lure that amusement-park owners build into their attractions. Yet to Walt Disney the goal of building a landscape represented a greater ideal. The cartoon fantasy of Disney World was a wienie designed to draw people to a new and more rational vernacular, an imaginary landscape of the future (Pawley 1988: 38–9; cf. Brown 1989).

Planned by Disney in 1958, the Experimental Prototype Community of Tomorrow (EPCOT) demanded such expensive and such complex technology that it was not built at Disney World until the early 1980s. Automated people-movers that transport the milling crowd, robots who perform speaking parts in historical panoramas, a release of sensations (smell, touch, sight, motion) that make the exhibits 'come alive': EPCOT offers an image of the future that can be controlled. In this sense Disney's plan is continuous with the stage-set tradition of amusement parks and world's fairs since the Columbian Exposition in Chicago in 1893. But EPCOT is both an object of visual consumption and a moral order. At Disney World, the landscape of consumption mediates between desire and control. This is a landscape for the eye of the adult in the mind of a child.

None the less, the EPCOT that Disney planned differs significantly from the landscape that was finally built. In 1966 Walt Disney envisaged:

a city that caters to the people as a service function. It will be a planned, controlled community, a showcase for American industry and research, schools, cultural and educational opportunities. In EPCOT there will be no landowners and therefore no voting control. No slum areas because we will not let them develop. People will rent houses instead of buying them, and at modest rentals. There will be no retirees. Everyone must be employed. (*Pawley 1988: 39*)

Issues of legal responsibility soon dissuaded the Disney Company from building a model new town. Instead, the utopian place that Disney defined in terms of social institutions (that is, employment, rental tenure, schools) was transformed into a tourist market. The permanent, planned community became a temporary haven for hotel and motel visitors, campers, time-share buyers, and even pensioners. But it was no less planned.

Besides the planning done by Disney imagineers, corporate sponsors built individual exhibits linked to their core products. They had almost immediately agreed to built exhibits at Disney World when plans for EPCOT were announced. They hoped to impress the public in Disney's Future World as their pavilions had done in World of Tomorrow at the 1939 World's Fair. Those separate, paying events had offered futuristic visions of science and technology scaled for domestic consumption by General Motors, General Electric, Eastman Kodak, and AT&T. By all accounts, they succeeded in imposing a coherent perspective – Technology = Progress – on a landscape that had been ravaged by the Depression, drought, migration, and mechanization. Although automation was the major cause of unemployment at the time in the United States, visitors to the 1939 World's Fair found that machines had moved beyond production into the landscape of consumption. A review of these exhibits in *Business Week* found the presentations of companies that produced consumer goods even more effective than those of industrial goods producers. A half-century later, at Disney World, the future still belongs to the major corporations. The public ride through Exxon's exhibit in solar-powered cars, and take a boat ride through lettuce cultivated in space-laboratory conditions by Kraft. They listen, at the same time, to didactic guided tours that offer the corporate sponsors' views of poverty, plenty, and progress (Susman 1984; Newson 1986; Wallace 1985).

The major corporate sponsor at EPCOT, however, is the Disney Company itself. Disney developed the 28,000 acres of Disney World in Orlando and built most of the accommodation for the 150,000 daily visitors who park in 20,000 surface parking spaces. Each night 30,000 guests sleep at Disney World in complexes that are theme parks in themselves. The Magic Kingdom includes ten resort hotels with 5,700 rooms, 1,190 camp sites, 580 time-share vacation villas, and three convention centres. Lake Buena Vista and Walt Disney World Village provide an additional seven hotels with 3,500 rooms. Between 1988 and 1990, three more super-hotels were built: the Grand Floridian, a modern 'Victorian' hotel with 900 rooms, and the Dolphin and Swan, which together have 2,300 rooms and a 200,000 square foot convention centre. The Dolphin and Swan form a temporary residential community for 10,000 people, making the Disney Company the largest hotel and convention centre developer in the south-eastern United States. The developer in charge of construction and the source of financing, however, is an international syndicate made up of the Tishman Company, Metropolitan Life Insurance, and the Aoki Corporation, a Japanese construction and real estate development firm.

The hotels' design by Michael Graves, a leading postmodern architect, is a cultural oscillation between the Disney model of cartoon animation and James's paradigm of hotel civilization. On the one hand, Graves chose friendly animal-and-water motifs that mediate the natural environment of southern Florida and the artifice that created Mickey and Minnie as cultural icons. 'They have the kind of warmth that the whole Disney experience gives,' Graves says. On the other hand, the two hotels are fantasy architecture that is monumental in scale, lavish in their treatment of space. The Dolphin's façade incorporates a cascading waterfall that flows through a series of huge clam-shells into a shell-shaped pool supported by four large sculpted dolphins. Like Louis XIV, another architect associated with the project says. Alternatively, the chairman of Walt Disney Company claims, 'We want to create a sense of place that is unique' (Giovanni 1988; see also Pawley 1988).

Yet many years ago, in Palm Beach, Henry James glimpsed 'on a strip of land between the sea and the jungle' a landscape where 'the clustered hotels, the superior Pair in especial, stand and exhale their genius. One of them, the larger, the more portentously brave, of the Pair,' which could be Michael Graves's 26-storey Dolphin, 'is a marvel indeed, proclaiming itself of course, with all the eloquence of an interminable towered and pinnacled and gabled and bannered skyline, the biggest thing of its sort in the world.' This is truly an imaginary landscape for visual consumption: 'no world but a hotel-world could flourish in such a shadow' (James 1907: 443).

Instead of the men in business suits and the well-costumed ladies that James observed, Disney World features a middle-class world in leisure suits. Just as employees are rigidly controlled for a healthy look and an orientation to entertainment as a service industry, so the public whom they serve is also homogenized, abstracted from a diverse and conflicted American society. Most visitors to Disney World have professional or administrative jobs; an overwhelming majority are white; their median income in the mid-1980s was $35,700 a year. For them Disney World is kept noticeably, spotlessly clean (Wallace 1985: 53).

Like the world of the hotel and the world's fair, Disney World produces a coherent imaginary landscape on the basis of visual consumption. But two differences divide the modern spaces and their image from the postmodern landscape of Disney World. Only Disney World creates an entire, coherent landscape, a landscape that is created, moreover, to substitute for social reality. Neither a pure business venture nor a banal resort, Disney World abstracts an image of security from the vernacular of Main Street and maps it on an urbanized society where crime, drugs, and business betrayals constitute a major way of life. It also projects an image of continuity in the technology at EPCOT, mapping it on the regional dislocations and economic polarization associated with industrial retrenchment, the shift to low-paid service jobs, and direct investment in overseas production.

The re-mapping of the imaginary landscape at Disney World is a paradigm for the re-mapping of the real landscape in Orlando and Orange County. Disney's real estate and tourist developments have provided jobs and a growing tax base. They implode into the landscape as growth poles of ex-urban service economies. Orlando has attracted publishing firms as well as leisure activities; Orange County is a leading manufacturing centre for both high-tech military equipment and low-tech apparel, as well as an expanding centre of business and financial services. As the animation industry in the city of Los Angeles tries to cut costs by turning to computerized design and overseas production, the tourist industry that the cartoons inspired in nearby Orange County is booming. Disney's symbolic landscape, moreover, legitimizes the appropriation of these regions – carved from swamp and desert – as real urban forms. In 1963, the urban real estate developer James Rouse, who sponsored both the renovation of Faneuil Hall and the new town of Columbia, Maryland, praised Disney as an urban planner. And in April 1986, *Los Angeles Magazine* named him as one of '25 people who changed Los Angeles'.

Both structured by and structuring postmodernity, Disney

World uses symbols to create real economic value. The landscape at Disney World is connected to two circuits of cultural capital. It should be noted, once again, that this is not symbolic capital in Pierre Bourdieu's sense of tastes and credentials, but goods and services, images and values, that constitute cultural categories and, at the point of consumption, articulate with the production system. One circuit of real cultural capital is constituted by inputs and products of culture industries: movies, television, magazines, and the spin-off commodities that are reproduced by deriving a new product from a cultural commodity in another area (for example, the movie stars who provide the subject of magazine articles, the character in a cartoon who becomes a toy and sweatshirt, the movie soundtrack that is marketed as a compact disk). Another circuit is constituted by elements of the built environment – the architecture, machinery, exhibitions, hotels, and movie studio sets that become cultural monuments. Thus the landscape at Disney World is both a stage set for consumption and an actual stage set, an image of vernacular architecture and a new vernacular, a dreamscape and a social control of dreams.[10]

VISUAL CONSUMPTION AS SOCIAL CONTROL

The circulation of images for visual consumption is inseparable from centralized structures of economic power. Just as the earlier power of the state illuminated public space – the streets by artificial lamplight – so the economic power of major corporations – Disney, Sony, CBS – illuminates private space by electronic and manufactured images. With the means of production so concentrated and the means of consumption so diffused, communication of these images becomes a way of controlling both knowledge and imagination, a form of social control. Cultural representation by mass communications has to a great extent established the postmodernity we imagine (see Meyerowitz 1985; Schierelbusch 1988).

Until quite recently, visual consumption of landscape consisted of moving (or projecting) an image rather than moving the viewer. A series of projection devices – from the late-eighteenth-century 'Eidophusikon' to nineteenth-century panoramas and twentieth-century films – took a stable audience and artificially changed its perspective on the landscape. Today, however, the identity of the viewer is constructed around mobility. The collage by which we see a landscape constantly changes our perspective.

The new owner and publisher of the *New York Post*, for example, aim at a readership that has almost no connection with the city of neighbourhoods of the modern past. The *Post*, an afternoon news-paper, was traditionally sold to commuters going home from the centre of the city. Readers' primary attachment was to their home; this point determined their perspective on the city in the news. But readers, according to the *Post*'s publisher, now 'have a real and visceral connection to the city, that active mobile life style, no matter where they live'. The landscape of the city flattens and expands by means of consumption. 'There is a core to New York that is essen-tially Manhattan but interlocks with the other boroughs and the suburbs'; and the interlocked perspectives that he names are those of upper-middle-class communities. (In Los Angeles, by comparison, there are gentrified neighbourhoods and expensive suburbs; ghettos, including residential communities heavily populated by displaced industrial workers; and the desolate communities of *Gastarbeiter* and illegal immigrants.) Only middle-class residents of the 'first zone' enter into the newspaper publisher's calculations; they can afford to view landscape in the multiple perspectives derived from *markets*. Without this mobility, other residents are mired in the single perspective of *place*.[11]

Gentrification and Disney World represent prototypes of post-modern urban landscapes. The multiple perspectives that they create by a circulation of images map culture and power. They use motifs of visual consumption as implicit means of social control.

Cultural appropriation is less hostile to economically dependent groups than naked strategies of capital accumulation, epecially labour control. But it is no less dramatic in its exclusionary consequences. To the extent, moreover, that 'dominant' culture is a market culture, the socialized eye is an economic conformist. In the Disney land-scape, for example, 'there is a constant feedback of human multiplic-ity, one's own efforts of vicarious participation constantly thwarted by the mirror of others' eyes.' Yet with greater knowledge about cultural products, visual consumers experience a more vicarious cul-ture – and a more vicarious cultural consumption. 'Few children who ride the Mad Hatter's Teacup [in Disneyland] have read or ever will read *Alice*... Most of them will only know Alice's story through Disney film, if at all. And that suggests a separation of two ontolo-gical degrees between the Disneyland customer and the cultural artifacts he is presumed upon to treasure in his visit' (Doctorow 1971: pp. 287, 288).

Abstracted from the time and space of their creation, cultural images project control rather than desire. The original character of Mickey Mouse, for example, was to a great degree shaped by the

Depression. 'Mickey's good deed', the initial illustrated story in a series of Mickey Mouse publications, came out in 1932.[12] In this Dickensian tale, a penniless Mickey and his dog Pluto tramp hungrily through the snow on Christmas Eve. They pass a great house where a spoiled rich child amuses himself by teasing the household pets; the butler, a dignified mastiff in morning coat, hails Mickey and Pluto passing in front of the house and asks Mickey if he will sell Pluto. Mickey refuses until he passes another house, a poor house, where nine little kittens are sleeping, with neither visions of sugar plums nor visits from Santa Claus expected. Rushing back to the butler, Mickey sells his dog, buys a sack of toys, and leaves them for the sleeping kittens. Still hungry but satisfied with his 'good deed', Mickey sits in the snow ... where he is soon joined by Pluto, who has rebelled against the rich child's cruel mischief and run away with the Christmas turkey. Reunited and fed, the mouse and dog fall asleep in the snow.

If circumstances then inspired a somewhat oppositional identity, the rejuvenation of Mickey in the 1980s coincided with an extraordinary period of market socialization. The Disney Company celebrated Mickey's 60th anniversary at a crucial point: five years after EPCOT opened to great acclaim at Disney World, four years after the Disney Company itself emerged triumphant from a hostile corporate takeover attempt, two years after record profits made the Disney chairman one of the most highly remunerated US executives, and just as Michael Graves unveiled his drawings for the Dolphin and the Swan. Mickey's visage is by this point reproduced on an array of products from children's lunch boxes ($19) and bedroom slippers ($9) to adults' bathrobes ($60) and golf bags ($275). Sold, of course, at Disneyland and Disney World, these products are also marketed by mail-order catalogue and in Disney stores at twenty suburban shopping malls. Even the identity of a cultural icon is malleable.

SOCIO-SPATIAL IDENTITY

The process of deriving identity from place is, however, more constrained. It is limited by both the material history, shape, and form of space, and the social practice of those who would try to imagine an alternative.

Significantly, current strategies of cultural appropriation are rooted in modernity. In specific places, modernity is mapped by notions of centrality and power, as in New York and London, or comfort and power, as in Miami and Los Angeles. These are both recurrent visual motifs and cultural strategies of spatial appropriation. More generally, however, the cultural strategies of abstraction, internationalization, and a shift from production to consumption also begin in the past. Abstraction as a visual, cognitive, and even ideological motif begins with High Modernism at the peak of the industrial era (*pace* Baudelaire and Simmel). A related shift in the social meaning of consumption aided the development of standardized industrial production (at least in the United States and Western Europe, if not initially in South-east Asia). Similarly, internationalization was implicit in modern industrial systems from the outset, not from a moment of crisis. During a crisis, however, such as the economic and cultural crisis that began in the early 1970s, these elements appear both dangerous and dangerously new (Shoenberger 1988: 245–62).

Inversion of spatial identities is also a recurrent phenomenon. Just as in the nineteenth century trade and manufacturing created the 'annihilation of space by time', so has time been annihilated by space in gentrification and Disney World.

Some elements, moreover, remain constant in postmodernity. The capacity to impose multiple perspectives on a landscape remains wedded to economic power. This cultural and economic asymmetry is translated into individual careers by attachment to housing and labour markets, which continues to have different impacts on different social classes.[13] Spatially, the imposition of multiple perspectives facilitates the erosion of locality – the annihilation of the archetypal place-based community by market forces. But this process also reflects the social organization of modernity. The autonomous development of communities has never been nurtured by big cities, on the one hand, or big economic structures, on the other.

The continuing erosion of locality none the less raises a question about the future of vernacular in postmodernity. If landscape becomes more abstract, reflecting the diminution of local production cultures, will the 'institution with long-range purpose' on which vernacular relies be lost? Will the powerless be even more incapable of generating an imprint of their own?[14]

Disney World implies that people will be satisfied to live with only an image of vernacular abstracted from history. The enormous market attraction in the United States of self-enclosed communities based on a nineteenth-century, small-town model ('Main Street'), which is selective in terms of both consumers and their consumption of time, reinforces Disney World as a cultural model that establishes socio-spatial identity. 'The small town model prevails wherever possible,' *Progressive Architecture* says (April 1988: 43) about the mixed-use redevelopment of a 55-acre site in Connecticut that was formerly a wire factory; 'in the "town green" and the new main street, called Main Street, of course.'

A similar vision of history that never was is also appropriated in an advertisement by property developers in Virginia, near Washington, DC:

> Announcing the Return to Hometown America. Find it at Potomac Crossing in historic Leesburg. It's come back. That simple way of life. That nice way of living. It's Potomac Crossing. A *planned community set within historic Leesburg near the Potomac River* ... nestled in the rolling hills of Virginia horse country ... with a view of the Blue Ridge mountains. Potomac Crossing offers everything from townhomes to luxury single-family homes... This small community is big on recreation. Enjoy the pool, jogging trails and VITA-Course. The adjacent 174-acre regional park features tennis, basketball and a recreation field. *But most of all, enjoy the atmosphere.* (Washington Post, *11 Feb. 1989; emphasis added*)

Collective as well as individual identity is, then, defined by a strategy of cultural appropriation and both symbolized and realized by visual consumption. While the pastoralism of Main Street is a recurrent motif in American architecture and city planning (listen, for example, to the narration to *The City* that Lewis Mumford wrote in 1939), its articulation with a service economy gives a meaning to place that is abstracted from historic space and time.

As more people work in the service economy, we can expect them to divide their 'real' identities from the form of production at which they work. Yet as landscapes are converted by service-sector institutions, we can expect them to become more alike. New housing developments and redeveloped downtowns increasingly choose to attract investors by either the Disney or the gentrification model of visual consumption. Structurally, the decentralization of service industries, especially financial offices, depends on uniform practices of work and thought. To the extent that Bristol or Brighton is selected as a partial substitute for a London location, and Manchester or Edinburgh appeals as a regional business centre, the socio-spatial distinctiveness of the city is eroded. Developers, investors, and constructors of the built environment for the most part determine the conditions under which such sites are 'bought'. Their conversion to a postmodern landscape doesn't depend on gentrifiers or Disney so much as on Olympia and York, the developers of Canary Wharf,

Battery Park City, and the financial centre of Toronto, and Kumagai Gumi, developers in the United States, Japan, and Australia (Leyshon et al. 1988; see also Thrift 1987).

To the extent, however, that such cities as Sheffield, Liverpool, Bradford, and Cardiff retain an older vernacular, they maintain the possibility of generating alternative identities. But it is an open question whether these identities are oppositional or Orwellian relics.

By the same token, vernacular, like other traditions, may be invented on the basis of an imagined past, or restored as a basis of an entirely different landscape. Nowhere is this 're-imagined community' clearer than in the transformation of rural landscape. British harvest festivals, whose pagan roots have outlasted more modern agrarian social practices in the United States, no longer celebrate locally sown sheaves of wheat, nor even local garden produce. 'The decision [to permit members of the community to bring "token gifts only" to the festival] simply recognized the fact that the village gardens of 1987 are landscaped masterpieces featuring flowers rather than utilitarian plots designed to yield vegetable marrows, onions, runner beans, carrots, cauliflower and beetroot of prize quality,' a village festival participant almost quaintly notes. 'As we sang "Raise the song of harvest home" we found ourselves looking at more peaches, bananas, grapes and nectarines than parsnips and cabbages and home-grown apples' (Whitlock 1987).

The same dualities that are historically implied by modernity can be anticipated in postmodernity. We will have both the inversion of socio-spatial identities by cultural categories, and the transformation of cultural categories by socio-spatial appropriation.

ORWELLIAN RELICS OR RESISTANT IDENTITIES?

Resistance to the multiple perspectives of a postmodern landscape can authentically be shown by those who don't participate in dominant modes of visual consumption. But who today might possess such an unsocialized eye? The homeless, who have neither market nor place; those who remain attached to place in spite of market forces (for reasons of sentiment or history, legal entitlement, or barriers of race and class); those who are professionally committed to liminality.

Postmodernity offers a chance to select an identity from the electronic image of mass communications, the manufactured image of domestic consumption, and the projected image of vernacular architecture. In these images we consume what we imagine, and we imagine what we consume.

While modernity still evokes the paradigmatic modern landscapes of Parisian arcades, central railroad terminals, and Le Corbusier's towers, most of us who are writing about postmodernism today grew up in a landscape of derelict Victorian and bastardized modern architecture. Our moment of high modernism occurred around 1953. Yet at that very time Walt Disney was planning Disneyland, Fernard Léger painting *La partie de campagne*, and Jacques Tati filming *Mr Hulot's Holiday*. While at the time most cities appeared to be unchanging, in retrospect we see that the entire landscape was transformed. That period of generational modernity marked a turning-point toward the landscape of consumption. From mass consumption to abstract expressionism, desire was socialized by an imaginary landscape.

An Italian theorist of contemporary design today extols imaginary landscape as the only space left for creativity:

> If in fact post-industrial society is formed by a hyper-industrialized system having no exterior and no empty spaces, the only virgin territories in which project and production manage to develop are those of the imaginary, in other words those consisting of spatial narration and stage-sets of new islands of sense, of stylems and behavior which allow the pool of objects in the house and in the metropolis to be renewed and improved. (*Branzi 1988*)

Yet stage-sets evoke the social production of visual consumption, with its history of resort and fantasy architecture, its fictive nexus in Disney World, and its dependence on markets to foster products that in turn create a sense of place. In this landscape, socio-spatial identity is derived purely from what we consume.

NOTES

1 Although Turner carefully differentiated the *liminal* rites of collective passage in tribal and early agrarian society from the *liminoid* zones or marginality that are individually carved out in modern industrial society, his tendency to use the term broadly was criticized. See Turner 1982 and Agnew 1986: ch. 1.

2 Emphasis added; for a full conceptualization, see his essays in Jackson 1984.

3 Certainly the social construction of any urban landscape combines economic and political power with cultural legitimation; it varies from city to city and across national societies. In modern British cities, for example, cultural appropriation of the centre for public housing projects was more entrenched – for political reasons – than in the United States, where public housing projects were confined to specific stretches on the edges of the centre, where new working-class housing would not deflate property values. Here too, however, marginal locations reflected historic patterns of occupancy, especially by non-whites.

4 This provided the grist of much US urban sociology, mainly influenced by the Chicago School, from the 1920s. See e.g. Zorbaugh 1929; cf. the emphasis on symbolic attachments to place in Firey 1945: 140–8, and Firey 1947.

5 Some of the best descriptions of this socio-spatial recentralization (and decentralization) are in Smith 1984: 119–24 and Smith 1987; Thrift et al. 1987; Soja 1986 and Soja 1987. See also Davis 1990.

6 On a related transmigration of spatial categories, i.e. nature and culture at the seashore, see Urry 1988.

7 For a diversity of views, see e.g. Zukin 1988: chs 3–4; Smith and Williams 1986; and Lash and Urry 1987: ch. 10.

8 These uniquely conjoined styles of consumption are illustrated effectively in local magazines such as *Inside Islington* (whose first issue was published in spring 1986).

9 While in England this decor signifies the stately houses of the aristocracy, in the United States it merely betokens 'English', and hence upper-class, style.

10 An interesting link between the two circuits is the real estate developer who becomes a press baron; the developer's agency permits local newspapers to directly support new socio-spatial patterns of consumption that enhance property values. (Thanks to Ingrid Scheib-Rothbart and George Rothbart for pointing this article out to me.) See Diamond 1989: pp. 44–50.

11 The owner of the *New York Post* is one of those real estate developers who have recently bought newspapers. See Davis 1986: pp. 304–5: *New York Times*, 28 March, 1988.

12 Reprinted in a facsimile edition with an introduction by Maurice Sendak in *Mickey Mouse Movie Stories* (New York: Harry N. Abrams, 1988). Mickey's original appearance dates from the cartoon feature 'Steamboat Willie' (1928).

13 Besides the on-going debate over the underclass in the United States, the interesting issues of mobility between firms and attachment to the service-industry (e.g. Silicon Valley, Glen, or Fen) are discussed by Savage, Dickens and Fielding, 1988.

14 To the degree that homeless people and their supporters attempt to create a vernacular – e.g. the tent city protesters in New York's East Village or earlier squatting in New York, London, Amsterdam, Berlin – it is transient and often violates other vernacular conventions.

REFERENCES
<hr>

Agnew, Jean-Christophe 1986: *Worlds Apart: The Market and the Theater in Anglo-American Thought, 1550–1750.* New York: Cambridge University Press.

Alpers, Svetlana 1983: *The Art of Describing: Dutch Art in the Seventeenth Century.* Chicago: University of Chicago Press.

Banham, Rayner 1971: *Los Angeles: The Architecture of Four Ecologies.* London: Allen Lane.

Barrell, John 1972: *The Idea of Landscape and the Sense of Place, 1730–1840: An Approach to the Poetry of John Clare.* Cambridge: Cambridge University Press.

Bottles, Scott 1987: *Los Angeles and the Automobile.* Berkeley/Los Angeles: University of California Press.

Branzi, Andrea 1988: 'Lose e case', *Domos*, November, p. 18.

Brown, Patricia Leigh 1989: 'In fairy dust, Disney finds new realism', *New York Times*, 20 July.

Cooper, Derek, and Urry, John (eds) 1985: *Social Relations and Spatial Structures.* New York: St Martin's Press.

Curl, Donald W. 1984: *Mizner's Florida: American Resort Architecture.* Cambridge, Mass.: MIT Press.

Davis, Mike 1986: *Prisoners of the American Dream.* London: Verso.

Davis, Mike 1990: *City of Quartz: Excavating the Future in Los Angeles.* London: Verso.

Diamond, Edwin 1989: 'The New (Land) lords of the Press', *New York magazine*, 27 Feb.

Didion, Joan 1987: *Miami.* New York: Simon & Schuster.

Doctorow, E. L. 1971: *The Book of Daniel.* New York: Random House.

Feagin, Joe R. 1988: *Free Enterprise City: Houston in Political and Economic Perspective.* New Brunswick, NJ: Rutgers University Press.

Firey, Walter 1945: 'Sentiment and symbolism as ecological variables', *American Sociological Review*, 10.

Firey, Walter 1947: *Land Use in Central Boston.* Cambridge, Mass.: Harvard University Press.

Giovanni, Joseph 1988: 'At Disney, playful architecture is very serious business', *New York Times*, 28 Jan.

Gregory, Derek, and Urry, John (eds) 1985: *Social Relations and Spatial Structures.* New York: St Martin's Press.

Harvey, David 1989: *The Condition of Postmodernity.* New York: Blackwell.

Jackson, J. B. 1984: *Discovering the Vernacular Landscape.* New Haven, Conn.: Yale University Press.

Jackson, J. B. 1985: 'Urban circumstances', *Design Quarterly*, 128.

James, Henry 1907: *American Scene.* New York: Harper.

Jameson, Frederic 1984: 'Postmodernism, or the culturalloigic of late capitalism', *New Left Review*, 146, 53–92.

Jencks, Charles 1978: *Daydream Houses of Los Angeles*. New York: Rizzoli.

Lernoux, Penny 1984: 'The Miami connection', *The Nation*, 18 Feb.

Leyshon, Andrew, et al. 1988: 'South Goes North? The Rise of the British Provincial Financial Centre', Working Papers on Producer Services, 9. Centre for Study of Britain and the World Economy: Bristol University.

Mandel-Viney, Leslie 1988: 'On foot in a London village', *New York Times*, 20 Mar.

Meyerowitz, Joshua 1985: *No Sense of Place: The Impact of Electronic Media on Social Behaviour*. New York: Oxford University Press.

Mohl, Raymond A. 1983: 'Miami: the ethnic cauldron', in Richard M. Bernard and Bradley R. Rice (eds), *Sunbelt Cities: Politics and Growth since World War II*. Austin: University of Texas Press.

Newson, Steve 1986: 'Walt Disney's EPCOT and the World's Fair performance tradition', *Drama Review*, 30 (Winter), 106–46.

Novak, Barbara 1980: *Nature and Culture: American Landscape and Painting, 1825–1875*. New York: Oxford University Press.

Pawley, Martin 1988: 'Tourism: the last resort', *Blueprint*, Oct.

Rieff, David 1987: *Going to Miami: Exiles, Tourists, and Refugees in the New America*. Boston: Little, Brown.

Rowntree, Lester 1986: 'Cultural/human geography', *Progress in Human Geography*, 10, 580–6.

Sahlins, Marshall 1976: *Culture and Practical Reason*. Chicago: University of Chicago Press.

Savage, M. et al. 1988: 'Some Social and Political Implications of the Contemporary, Fragmentation of the "Service Class" in Britain', *International Journal of Urban and Regional Research*, 12: 455–76.

Scott, A. J., and Cooke, P. 1988: articles, *Society and Space*, 6, 241–367.

Shoenberger, Erica 1988: 'From Fordism to Flexible Accumulation: Technology, Competitive Strategies, and International Location', in *Society and Space*, 6.

Smith, Neil 1984: *Uneven Development*. New York: Blackwell.

Smith, Neil 1987: 'Of yuppies and housing: gentrification, social restructuring, and the urban dream', *Society and Space*, 5, 151–72.

Smith, Neil, and Williams, Peter 1986: *Gentrification and the City*. Boston: Allen & Unwin.

Soja, Edward W. 1986: 'Taking Los Angeles apart: some fragments of human geography', *Society and Space*, 4, 255–72.

Soja, Edward W. 1987: 'Economic restructuring and the internationalization of the Los Angeles region', in Michael Peter Smith and Joe R. Feagin (eds), *The Capitalist City*. New York: Blackwell, 178–98.

Soja, Edward J. 1989: *Postmodern Geographies*. London: Verso.

Susman, Warren I. 1984: 'The people's fair: cultural contradictions of a consumer society', in *Culture as History*. New York: Pantheon, 211–29.

Thrift, Nigel 1987: 'The Fixes: The Urban Geography of International Commercial Capital', in Jeffrey Menderson and Manuel Castells (eds), *Global Restructuring and Territorial Development*. London: Sage, 203–33.

Thrift, Nigel, et al. 1987: *'Sexy Greedy': The New International Financial*

System, the City of London and the South-east of England, Working Papers on Producer Services, 8. University of Bristol/University of London.

Turner, Victor 1982: *Play, Flow, Ritual: An Essay in Comparative Symbology*. New York: Performing Arts Journal Publications.

Urry, John, and Lash, Scott 1987: *The End of Organized Capitalism*. Cambridge: Polity Press.

Urry, John 1988: 'Cultural change and contemporary holiday-making', paper published in *Theory, Culture and Society*, 5/1 (1988): 35–55.

Wallace, Mike 1985: 'Mickey Mouse history: portraying the past at Disney World', *Radical History Review*, 32.

Weitze, Karen J. 1984: *California's Mission Revival*, California Architecture and Architects, 3. Los Angeles: Hennessey and Ingalls.

Whitlock, Ralph 1987: 'Harvest Isn't What It Was', *Manchester Guardian*, 8 November.

Wright, Patrick 1985: 'The ghosting of the inner city', in *On Living in an Old Country*. London: Verso.

Zorbaugh, Harvey W. 1929: *The Gold Coast and the Slum*. Chicago: University of Chicago Press.

Zukin, Sharon 1988: *Loft Living: Culture and Capital in Urban Change*, 2nd edn. London: Radius/Hutchinson; New Brunswick, NJ: Rutgers University Press, 1989.

Zukin, Sharon 1991: *Landscapes of Power: From Detroit to Disney World* Berkeley/Los Angeles: University of California Press.

10

A modern tour in Brazil

Paul Rabinow

Les Tropiques sont moins exotiques que démodés.
Lévi-Strauss 1955: 81

SURFACES

As part of its modernization programme, the Musée d'histoire naturelle, in the Jardin des Plantes in Paris, organized an exhibit on 'Plumes du Brésil' (Brazilian feathers), amply demonstrating the ceremonial and decorative uses of feathers by Brazilian Indians. Urban explorers in search of postmodern pastiche found if not a gold-mine at least its sign. In the central hall of the classical building, watched over by the statue of Buffon, were juxtaposed two rather diverse displays: hugging the walls, encased in Plexiglass cases, was a collage of photos and drawings of Indians on top of which were placed real feathers; running through the centre of the hanger-like space of the great hall were ancient rectangular display cases filled with resplendent stuffed birds of wondrous variety apparently long mouldering in the storage rooms where they had been deposited centuries earlier by explorers and scientific missionaries commissioned to add to the royal collections.

The polysemy of 'Plumes' – both feathers and writing tools – highlighted the juxtaposition of the building's classical space and representation with its high modernist reformulation, if by modernist we mean the attempt to efface history and cultural specificity through universal formal operations which are ultimately their own referent. Claude Lévi-Strauss, the great champion of *la pensée sauvage*, and the man who, it could be argued, gave the Other her most fully modernist form, inaugurated the exposition. It was part of an effort to publicize the plight of Brazil's Indian populations, increasingly threatened by rampant expansion into the Amazon. Lévi-Strauss, notoriously disdainful of political action, even travelled to Brazil to plead the Indians' case and indeed was given wide press coverage there. In addition to the classical space and the structuralist script, a third dimension was also present: a mock-up mini-jungle of vines and recorded sounds of the wild surrounding the ticket booth one passed through before entering the hall. The result was post-modern pastiche, if by pastiche we mean 'an imitation of dead styles deprived of any satirical impulse', and if by postmodern we mean, simply, after modernism (Bruno 1987: 62). Classical, modernist, postmodern: these three forms are highlighted today by the re-eruption of the term around which they all cluster – modernity. This essay explores some of the terrain.

My entry into Rio, where I was to be a visiting Fulbright Professor for the Spring 1987 term, was delayed as customs officials, following their own opaque practices, ignored the cascading jumble of electronics equipment our 747 full of Brazilians returning from Disney World had crammed into every corner of the plane, but carefully searched through my books (copies of *Writing Culture* and *Tristes Tropiques*), lingering suspiciously over the macaroni-shaped plastic filling in the box, perhaps a left-over habit from the days of the military dictatorship they had been unable to kick. Outside J., an anthropologist from the National Museum, was there to meet us, waiting patiently for the customs ritual to be over. Gracious, famil-iar, respectful, he was the first of a long line of intellectuals whose non-dramatized dignity only grew more impressive as my awareness of the difficulty of navigating Brazil's troubled waters slowly grew. We spoke French.

Driving into Rio through the major highway system the military had constructed: reverberating memories of Casablanca; long wide avenues leading through the mottled texture of the city; old cars (Volkswagen had won the right to build its factories in Brazil); long lines of fuming buses; hodge-podge mix of 1970s skyscrapers, shanty towns undatable to a tourist, and palm trees; ample graffiti, the product of a recent soccer championship. Today, despite its pockets of enormous wealth, Rio is infrastructurally shabbier and less co-herently laid out than Casablanca (both topography and politics involved in that). The comparison of the cities is not gratuitous, as it might seem; they were partially planned by two French architects, Henri Prost and Alfred Agache, who were friends and who both contributed to the emergence of modern French urban planning. Indeed, the history of modern French planning and social science before high modernism was one of the topics I was to lecture on. Lunch-hour traffic clogged Rio's pitted arteries (schools have multiple sessions and middle-class children are transported from school to school, school to home, home to lesson, lesson to home throughout the day). Horns blared, cars lurched, hands gesticulated; it felt like New York. Drained, we parked on a small dead-end street abutting one of the many formerly coffee-covered hills punctuating the topography around which modern Rio has expanded and in whose newly wooded groves the syncretic *candomblé* cult is practised nightly, looked up to see a purple orchid growing on the overhanging tree. Exotic.

The first task was an obligatory visit to the American Consulate located downtown in the bustling business district with its turn-of-the-century office buildings, imitation Paris Opera house, abutting the bay and the ceremonial park (taxi drivers washing in the early twentieth-century fountains), laid out according to another French-inspired plan. We passed several security checks: long lines of well-groomed people waiting outside for visas. A briefing packet informed us that untreated sewage from seven (nine?) million people pouring into the bay of Rio and open industrial sewage on its far side (Niteroi) made swimming in Rio's Guanabara Bay inadvisable (for Americans): epidemics of two types of hepatitis, meningitis, dengue, typhoid and a cornucopia of intestinal diseases. A knowledgeable Brazilian woman working at the Consulate, who was unobtrusively and patiently to become our guide, explained gently with consummate tact how one should not wear wedding rings or carry anything of value, photocopy all documents etc. Bands of young men brazenly prowl the beach looking for tourists (recognizable by the fact that they haven't been sun-tanned since early childhood) and rob them with the blasé complicity (a combination of habit and lack of alternatives) of the police and other beach-goers, working on their tans and perfecting their volleyball techniques. Ordinary life.

Others explained how real estate values on the fashionable beaches of Ipanema and Leblon, now adorned with the worst of 1970s skyscrapers quickly slapped in place once the military had lifted zoning restrictions, were (despite the crime and six-lane highway adjoining the beach) higher than in New York or Paris. Still others explained that the fabled Rio sex scene is depressed, as the seriousness of the largely uncharted but clearly massive AIDS epidemic is slowly sinking in. Carnival had been less exhilarating this year. However, no screening of the blood supply was yet enforced. One television report claimed 60 per cent of Rio's transvestites, to be found in the Bois de Boulogne, were infected. Samples at blood banks revealed high levels of AIDS, as well as syphilis; as in the US, blood is a commodity bought and sold. The Church opposed a safe sex campaign. The government was reluctant to intervene: presumably it would be bad for tourism. This litany of dangers was sobering but expressed as well a familiar big-city cultural form evincing a heroism of endurance of small, if mounting, troubles as a sign of greater worth, tougher fabric, stronger hide. Modern life.

Here, as in so many other areas of Brazilian life, the answer for the dominant classes was privatization, a tactic familiar enough to North Americans. Hoard your own blood; buy your own protection. For example: a leading specialist on carnival and ethnographic lyricist of the integrity of popular culture lives 50 kilometres outside of Rio in a compound surrounded by large reinforced fences. At the gate, two armed guards check one's licence number and telephone ahead to the house to make sure one is expected. Raised humps in the road every 50 metres ensure a leisurely pace. During the drinks and chat on the verandah of the American-style suburban house, one hears exotic birds and sees men with rifles patrolling the empty street. His lament, performed on television, over 'the Brazilian street', where classes and races mixed, is less cant than loss and nostalgic reconstruction. During dinner, served buffet-style, the television showing an American grade B war film provided background noise to the outside silence. Suburbs.

Returning across Rio's fabled bay after this evening of alternating professional chat and silences, across the long bridge constructed under the military as part of its modernization programme, I remarked on its emptiness: people were reluctant, it seems, to cross the bridge at night as gangs accosted crossing cars, robbing their occupants. Whether or not this was yet another macho urban stylization remained unclear as we cruised unaccompanied for miles over New Jersey-like industrial landscapes back towards mythic Rio. Michel de Certeau might have seen the local production of discourses about this forced modernization and its discontents as 'resistance'. I was in no position to judge. Reserve.

The inhabitants of Rio's shanty-towns, cascading down the slopes of Rio's hills – compared fifty years earlier to the teeth in the mouth of an old hag by Lévi-Strauss, who remarked as well on the reversal of the usual pattern in which the rich live on the lower terrain and the poor the higher – are considered by sociologist and *favela*-dweller alike to be comparatively well off: some have water, electricity, buses, access to schools, neighbourhood political action groups; a few even have formal rights. The last governor of Rio encouraged recognizing occupation as a de facto title to ownership as had been tacitly the practice for some time. However, with more drought in the north-east, with more peasant land being stolen – anthropologists report systematic killings – even greater numbers of poor continue to flee south to Brazil's great cities. New 'invasions' of the cities' parks, tunnels, metros, bridges ensued in the 1980s. After a detailed account of the tens of thousands of illegal occupations by the poor, the *Jornal do Brasil* added that the rich were engaged in similar illegal occupations of land, building luxury villas and apartment houses increasingly higher along the slopes of the former coffee plantations which dot the jagged hills of Rio and beaches south along the coast, now filling in with large complexes of box-like towers and well-guarded shopping centres. Justice.

The frontiers of social chaos are always relative: even for a North American, wild west *laissez-faire* extends quite far in Brazil. Whether people will stop at red lights is a question directly posed to the pedestrian at each crossing. Why bother? Others recount stories – everyone seems to know of a particular example – of a driver waiting at a red light feeling the cold barrel of a pistol against his temple, if he were lucky just losing the car (others left nude in the city's outskirts). This car rustling is the result of massive poverty as well as organized business growing out of a protectionist trade policy; the stolen cars are apparently shipped off to Paraguay, where they are rebuilt, smuggled back in and resold. Frustrated, underpaid bus drivers, their salaries always trailing far behind the 1,000 per cent inflation in 1987, frequently roar off into an open lane of oncoming traffic. Brazil makes the United States seem like an old, historically saturated society, imbued with the Republican civic virtue invoked by Robert Bellah. Commerce.

Incessant noise. The *Jardim Botanico* quarter is reputed for its tranquillity but is almost never quiet. The hammering of jackhammers and hand-held ones used in the construction of new apartment buildings continues until late into the night (São Paulo has the highest rate of industrial accidents in the world and Rio can't be far behind). Every private house (as they are harder to protect they are losing their value as crime rises) has a barking dog to greet those who pass by – many of these incongruous German shepherds, panting from the heat, having lost their vocal power from continual barking, heroically continue to mime the gestures. The grinding and sputtering car and bus noise is constant. Engines run on alcohol, which seemed a wise shift before the fall of oil prices made alcohol only marginally cheaper than gasoline, are much harder on the engine and require ten to fifteen minutes of high-pitched revving, before starting off in the morning as their noise and thin fumes fill the tropical air. Skateboards are a must for the children of the upper middle classes. There is intermittent music in the street from high-quality sound equipment; almost invariably North American, more Simon and Garfunkel than Gilberto Gil. Environment.

All very 'Third World' except that Brazil with the eighth-largest gross national product in the world, with a booming export arms industry, substantial computer and automobile sectors, with vast mineral and agricultural wealth, modern cities, great cultural and ethnic diversity (São Paulo has 1 million Japanese), with a short and thin history, with its ceaseless migration of populations, with its genocide of the Indians (some 200,000 remain studied by over half the 700 anthropologists in Brazil), its never-achieved (except in song and story) integration of the slaves it imported (twenty times more than the US), its fantastic cultural creativity, is truly the New World – much closer to California than to Morocco or India. First, Second, Third? Movies like *Brazil* and *Blade Runner* are more postmodern realism than science-fiction fantasy. As Mort Sahl used to say: the future lies ahead. Progress.

Apparently some 2 million people are dancing funk every night in Rio – accompanied by another formulaic discourse about the insatiable rhythm of the poor – but the northern working-class areas are not safe to go to for middle-class types, said the urban anthropologist. Instead, we went to hear Paulinho da Viola, one of Brazil's best-known musicians. Ushered into a parking spot in front of an old crumbling aqueduct in a downtown area several blocks from the business district by a young black boy, one felt protected. In the club a show was already under way – a black musician belted out Frank Sinatra songs – to an audience, another Museu anthropologist observed, of lower middle-class store owners and their rotund bejewelled wives: had we been transported to Miami Beach? Then the main act: all the magic was there. Extraordinarily subtle and sweet music, the audience transformed into a singing, dancing, array of alive human beings: professional black samba dancers, on their break from another club, escorted white, no longer young, women across the floor; the store owners loosened up, and even, to quote Frank Sinatra, danced with their wives; but this was not Chicago but for a moment at least, magical Rio of the tourist posters. Culture.

It was too hot to cook. Mounted electronic advertising placards dot the city vaunting the virtues of Seiko or Sony and reminded you objectively of how hot it really was: 40, 38, 36, 32 degrees centigrade at night. The restaurants in Ipanema and Leblon recommended by the guide-books were expensive, regularly ringed with begging children, and the Italian food was indistinguishable from the Brazilian. We soon discovered the Tocao (the Den), located near the television studios in our neighbourhood. Through the front room whose tables provided a view of the street, past the ovens and roasting spits, one enters into a poorly painted back room decorated with travel posters. Rarely too crowded, excellent beer and the basic meat, chicken and manioc at very reasonable prices, friendly but not fawning service: it became our haunt. The regulars included television employees and some older couples from the neighbourhood: friendly hum of conversation, plates arriving, beer glasses refilled, fan humming above, from time to time samba songs whose words everyone knew. City life.

OTHERS

First visit to the Museu Nacional: the former imperial residence, still painted in the Royal Pink, the large two-storey compound is set in the middle of an extensive formally laid out park with cupolaed bandstands. Today, the surrounding neighbourhood is reputedly dangerous and unsavoury; this description seemed affirmed by the platoons of young, sweating troops exercising on the park's ceremonial avenues. The museum's interior courtyard, sparsely dotted with trees, housed a large metallic cage, home to two parrots, who, exotic and resplendent in their red plumage, begin an unspeakable hollering around eleven each morning demanding to be fed. Before their demands are honoured all other teaching and conversation stops. As the birds and their cage belong to the government and consequently cannot be moved outside the reverberating courtyard without official approval, which although applied for somehow never comes, a mildly embarrassed shrug before visitors is patiently performed, and stories told. The exoticism compensated for the bother. A group of Amazonian Indians, paying an official visit to the anthropology department, covetously eyed the birds' feathers, restrained only by the reminder that the feathers were government property as well. In the Indians' village, the anthropologist who worked there recounted, were found over a hundred such parrots, choice feathers stripped, dinning for food.

After being guided past display cases containing piles of unlabelled bones and stacks of human skulls, I entered the office of Professor M., a leading anthropologist whom I had known at Berkeley. I was greeted by a well-rehearsed analysis of a photo of Lévi-Strauss and a group of anthropologists in front of a balcony with the park in the background at the Museu in the 1930s – nature and culture, you see. The manicured royal park and zoo hardly seemed unmediated nature. On to culture: the three Brazilians were grouped together on one side of the frame; an unidentified mediating woman was in the centre; the American anthropologist stood stiffly to her left; an aloof Lévi-Strauss observed the group from a vantage-point one half-step to the side, at the edge of the picture. M., the holder of a Harvard Ph.D., simultaneously insecure and self-congratulatory, remained nonplussed by the cool reception he had received when he performed his little theatre for the master. The skit underlines an uneasy identification (half-asserted, half-denied) of a lineage which still carries a hefty symbolic charge in Brazil. M.'s structuralism is a talisman turned back on Lévi-Strauss and other foreigners, simultaneously claiming and denying seriousness, welcoming and warning at the same time. Still, M. seemed more like a pompous provincial than an exotic trickster. Lévi-Strauss's formula, put forth fifty years early, that the tropics were not so much exotic as démodé, rang true.

This conceit, typically paternalist and historically thin, was itself, as with so much of high modernism, démodé. The tropics were merely hot, not exotic. Further, M. was not typical. The other anthropologists at the Museu (as well as São Paulo, Bahia and Brasilia) were uniformly more hospitable, convivial and scientifically serious. The extraordinary sumptuousness of American material conditions contrasted with the infrastructural difficulties in Rio, as did inversely the tempered, complex judgements and cosmopolitan openness frequent among Brazil's intellectuals compared to the comfortable and well-tended provincialism typical of much of the American university world. In part because of this seriousness of tone, in part because of the cloistered setting of the Museu Nacional, and in part because they have been less directly involved in governmental affairs than the anthropologists in São Paulo (several of whom have held high positions in state and national government), the Museu's anthropologists are referred to by the rest of the Brazilian anthropological community as the Garden of the Finzi-Continis. The reference to a film portraying rich and cultivated Jews in Italy refusing to face the rise of fascism is generally meant as a mild, if affectionate, rebuke, tinged, it is true, with a certain envy. Its use of reference is symptomatic of the European orientation in Brazil: Paris was, and is, culturally closer than Buenos Aires.

A Ford Foundation-sponsored tour, designed to explore social science under authoritarian conditions (Chile, Argentina, Brazil), brought four prominent members of the African Social Science

Association to a sweltering, polluted Rio. Seated around the large oval wooden table at the museum were these four, plus two representatives from Ford (their Brazil man and their Africa man), five of the Museu's anthropologists and myself. The Africans were unequivocal: despite its reputation for racial harmony, Brazil was the most racist country they had ever seen; South Africa had more blacks on its campuses and its faculties; the US had a civil rights movement and active public discussion of racial problems. The talk of Brazil's multiracial democracy was propaganda and the complacency of the Brazilian middle classes in the face of such discrimination was complicity. The discursive assault was shocking; only I was prepared by having recently read Simone de Beauvoir's similar pronouncements written decades earlier.

None of this litany was directly answered, rebutted, refuted or even contested by the anthropologists around the table. Later, M. asserted that racial inequality in Brazil was all a socio-economic question; or, alternatively, it was contextual: you were black in one context and white in another. Another anthropologist half-heartedly referred to Brazil's much studied complexity of colour classification: a multitude of different classificatory terms depending on a subtle and complex perception of context were employed with artful dexterity and imagination. After this eye-opening encounter, whenever I was in a middle-class setting (club, restaurant etc.) I asked if there were any blacks present. No one ever answered, 'It's too complicated a question, it all depends on context.' The answer was always 'No'. Obviously not South Africa, as no laws or overt ideology preaches or enforces discrimination; paternalism or, better, nostalgia for paternalism holds sway.

Brazil was the last nation in the hemisphere to abolish slavery and then admittedly for predominantly economic reasons. The Ford Foundation was attempting to mount a commemoration of the one hundredth anniversary of the abolition of slavery through a major exhibit at the Museu, where one can still find blatantly racist exhibits dating from fifty years ago. The response was not negative, only evasive: no doubt a coping strategy, a commitment to their own work, a space of reserve. The solution: hire the anthropologist who runs the Ford office and let him do it. A most unusual and special man, British born and trained, he has lived over fifteen years in Brazil and taken out Brazilian nationality. Ford was instrumental in preserving independent social science in Brazil under the dictatorship, financing a research institute in São Paulo which served as a haven for many of those expelled from the university. Arguing that these social scientists should now give up their privileges and return to the university to fight its battles as well as teach its students, he argues for an educational celebration to commemorate the end of slavery while demonstrating how far Brazil's blacks are from having achieved full social equality.

A., stocky and compact, dignified, reserved but with almost pleading eyes, explained in quiet tones (his passion for justice filtered and moulded and sifted through a technical vocabulary he had learned from Pierre Bourdieu) how massacres of peasants were organized in the North East. The pervasive brutality of economic expansion and the utter arrogance of its perpetrators, the mythic trekking south, the occasional philanthropic gesture, the precariousness of smallholders, emerged modulated into perfectly formed French sentences punctuated by words like 'habitus' and 'socio-economic'. His office had a view of the zoo, which was being modernized; the office itself had a fan which moved the tepid air in slow currents over yellowed books, witnesses to communities long since destroyed. He was now working on the wave of interest in the para-scientific that was sweeping certain factions of certain classes in Brazil – sightings of extraterrestrials, miracle drugs, past lives. The television and media spread these discourses infinitely more rapidly than the time it took for people to come south and long to return north. Everything was speeding up. We Americans had a lot in common.

MAIDS

V. S. Naipaul writes of his frustration and disappointment in India: [that Delhi evening] 'I had gone to that apartment expecting ideas, discussion. I had found no ideas, only obsessions, no discussion, only disingenuous complaint and an invitation to wallow, the sweet surrender to tragedy' (1978: 150). Whether or not this is an accurate description of India, I cannot say. It certainly is not of Brazil. Social-structurally as well as spatially the Brazilian middle and upper-middle classes are constructing themselves into a position in which many will no doubt spend their evenings in comfortable fear, emoting from afar, that is, projecting. Such corrosive and debilitating cynicism was absent from the intellectuals who, having generally discarded messianic visions of revolution when *favela*-dwellers supported the military, abjure the Manicheanism Naipaul often embraces, displaying instead an impressive maturity (lucid and humorous) about their situation. Many had served at one level or another of government; the local Foucault specialist had helped organize the delivery of food services in one of the peripheral shanty-towns. The understanding of limits and the lack of cynicism was a marvel.

The social space between the high-rise fortresses of the middle classes and the *favela* camps of the poor is increasingly a battlefield, traversed and mediated by maids, doormen and the ever-increasing floating population of new immigrants, those invading the public spaces of Brazil's cities, as well as a few anthropologists. The constant nostalgic plaint of the middle classes for the days of more settled, paternalistic relations forms a conversational leitmotif. Here, as with race, one encounters the pathos of a quietly obsessive discourse of paradise lost: the good old days when we were raised and fondled by loving and loyal maids, slept and danced with the Orphic blacks. This gesture to a harmonious holism Brazilian intellectuals (or most of them) know they have lost (which anyway never really existed) persists as a wistful, openly regressive retreat from a very different contemporary reality. Everyone can sing the carnival samba songs together.

The first evening in São Paulo I enjoyed one of those evenings Naipaul claims to have expected but never encountered. The dinner guests were two sociologists who, along with my hosts, an anthropologist and her doctor husband, wonderfully confirmed all the Brazilian clichés about São Paolo. They were urbane, sophisticated, talkative, analytic, hard-working, with lots of jokes and global curiosity; everyone was smoking cigarettes with a degree of addiction last seen in some French New Wave movie of the early sixties. All the social scientists were articulate women. At one point, the conversation turned to professional women and their changing domestic lifestyles. Articles in women's magazines had alerted us to the topic; upbeat articles on how to clean your house were accompanied by descriptions of how to use condoms properly in your casual affairs in order to avoid AIDS.

Brazilian professional women don't cook. Brazilians were investing in massive freezers in which a month's meals could be stored (assuming there was no massive power failure). 'Freezerladies': these women come to your house and cook for fourteen or sixteen hours; they are paid roughly one dollar an hour. There were amusing stories told of a double portion of salt mistakenly added, spoiling the entire month's meals. A French sociologist recounted how one of her interviewees told how she was coping with her life by purchasing all the latest technologies: dishwasher, vacuum cleaner, refrigerator and *congeladora*. The key is there: the nostalgia for the paternalistic as a sign of the technological. The sociologically objective absurdity of intelligent people lamenting their future maid-less state when millions upon millions of Brazilians are living near or below subsistence can only be understood as a comment on a changing discourse of social relations. Hierarchical class relations were hardly disappearing, only modernizing and becoming transparent. People knew this. No one seemed to know what to do about it.

SPACES

Between the crumbling city of Salvador – capital of Jorge Amado's mysterious, magical and sensual Bahia – reachable only by sea until the 1950s, and its ultramodern and architecturally striking modern airport designed (before the oil crisis to which these plans have succumbed) to make this capital of black culture in Brazil an international tourist attraction, lie some of the most beautiful fine-grained white sand, palm-lined, sea breeze-cooled beaches in the world as well as some of Brazil's newest squatter settlements. Our guide and host in Salvador was an insightful and gracious, exiled Portuguese anthropologist, who when asked if he felt at home in Salvador after fifteen years of residence, responded 'not at all'. He was passionately interested in Indians, accumulating ethnographic detail in his writing both as a witness to what was being destroyed and for the sheer joy it seemed to produce for him. Another world. The university, perched on a hillside overlooking the ocean or at least partially overlooking the ocean, because there now stands a massive international-style hotel on the beach in clear and absolutely illegal occupation of state-protected land, is drastically underfunded. Comparing the costly extravagance of this multinational clone with the lack of shutters in the classroom, a shrug made visible both his pain and his patience.

On the way to the luxurious and elegantly designed airport, expanded under the military to become a stop on the international tourist route, a plan which never materialized, he had the driver stop alongside the broad new highway at the site of a *ville nouvelle*; actually a well organized occupation of a large piece of land cradling the rolling dunes above and adjacent to a swampy inlet. The low dune scrub had been scorched off; then streets were traced and lots drawn, as for any speculative housing development in the new world and latterly in the old. Only then was the land 'invaded', and the lots were gradually filling with a variety of constructions from tents to tin and cardboard shelters supplemented by palm fronds and blue plastic sheeting. Obviously there was no electricity, but water from the swampy inlet was supplemented by pools formed in a ditch lying in the landscaped area between lanes on the highway. As the new city is some 15 kilometres from the outskirts of Salvador, the possibility of finding work in the immediate vicinity was nil. However, as the land was not slated for development and lay adjacent to the highway, it could conceivably be serviced by buses one day if enough political pressure could be mobilized. The contrastive tension between the orderliness of the situation and its material desperation was at first paralysing. The poverty was all too evident; less evident (although highly visible) is the modern dream – shared by planners, speculators and some anonymous entrepreneurial groups of the poor – of a better life through an efficient, rational and readable structuring of space. Modernism's messianism, its grim fetishism, lies exposed in these spaces etched with hope.

BRASILIA: PRESERVING MODERNISM

Despite what the guide-books say, the approach to Brasilia has nothing breathtaking about it; the fabled airport shape of the city itself may be readable from the plans but is hard, if not impossible, to read from the air. Here as in so many other instances in Brazil, an official discourse flies far from the signified to which it is supposedly attached. Representation has achieved a high degree of autonomy in Brazil. The city's efficiency is immediately apparent upon arrival. One is out of the airport and into the empty highway system in minutes. My host, another learned, affable and hospitable Portuguese anthropologist, whisked us immediately to the French consulate just in time to watch two films made in the late 1930s by Lévi-Strauss (or more precisely his wife). Ten people sat in the large barn-like conference hall; the first film was a jerkily shot sequence of a woman weaving, the second of a cosmological rite. The French cultural attaché seemed at a loss for words in his commentary. Our hosts later explained at length what we had seen, as well as how Indians from the same villages were fighting for institutional protection in the new constitution being debated nearby in the parliament. The Indian leaders came to Brasilia, pitched their hammocks in the black-tiled, cool, open spaces of the anthropologist's small modern apartment, as they jointly planned strategy for the constitutional convention. Women were prominently leading this fight from the anthropological side.

In Brasilia, the principles of Planning are everywhere writ large, always spelled with capital letters. Traffic does flow (perhaps the only place in Brazil) through the city's underpasses and freeways; air and light do circulate through the large empty parks, totally out of scale with population density, designed to compensate for the stresses of urban life (absent, successfully planned out of existence in Brasilia; suburban stress is another matter). Zoning is carried to perfection and to absurdity; the ministries, ceremonially grouped in erect slabs, although now inadequate for current needs, are easily reachable from the housing zones. The city's cemetery, located next to the hospital, is itself laid out in a grid corresponding to Brasilia's super-quadra housing pattern, pushing efficiency – and lack of satire – to its limits.

The fundamental contradiction of this modernist city is the fact that those who built it and those who keep it running basically cannot live in it. There is almost no low-income housing in Brasilia and those who service the city are forced to live some twenty miles away in the semicircular ring of impoverished and unplanned satellite towns. Zoning provides strict controls for land use within the original perimeter of the city. There is almost no low-income housing although Oscar Niemeyer, the communist architect, did provide space in each apartment for maids. These modern rooms have no windows, but, as opposed to the equally omnipresent maids' rooms in Rio, they often do have space for a dresser or chair as well as the bed. In Niemeyer's (and his followers) six-storey super-quadra buildings there are two systems of elevators: one for the maids – these don't stop at the main floor, only the underground garage level – as well as the regular elevators for Brasilia's modern citizens. The variation within unity found in Brasilia in the residential architecture is its most successful aesthetic achievement. As with so much else of high modernism, its demands have proved too heroic for middle-range functionaries and more and more decorative elements are being added to exterior façades. Brazilian kitsch, a kind of middle-class structural graffiti, slowly gaining ground.

The city is not as sterile as it is often reported to be. The recurring use of the naturally sparse high plateau vegetation as a unifying motif allied with the height restrictions works well; the occasional patches of colour – a burst of bougainvillea, so rare in Rio – are pleasing, the modernist restraint successful in its sparseness. The landscaping at the stunning 800 metre-long single-building, snaking, low-slung university is impressive in its economic use of restrained planting to achieve a cultivated sense of harmony and beauty: a sunken level paralleling and echoing the two-storey snake and protected by low trees is a wonder, a triumph of another order than the interior neo-Moorish gardens of Casablanca's 1920s Hôtel de Ville, themselves stunningly beautiful in their profusion and multitude of levels as well as cultural references.

Truly impressive visually, the university has noise problems; the walkway adjacent to the offices and classrooms on the second floor, carrying students back and forth to their classes, disturbs every single office artfully nestled against it. The classroom acoustics are terrible, almost a kind of Jean-Luc Godard parody of modern life as if designed to prevent conversation. The use of glass walls in the earlier super-quadra housing also ignored noise as a potential problem; the large thoroughfares carrying the morning traffic to work provide a sonic rush to those a hundred metres away and six floors up over the empty, visually appealing and efficient formal spaces.

Brasilia is not neo-anything: it is high modernism in all its purity. It is not the utopia of the twentieth century the publications of the Ministry of Culture quote Umberto Eco as saying it is. It is not utopian at all, it is explicitly far away – not just anywhere. A group of architects working at the Ministry of Culture have submitted a proposal to Unesco to make the region of Brasilia a historical monument, part of the *patrimoine mondial*, like the crumbling pastel centre of Salvador: 'Attendu que Brasilia est déjà née capitale et dans une conception monumentale de l'espace, le rôle de témoin historique de son temps y est inséré. La préservation de ce temoignage se fonde tant sur sa condition de ville entièrement neuve que du fait qu'elle traduit pleinement les principes du Mouvement d'Architecture Moderne contenus dans la Charte d'Athènes (Conjunto 1986).' Modernism has been overcome by modernity; the universal principles of urban planning and architecture embodied in Brasilia are now defended for their cultural and historical particularities.

This modernist monument can be protected against its middle-class inhabitants who want to decorate it, government officials who want to add office buildings, speculators who want to fill its empty spaces with profitable apartment towers, workers and maids who want to live where they work, only by an appeal to an equally modern (if not modernist) set of legitimations – history and an international agency. Going beyond the tenets of modernism itself, the preservers argue that the pre-modern conditions of the site should be marked as well as those constructions which embody the process of historical emergence. The documents argue for the preservation of: the natural site, that is, the parks and the native regional vegetation; the few remaining farmhouses from the pre-development era; the workers' camps erected during the heroic period of Brasilia's construction. They argue neither for the museumification of Brasilia nor for its abandonment to the free market. Given what has been done to Rio in the last twenty years of Brazil's economic miracle (no one talks of a political or social miracle), one can only hope they succeed.

In this process of historicizing and culturally situating high modernism's claims to be ahistorical, utopian and universal, a process which underlines the macro-level influences as well as individual talents which melded together in the construction of Brasilia, one can perhaps discern the re-emergence of the anthropological dimension – particulars as the ground from which the universals of Reason, Art and Economics grow. We are now all resolutely post-high modernist: whether this means we are moving toward the postmodern culture of pastiche and schizophrenia Fred Jameson describes, or in the midst of modernity, challenged to change it and ourselves without an authorized plan, as Foucault suggests, is a matter of opinion. In either case, Baudelaire's ironic dictum to participant observers of modern life – you have no right to despise the present – remains appropriate advice.

CODA

Two French friends to whom I showed an earlier version of this piece disliked it intensely. Such reactions are frequently interesting. The first, an older gentleman, was outraged at what he saw as my judgemental tone. Ethnographers should never condemn, he reminded me. I was perplexed: I hadn't meant to condemn and I had made no claims that the piece was ethnographic. I was and still am haunted and humbled by Brazil and the Brazilians I had had the pleasure of meeting. The second friend, a younger urbanist with a good deal of experience in African cities, thought I came across too much as the American unused to the daily life of Third World cities, that is to say, the worst thing one could be in Paris – naive. Guilty. The only thing worse, for me, was to be blind or jaded. Verdict out.

NOTE

I would like to thank Anthony Vidler for suggesting the idea of attempting a *post scriptum* to Lévi-Strauss.

REFERENCES

Bruno, Giuliana 1987: 'Ramble City: postmodernism and blade runner', *October*, 41 (Summer).
Conjunto Representativo do Patrimonio Historico, Cultural, Natural e Urbano de Brasilia: *Dossier ao Comite do Patrimonio Mundial, UNESCO*, 1986, Part I, 8.
Lévi-Strauss, Claude 1955: *Tristes Tropiques*. Paris: Plon.
Naipaul, V. S. 1978: *A Wounded Civilization*. New York: Vintage.

11

Postmodernism and the aestheticization of everyday life

Mike Featherstone

INTRODUCTION

Despite the oft-remarked looseness and imprecision of the term postmodernism, it does have the merit of directing our attention towards the nature of contemporary cultural change. It sensitizes us to the variability of the culture–society relationship and the metatheoretical status of culture (Featherstone 1988a, b). At the same time there is the danger of encouraging a looser, more speculative mode of theorizing in which postmodernism is presented as the harbinger of a profound or even epochal social change. In some cases generalizations are produced from evidence of particular changes in cultural practices, experiences and theories to suggest a major trans-formation of the cultural sphere or even the emergence of a new social formation or totality is taking place. There is also a tendency to read off cultural changes in terms of what are perceived as more basic economic or technological changes with which they are held to be in, or out of, synchronization – as is the case in the work of Jameson, Bell and Baudrillard (see Kellner 1988). Rather than con-ceive postmodernism as the product of a cultural logic, capital logic or other 'logic' at work within the historical process, we need also to understand it in terms of the practices and experiences of particular groups of people (Featherstone, 1989a). In short we need to focus upon the generation of the carriers of and audiences for postmodern-ism, upon cultural producers, consumers and intermediaries. This suggests that, firstly, we should adopt a certain degree of reflexivity and attempt to understand sociologically the changing power struggles and interdependencies involving cultural specialists (artists, intellectuals, academics) and other groups which help to produce postmodern theories, cultural artifacts and sensibilities. This implies that, secondly, the focus should not merely be on the alleged discontinuities implicit in the emphasis given in the prefix *post*, which suggests that something has happened to the modern to the extent that we can perceive its limits and exhaustion and search out the new cultural practices and experiences that the postmodern allegedly heralds. Rather we need also to focus upon some of the continuities between the modern and postmodern and situate the postmodern in terms of the long-term process of the development of the cultural sphere, which has seen a significant expansion of the power potential of cultural specialists and shifts in the struggles of interdependencies between this group and other groups, most notably economic specialists (Featherstone, 1988a, 1989b).

One of the possible dangers of the focus upon the cultural carriers is that it can lead to a certain cynicism in which postmodernism is merely regarded as an arbitrary invention, another product of avant-garde strategies, another tactic in the distinction games played by intellectuals, artists and academics. It is therefore also important to focus upon the form and content of the experiences, sensibilities and practices labelled postmodern. While it can be argued that cultural specialists may have a stake or interest in inventing new movements and in educating audiences and publics to appreciate the resultant new sensibilities, cultural specialists are not only, nor the only, cultural producers. We also need to focus upon their role as interpreters who are sensitized to searching the cultural domain in its multifarious dimensions (specialist culture, mass-produced culture, popular culture and everyday culture) for signs and traces of new sensibilities and experiences. Attention then needs to be given to the specificity of those experiences and practices labelled postmodern and to the way in which this aspect relates to the process whereby they are subjected to definition and formulation by cultural specialists and generalized and proliferated to wider audiences and publics. To understand postmodernism therefore demands that we adopt a degree of reflexivity in which we acknowledge the double role of symbolic specialists and cultural intermediaries. In the first place their capacity to innovate and adopt avant-gardist strategies becomes heightened under conditions of the de-monopolization of symbolic hierarchies, the opening up of sealed-off enclaves of cultural goods to wider markets coupled with more general tendencies towards cultural de-classification, which help to create a more critical attitude towards the rationale for the existing canon (high culture, modernism) and its exclusions (popular culture, mass culture), while still maintaining the overall status and societal valuation of culture and cultural capital. Secondly they are involved in an interpretive role in terms of making sense and articulating new experiences and cultural signs with which to fashion new cultural goods in various media which have relevance as means of orientation for particular audiences and publics.

If we examine definitions of postmodernism we find an emphasis upon the effacement of the boundary between art and everyday life, the collapse of the distinction between high art and mass/ popular culture, a general stylistic promiscuity and playful mixing of codes. These general features of postmodern theories which stress the equalization and levelling out of symbolic hierarchies, anti-foundationalism and a general impulse towards cultural de-classification, can also be related to what are held to be the character-istic postmodern experiences. Here one can build upon the use of the term *modernité* by Baudelaire to point to the new experience of modernity, the shocks, jolts and vivid presentness captured by the break with traditional forms of sociation which the modern cities such as Paris seemed to bring forth from the mid-nineteenth century onwards. In a similar way one might also be able to speak of the experience of *postmodernité* and draw upon perceived shifts in cul-tural experiences and modes of signification. Here we find an emph-asis upon the aestheticization of everyday life and the transformation of reality into images in the work of Baudrillard (1983a, b). Jameson too (1984a, b) emphasizes the loss of a sense of history and the fragmentation of time into a series of perpetual presents in which there is the experience of multi-phrenic intensities. A similar aesthe-ticization of experience and breaking down of the ordered chain of signifiers can be detected in the writings of their followers, where one finds an emphasis upon 'the liquefaction of signs and commod-ities', 'the effacement of the boundary between the real and the image', 'floating signifiers', 'hyperreality', 'depthless culture' 'be-wildering immersion', 'sensory overload', and 'affect-charge intensi-ties' (Kroker and Cook 1987; Crary 1987). While many of these examples draw this inspiration from the intensification of image production in the media and consumer culture in general, one also finds it in descriptions of the contemporary city. Here the emphasis is not only on the type of new architecture specifically designated postmodern, but also on the more general eclectic stylistic hodge-podge which one finds in the urban fabric of the built environment. In addition a similar de-contextualization of tradition and a raiding of all cultural forms to draw out quotations from the imaginary side of life are found amongst the young 'de-centred subjects' who enjoy the experimentation and play with fashion and the stylization of life as they stroll through the 'no place' postmodern urban spaces (Chambers 1987; Calefato 1988). There are clearly strong linkages and cross-overs between the project of the aestheticization and stylization of everyday life on the part of such groups and the romantic, bohemian art school tradition that has fed into rock music, particularly since the 1960s, which has sought in various ways to transgress the boundary between art and everyday life (see Frith and Horne 1987). This suggests, then, that the experience of *postmodernité*, in particular the emphasis upon the aestheticization of everyday life and its formulation, articulation and promotion by cultural specialists, may have a long history. In short it would be useful to explore the *genealogy* of *postmodernité* and in particular examine the linkages between *modernité* and *postmodernité* which may yet direct us back to still earlier forerunners. This is not to argue that the postmodern does not exist or that it is a misleading concept. Rather it is only by exploring its antecedents and the long-term cultural process, in which there may have been earlier similar developments, that we can attempt to understand, and differentiate between, what is specific to the postmodern and what may represent an accumulation and intensification of tendencies long present within the modern, and even pre-modern.

THE AESTHETICIZATION OF EVERYDAY LIFE

There are three senses in which we can speak of the aestheticization of everyday life. Firstly we can refer to those artistic subcultures which produced the Dada, historical avant-garde and surrealist movements in World War I and the 1920s which sought in their work, writings, and in some cases lives, to efface the boundary between art and everyday life. Postmodern art in the 1960s, with its reaction to what was regarded as the institutionalization of modernism in the museum and the academy, built on this strategy. It is interesting to note that Marcel Duchamp, who was centrally involved in the earlier Dada movement with his infamous 'ready-madies', became venerated by the New York postmodern trans-avantgarde artists in the 1960s. Here we detect a double movement. In the first place there is the direct challenge to the work of art, the desire to de-auraticize art, to dissemble its sacred halo and challenge its respectable location in the museum and the academy. There is also, secondly, the assumption that art can be anywhere or anything. The detritus of mass culture, the debased consumer commodities, could be art (here one thinks of Warhol and pop art). Art was also to be found in the anti-work: in the 'happening', the transitory 'lost' performance which cannot be museumified, as well as in the body and other sensory objects in the world. It is also worth noting that many of the strategies and artistic techniques of Dada, surrealism and the avant-garde have been taken up by advertising and the popular media within consumer culture (see Martin 1981).

Secondly the aestheticization of everyday life can refer to the project of turning life into a work of art. The fascination of this project among artists and intellectuals and would-be artists and intellectuals has a long history. It can, for example, be found in the Bloomsbury Group around the turn of the century in which G. E. Moore argued that the greatest goods in life consisted of personal affections and aesthetic enjoyment. A similar ethic of life as a work of art can be detected in the late nineteenth-century writing of Pater and Wilde. Wilde's assumption was that the ideal aesthete should 'realize himself in many forms, and by a thousand different ways, and will be curious of new sensations' (Shusterman 1988). It can be argued that postmodernism – especially postmodern theory – has brought aesthetic questions to the fore, and there are clear continuities between Wilde, Moore and the Bloomsbury Group and the writings of Rorty, whose criteria for the good life revolve around the desire to enlarge one's self, the quest for new tastes and sensations, to explore more and more possibilities. We can also detect the centrality of the aesthetic approach to life in the work of Foucault, as Wolin (1986a) has argued. Foucault (1986: 41–2) approvingly refers to Baudelaire's conception of modernity in which a central figure is 'the dandy who makes of his body, his behaviour, his feelings and passions, his very existence, a work of art'. In effect the modern man is 'the man who tries to invert himself'. Dandyism, which first developed with Beau Brummel in England in the early nineteenth century, stressed the quest for social superiority through the construction of an uncompromising exemplary lifestyle in which an aristocracy of spirit manifests itself in a contempt for the masses and the heroic concern with the achievement of originality and superiority in dress, demeanour, personal habits and even furnishings – what we now call lifestyle (see Williams 1982: 107ff). It became an important theme in the development of artistic counter-cultures, the Bohemias and avant-gardes in mid- to late nineteenth-century Paris; and one finds a fascination with it in the writings and lives of Balzac, Baudelaire, the Comte d'Orsay, down to Goncourt, Montesquieu and des Esseintes. This dual focus on a life of aesthetic consumption and the need to form life into an aesthetically pleasing whole on the part of artistic and intellectual counter-cultures should be related to the development of mass consumption in general and the pursuit of new tastes and sensations and the construction of distinctive life-styles which has become central to consumer culture (Featherstone 1987).

The third sense of the aestheticization of everyday life refers to the rapid flow of signs and images which saturate the fabric of everyday life in contemporary society. The theorization of this process has drawn much from Marx's theory of the fetishism of commodities which has been developed in various ways by Lukács, the Frankfurt School, Benjamin, Haug, Lefebvre, Baudrillard and Jameson. For Adorno the increasing dominance of exchange value not only obliterated the original use-value of things and replaced it by abstract exchange-value, but it left the commodity free to take on an ersatz or secondary use-value, what Baudrillard was later to refer to as 'sign-value'. The centrality of the commercial manipulation of images through advertising, the media and the displays, performances and spectacles of the urbanized fabric of daily life therefore entails a constant re-working of desires through images. Hence the consumer society must not be regarded as only releasing a dominant material-ism, for it also confronts people with dream-images which speak to desires, and aestheticize and de-realize reality (Haug 1986: 52; 1987: 123). It is this aspect which has been taken up by Baudrillard and Jameson, who emphasize the new and central role which images play in the consumer society which gives culture an unprecedented im-portance. For Baudrillard it is the built-up, dense and seamless, all-encompassing extent of the production of images in contempor-ary society which has pushed us towards a qualitatively new society in which the distinctions between reality and image become effaced and everyday life becomes aestheticized: the simulational world or postmodern culture. It is worth adding that this process has general-ly been evaluated negatively by the above writers, who stress the manipulative aspects (Benjamin to some extent and Baudrillard in his later writings being exceptions). This has prompted some to argue for a more progressive integration of art and everyday life – as, for example, we find in Marcuse's (1969) *Essay on Liberation*. We also find this in the notions of cultural revolution developed in various ways by Henri Lefebvre (1971), with his plea to 'let everyday-life become a work of art', and the International Situationists (see Poster 1975).

This third aspect of the aestheticization of everyday life is of course central to the development of consumer culture, and we need to be aware of its interplay with the second strand we have identified: In effect we need to examine the long-term process of their relational development which has entailed the development of mass consumer culture dream-worlds and a separate (counter-) cultural sphere, in which artists and intellectuals have adopted various strategies of distantiation; we should also attempt to thematize and comprehend this process. First we will examine in more detail the writings of Baudrillard to gain a stronger sense of the meaning of the aestheticization of everyday life in relation to postmodernism.

In his earlier writings on the consumer society Baudrillard developed a theory of the commodity-sign, in which he pointed to the way in which the commodity has become a sign in the Saussurean sense, with its meaning arbitrarily determined by its position in a self-referential set of signifiers. In his more recent writings Baudrillard (1983a, b) has pushed this logic even further to draw attention to the overload of information provided by the media, which now confront us with an endless flow of fascinating images and simulations, so that 'TV is the world'. In *Simulations* Baudrillard (1983b: 148) states that in this hyperreality the real and the imaginary are confused and aesthetic fascination is everywhere, so that 'a kind of non-intentional parody hovers over everything, of technical simulating, of indefinable fame to which is attached an aesthetic pleasure'. For Baudrillard (1983b: 151) art ceases to be a separate enclaved reality; it enters into production and reproduction so that everything, 'even if it be the everyday and banal reality, falls by this token under the sign of art, and becomes aesthetic'. The end of the real and the end of art moves us into a hyperreality in which the secret discovered by surrealism becomes more widespread and generalized. As Baudrillard (1983b: 148) remarks:

> It is reality itself today that is hyperrealist. Surrealism's secret already was that the most banal reality could become surreal, but only in certain privileged moments that are still nevertheless connected with art and the imaginary. Today it is quotidian reality in its entirety – political, social, historical and economic – that from now on incorporates the simulating dimension of hyperrealism. We live everywhere already in an 'aesthetic' hallucination of reality.

The contemporary simulational world has seen the end of the illusion of relief, perspective and depth as the real is emptied out and the contradiction between the real and the imaginary is effaced. Baudrillard (1983b: 151) adds: 'And so art is everywhere, since artifice is at the very heart of reality. And so art is dead, not only because its critical transcendence is gone, but because reality itself, entirely impregnated by an aesthetic which is inseparable from its own structure, has been confused with its own image.'

In this third stage of simulational culture, which Baudrillard now calls postmodern (Kellner 1988), one of the forms often used as an illustration is MTV (music television) (see Chen 1987; Kaplan 1986, 1987). MTV provides round-the-clock videos of rock music. According to Kaplan (1986) MTV seems to exist in a timeless present with video artists ransacking film genres and art movements from different historical periods to blur boundaries and the sense of history. History becomes spacialized out, aesthetic hierarchies and developments are collapsed with the mixing of genres and high art, popular and commercial forms. It is argued that the continuous flow of diverse images makes it difficult to chain them together into a meaningful message: the intensity and degree of saturation of signifiers defy systematization and narrativity. Yet we should raise the question of how those images work: has MTV moved beyond a sign system which forms a structured language in the Saussurean sense?

The distinction between *discourse* and *figure* which Scott Lash (1988) takes from the work of Lyotard (1971) may go some way towards helping to answer this question. Lash points to a number of features that it emphasizes which make postmodern culture figural: primary processes (desire) rather than secondary (the ego); images rather than words; the immersion of the spectator and investment of desire in the object as opposed to the maintenance of distance. Lash also associates these qualities with the process of de-differentiation. This notion is based on a reversal of the process of cultural *differentiation* referred to by Weber and Habermas (which entails the differentiation of aesthetic forms from the real world); *de-differentiation* implies a reversal to favour the de-auraticization of art, and an aesthetics of desire, sensation and immediacy. De-differentiation and figural regimes of signification then for Lash point to the way in which images unlike language are based upon perceptual memories which draw on the unconscious, which is not structured like language with systematic rules. Images signify iconically, that is through resemblances. While the figural is found in visual regimes of signification such as the cinema, television and advertisements, it can also be said to be a general feature of consumer culture. Here we can refer to Benjamin's emphasis upon the sense of intoxication and the poetization of the banal in the dream worlds of mass consumption, which is central to his discussion of the mid-nineteenth-century Paris arcades in his *Passagen-Werk* (1982b). This study, with its focus on nineteenth-century Paris, brings together in time and space the origins of the second and third sense of the aestheticization of everyday life we have discussed.

The aestheticization of everyday life through the figural regimes of signification, which Lash (1988) holds as central to postmodernism, then, may have its origins in the growth of consumer culture in the big cities of nineteenth-century capitalist societies, which became the sites for the dream worlds, for the flow of commodities, images and bodies (the *flâneurs*) which were constantly changing and being renewed. In addition those big cities were the sites of the artistic and intellectual counter-cultures, the Bohemias and artistic avant-gardes whose members became fascinated by and sought to capture in various media the range of new sensations, and who also acted as intermediaries in stimulating, formulating and disseminating these sensibilities to wider audiences and publics (see Seigel 1986). While the literature on modernity pays attention to the centrality of this experience of *modernité*, the shocks, jolts and phantasmagoria of the new urban centres captured in Baudelaire's discussion of the *flâneur* and Benjamin's discussion of the arcades, we need to consider how relevant it is to understanding the experience of *postmodernité*.

Hence we need to investigate the continuities and discontinuities with late twentieth-century practices and sites. This would point us towards a consideration of urban renewal through the process of postmodernization (Cooke 1988; Zukin 1988b) with the gentrification of inner city areas and the emergence of simulational environments which use spectacular imagery in malls, shopping centres, theme parks and hotels. In addition it has been argued that significant changes are taking place in institutions which (formerly were) designated as restricted spaces for the educated connoisseur and serious viewer: museums. Today museums seek to cater for larger audiences and discard their exclusively high-culture label to become sites for spectacles, sensation, illusion and montage; places where one has an experience, rather than where knowledge of the canon and established symbolic hierarchies are inculcated (Roberts 1988.) We also need to enquire into the process of the articulation, transmission and dissemination of the experience of these new spaces by intellectuals and cultural intermediaries to various audiences and publics and examine the way in which pedagogies of these 'new' sensibilities are incorporated into everyday practices.

This points to the need to investigate the aestheticization of everyday life in specific locations in time and space. While the total aestheticization of everyday life would entail the breaking down of the barriers between art, the aesthetic sensibility and everyday life so that artifice becomes the only reality available, we should not assume this is a given, or something in the nature of human perception which once discovered can be read back into all previous human existence. Rather we should investigate the process of its formation.

It is therefore necessary to raise the stark sociological questions of the specific locations and degree of generality. Here we investigate the socio-genetic historical origins of particular cognitive styles and modes of perception which arise in the changing interdependencies and struggles between figurations of people. Let us take two brief examples. As Robbins (1987) has shown in his study of nineteenth-century British mountaineers, the process whereby mountains, long regarded with indifference by travellers and locals alike, became objects of beauty which would yield up aesthetic pleasures was a definite social process involving the development, education and institutionalization of new tastes in the middle classes. Likewise in the early eighteenth century the emergence of the Grand Tour began to attract nobles and upper-class people who desired to experience the ruins and art treasures of Europe, whereas previously the general attitude had been a reluctance to leave one's own locality which was usually conceived of as providing all the sensations and pleasures that one could possibly ever need (Hazard 1964: 23).

It is clear that we need to work towards a more precise sense of what is meant by the aestheticization of everyday life. More generally aesthetics has sought to investigate the nature of art, beauty, aesthetic experience and the criteria for aesthetic judgement (Wolff 1983: 13, 68ff). Since the development of modern aesthetics in the eighteenth century, one influential tradition has developed from Kant's *Critique of Judgement* in which the distinguishing characteristic of aesthetic judgement of taste is disinterestedness. From this perspective anything can be looked at in the aesthetic attitude, including the full gamut of objects in everyday life. Hence Simmel shows the influence of this tradition when he refers to the pleasures involved in looking at objects from a detached, contemplative point of view, without direct immersion (Frisby 1982: 151). This distanced, voyeuristic attitude is to be found in the stroller in the large cities whose senses are overstimulated by the flood of new perspectives, impressions and sensations that flow past him. Yet we also face the question of the necessity of distantiation and whether the reversal of it in the figural can also be described as entailing an aesthetic orientation. In the same way that Lash (1988) speaks about de-differentiation, it may also be useful to refer to de-distantiation or instantiation – that is, the pleasure from immersion into the objects of contemplation. (Here we are using distantiation in a different way from that used by Mannheim (1956) in his discussion of the democratization of culture.) De-distantiation has the benefit of capturing the capacity to view objects and experiences usually placed outside the range of institutionally designated aesthetic objects in the way it points to the immediacy of the object, the immersion into the experience through the investment of desire. Effectively it involves the capacity to develop a de-control of the emotions, to open oneself up to the full range of sensations available which the object can summon up. A further question needs to be considered. To what extent can the figural and de-differentiation discussed by Lash, as well as the above use of de-distantiation, be used to suggest further related categories: pre-differentiation and pre-distantiation? May we infer a similar immersion and abandonment of coded controls and enframing of experiences which occurs prior to differentiation and distantiation processes, or can be said to emerge and be cultivated along them in circumscribed liminal moments. On a theoretical level it may be useful to approach this at a later point in terms of the changing balances that occur between involvement and detachment. Elias (1987) points to the way in which the artist swings between extreme emotional involvement and detachment. Indeed it is a central capacity generated within artistic subcultures to cultivate and manage the capacity to shift between the full exploration and control of the emotions both in the process of producing the work of art and in developing an associated style of life. (This will be discussed in more detail below.) Finally it should be added that if aesthetics is held to revolve around questions of taste, Bourdieu (1984) has developed an opposition between the high Kantian aesthetics (involving cognitive appreciation, distantiation and the controlled cultivation of pure taste) and what it denies: the enjoyment of the immediate, sensory, 'grotesque' bodily pleasures of the popular classes. In terms of the aestheticization of everyday life we have to ask how far the direct impressions, sensations and images of the consumer-culture 'dream worlds' in the big cities, which find resonances in postmodernism's figural regimes of signification, are something with a much longer history within the process of development of the popular classes and their culture. But first we must turn to a brief consideration of the experience of *modernité* in the large cities of mid- and late nineteenth-century Europe as discussed by Baudelaire, Benjamin and Simmel.

MODERNITÉ

Baudelaire, Benjamin and Simmel all sought to account for the new experiences of *modernité* in the big cities of the mid- to late nineteenth century. Baudelaire focused on the Paris of the 1840s and 1850s, which was subsequently to fascinate Benjamin. Baudelaire's world with its growth of mass culture became the subject of Benjamin's (1982b) unfinished *Passagen-Werk*. Simmel's *Philosophy of Money* (1978), written in the 1890s and published in 1900, also focuses on the experience of strollers and consumers in the new crowded urban spaces of Berlin. Simmel's Berlin was also the subject for Benjamin's reflections on his childhood: *Berliner Kindheit um 1900*, and 'Berlin Chronicle' (Benjamin 1979).

Baudelaire was fascinated by the fleeting, transitory beauty and ugliness of life in mid-nineteenth-century Paris: the changing pageants of fashionable life, the *flâneurs* strolling through the fleeting impressions of the crowds, the dandies, the heroes of modern life – referred to by Lefebvre (1978) as 'spontaneous [as opposed to professional] artists' – who sought to turn their lives into works of art (quoted in Frisby 1985a: 19). For Baudelaire art should endeavour to capture these modern scenarios. He despised contemporary artists who painted pictures with the costumes and furnishings of ancient Rome, Greece, the Middle Ages or the Orient. Rather the artist should be aware that 'every age has its own gait, glance and gesture ... not only in manners and gestures, but even in the form of the face' (Baudelaire 1964: 12). Likewise every trade or profession stamps its marks in terms of beauty or ugliness on the face and body. Hence the painter of modern life, such as Constantine Guys, whom Baudelaire admired, should endeavour to seek out the transitory, fleeting beauty which is being ever more rapidly reconstituted.

Baudelaire was fascinated by the crowd. Benjamin contrasts the distaste Engels felt for the crowd and Poe's depiction of the fear and menace of the crown with Baudelaire's *flâneur*, who inhabited a different crowd in the arcades where he had elbow-room to stroll in comfort and leisure (Benjamin 1973: 169, 194). The new Parisian arcades were the subject of Benjamin's *Passagen-Werk* (1982b). Literally they are passages, worlds without windows which are 'soul spaces of the psyche' (van Reijen 1988). These consumer-culture 'dream worlds', the arcades and department stores, were for Benjamin materializations of the phantasmagoria which Marx talked about in his section on 'the fetishism of commodities' in *Capital* (vol. I). The new department stores and arcades were temples in which goods were worshipped as fetishes. Benjamin sought to give expression to the 'sex appeal of the anorganic in the fetish character of commodities' (van Reijen 1988). (For a discussion of the department store and arcades see Williams 1982; Geist 1983.)

Within the age of industrialism art's power as illusion, its authority as an original work, the source of its 'aura', became shifted over into industry, with painting moving into advertising, architecture

into technical engineering, handicrafts and sculpture into the industrial arts to produce a mass culture. Paris exemplifed this new urban
panorama of visual representations. As Buck-Morss (1983: 213) remarks:

> One could say that the dynamics of capitalist industrialism had
> caused a curious reversal in which 'reality' and 'art' switch
> places. Reality becomes artificial, a phantasmagoria of com-
> modities and architectural construction made possible by
> the new industrial processes. The modern city was nothing
> but the proliferation of such objects, the density of which
> created an artificial landscape of buildings and consumer items
> as totally encompassing as the earlier, natural one. In fact for
> children (like Benjamin) born into an urban environment, they
> appeared to be nature itself. Benjamin's understanding of com-
> modities was not merely critical. He affirmed them as utopian
> with images which 'liberated creativity from art, just as in the
> XVIth century the sciences freed themselves from philo-
> sophy' (Passagen-Werk: 1236, 1249). This phantasmagoria of
> industrially-produced material objects, buildings, boulevards,
> all sorts of commodities from tour-books to toilet articles – for
> Benjamin *was* mass culture, and it is the central concern of the
> Passagen-Werk.

The mass media of the twentieth century, with Hollywood films, the
growing advertising industry and television, could replicate this commodity world endlessly, although Benjamin still held that the mass
media, especially film, could be used in a more critical way, not to
duplicate the illusions but to demonstrate that reality was illusion.

The constant recycling of artistic and historical themes in the
aestheticized commodity world meant that the city landscape confer-
red on childhood memories the quality of alluring half-forgotten
dreams. In the mythical and magical world of the modern city the
child discovered the new afresh, and the adult rediscovers the old in
the new (Buck-Morss 1983: 219). The capacity of the ever-changing
urban landscape to summon up associations, resemblances and
memories feeds the curiosity of the stroller in the crowds. To the
idler who strolls the streets, objects appear divorced from their
context and subject to mysterious connections in which meanings are
read on the surface of things (Buck-Morss 1986: 106). Baudelaire
(1964: 4) sought to capture this in his use of the metaphor of the
post-illness ability to see everything anew in its immediacy. Con-
valescence, he tells us, is like a return to childhood: the 'convales-
cent, like the child, is possessed in the highest degree of the faculty

of keenly interesting himself in things, be they apparently of the most trivial... The child sees everything in a state of newness, he is always *drunk*' (quoted in Frisby 1985a: 17). This passage is interesting because it resembles one in which Fredric Jameson (1984b: 118) talks about 'intensities' as in schizophrenia being one of the key features of postmodern culture and refers to vivid powerful experiences charged with affect. This leads to a breakdown of the relationship between signifiers and the fragmentation of time into a series of perpetual presents which is found in schizophrenia or post-illness perceptions. This, then, would seem to be a good example of the figural aesthetic.

In his discussion of Georg Simmel as the first sociologist of modernity, David Frisby (1985b) points to the way in which the themes of neurasthenia, the big-city dweller and the customer which Benjamin (1973: 106) detected in Baudelaire's work are also paramount in Simmel's discussion of modernity. Simmel develops interesting insights into the aesthetic dimensions of the architecture of world exhibitions whose transitory and illusory nature echoes the aesthetic dimension of commodities we have already spoken of. A similar process of the introduction of aesthetics into non-aesthetic areas can also be found in fashion. The intensified pace of fashion increases our time consciousness, and our simultaneous pleasure in newness and oldness gives us a strong sense of presentness. Changing fashions and world exhibitions point to the bewildering plurality of styles in modern life. For the middle classes the retreat to the interior of the household offered little refuge from style, for at the turn of the century when Simmel was writing, the contemporary *Jugendstil* movement (in Britain there was the parallel movement known as Aestheticism) sought to stylize 'every pot and pan'. The stylization of the interior was a paradoxical attempt to provide a toning down and relatively stable background to the subjectivism of modern life (Frisby 1985a: 65).

For Frisby (1985a: 52) Simmel's theory of cultural modernity is preferable to that of Habermas. Although Habermas (1981) discusses the aesthetics of modernity in terms of Baudelaire, his definition of cultural modernity draws on Max Weber's theory of modernity involving the differentiation of the spheres of life (Habermas 1984). For Frisby Simmel's position is preferable as it attempts to ground the aesthetic sphere in the modern life world rather than seeing it as separate from the other spheres of life.

We can use these contrasting positions to make a number of points with which to conclude the section. Firstly it may not be a question of Habermas or Simmel, but rather that both are looking at different aspects of the same process. Habermas's position builds on Weber's discussion of the emergence of separate artistic counter-cultures such as the Bohemias of the mid-nineteenth century. While the term cultural sphere, which includes science, law and religion as well as art, may direct us away from the interdependencies it has with the rest of society, it has the merit of focusing attention on the *carriers* – to the growth in numbers and power potential of specialists in symbolic production, and in particular, for our purposes, artists and intellectuals. The artistic counter-cultures were also spatially located in the big cities of the nineteenth century, and in particular in Paris (Seigel 1986), which Benjamin called 'the capital of the nineteenth century'. We therefore have to consider the position of the artist and intellectual as stroller, moving through the new urban spaces and taking in the shocks, jolts and flows of the crowd and dream worlds we have talked about.

What is important about this group, which are by trade predisposed to observe and record experiences, is that the experiences they captured while floating through the urban spaces were taken to be *the* definitive experiences of these places. In Baudelaire, Simmel and Benjamin we have numerous references to the observer's sense of detachment, then swings of immersion (involvement); but they all presume the city crowd to be a mass of anonymous individuals which they can slip into and which carries them along. Baudelaire (1964: 9), for example, talks of the pleasure of seeing 'the world, to be at the centre of the world, and yet to remain hidden from the world'. Yet the spectator is not invisible, and we could follow Bourdieu (1984) and cite good reasons why the petit bourgeois intellectual or artist may seek such invisibility and feel he is floating in the social space. He is, however, not a perfect recorder, or camera taking snapshots; he (and we need to use the term advisedly, as Janet Wolff (1985) points out in her essay 'The Invisible *Flâneuse*') is an embodied human being whose appearance and demeanour give off readable impressions and signs to those around him. These signs are to be found not only inscribed in the professions and the prostitute, but in the artist and intellectual too. Although the crowd with its rapid flow of bodies may be a place of unspoken encounters, the process of decoding and delight in reading other persons' appearance goes on apace, as Baudelaire points out. Baudelaire was not only aware of the ways in which intellectual and artistic activities, including his own work, had become commodified; he disdained the attempts of the ethereal, spiritually minded artist to escape the process of appropriation in public life. Hence in his prose piece 'Loss of a Halo' he mocks the poet who thinks he can float invisibly through the crowds and shows that his art is profane and his persona socially recognizable (see Spencer 1985: 71; Berman 1982: 155).

Once we move from this liminal sphere into direct social encounters in shops, offices, institutions the flow is slowed down and the reading process goes on more precisely, as participants are able to detect, monitor and react to the symbolic power manifest in the unconscious bodily signs and gestures: the dress, style, tone of voice, facial expression, demeanour, stance, gait all incorporated in body volume, height, weight etc., which betray the social origins of the bearer. In effect the artist and intellectual must be understood in terms of their lifestyle, which is socially recognizable and locatable in the social space. They also have a social interest in: (1) the wider acceptance of their perceptions on life, namely the value of the aesthetic gaze, even while challenging and negating it; the value of cultural and intellectual goods in general and the need for instruction into how to use and experience them; and (2) the proclamation of the superiority of their lifestyle manifest in their subcultures so that others will adopt the off-duty fashions, styles and perceptions they embody – if not those of the very moment, put forth by the avant-garde, then those of yesterday which would maintain the useful distance between the cognoscenti and their eager, but lagging behind, audiences and followers.

While we can use Weber and Habermas to direct us towards the artists' and intellectuals' tastes and lifestyles, and their interest in the generalization of aesthetic perceptions and sensibilities, Simmel and Benjamin can be used to direct us towards the way in which the urban landscape has become aestheticized and enchanted through the architecture, billboards, shop displays, advertisements, packages, street signs etc. and through the embodied persons who move through these spaces: the individuals who wear, to varying degrees, fashionable clothing, hair-styles, make-up, or who move or hold their bodies in particular stylized ways. The aestheticization of everyday life in this second sense points to the expansion and extension of commodity production in the big cities, which has thrown up new buildings, department stores, arcades, malls etc. and produced an endless array of goods to fill the shops and clothe and cater for those who pass through them. It is this double capacity of the commodity to be exchange-value and ersatz use-value, to be the same and different, which allows it to take up an aestheticized image, whatever may be the one currently dreamt up. Sennett (1976), for example, tells of how in the first Paris department store, Bon Marché, shortly after it was opened in the 1850s one of the first window displays featured pots and pans. The pots and pans were stylistically arranged into a South Sea Island display with shells, coral beads, palms etc. to produce an aesthetic effect. We have also to ask the question: 'Who arranged the display?' The answer would be dressers, but we can also point to other related workers in advertising, marketing, design, fashion, commercial art, architecture, journalism, etc., who help to design and create the dream worlds. In many ways their tastes, dispositions and classificatory schemes are similar to those of the artists and intellectuals, and they usually keep in touch with the latest developments in this sphere. Hence in many overt and subtle ways they also transmit aesthetic dispositions and sensibilities, and the notions of 'the artist as hero' and the importance of the 'stylization life' to wider publics (see Allen 1983; Frith and Horne 1988; Zukin 1988a). In effect as cultural intermediaries they have an important role in educating the public into new styles and tastes.

The second point we can note is that many of the features associated with the postmodern aestheticization of everyday life have a basis in modernity. The predominance of images, liminality, the vivid intensities characteristic in the perceptions of children, those recovering from illness, schizophrenics etc. as well as figural regimes of signification can all be said to have parallels in the experiences of *modernité* as described by Baudelaire, Benjamin and Simmel. In this sense we can point to the links between modernism and postmodernism as Lyotard (1984: 72) does when he says that postmodernism 'is not modernism at its end but in the nascent state, and that state is constant'. While Lyotard is referring to artistic modernism and takes a Kantian perspective on postmodernity as the avant-gardist attempt constantly to express the inexpressible and represent the unrepresentable, we can also extend this to late twentieth-century spectacles and simulated environments in malls, shopping centres, department stores, theme parks, 'Disney's Worlds' etc. (see Urry 1988) which have many features in common with the department stores, arcades, world's fairs etc. described by Benjamin, Simmel and others. To mention a brief example: the Paris Exposition of 1900 involved a number of simulations including: an exotic Indian landscape with stuffed animals, treasures and merchandise; an exhibit representing Andalucian Spain at the time of the Moors, with simulated interiors and courtyards; a Trans-Siberian panorama which placed spectators in a real railway car which moved along a track, while a canvas was unrolled outside the window to give an impression of Siberia. There was also an early demonstration of Cinerama (see Williams 1982).

Thirdly, the figural emphasis upon primary processes, the flows of images, the dreamlike quality of modernity with its vivid intensities and sense of wonder at the commodity aesthetics on display may itself be traceable back further than modernity. We will shortly look at the forerunners in carnivals, fairs, theatres and other public spaces. Such locations offered excitement, a new range of sensations, and the general de-control of the emotions, a contrast and temporary relief from the general control of affects which results from civilizing processes.

Fourthly, we will have little to say about the progressive or retrogressive aspects of this process, save to note that a good deal has been made of the antinomial, transgressive qualities of the artistic and intellectual subcultures of modernism, and their invasion of everyday life through the development of consumer culture. In effect for Bell (1976) art has undermined morality and the puritan work ethic gives way to the hedonistic search for new sensations and gratifications on the part of the 'untrammelled self'. It is possible that Bell has overemphasized the social threat and de-moralizing effect on society through an overemphasis on the transgressive socially destabilizing qualities of art and an overestimation of the role of beliefs as opposed to practices in producing a viable social order. In addition, despite many attempts by artists to outbid each other in their quest to scandalize the petite bourgeoisie, it can be argued that rather than being a naive, uncontrolled emotional regression many of the practices and lifestyles of artists necessarily involve 'a controlled de-control of the emotions', which may entail, and indeed require, the mutual respect and self-restraint of the participants as opposed to a narcissistic regression which threatens to destroy the social bond (see Wouters 1986).

THE MIDDLE CLASSES AND THE CONTROL OF THE CARNIVALESQUE

For Daniel Bell (1976) modernism with its antinomial and transgressive qualities has dominated in the arts since the mid-nineteenth century. Certainly since the mid-nineteenth century, especially in Paris after the 1848 revolution, we see the emergence of Bohemias which adopt the strategies of transgression in their art and lifestyle (Seigel 1986). The representation of the *bohème* existed outside the limits of bourgeois society and identified with the proletariat and the left. Hauser (1982) refers to the bohemians as the first true artistic proletariat, consisting of people whose existence was completely insecure. Indeed they lived cheek by jowl with the lower orders in the low-rent areas of the large cities. They cultivated similar manners, valuing spontaneity, an anti-systematic work ethos, lack of attention to the sense of ordered living space and controls and conventions of the respectable middle class. Yet while the symbols and lifestyle may have seemed to be new within the middle classes, there is a long history of the transgressive strategies they adopted. Within the middle classes there are attempts to use transgressive symbols to shock which runs parallel to civilizing processes which sought to bring about the control of emotions through manners. It is therefore possible, following Stallybrass and White (1986) to see Bohemias as producing 'liminoid symbolic repertoires' similar to those afforded by earlier carnival forms. Middle-class Bohemias, especially surrealism and expressionism, took over in a displaced form much of the symbolic inversion and transgressions which were found in the carnival. It may be possible therefore to trace back to the carnival of the Middle Ages many of the figural aspects, the disconnected succession of fleeting images, sensations, de-control of the emotions and de-differentiation which have become associated with postmodernism, and the aestheticization of everyday life.

In their *Politics and Poetics of Transgression* (1986) Stallybrass and White discuss the relational nature of carnivals, festivals and fairs which are seen as symbolic inversions and transgressions in which the distinction between high/low, official/popular, classical/grotesque are constructed and deformed. They draw on Bakhtin's (1968) work to point to the ways in which the carnival involves the celebration of the *grotesque body* – fattening food, intoxicating drink, sexual promiscuity – in a world in which official culture is turned upside down. The grotesque body of the carnival is the lower body of impurity, disproportion, immediacy, orifices, the material body, which is the opposite of the *classical body*, which is beautiful, symmetrical, elevated, perceived from a distance and is the ideal body. The grotesque body and the carnival represent the Otherness which is excluded from the process of formation of middle-class identity and culture. With the extension of the civilizing process into the middle classes the need for greater controls over the emotions and bodily functions produced changes in manners and conduct which heightened the sense of disgust at direct emotional and bodily expressivity (Elias 1978, 1983; Bogner 1987). In effect the Other which is excluded as part of the identity-formation process becomes the object of desire.

Stallybrass and White provide an interesting discussion of the dual role of fairs: firstly as the open space of the market place in which commercial exchanges take place in a local market which is connected to, and displays wares from other national and international markets; secondly as sites of pleasure which are local, festive and communal, and are unconnected to the real world. Fairs were therefore not just guardians of local traditions; they were sites of transformation of popular tradition through the intersection of different cultures. They were sites of what Bakhtin refers to as *hybridization*, which brought together the exotic and familiar, the villagers and townsmen, the professional performer and bourgeois observer. As agents of cultural pluralism they were not, then, just 'Otherness' to official discourse, but involved the disruption of provincial habits and local traditions via the introduction of different, more cosmopolitan people and cultural objects. They displayed the exotic and strange commodities from different parts of the world and along with a flood of strange signs, bizarre juxtapositions, people with different dress, demeanour and languages, freaks, spectacles and performances stimulated desire and excitement. They were in effect outdoor forerunners of the department stores and world exhibitions of the late nineteenth century, and we can surmise produced some of the same effects in a more tamed and controlled manner. Aspects of the untamed emotions, inversions and transgressions which still produced a kind of 'social vertigo' and festive disorder survived in the music halls (see Bailey 1986a, b; Clark 1985). The excitement and fears the fair can arouse are still captured today in films which highlight the way in which these liminal spaces are sites in which excitement, danger and the shock of the grotesque merge with dreams and fantasies which threaten to overwhelm and engulf the spectators. Today fun fairs and theme parks such as Disneyland still retain this aspect, albeit in a more controlled, safer way, to provide enclaved environments for the controlled de-control of the emotions, where adults are given permission to behave like children again.

Elements of the carnivalesque were displaced from the fair into literature. Writing about the fair could be an act bent on producing carnivalesque outrage or dissociation from these lower pleasures. In the seventeenth century we also find attempts by Dryden and others to transform theatre audiences from the inattentive, noisy carnivalesque rabble into the disciplined, controlled, polite and appreciative bourgeois theatre public. These contrary pulls towards popular culture and a more genteel educative culture in the middle classes opened up spaces for cultural entrepreneurs. Sir Robert Southwell in 1685 wrote to advise his son that he should consider Bartholemew Fair as a suitable subject for a profitable book. To write the book his son would have to learn the rules of resemblances and differentiation of the fair by watching it from some high window to survey the crowd. He was also advised to read Ben Jonson's play on the fair

(Stallybrass and White 1986: 118–19). Here we have an early example of the education project of the middle class in developing structured accounts and pedagogies for new publics about how to read popular cultural experiences in an aestheticized way. Southwell is clear about the dangers of the enterprise, that his son will be lost in endless distinctions which end in 'blank confusion'. This is the threat of disorder which demands elevation and not immersion in order to produce the detached aesthetic appreciation.

We find a similar example in Wordsworth's account of Bartholemew Fair in *The Prelude* (1805). While the fair is 'monstrous', he revels in the 'colour, motion, shape, sight and sounds' of the wonders from all parts of the world which are jumbled up together to produce a transgression and confusion of boundaries in which animals become human, humans become animals etc. (Stallybrass and White 1986: 120). For Wordsworth the proliferation of differences and erosion of boundaries in the fair and the city threaten to 'cast loose the chain of signifiers' and dissolve his identity into 'blank confusion' (Stallybrass and White 1986: 123). The fear of total immersion, the loss of boundaries and the loss of self is resolved by Wordsworth by invoking the classical 'Muse'. In effect the symbolic hierarchies of a classical aesthetic are invoked to retain some neoclassical notion of an education project in which the lower orders and forms will be raised up and ennobled by the poet. For the varieties of modernism that developed in the late nineteenth century and postmodernism in the late twentieth century the neoclassical option was ruled out and the figural disorders were explored and cultivated. This is not to imply that the educative mission was abandoned; far from it. Rather the educative project becomes one in which the techniques necessary for a controlled de-control of the emotions are developed. Techniques of the self can be developed to foster sensibilities which allow us to enjoy the swing between the extremes of aesthetic involvement and detachment; thus the pleasures of immersion and detached distantiation can both be enjoyed.

The civilizing process therefore involved an increasing control of the emotions, sense of disgust at bodily betrayal, the smells, sweating, and noises of the lower body, and sensitivity to one's own bodily space. It involved the middle class in a process of complex distancing from the popular, the grotesque Other. Yet Stallybrass and White (1986: 191) argue that this rise in the threshold of the disgust function which Elias (1978) talks about also bears the offprint of desire for the expelled Other which became the source of fascination, longing and nostalgia. Hence we have the attractions of the forest, fair, theatre, circus, slum, savage, seaside resort for the bourgeois. If the experience of these sites were not acknowledged, if the structures of the civilizing process were too strong, then there was the possibility that this danger zone *outside* of consciousness would become one *inside*, in the subconscious fed by the struggle to exclude it. Hysteria in late nineteenth-century middle-class women is an example of the price of excluding the lower body and associated symbolic disorders. We should also add that rather than see a strong polarization derived from the 'binaryism of symbolic functioning' which is held by Stallybrass and White (1986: 189) to be at the centre of cultural production, it is also possible to detect shifts in the balances between civilizing and informalizing (emotional de-controlling) processes which themselves represent a higher level of control of the emotions and not a regression: that is, a 'controlled de-control of the emotions' (Wouters, 1986). In this sense as I have argued elsewhere (Featherstone, 1989b), postmodernism has drawn much from the social and cultural wave of informalization in the 1960s. The elements of the carnivalesque which became displaced into art, and retained in consumer cultural sites and spectacles, and in the media of film and television, now have larger middle-class audiences who have moved away from the more rigid personality structure associated with the puritan ethic which Bell (1976) speaks of, and are better able to cope with threatening emotions. In effect fractions of the new middle class have become more educated into a controlled de-control of the emotions and the sensibilities and tastes that support a greater appreciation of the aestheticization of everyday life (see Featherstone, 1989b).

CONCLUDING REMARKS

In this essay I have attempted to sketch out some of the features of the aestheticization of everyday life and have argued that it is not unique to postmodernism but that it can be traced back to the experience of the big cities of the mid-nineteenth century as described by Baudelaire, Benjamin and Simmel. I have argued that similar aesthetic experiences seem also to have been generated in the carnivals and fairs in which the emergent middle classes struggled to grapple with the symbolic inversions and the grotesque body of the lower orders, which remained an ever present Otherness running parallel to the civilizing process. In effect, to construct an identity, to know who you are, you need to know who you are not; and the material excluded or confined to the boundaries may continue to exert a fascination or allure and stimulate desires. Hence the attraction of the sites of 'ordered disorder': the carnival, fairs, music halls, spectacles, resorts, and, today, theme parks, malls, tourism. As Stallybrass and White (1986) wryly comment, the bourgeoisie never really returned from Bougainville's voyage and still succumb to the fascination of the constructed exotic Otherness.

NOTE

I would like to thank David Chaney, Peter Bailey, Steve Best, Bryan Turner and Andy Wernick for commenting on an earlier version of this essay. Previous versions were given at the Popular Culture Association Conference, New Orleans, March 1988 and the Conference on Modernity as History, Copenhagen, October 1988.

REFERENCES

Allen, J. S. 1983: *The Romance of Commerce and Culture*. Chicago: University of Chicago Press.

Bailey, P. 1986a: 'Champagne Charlie', in J. S. Bratton *Music Hall: Performance and Style*. Milton Keynes: Open University Press.

Bailey, P. 1986b: *Music Hall: The Business of Pleasure*. Milton Keynes: Open University Press.

Bakhtin, 1968: *Rabelais and His World*. Cambridge, Mass.: MIT Press.

Baudelaire, C. 1964: *The Painter of Modern Life and Other Essays*. Oxford: Phaidon.

Baudelaire, C. 1965: *Art in Paris 1845–1862*. Oxford: Phaidon.

Baudrillard, J. 1983a: *In the Shadow of the Silent Majorities*. New York: Semiotext(e).

Baudrillard, J. 1983b: *Simulations*. New York: Semiotext(e).

Bell, D. 1976: *The Cultural Contradictions of Capitalism*. London: Heinemann.

Benjamin, W. 1973: *Charles Baudelaire: A Lyric Poet in the Era of High Capitalism*. London: New Left Books.

Benjamin, W. 1979: 'Berlin chronicle', in *One Way Street and Other Writings*. London: New Left Books.

Benjamin, W. 1982a: 'On some motifs in Baudelaire', in *Illuminations*. London: Cape.

Benjamin, W. 1982b: *Das Passagen-Werk*, 2 vols. Frankfurt a.M.: Surhkamp.

Berman, M. 1982: *All that Is Solid Melts into Air: The Experience of Modernity*. New York: Simon & Schuster; 1983: London: Verso; 1988 (2nd edn): Harmondsworth: Penguin.

Bogner, A. 1987: 'Elias and the Frankfurt School', *Theory, Culture and Society*, 4/2–3.

Bourdieu, P. 1984: *Distinction: A Social Critique of the Judgement of Taste*. London: Routledge.

Buck-Morss, S. 1983: 'Benjamin's Passagen-Werk', *New German Critique*, 29.

Buck-Morss, S. 1986: 'The flaneur, the sandwichman and the whore: the politics of loitering', *New German Critique*, 39.

Calefato, P. 1988: 'Fashion, the passage, the body', *Cultural Studies*, 2/2.

Chambers, I. 1987: 'Maps for the metropolis: a possible guide to the postmodern,' *Cultural Studies*, 1/1.

Chen, K. H. 1987: 'Baudrillard's implosive postmodernism', *Theory, Culture and Society*, 4/1.

Cooke, P. 1988: 'Modernity, postmodernity and the city', *Theory, Culture and Society*, 5/2–3.

Clark, T. J. 1985: *The Painting of Modern Life*. London: Thames & Hudson.

Crary, J. 1987: 'The eclipse of the spectacle', in B. Wallis (ed.), *Art After Modernism*, New York: Godine.

Denzin, N. 1988: '*Blue Velvet*: postmodern contradictions', *Theory, Culture and Society*, 5/2–3.

Elias, N. 1978: *The Civilizing Process*, vol. 1: *The History of Manners*. Oxford: Blackwell.

Elias, N. 1983: *The Civilizing Process*, vol. 2: *State Formation and Civilization*. Oxford: Blackwell.

Elias, N. 1987: *Involvement and Detachment*. Oxford: Blackwell.

Featherstone, M. 1987: 'Lifestyle and Consumer Culture', *Theory, Culture and Society*, 4/1.

Featherstone, M. 1988a: 'Cultural production, consumption and the development of the cultural sphere', paper presented at the Third German–American Theory Group Conference, Bremen.

Featherstone, M. 1988b: 'In pursuit of the postmodern', *Theory, Culture and Society*, 5/2–3.

Featherstone, M. 1989a: 'Postmodernism, cultural change and social practice', in D. Kellner (ed.), *Jameson/Postmodernism/Critique*. Washington, DC: Maisonneuve Press.

Featherstone, M. 1989b: 'Towards a sociology of postmodern culture', in H. Haferkamp (ed.), *Culture and Social Structure*. Berlin: de Gruyter.

Foucault, M. 1986: 'What is enlightenment', in P. Rabinow (ed.), *The Foucault Reader*. Harmondsworth: Penguin.

Frisby, D. 1982: *Sociological Impressionism: A Reassessment of Georg Simmel's Social Theory*. London: Heinemann.

Frisby, D. 1985a: *Fragments of Modernity*. Cambridge: Polity Press.

Frisby, D. 1985b: 'Georg Simmel, first sociologist of modernity', *Theory, Culture and Society*, 2/3.

Frith, S. and Horne, H. 1987: *Art into Pop*. London: Methuen.

Geist, H. 1983: *Arcades: The History of a Building Type*. Cambridge, Mass.: MIT Press.

Habermas, J. 1981: 'Modernity versos Postmodernity', New German Critique, 22: 3–14.

Habermas, J. 1984: *The Theory of Communicative Action*, vol. 1. Cambridge: Polity Press.

Hassan, I. 1985: 'Postmodern culture', *Theory, Culture and Society*, 2/3.

Haug, W. F. 1986: *Critique of Commodity Aesthetics*. Cambridge: Polity Press.

Haug, W. F. 1987: *Commodity Aesthetics, Ideology and Culture*. New York: International General.

Hauser, A. 1982: *The Sociology of Art*. London: Routledge.

Hazard, P. 1964: *The European Mind 1680–1715*. Harmondsworth: Penguin.

Jameson, F. 1979: 'Utopia and mass culture', *Social Text*, 1/1.

Jameson, F. 1984a: 'Postmodernism, or the cultural logic of late capitalism', *New Left Review*, 146.

Jameson, F. 1984b: 'Postmodernism and the consumer society', in H. Foster (ed.), *Postmodern Culture*. London: Pluto.

Kaplan, E. A. 1986: 'History, spectator and gender address in music television', *Journal of Communications Inquiry*, 10/1.

Kaplan, E. A. 1987: *Rocking Around the Clock: Music Television, Postmodernism and Consumer Culture*. London: Methuen.

Kellner, D. 1988: 'Postmodernism as social theory: some challenges and problems', *Theory, Culture and Society*, 5/2–3.

Kroker, A. 1985: 'Baudrillard's Marx', *Theory, Culture and Society*, 2/3.

Kroker, A. and Cook, D. 1987: *The Postmodern Science*. New York: St Martin's Press.

Lash, S. 1988: 'Discourse or figure? Postmodernism as a regime of signification', *Theory, Culture and Society*, 5/2–3.

Lefebvre, H. 1978: *Everyday Life in the Modern World*. London: Allen Lane.

Lyotard, J. F. 1971: *Discours, figure*. Paris: Klincksiek.

Lyotard, J. F. 1984: *The Postmodern Condition*. Manchester: Manchester University Press.

Mannheim, K. 1956: 'Democratic culture' in *Essays on the Sociology of Culture*. London: Routledge & Kegan Paul.

Marcuse, H. 1969: *An Essay on Liberation*. Harmondsworth: Penguin.

Martin, B. 1981: *A Sociology of Contemporary Cultural Change*. Oxford: Blackwell.

Megill, A. 1985: *Prophet of Extremity*. Berkeley: University of California Press.

Poster, M. 1975: *Existential Marxism in Postwar France*. Princeton: Princeton University Press.

Robbins, D. 1987: 'Sport, hegemony and the middle class: the Victorian mountaineers', *Theory, Culture and Society*, 4/4.

Roberts, D. 1988: 'The museum as montage', *Theory, Culture and Society*, 5/2–3.

Rorty, R. 1986: 'Freud and moral reflection', in J. H. Smith and E. Kearigan (eds), *Pragmatism's Freud*. Baltimore: Johns Hopkins University Press.

Rosengren, K. E. 1987: 'Literary criticism: future invented', *Poetics*, 16.

Said, E. W. 1978: *Orientalism*. London: Routledge & Kegan Paul.

Seigel, J. 1986: *Bohemian Paris*. New York: Viking.

Sennett, R. 1976: *The Fall of Public Man*. Cambridge: Cambridge University Press.

Shusterman, R. 1988: 'Postmodernist aestheticism; a new moral philosophy?', *Theory, Culture and Society*, 5/2–3.

Simmel, G. 1978: *The Philosophy of Money*. London: Routledge & Kegan Paul.

Spencer, L. 1985: 'Allegory in the world of the commodity: the importance of *Central Park*', *New German Critique*, 34.

Stallybrass, P. and White, A. 1986: *The Politics and Poetics of Transgression*. London: Methuen.

Stauth, G. and Turner, B. S. 1988: *Nietzsche's Dance*. Oxford: Blackwell.

Urry, J. 1988: 'Cultural change and contemporary holiday-making, *Theory, Culture and Society*, 5/1.

Vattimo, G. 1988: 'Hermeneutics as koine', *Theory, Culture and Society*, 5/2–3.

van Reijen, W. 1988: '*The Dialectic of Enlightenment*, read as allegory', *Theory, Culture and Society*, 5/2–3.

Williams, R. 1982: *Dream Worlds*. Berkeley: University of California Press.

Wolff, J. 1983: *Aesthetics and the Sociology of Art*. London: Allen & Unwin.

Wolff, J. 1985: 'The invisible *flaneuse*', *Theory, Culture and Society*, 2–3.

Wolin, R. 1986a: 'Foucault's aesthetic decision', *Telos*, 67.

Wolin, R. 1986b: *Walter Benjamin*. New York: Columbia University Press.

Wouters, C. 1986: 'The formalization of informalization: changing tension balances in civilizing processes', *Theory, Culture and Society*, 3/2.

Wouters, C. 1987: 'Differences in the behavioural codes between the sexes: the formalization of informalization in the Netherlands, 1930–1985', *Theory, Culture and Society*, 4/2–3.

Zukin, S. 1988a: *Loft Living: Culture and Capital in Urban Change*, 2nd edn. London: Radius/Hutchinson.

Zukin, S. 1988b: 'The Postmodern debate over urban form', *Theory, Culture and Society*, 5/2–3.

Part IV

Modernity and the voice of the Other

12

We, the people: popular culture and popular identity in modern Europe

Peter Burke

This essay examines one important form of collective identity in post-medieval Europe, that of 'the people'. More exactly, it examines two forms of collective identity, since the term 'the people' is ambiguous, and has been so from ancient Roman times at least. In the first place, it signifies everyone in a particular city, region or nation, as opposed to other peoples. As the Roman lawyers used to say, 'the safety of the people is the highest law', *Salus populi suprema lex*. In the second place, the term 'people' signifies the members of the subordinate as opposed to the ruling classes, as in the classical phrase distinguishing the Roman Senate from the people, *Senatus Populusque Romanus* (Boas 1984; Payne 1976).

This essay is therefore divided into two parts, corresponding to these two concepts of the people, the inclusive (one might say) and the exclusive, the first of them generally linked with right-wing politics and the second with the left. Today, the study of popular culture is associated with left-wing politics, as in the contemporary British examples of Edward Thompson, Raymond Williams, Raphael Samuel and Stuart Hall. In the nineteenth century, on the other hand, students of what they called 'folklore' were often conservatives, who saw themselves as defending traditional values against the assaults of modernization.

Discussing the two concepts of the people necessarily involves dealing in turn with two of the best-known – not to say hackneyed – themes in modern history, the so-called rise of nationalism, and the so-called making of the working class. My purpose, however, is to consider these two movements from the somewhat oblique perspective of the cultural construction of identity.

From this point of view, what is significant is the coexistence of these two rival claims to identity, a rivalry which the use of the term 'people' was unable to disguise altogether. Ordinary people in many parts of Europe were invited at much the same time to identify themselves as members of a class and as members of a nation. Historians have come to recognize, with some reluctance, that neither invitation received as enthusiastic a response as was expected. To what extent did the two movements neutralize each other? To what extent did the same people identify themselves in different ways in different situations (from strikes to wars)?

In this essay I shall place particular emphasis on the spread of the idea of the people (in both its senses) among the subordinate classes. I shall argue that the spread of this idea indicates major changes in collective self-consciousness, and also that these changes in consciousness were essentially reactions to attempts by other people to change their culture or way of life.[1] The inclusive concept of the people was associated with acceptance of these changes, while the exclusive concept was associated with resistance to 'modernization'.

IDENTITIES OF CONSENSUS, OR THE RISE OF NATIONALISM

It is commonplace to call the nineteenth and twentieth centuries the age of the rise of nationalism, first in Europe and then in other parts of the world. The social, cultural and political conditions for this movement, from the rise of print to the decline of the 'society of orders' have been analysed in several recent books (Anderson 1983; Gellner 1983; Smith 1986). Other studies have been more concerned with the cultural consequences of nationalism, for example with the attempt to use the schools to encourage national consciousness and a national language, and especially to turn 'peasants' rooted in a regional culture into Frenchmen, Italians or whatever (De Mauro 1960: 81ff.; Weber 1976: esp. ch. 19). What I should like to discuss here is the relation between the twin – but sometimes conflicting – concerns for national identity and popular culture.

In some parts of Europe, the words for 'people' and 'nation' are identical; *narod in Slav* languages such as Russian, Polish, Czech and Serbo-Croat, *nép* in Hungarian (*Volk* in German is also ambiguous, but coexists with the term *Nation*). It is difficult to know whether to translate the titles of some collections of what we call 'folk-songs' as 'popular songs' or 'national songs'.[2] This ambiguity papers over the cracks between the two concepts of the people, which are more apparent in the Romance languages.

All over Europe, however, the movements of so-called national 'revival' of the nineteenth century, from the Celtic Revival in Ireland to the 'Renaissance' in Catalonia and Occitania, were associated with what it may be useful to call the 'discovery of popular culture' by the intellectuals and more generally by the upper and middle classes (for details see Burke 1978: ch. 1).

It should be explained at this point that in this essay 'culture' is taken to mean attitudes, values and mentalities, as they are expressed, embodied and symbolized in artifacts, performances and the practice of everyday life. Social anthropologists today place most emphasis on cultural practice. It is probably fair to say, however, that the discoverers, men of letters for the most part, from Herder to Scott and from Mistral to Yeats, took particular notice of popular poetry and music. The discovery of folk art and artifacts came relatively late in the nineteenth century, with the foundation of the great open-air museums in Sweden, Norway and other parts of Europe, and the increasing interest in folk costume on the part of tourists.

There was, it is true, considerable middle-class interest, whether nostalgic or patronizing, in the world-view or mentality of the peasants, but this interest was much less differentiated or specific than the interest in their costumes or ballads. The attitudes and customs of the farmers and agricultural workers of their day – ironically enough, a period when the countryside was increasingly penetrated by capitalism – were interpreted by nineteenth-century scholars as simple 'survivals' of an archaic or 'pagan' way of thinking, assumed to be more or less the same all over Europe or even Eurasia. According to Sir James Frazer, for example, 'the popular superstitions and customs of the peasantry are by far the fullest and most trustworthy evidence we possess as to the primitive religion of the Aryans' (Frazer 1890: Preface).

From the perspective of modern anthropology, we might describe the European discovery of popular culture as a series of 'nativistic' movements in the sense of movements to revive traditional culture, often in societies which were under foreign domination, or domination which was perceived as foreign by some at least of the dominated (Linton 1943; Fernandez 1966).

There are clear links between the publication of some famous collections of folk-songs and the rise or, not to make it sound too spontaneous, the 'mobilization' or even the 'constitution' of national identity. The anthology *Des Knaben Wunderhorn*, for example, first published in 1806, was intended by at least one of its editors, the Prussian nobleman Achim von Arnim, to encourage German national consciousness and unite a 'divided people', while the Prussian statesman the Freiherr von Stein recommended it in similar terms. The collection *Svenska Folkvisor*, published in 1814, was the work of two members of the Gothic Society, founded to revive the traditional Swedish or 'Gothic' virtues of a past age when, as one of the editors put it, 'the whole people sang as one man' (in this case, the stimulus to the revival was not a foreign invasion or a revolt against a colonial power but the loss of a colony, Finland, to another empire, that of Russia).

It was also in 1814, at the time of the suppression of a Serbian rising against Austrian domination, that Vuk Stefanovic Karadžić published his famous collection of Serbian folk-songs. The first anthology of Polish folk-songs, Gołębiowski's *Lud Polski* (1830), was also published at the time of an unsuccessful rising, this time against Russian domination. An important edition of Italian folk-songs, *Canti popolari*, was published in 1841 by Niccolò Tommaseo, an exile because of his opposition to Austrian rule in Italy.

A particularly famous case of a man of letters playing a fundamental role in the construction of national identity is that of the Finn Elias Lönnrot, who began by collecting folk-songs, which he published in 1829 in a collection he called *The Finnish Harp*, and went on to write the *Kalevala*, a poem which has been canonized as the Finnish national epic, and has also been described as 'the nearest to popular tradition of all the world's national epics because almost every one of its lines has an equivalent in the folk songs' (Hautala 1969: 26).[3] Like the brothers Grimm in Germany, Lönrott believed that folk-songs were the collective work of the people.

It is perhaps no accident that some of the great national histories of the nineteenth century were written by scholars with a great interest in folk-songs, notably Erik Gustav Geijer, František Palacký and Jules Michelet, who were respectively the authors of histories of the Swedish, Czech and French 'peoples'. All the same, we should not be too quick to assume an identity of purpose among these three historians, and others like J. R. Green, author of *A Short History of the English People* (1874). Green, a liberal Church of England clergyman with a working-class parish in Stepney, wrote a history of England which found room for an account of the daily lives and aspirations of ordinary people and was intended to be read by ordinary people – the book was in fact a best-seller. Palacký, on the other hand, was concerned with an ethnic group. His multi-volume *History of the Czech People* (1836 onwards) was organized around the theme of contacts and conflicts between the Czechs and their German neighbours.

Michelet's notion of 'people' is perhaps the most ambiguous of all.

Jules Michelet was a man of the left, working-class in origin (his father was a printer), a hater of priests and kings, a supporter of the French revolutions of 1830 and 1848 as well as 1789. He was also the author of an eleven-volume history of France which celebrated achievements such as the Renaissance, hardly the work of the 'people'.[4]

In some cases, folk-songs (and sometimes their collectors) were implicated in political movements which we tend to call 'regionalist' because these areas have not achieved independence; Brittany, for example, or Catalonia. The Breton folklorist T. H. C. Hersart de Villemarqué published his famous collection, *Barsaz Breiz*, in 1839. The Catalan Manuel Milà i Fontanals was involved in the movement of cultural (or national) revival known by Catalans as *La Renaixença*. It has been argued that the growing interest in the traditional culture of nineteenth-century Catalonia had political roots, indeed that a 'myth of popular tradition' was created to justify claims for autonomy from Madrid (Prats 1988).[5] From the point of view of the modern centralized national state, popular culture was a two-edged weapon. It assisted the revolt against multicultural empires like those of the Habsburgs or Ottomans, but it left the national state, which generally lacked linguistic (not to mention cultural) homogeneity, extremely vulnerable to movements of regional revolt.

All these examples of the discovery of popular culture might very well be analysed in terms of the idea of the 'invention of tradition', not because the songs were faked – although this also happened from time to time – but because they were attributed to particular peoples, despite the fact that many ballads (such as 'Manuel the Mason' in the Balkans) did not respect political or even linguistic frontiers (Hobsbawm and Ranger 1983). Like archaeological remains, ballads were and are objects of conflicting claims to ownership on the part of different nations, claims which have tended to seem more than a little absurd to outsiders, but had and still have great importance for participants precisely because they are claims to identity – given that who we are depends on who 'we' were.

This international movement of national self-discovery is full of paradoxes and ironies. Intellectuals all over Europe tended to regard peasants in particular as 'the nation's most adequate representatives' on the grounds that the peasants were the least contaminated by foreign influences and the most in touch with the nation's distant past (Falnes 1933: 55). There was a boom in paintings of peasants – often the work of middle-class artists, and generally intended for a middle-class public.[6]

On the other hand, the intellectuals' knowledge of the peasants was often second-hand. It has been suggested, for example, that 'Much of what Yeats believed about the Irish peasantry ... was formed by the literature produced by the more cultivated sections of the nineteenth-century landlord class' (Deane 1985: 34). When they did make contact with the peasant, they sometimes discovered that he (or doubtless she) was in the course of acquiring a taste for the products of modern international industrial culture, such as curtains, mirrors, clocks and stoves. They felt that 'he was deserting his role just as the cultured awoke to appreciate it'. Popular consciousness of the appropriate kind had in some cases (Falnes 1933: 58ff.) to be encouraged by means of journals like the Norwegian *Folkevennen* (Friend of the People). One group of the middle class, the reformists, tried to persuade ordinary people to modernize, while another group or generation, the populists, tried to persuade them to remain faithful to tradition.

IDENTITIES OF RESISTANCE, OR THE MAKING OF THE WORKING CLASS

In many parts of the world, collective identities have been formed or re-formed in the course of resistance to the West. In Latin America in the nineteenth century, for example, there was a long and intense conflict between Westernizing elites, who attempted to reform their countries along foreign lines, and those who fought to preserve their traditional local cultures from modernization. In this case the conflict between centre and periphery and the conflict between dominant and subordinate classes virtually merged into one (Burns 1980).

However, 'identities of resistance' of this kind existed in the West itself. In East and Central Europe in the nineteenth century, the situation was not unlike the Latin American one, with a wide gap, indeed a sharp conflict, between the elites, who generally identified themselves with the 'West', and the peasants, who still saw their own villages as the centre of the universe (Hofer 1984; Fel and Hofer 1969). This conflict led to the peasants becoming conscious of themselves as peasants, and on occasion, as in Croatia and Hungary, joining political parties founded to promote their interests.

In Europe generally, one of the most important identities of resistance was and is that of 'the people' in the exclusive sense, the people as opposed to the ruling class. It is not difficult to find examples, from the late Middle Ages onwards, of the ruling class using the term 'the people' to refer to the remainder of the population, to describe them as ignorant, superstitious, disorderly and so on. The problem is rather to discover whether, or more exactly when and where, this remainder of the population identified themselves as 'the people' or the 'working class'.

Much has been written on the rise of class consciousness in nineteenth-century Europe. One of the major contributions to the subject is Edward Thompson's famous book *The Making of the English Working Class*, first published in 1963. Thompson's study is a pioneering piece of history from below. It sets out, in its author's words, 'to rescue the poor stockinger, the Luddite cropper, the "obsolete" hand-loom weaver . . . from the enormous condescension of posterity'. It tries to reconstruct their experiences, their culture – their religion (Methodism or millenarianism), their reading (chapbooks and almanacs), the ethos expressed in their rituals of 'mutuality', and so on. Its central theme is that of modernity and identity, in the sense that it argues that 'In the years between 1780 and 1832 most English working people came to feel an identity of interests as between themselves, and as against their rulers and employers' (Thompson 1963: 11–12).

Thompson's attention to culture and to language, still unusual in social history in the early 1960s, has inspired later historians, though some of them feel that he has dated the making of the working class too early, and that ordinary people in England and indeed elsewhere identified themselves more vaguely as the poor or the people as opposed to the rich and privileged.

William Sewell's *Work and Revolution in France*, for example, is essentially concerned with the 'language of labour', especially the description of occupations as moral communities. Sewell argues that the 1830s were the first stage in the making of the French working class, in which manual workers were identified as the people *par excellence*. The language of class was not current until the later nineteenth century (Sewell 1980: esp. 281ff.).

Gareth Stedman Jones (1983) has also listened carefully to contemporary languages in his study of the English Chartists, which suggests that they inherited and adapted an earlier 'vocabulary of grievance'. In this vocabulary traditional terms such as 'freedom' and 'people' were prominent, but the people were redefined as the 'labouring classes'. Patrick Joyce (1980) has also emphasized the importance of popular identities other than class in nineteenth-century England.[7]

This sense of belonging to the people, well-documented in England and France in the 1830s and 1840s, was not altogether new. As Sewell, Stedman Jones and Joyce know very well, the term 'people', in opposition to that of the privileged classes, was common enough in political discourse in the age of the French Revolution, from Tom Paine to the Comte de Volney (1791: ch. 15) and of course Rousseau. It can occasionally be found still earlier (Morgan 1988).

In the English Revolution of the 1640s, for example, the Levellers declared that 'all power is originally and essentially in the whole body of the people'. This declaration seems to follow the principle laid down by St Thomas Aquinas, that political legitimacy depends on the consent of the people, in the inclusive sense of that term. What gives the doctrine a new twist is the fact that the Levellers generally used the term 'people' in its exclusive sense, to refer to yeomen and craftsmen.[8] In Germany (Blickle 1975: 177ff.) in the age of Luther and the great Peasant War of 1525, a term in common use was 'the common man' (*der gemeine Mann*).

To go back still further, the chronicles of the Italian city states of the late Middle Ages and the Renaissance, Florence in particular, record the political slogan *Popolo e libertà* (the people and freedom). A distinction was commonly made between the *popolo grasso* or 'fat people' (the rich, or the members of the major guilds), the *popolo minuto* or 'little people' (the members of the lesser guilds), and the *plebe* or 'plebs', in other words the unskilled workers outside the guild system altogether.[9] The phrase *governo popolare*, literally 'a popular regime', meant a regime in which the guildsmen participated, as opposed not only to *governo ristretto*, or oligarchy, but also to *governo universale*, or democracy.

However, there are good reasons for identifying the years around 1800 as a turning-point in many parts of Europe. It was at about this time that ordinary people seem to have become aware of what we call 'popular culture' as *their* culture, in the course of resisting what they regarded as attempts by the privileged classes to take this culture from them.

In 1500, the popular culture of songs, tales, festivals and so on was still popular in the inclusive sense, open to all, like the tavern and the piazza where so many performances took place. It was everyone's culture, although certain elites had cultures of their own to which access was restricted (via grammar schools, universities, seminaries, noble academies, etc.). However, in the course of the early modern period, as what Norbert Elias calls the 'civilizing process' affected their behaviour more and more deeply, the European elites gradually withdrew from participation in popular culture for the same reasons that led them to try to reform it. They came to see it as dirty, barbarous, irrational, uncivilized, everything which they thought their own culture was not. They tried to distance themselves from it in the literal, spatial sense as well as the metaphorical, psychological one. Hence the elites abandoned street festivals to ordinary people or watched them from a safe distance, from a balcony, perhaps, rather than taking part in them. They celebrated carnival in their own houses, instead of going down to the market-place. One sign of this social 'apartheid' in mid-nineteenth-century England was the division of public houses into compartments, the middle-class 'private bar' or 'saloon bar' being separated from the working-class public bar (Girouard 1975: 57ff.). In the eighteenth and nineteenth centuries European elites spoke less and less dialect, and they stopped listening to, or reading, certain kinds of story, leaving these 'folk-tales' to their children and to the common people (a significant equation). By the early nineteenth century, the cultural distance between elites and people had widened to such a degree that it was possible for European intellectuals to discover popular culture as something exotic and enthralling (Burke 1978: 270ff.).

As a result of this withdrawal by the upper classes, and the increasing elaboration of a bourgeois ethic in the eighteenth and nineteenth centuries, what I have elsewhere called the 'reform of popular culture' (in the sense of recurrent attempts by the clergy and the magistrates to eliminate 'superstition', immorality, violence and disorder), changed its significance (Burke 1978: ch. 8).[10] According to some historians, it became an attempt by the bourgeoisie to impose its own ethos on the working class, especially such qualities as discipline, rationality, cleanliness, temperance, respectability, self-control, and a precise sense of time. This attempt to convert the working class to middle-class values stemmed in part at least from the need for labour discipline in the nineteenth-century factory.[11]

This interpretation is not unproblematic. In fact, it raises at least three major problems. The first problem, already discussed, is whether 'class' is an appropriate conceptualization of ordinary people before the late nineteenth century. The second problem concerns the explanation of change. Was it the work of the middle class alone, or the joint work of the clergy, the middle classes and the state? The rise of nationalism and the nation-state, already discussed, was generally associated with attempts to impose a standardized form of the national language (English, French, German, Italian, etc.) on speakers of dialect or, in some cases, of other languages. In Breton schools at the end of the nineteenth century, for example, the children were punished for speaking their native language at playtime (Hélias 1976).

The third problem is whether the simple dichotomy between rulers and ruled, elite culture and popular culture is adequate or whether it needs to be broken down into a series of oppositions.

To amplify this point: ordinary people should not be described as nothing but passive 'objects' of reform. Some of them were active supporters of the new values, and worked to convert their fellows. Some Breton peasants insisted that their children speak French at school, because French was associated with upward social mobility. English spread in Ireland, as in Wales, for similar reasons (Wall 1969: 81–90). On the other hand, as we have seen, some members of the upper and middle classes had discovered the virtues of traditional popular culture and were concerned to defend it from the reformers. Some, like the Russian *narodniks*, went so far as to argue that they should go to the people and learn from them instead of trying to teach them, an attitude linked to the so-called Slavophil movement of resistance to Westernization. It may be convenient to call the fraction of the middle class who defended popular culture the 'populists', as opposed to the 'reformists'.

However, from the point of view of this essay, which focuses on collective mentalities and collective identities, what matters is not so much what 'actually happened' as what ordinary people thought was happening. The point is that the movement of reform was widely perceived as a middle-class attack, as an attempt by 'Them' to destroy 'Our' culture. In the course of resistance to this attack, traditional culture came to be identified all the more strongly with the traditional community, and novelties with the enemies of the community. Breton peasants sometimes described French as the language of the bourgeoisie, thus assimilating the conflict between dominant and subordinate languages to that between dominant and subordinate classes.

Particularly revealing as well as particularly elusive are the reactions of ordinary people not only to the middle-class reformers but also to the middle-class populists, visitors in search of picturesque folklore (or later, rural antiques), armed with notebooks, sketchbooks (or later, tape recorders and cameras). Like anthropologists, social historians have to take account of their own impact (or the impact of people like them) on the 'phenomena' (in other words, the people) they are trying to study.[12]

We owe an early record of this kind of encounter to the naivety (whether genuine or false) and to the sharp observation of James Boswell. Boswell and Johnson embarked on a tour of the Hebrides in 1773. They had already formed an image of the place from reading about it, and expected 'to find simplicity and wildness', and 'a system of life almost totally different from what we had been accustomed to see'. Following the tradition of Western travellers into remote parts, Boswell 'observed to Dr Johnson' at Auchnasheal (where the villagers spoke no English), that 'it was much the same as being with a tribe of Indians'. But he also noticed that their host at Glenmorison seemed offended with them: 'his pride seemed to be much piqued that we were surprised at his having books'. It would have been good to have had an account of the incident from the host's point of view, but even this small scrap of information has its uses (Boswell 1786).

THE STRUGGLE OVER POPULAR CULTURE

The remainder of this essay will consider popular responses to the attack on popular culture – responses which deserve to be investigated in more depth and from a more comparative point of view – with special reference to England in the nineteenth century.

The English case reveals a struggle over popular culture, a struggle which is most visible when it involves competing uses of space, especially the use of public space in the centre of towns for traditional festivals. In Derby, for example, the custom of playing football in the streets on Shrove Tuesday was suppressed in the late 1840s, on the grounds that it led to 'moral degradation', 'the assembling of a lawless rabble', 'terror and alarm', and damage to property. The supporters of the 'rational recreation' movement suggested that the game be replaced by athletic sports outside the town or by a free railway excursion: in other words that it be displaced from the centre of the city, as if this was middle-class territory.

The conflict over street football in Derby did not exactly follow class lines. Some of the respectable working class criticized the sport, while it was supported by some middle-class populists, including the local factory-owner Joseph Strutt. All the same, there is evidence that some ordinary people resented being deprived of their recreation. As one of them remarked, 'This is the way they always treat poor folks' (Delves 1981: 94).[13]

Derby was a microcosm of the cultural conflicts in mid-nineteenth-century Britain, and other parts of Europe as well. There was a powerful movement to reform popular culture, the culture of custom, drinking, violence, irreverent humour, and what might be called more generally the 'carnivalesque'.[14] Indeed, there were several movements of reform, concerned, for example, with the evils of drink, with breaches of the Sabbath, and with the cruelty to animals involved in the popular sports of cock-fighting, dog-fighting and bull-baiting.[15] However, these movements were all 'predominantly evangelical in inspiration and middle class in membership' (Bailey

1978: 31; cf. Malcolmson 1973; Cunningham 1980: 76ff.; Yeo and Yeo 1981: 128–54; Golby and Purdue 1984: esp. ch. 2). The reformers tended to be middle-class, but the reformed tended to be working-class. For example, participants in Guy Fawkes demonstrations who were arrested by the police tended to be artisans and labourers (Storch 1982: 75). The police were the object of much popular hostility precisely because they were the agents enforcing the new urban discipline (Storch 1975). It is not difficult to see how a conflict between cultures came to be seen as, and thus to turn into, a conflict between classes.

The conflict between classes was made all the sharper by the changes in the organization of space in the rapidly growing cities of the nineteenth century. In pre-industrial cities, rich and poor lived relatively close together, often in adjoining streets, and shared the central spaces. In the nineteenth century, however, the division between middle-class and working-class neighbourhoods became sharper. Street widening and the erection of monumental buildings (from railway stations to concert halls) in the centre of cities generally involved the displacement of poor people to distant suburbs, and the increasing regulation of activities in the centre. The most spectacular example of this displacement was not in Britain but in Haussman's Paris, where some 350,000 people were moved to make way for the new boulevards, deliberately designed to destroy the old popular culture of riots and barricades (Kellett 1969; Clark 1985: 37ff.). It is not surprising that the working classes felt that they were being deprived of 'their' territory.

This chapter has sketched an argument about the uses of various kinds of popular culture, from dialects to festivals, in defining popular identity. In order to avoid possible misunderstandings, a few qualifications to this argument need to be made explicit.

In the first place, by employing the term 'uses', I do not mean to imply that dialects or ballads or festivals or costumes were self-consciously utilized as objects to mark an identity which already existed; they helped create this identity. Nor do I mean to imply that popular culture was the true agent and ordinary people merely its tools, for a phrase like 'the rise of class-consciousness' or 'national identity' is no more than shorthand for innumerable individual acts of identification. It is hard to find a simple formula which does not overemphasize either liberty or constraint.

In the second place, this argument about the cultural roots of popular identity does not imply that other roots were non-existent. The spread of the railways, for example, and the work of trade unions and political parties played important roles in weakening some kinds of identity and strengthening others. These points have often been discussed. The aim of this essay is simply to ensure that popular culture is not left out of the story of the construction and reconstruction of popular identity.

As I have tried to suggest already, the term 'identity' should be used in the plural. Popular identities included a sense of membership in a nation, a region, a town or village, a craft, and finally a class. National identities and class identities both became stronger in the nineteenth century. This may appear a contradiction, but only on the assumption that identity is something simple and fixed, so that one identity necessarily excludes another. I would prefer to argue that identities are multiple and fluid or 'negotiable' and that the same individual or group may privilege one identity over another according to the situation and the moment. My examples have come from Europe in the past, but recent studies of ethnicity in Africa and elsewhere would suggest that the story of the creation of popular identity is repeating itself – with local variations – in many parts of the world today.

NOTES

1 For further details and references, see Burke 1978. This essay will also make use of some of the considerable body of work on the history of popular culture which has appeared since that time.
2 Early examples include N. A. Lvov, *Sobranie Narodnykh Russkikh Pesen* (1790); J. Erdélyi, *Nepdalok és Mondak* (1846). The famous Serbian collector Vuk Karadžić called his collection of 1814 'Prostanarodna Pesnaritsa' (the songs of the 'simple' or 'plain' people), just as the Russian V. F. Trutovsky called his book (1776) *Sobranie Russkikh Prostykh Pesen* (a collection of plain Russian songs).
3 Professor Michael Branch is working on a full-scale study of Lönnrot.
4 On Michelet's notion of the people, see Viallaneix 1959.
5 I should like to thank Dr Prats for sending me a copy of his study (1988).
6 Two leading painters of rural life, Jean-François Millet and Gustave Courbet, were, however, of peasant stock.
7 Cf. also Joyce, *Society Signified* (forthcoming). I am grateful to Patrick Joyce for letting me see part of this book in draft form.
8 On popular sovereignty, see Skinner 1978: 62ff; on the Levellers, see Hill 1972: ch. 7.
9 There is a substantial literature on the *popolo* of urban Italy at this time,

summarized in Hyde 1973: 108f, with references on p. 210. On Florence
around 1500, see Gilbert 1965: 21ff.

10 On the middle-class ethic, see the important Swedish case-study by Frykman and Löfgren (1987).

11 A famous discussion is Thompson 1967. On 'rational recreation', see Bailey
1978.

12 For a vivid account by an extraordinary 'ordinary person' of his reactions
to the invasion of Brittany by tourists, see Helias 1976: ch. 8.

13 Joseph Strutt (1765–1844) was apparently no relation of his namesake
(1749–1802), the author of Sports and Pastimes of the People of England
(1801).

14 On custom and conflicts over its control, see Bushaway 1982. On the
carnivalesque in Europe, see Burke 1978: 191ff; in Birmingham, Reid 1982.

15 On the rise of compassion for animals, see Thomas 1983: 150ff.

REFERENCES

Anderson, B. 1983: *Imagined Communities*. London: Verso.

Bailey, P. 1978: *Leisure and Class in Victorian England*. London: Routledge.

Blickle, P. 1975: *Die Revolution von 1525*. Munich: Oldenbourg.

Boas, G. 1984: 'Vox populi', in P. Weiner (ed.), *Dictionary of the History of Ideas*, 4 vols. New Haven, Conn.: Yale University Press.

Boswell, J. 1785: *The Journal of a Tour to the Hebrides*. London: Charles Dilty. Often reprinted.

Burke, P. 1978: *Popular Culture in Early Modern Europe*. London: Temple Smith.

Burns, E. Bradford 1980: *The Poverty of Progress: Latin America in the Nineteenth Century*. Berkeley: University of California Press.

Bushaway, B. 1982: *By Rite: Custom, Ceremony and Community in England*. London: Junction Books.

Clark, T. J. 1985: *The Painting of Modern Life: Paris in the Art of Manet and His Followers*. London: Thames & Hudson.

Cunningham, H. 1980: *Leisure in the Industrial Revolution*. London: Croom Helm.

Deane, S. 1985: *Celtic Revivals*. London: Faber.

Delves, A. 1981: 'Popular recreation and social conflict in Derby', in Yeo and Yeo 1981: 89–127.

Falnes, O. J. 1933: *National Romanticism in Norway*. New York: Faculty of Political Science of Columbia University.

Fel, E. and Hofer, T. 1969: *Proper Peasants*. Chicago: University of Chicago Press.

Fernandez, J. W. 1966: 'Folklore as an agent of nationalism', in I. Wallerstein (ed.), *Social Change: The Colonial Situation*. New York: Wiley.

Frazer, J. G. 1890: *The Golden Bough*, 2 vols. London: Macmillan.

Frykman, J., and Löfgren, O. 1987: *Culture Builders*. New Brunswick, NJ: Rutgers University Press.

Gilbert, F. 1965: *Machiavelli and Guicciardini*. Princeton: Princeton University Press.

Girouard, M. 1975: *Victorian Pubs*. London: Studio Vista.

Golby, J. M., and Purdue, A. W. 1984: *The Civilisation of the Crowd: Popular Culture in England, 1750–1900*. London: Batsford.

Hautala, J. 1969: *Finnish Folklore Research, 1818–1919*. Helsinki: Societas Scientiarum Fennica.

Hélias, P.-J. 1976: *Le Cheval d'orgueil*. Paris: Plon.

Hill, C. 1972: *The World Turned Upside Down*. London: Temple Smith.

Hobsbawm, E., and Ranger, T. (eds) 1983: *The Invention of Tradition*. Cambridge: Cambridge University Press.

Hofer, T. 1984: 'The perception of tradition in European ethnology', *Journal of Folklore Research*, 21, 133–47.

Hyde, J. K. 1973: *Society and Politics in Medieval Italy*. London: Macmillan.

Joyce, P. 1980: *Work, Society and Politics*. Brighton: Harvester.

Joyce, P. n.d.: *Society Signified*.

Linton, R. 1943: 'Nativistic movements', *American Anthropologist*, 45.

Malcolmson, R. W. 1973: *Popular Recreations in English Society*. Cambridge: Cambridge University Press.

Mauro, T. De 1960: *Storia linguistica dell'Italia unita*. Milan: A. Guiffrè.

Morgan, E. 1988: *Inventing the People*. New York: Norton.

Payne, H. C. 1976: *The Philosophes and the People*. New Haven, Conn.: Yale University Press.

Prats, L. 1988: *El mite de la tradició popular*. Barcelona: Edicions 62.

Reid, D. A. 1982: 'Interpreting the festival calendar', in R. D. Storch (ed.), *Popular Culture and Custom in Nineteenth-century England*. London: Croom Helm, 125–53.

Sewell, W. H. 1980: *Work and Revolution in France*. Cambridge: Cambridge University Press.

Skinner, Q. 1978: *The Foundations of Modern Political Thought*, vol. 1. Cambridge: Cambridge University Press.

Storch, R. 1975: 'The policeman as domestic missionary: urban discipline and popular culture in northern England, 1850–80, *Journal of Social History*, 9, 481–509.

Storch, R. 1982: 'Please to remember the Fifth of November', in Storch (ed.), *Popular Culture and Custom in Nineteenth-century England*. London: Croom Helm.

Thomas, K. V. 1983: *Man and the Natural World*. London: Weidenfeld & Nicolson.

Thompson, E. P. 1963: *The Making of the English Working Class*. London: Gollancz.

Thompson, E. P. 1967: 'Time, work-discipline, and industrial relations', *Past and Present*, 38, 56–97.

Viallaneix, P. 1959: *La Voie royale*. Paris: Librairie Delagrave.

Volney, C. 1791: *Les Ruines, ou méditations sur les révolutions des empires*. Paris: Desenne.

Wall, M. 1969: 'The decline of the Irish language', in B. O'Cuív (ed.), *A View of the Irish Language*. Dublin: Stationery Office.

Weber, E. 1976: *Peasants into Frenchmen*. London: Chatto & Windus.

Yeo, E., and Yeo, S. 1981: 'Ways of seeing: control and leisure versus class and struggle', in Yeo and Yeo (eds), *Popular Culture and Class Conflict*. Brighton: Harvester.

13

Past, present and emergent identities: requirements for ethnographies of late twentieth-century modernity worldwide

George Marcus

The following passage from a recent paper by Charles Bright and Michael Geyer, 'For a unified history of the world in the twentieth century' (1987: 69–70) is a typical statement of a problematic current within the interdisciplinary space that is often labelled in the US and Britain as cultural studies:[1]

> the problem of world history appears in a new light. At its core is no longer the evolution and devolution of world systems, but the tense, ongoing interaction of forces promoting global integration and forces recreating local autonomy. This is not a struggle for or against global integration itself, but rather a struggle over the terms of that integration. The struggle is by no means finished, and its path is no longer foreordained by the dynamics of western expansion that initiated global integration. The world has moved apart even as it has been pulled together, *as efforts to convert domination into order have engendered evasion, resistance and struggles to regain autonomy. This struggle for autonomy – the assertion of local and particular claims over global and general ones – does not involve opting out of the world or resorting to autarky.* It is rather an effort to establish the terms of self-determining and self-controlled participation in the processes of global integration and the struggle for planetary order.
> *At the center of this study is the question of who, or what, controls and defines the identity of individuals, social groups,*

nations and cultures. This is as much a political as an intellectual formulation, for it involves a critical reassessment of the practice of globalism. (*emphases mine*)

The paradoxical, even vertiginous, equality of the above passage's manifesto-like formulations asks the scholar of world history to keep similarity and difference, the global and the local, in mind simultaneously, requiring of him or her the ability to see 'everything everywhere' as the key to perceiving diversity also. Indeed, it recalls the cognitive framework with which classic aesthetic modernists revolted against realism in art and literature, and signals to me the penetration, at long last, of this critical framework into the modes of representation that the social sciences and history have employed to construct their subjects and explain them. This is occurring just as aesthetic modernism in art and literature has been suffering a moment of exhaustion in the continuing efforts to define a post-modernism.[2] Marshall Berman, in *All that Is Solid Melts into Air* (1982), has creatively redeemed the power of classic modernism to speak to contemporary history and culture, against the so-called postmodern condition. In Berman's words (1982: 14):

> Modern irony animates so many great works of art and thought over the past century; at the same time, it infuses millions of ordinary people's everyday lives. This book aims to bring these works and these lives together, to restore the spiritual wealth of modernist culture to the modern man and woman in the street, to show how, for all of us, modernism is realism.

The vision of social life with which a nineteenth-century avant-garde tried to tax the progress-orientated narratives of bourgeois life in European industrial society has now become, or at least has come to be appreciated as, the empirically describable conditions of modernity, not only in consumer societies in the West, but for vast areas of an increasingly transcultural globe. This is perhaps the one area where the current attempts to recast the framing of description and analysis in the social sciences and history inspired by modernist challenges to the assumptions of realist narrative intersect with the parallel effort in the arts to define a postmodernism: postmodernism distinguishes itself from modernism on the perception that there can no longer be avant-gardes for the cultural productions of classic modernism. Ironic statement, parody, spectacle, ruptures, and shock effects now are produced for large, even popular culture 'reception' classes which exhibit a sensibility for, or at least a recognition of, such productions. Such 'reception' classes include, of course, academics and scholars, among whom are those social scientists and historians who understand the social lives of their subjects (who also understand their own lives) in terms akin to the classic avant-garde experimenters, and who as analysts and describers of culture and society seek techniques of representation from the same source. Thus, while Berman, like others who study the legacy of modernist expression in contemporary life, departs from the postmodernist project in literature and the arts, his ground for defending the relevance of classic modernism is the common insight with postmodernism that the conditions of life worldwide are fundamentally and increasingly self-consciously modernist. However, what is apparently a predicament for the artist in this recognition is an opportunity for the social scientist and historian.

In the Bright and Geyer passage, the modernist problem in historical and social scientific research is foregrounded specifically as one of identity formation, 'the question of who, or what controls and defines the identity of individuals, social groups, nations and cultures'. And with this formulation, we also come to a salient 1980s trend in ethnographic research and writing within anthropology, on which I want to focus this essay. In *Anthropology as Cultural Critique* (1986), Mike Fischer and I paralleled Bright and Geyer in our documentation of a diverse and complex trend in contemporary ethnographic research which attempts to synthesize, through the current play of strategies by which ethnographies are constructed,[3] major theoretical interests in the description of culture at the level of experience, or shared categories of experience (the prominence of studies of the 'self'). The trend also has equivalent concerns with how the conventional ethnographic studies of locales, regions, communities, and diverse peoples generally fit into the formation of a world-historical political economy (viz. the major anthropological statement by Eric Wolf (1982) of the influential metanarrative about world-historical political economy introduced by Wallerstein, after Braudel, in the early 1970s). By the mid-1980s, these cross-cutting interests in culture as lived *local* experience and the understanding of the latter in *global* perspective have come specifically to be about how collective and individual identities are negotiated in the various places that anthropologists have traditionally, and now not so traditionally, conducted fieldwork. Such ethnography bears the burden of explaining how in the conventional local contexts and sites familiar to ethnographic research paradoxical diversity emerges in the saliently transcultural world that Bright and Geyer envision. Thus, in the face of global creolization processes, there is renewed interest among anthropologists in such topics as ethnicity, race, nationality, and colonialism. While such primordial phenomena as traditions, communities, kinship systems, rituals, and power structures continue to be documented, they can no longer in and of themselves serve as the grounding tropes which organize ethnographic description and explanation. The most venturesome works in the trend of ethnographies are profoundly concerned with the shaping and transformation of identities (of one's subjects, of their social systems, of the nation-states with which they are associated, of the ethnographer and the ethnographic project itself). These are the most radically questioning of analytic and descriptive frameworks which rest on, and privilege, a particular 'solidity that does not melt into the air' – that is, exclusive identities, emergent from an authoritative cultural structure, which can always be discovered and modelled. The modernist problematics of ethnography, outlined in the next section, instead emerge from a systematic *disqualification* of the various structuring devices on which ethnographic realism has depended.

That the problem of collective and individual identity has itself become the identity at the moment of this leading trend of ethnography is worthy of comment.[4] The very notion of identity, after all, has been a rather generic one in the history of Western social theory. At moments such as this, when change and its character as a process become the predominant theoretical and empirical concern of social scientists, how identities at different levels of organization take shape also seems to become the goal of study. But the treatment of identity formation, for example, in ethnographies written under the reign of the development and modernization paradigm of the 1950s and 1960s is far different from what might be seen as their 1980s heirs, the ethnographies of identity processes under a theoretical regime focused on modernity, a term with quite different implications than modernization. The differences are probably as much political as intellectual. The regime of modernization dealt in progressive stage frameworks, based on Western experience and applied to the rest of the world. Under this regime, change was of course disruptive to identity – personal, communal, or national – but there was a clear valuation on the re-establishment through whatever process of the coherence and stability of identity. The 'homeless mind' was clearly a condition of change, but was profoundly unsettling to the theorist/ analyst and had to be resolved in community or its possibility, in the reinvention of tradition in which one could have faith, or in the notion that history, however complex events may be, operates by something akin to laws. The theoretical conception of this process depended on arguing between dualities such as traditional–modern, rural–urban, *Gemeinschaft–Gesellschaft* and the like – the form that the intellectual capital of nineteenth-century social theory commonly took in translation and deployment in twentieth-century Anglo-American social science.

The regime of modernity globalizes specific histories of the modern and encompasses the dualities of modernization theories and their creation as kinds of ideologies and discourses that are themselves products of the modern. The study of the modern or modernity requires a different frame of reference and this recognition is what has occupied so much of social theory in the twentieth century, in itself a project of self-identity that is not yet completed, or perhaps is uncompletable. Thus identity processes in modernity concern a 'homeless mind' that cannot be permanently resolved as coherent or as a stable formation in theory or in social life itself. However, its changing permutations, expressions, and multiple determinations indeed can be systematically studied and documented as the ethnography of identity formation anywhere, but only in terms of a different set of strategies for the writing of ethnography, to which we now turn.

Referring once again to the Bright and Geyer passage, we find that the key question of identity formation is pursued through a specific conceptual rhetoric of 'resistance and accommodation'; as they say, 'efforts to convert domination into order have engendered evasion, resistance and struggles to regain autonomy. This struggle for autonomy ... does not involve opting out of the world or resorting to autarky.' Distinguishing the elements of resistance and accommodation in the formation of collective or personal identities at the site of any ethnographic project has become the almost slogan-like analytic formula for addressing the paradoxical modernist vision of 'everything everywhere, yet everywhere different' (see Marcus n.d.).

The resistance and accommodation formula, however, can be explored with more or less radical departures from the conventional framing assumptions of realist ethnography. In its more conservative use, this formula negotiates the simultaneity of cultural homogenization and diversification in any locale through preserving the foundational framing power of such notions as community, subculture, tradition, and structure. Local identity emerges as a compromise between a mix of elements of resistance to incorporation into a larger whole and of elements of accommodation to this larger order. The irony of unintended consequences is often brought into play in ethnographies to account for the articulation of such parsed elements of identity formation to each other in a local setting and, in turn, for their combined articulation of a small, local world to a larger order. (See my analysis (1986) of Paul Willis, *Learning to Labour*, for an account of how a very sophisticated use of the resistance and accommodation strategy operates along conservative, realist lines.)

Resistance and accommodation ethnographies often do privilege some form of stable community, or cultural structure, over any logic of enduring contradiction. The two poles of the strategy most importantly serve to position traditional studies in a satisfactory ideological way in the face of the modernist problematic as stated in the Bright and Geyer passage. On the one hand, admitting accommodation avoids the nostalgia for the whole, for the community, and more broadly avoids the allegory of the pastoral which, as Jim Clifford has shown (1986b) has organized so much ethnography as narrative. On the other hand, admitting resistance avoids the 'iron-cage' pessimism of the totally administered world vision of modernity in the Frankfurt School critical theory of Theodor Adorno or in the theory of power and knowledge in the later work of Michel Foucault. However, what is really avoided or refused in the more conventional or conservative resistance and accommodation ethnographies is an exploration of the uncompromising sense of paradox in the intertwining of diversity and homogeneity that will not allow an easy parsing of these two terms.

In the following section, I will briefly and schematically lay out a set of requirements for shifting the chronotope of ethnography, to use Bakhtin's concept, toward modernist assumptions about the organization of contemporary social reality. This will involve both changing certain parameters in the way that ethnographic subjects are analytically constructed as subjects and altering the nature of the theoretical intervention that the ethnographer deploys in the text he or she creates. This duality of alteration encompassing both the observer and the observed is fully consistent with the simultaneous levels on which modernist perspectives work – the writer shares conditions of modernity, and at least some identities, with his or her subjects, and no text can be developed without some registering of this.

Thus, three requirements will deal with the construction of the subjects of ethnography through problematizing the construction of the spatial, of the temporal, and of perspective or voice in realist ethnography. And three requirements will concern strategies for establishing the analytic presence of the ethnographer in his or her text: the dialogic appropriation of analytic concepts, bifocality, and the critical juxtapositions of possibilities. These requirements are by no means exhaustive, nor are there necessarily any existing ethnographies that satisfactorily enact any or all of them. I am particularly interested in how a distinctly modernist text is created in each work where it is shown how distinctive identities are created from turbulence, fragments, intercultural reference, and the localized intensification of global possibilities and associations.

Remaking the observed

Problematizing the spatial: a break with the trope of community in realist ethnography The concept of community in the classic sense of shared values, shared identity, and thus shared culture has been mapped literally onto locality to define one basic frame of reference orientating ethnography. The connotations of solidity and homogeneity attaching to the notion of community, whether concentrated in a locale or dispersed, has been replaced in the framework of modernity by the idea that the situated production of identity – of a person, of a group, or even a whole society – does not depend alone, or even always primarily, on the observable, concentrated activities within a particular locale or a diaspora. The identity of anyone or any group is produced simultaneously in many different locales of activity by many different agents for many different purposes. One's identity where one lives, among one's neighbours, friends, relatives, or co-strangers, is only one social context, and perhaps not the most important one in which it is shaped. For a modernist approach to identity in ethnography, it is this process of dispersed identity in many different places of differing character that must be grasped. Of course, such a requirement presents new and some very difficult problems of research method and textual representation in ethnography. To capture the formation of identity (multiple identities, really) at a particular moment in the biography of a person or the history of a group of people through a configuration of very differing sites or locales of activity recognizes the powerful integrating (rationalizing) drives of the state and economy in modernity. It also takes account of constant technological innovations to power these drives, and the resulting dispersals of the subject – person or group – in multiple overlapping fragments of identity that are also characteristic of modernity (see Marcus 1989). There are a number of questions for study in this so to speak parallel processing, of identity at many sites. Which identities coalesce and under what circumstances? Which become defining or dominant and for how long? How does the play of unintended consequences affect the outcome in the coalescence of a salient identity in this space of the multiple construction and dispersed control of a person's or group's identities? And what is the nature of the politics by which identity at and across any site is controlled, perhaps most importantly at the site where identity in a literal sense is the embodiment of a particular human actor or group? Cultural difference or diversity arises here not from some local struggle for identity, but as a function of a complex process among all the sites in which the identity of someone or a group anywhere is defined in simultaneity. It is the burden of the modernist ethnography to capture distinctive identity formations in all their migrations and dispersions. This multi-locale, dispersed identity vision thus reconfigures and complexifies the spatial plane on which ethnography has conceptually operated.

Problematizing the temporal: a break with the trope of history in realist ethnography   The break is not with historical consciousness, or a pervasive sense of the past in any site or set of sites probed by ethnography, but rather with historical determination as the primary explanatory context for any ethnographic present. Realist ethnography has become dependent on, to some degree has been revived by, its incorporation within existing Western historical metanarratives. There is a lively effort these days, in contradistinction to the classic period in the development of ethnography in Anglo-American anthropology, to tie the site of ethnographic close observation to a stream of history within which it can be explained by reference to origins, not in the generic sense of earlier anthropology, but in the framework of historical narrative. Modernist ethnography is not so sanguine about the alliance between conventional social history and ethnography. The past that is present in any site is built up from memory, the fundamental medium of ethnohistory. In modernist ethnography, collective and individual memory in its multiple traces and expressions is indeed the crucible for the local self-recognition of an identity. While this significance of memory as the linking medium and process relating history and identity formation is well recognized by contemporary ethnographers, analytic and methodological thinking about it is as yet very undeveloped. It is another diffuse phenomenon of the conditions of modernity which none the less encompasses the possibility of comprehending the processes of diversity that derive not from rooted traditions or community life, but from their emergence amid other associations in collective and individual memory. The difficulty of descriptively grasping memory as a social or collective process in modernity is not unrelated to the inadequacy of the trope of the community to conceptualize the spatial plane of ethnography, as noted in the last section. In the electronic information age there is an erosion of the public/ private distinction in everyday life (on which community is constructed in Western narratives) as well as displacement of the long-term memory function of orality and story-telling (again a condition of life in community as traditionally conceived). This makes the understanding and description of any straightforward 'art of memory' especially problematic in modernity. Collective memory is more likely to be passed through individual memory and autobiography embedded in the diffuse communication between generations than in any spectacles or performances in public arenas, the power of which relies on ironic references to the present or what is emergent, rather than on exhortations of varying subtlety to remember. Collective representations are thus most effectively filtered through personal representations. With this insight, the modernist ethnography transforms the conventional realist concern with history as it infuses, expresses, and even determines social identities in a locale into a study that is synonymous with addressing the construction of personal and collective identity itself. It is probably in the production of autobiography, as this genre has returned to prominence, with a salient focus on ethnicity (see Fischer 1986), that the sort of historical experiences carried in memory and shaping contemporary social movements can best be appreciated.

The return of an ethnographic present, but a very different ethnographic present from the one that largely ignored history in the classic functionalist anthropology of traditional, tribal society, is thus a challenge to the construction of the temporal setting for modernist ethnography. This is a present that is defined not by historical narrative either, but by memory, its own distinctive narratives and traces. This art of memory is synonymous with the fragmented process of identity formation in any locale – one whose distinctly social forms are difficult to grasp or even see ethnographically – and that thus sets another problematic to be explored in the production of modernist works.

Problematizing perspective/voice: a break with the trope of structure in realist ethnography Ethnography has opened to the understanding of perspective as 'voice', just as the distinctly visual, controlling metaphor of structure has come into question. The trope of structure – that is, either social structure on the surface derived from patterns of observed behaviours, or structures as underlying systematic meanings or codes that organize language and social discourses – may well continue to be indispensable in rendering descriptions of the subject-matter even of modernist ethnography. Nevertheless the analytic weight or heft of an account shifts to a concern with perspective as voice, as embedded discourse within the framing and conduct of a project of ethnographic enquiry.

In part, this came about as a result of questioning the adequacy of structural analysis of whatever kind to model the complexity of intracultural diversity. A Wittgensteinian family of resemblances problem confronted the ethnographer who would represent reality as organized by the operation of cultural models or codes (usually one key or central model) and the more or less orderly transformations of their components. Controlling for context and the empirical recording of actual montage flows of association in data on discourse have challenged the adequacy of structural or semiotic models to account for associations that resist assimilation to a model of limited dimensions.

In part, the modernist alternative in voice, accepting the montage of polyphony as the problem of simultaneous representation and analysis, probably has had as much to do with the changing ethics of the ethnographic enterprise as with a dissatisfaction concerning the structural analysis of cultural phenomena. These changes are rooted in a marked sensitivity to the dialogic, oral roots of all anthropological knowledge, transformed and obscured by the complex processes of writing which dominate ethnographic projects from field to text, and of the differential power relationships that shape the ultimate media and modes of representing knowledge. Here, I merely want to comment on this shift in terms of the analytic difference in the way modernist ethnography creates its chronotope regardless of one's assessment of the possibilities for success in representing ethically as well as authoritatively voice and its diversity.

In the mode of cultural analysis that Raymond Williams developed (1977), a structure of feeling (the use of structure is quite idiosyncratic) would be the goal of ethnography, focused on what is emergent in a setting from the interaction of well-defined dominant and residual formations with that which is not quite articulable to subjects or to the analyst. (Such formations could be systems of social relations in the British sense of structure, but they also refer to possible and established modes of discourse.) Making it more sayable/visible is one of the critical functions of ethnography. The modernist ethnography in this vein, recognizing such properties of discourses as dominance, residualness, and emergence (or possibility), would map the relationships of these properties in any site of enquiry not by immediate structural appropriations of discourse formations, but by exposing, to the extent possible, the quality of voices by means of metalinguistic categories (such as narrative, trope, etc.). Voices are not seen as products of local structures, based on community and tradition, alone, or as privileged sources of perspective, but rather as products of the complex sets of associations and experiences which compose them. To enact this refocusing of ethnography from structure to voice/discourse involves different conceptions of the relationship of the observer to the observed, to which we now turn.

Remaking the observer

It should not be lost on one that while a more complex appreciation of the dynamics of identity formation is the object of the modernist strategies of remaking the observed, the parallel strategies of remaking the observer are no less directed toward the dynamics of identity formation of the anthropologist in relation to his or her practice of ethnography.

The appropriation through dialogue of a text's conceptual apparatus
The realist ethnography has often been built around the intensive exegesis of a key indigenous symbol or concept pulled from its contexts of discourse to be reinserted in them, but according to the dictates of the ethnographer's authoritative analytic scheme. Much in recent cultural ethnography has depended on this central organizing and analytic technique so common in ethnographic accounts. On the quality and thoroughness of such exegesis often depends the professional assessment of the value of a particular ethnographic work.

In one sense, exegesis at the centre of ethnography is a gesture toward recognizing and privileging indigenous concepts over anthropology's own. Most importantly, such targeted concepts come to act as synedoche for identity – they stand for a system of meanings but also for the identity of a people in the anthropological literature and sometimes beyond it. Keying an account to particular concepts, myths, or symbols thus tends to impose an identity upon a people as a contribution (or curse) of anthropology.

One alteration of the modernist ethnography is to remake this exercise into a fully dialogic one in which exegesis is foregrounded in the ethnography and frame of analysis as arising from at least the dual voices party to dialogue. In this basic process of cultural translation – one of the favoured metaphors for characterizing the interpretive task in ethnography – the purpose is not so much to change indigenous concepts (that is the responsibility of the anthropologist's interlocutors) as to alter the anthropologist's own. In no ethnography of which I am aware (maybe Maurice Leenhardt's *Do Kamo*, but then the whole project of ethnography is redefined in his work) does the central exegetical task lead to the recreation of concepts in the apparatus of social theoretic discourse. For example, in the face of the apparent exhaustion of our concepts to map late twentieth-century realities, Fredric Jameson in an interview responds thus to a comment (1987: 37):

Q: It is obvious, nevertheless, that postmodernist discourse makes it difficult to say things about the whole.

FJ: One of the ways of describing this is as a modification in the very nature of the cultural sphere: a loss of autonomy of culture, a case of culture falling into the world. As you say, this makes it much more difficult to speak of cultural systems and to evaluate them in isolation. A whole new theoretical problem is posed. Thinking at once negatively and positively about it is a beginning, but what we need is a new vocabulary. The languages that have been useful in talking about culture and politics in the past don't really seem adequate to this historical moment.

From where might this vocabulary come, for the sake of Western social theory and cognition? Maybe from a modernist reshaping of the translation of concepts at the core of realist ethnographies. Perhaps moments of exegesis, of definitions in context, would be replaced by the exposure of moments of dialogue and their use in the ethnographer's revision of familiar concepts that define the analytic limits of his or her own work, and of anthropological discourse more generally. Such a move would open the realm of discussion of ethnographies to organic intellectuals (to use Gramsci's term) and readerships among one's subjects, wherever this is now feasible.

Modernist exegesis, distinctively tied to a recognition of its dialogic character, becomes a thoroughly reflexive operation. While one explores the changing identity processes within an ethnographic setting, the identity of one's own concepts changes. The process of constructing an analysis thus can take on and parallel aspects of the process it describes. The key challenge here is whether an identity can ever be explained by a reference discourse when several discourses are in play, not the least of which is the ethnographer's in dialogue with specific other subjects. There are several resolutions in the way this activity might be represented textually, but the modernist innovation is that the identity of the ethnographer's framework should not remain intact, 'solid', if the subject's is 'melting into air'. This leads to a consideration of the bifocal character of any project of ethnographic research, a character that is heightened by the modernist sense of the real – that the globe generally and intimately is becoming more integrated and that this paradoxically is not leading to an easily comprehensible totality, but to an increasing diversity of connections among phenomena once thought disparate and worlds apart.

Bifocality Looking at least two ways, an embedded comparative dimension, has always been a more or less implicit aspect of every ethnographic project. In the evolving global modernity of the twentieth century in which anthropology has been pursued almost from its professional inception, the coevalness of the ethnographer with the Other as subject has for the most part been denied (Fabian 1983). There is indeed a history in ethnography of a developing critical juxtaposition, made explicit between one's own world and that of the Other as subject, but the construct of separate, distant worlds in analytically making such juxtapositions has been sustained. Only in the periodic internal critique of anthropology's relationship to Western colonialism has the thoroughly blurred historic relationship of the anthropologist's own society and practices to the subject's under colonial domination been argued.

Now that Western modernity is being reconceptualized as a global and thoroughly transcultural phenomenon the explicit treatment of bifocality in ethnographic accounts is becoming more explicit and openly transgressive of the us–them, distanced worlds in which it was previously constructed. In other words, the identity of the anthropologist and his or her world by whatever complex chain of connection and association is likely to be profoundly related to that of any particular world he or she is studying. However, only the modernist remaking of the observed, outlined in the previous section, makes possible this revision of the bifocal character of ethnography. For example, the multilocality of identity processes across various levels of conventional divisions of social organization – the pathway of the transcultural – creates a mutuality of implication for identity processes occurring in any ethnographic site. The chain of pre-existing historic or contemporary connection between the ethnographer and her or his subjects may be a long or short one, thus making bifocality an issue of judgement and a circumstance even of the personal, autobiographical reasons for pursuit of a particular project, but its discovery and recognition remains a defining feature of the current modernist sensibility in ethnography. The mere demonstration of such connections and affinities, the juxtaposition of two identity predicaments precipitated by the ethnographer's project, itself stands as a critical statement against conventional efforts to sustain distanced worlds and their separate determinations, despite the modernist insight about global integration through paths that are transcultural as well as technological, political, and economic in nature.

Critical juxtapositions and contemplation of alternative possibilities
The function of the modernist ethnography is primarily one of cultural critique, of one's disciplinary apparatus through an intellectual alliance with the subject, or of one's society that in the increasing condition of global integration is always bifocally related in transcultural process and historical perspective (or rather retrospective) to the site of ethnographic attention. The cultural critique is also directed to conditions within the site of ethnographic focus – the local world which it treats. Given the general commitment of modernist ethnographies to explore the full range of possibilities for identities and their complex expressions through voice in any setting, such exploration is a key form of cultural critique also. This move is indeed the distinct and committed voice of the ethnographer in his or her text, and it operates from the critical attitude that things as they are need not have been or need not be the way they are, given the alternatives detectable within the situations – there are always more possibilities, other identities etc. than those that have come to be enacted. Exploring through juxtapositions all actual and possible outcomes is itself a method of cultural critique which moves against the grain of the given situation and its definition in dominant identities which might otherwise be mistaken as authoritative models from which all variation is derived. The modernist treatment of reality allows, rather, for the traces of the roads not taken or the possibilities not explored. Indeed this kind of critical thought experiment incorporated within ethnography, in which juxtaposed actualities and possibilities are put analytically in dialogue with one another, might be thought to border on the utopian or the nostalgic if it were not dependent, first of all, on a documentation that these traces do have a life of their own, so to speak, and are integral to the processes that form identities, including the ones that appear defining or dominant. Such clarification of possibilities against the objective, defining conditions within the limits of the discourses 'that matter' in any setting, is the one critical intervention and contribution that the ethnographer can make that is uniquely his or her own.

In line with the preceding sets of requirements for modernist ethnography, what the diverse kinds of contemporary works that might be identified as such share is an experimental attitude. This is brought to bear in writing and analysis precisely at those points or moments when one is compelled to explain how structure articulates with the particular cultural experiences encompassed in the account (including the reflexive ones made explicit by the author); how the global articulates with the local; or, as the problematic is currently and commonly expressed, how identities are formed in the simultaneity of relationship between levels of social life and organization (that is, the coevalness, to use Fabian's term (1983), of the state, the economy, international media and popular culture, the region, the locale, the transcultural context, the ethnographer's world and his subjects' *all at once*).

What makes the operations in such works different from, and more daring than say, the work of Anthony Giddens, a theorist who is also very much concerned with the same general problem, is that at the just noted points of articulation they do without, or are open to the possibility of doing without, an imagery of structure to see their accounts through. While understanding the play of structures and unintended consequences in the shaping of any domain or site of social life, they do not need a linking theory of structure as a determination of process, as does Giddens in his resolution of the problem of structure and action in 'structuration'. It is precisely at this theoretic point in their accounts that the relationship between world and experience, text and reality, structure and action remains uncompromisingly problematic in a way that allows no given or traditional social theoretic solutions to impose order on what is not orderly.[5] Here, then, at the site of articulation where the global and the local are entwined, without grounding reference to a determining culture or history that went before, resides the main experimental problem of modernist ethnography. Here also is the possibility of treating what have been the deepest sorts of issues in traditional social theory as problems of form in which conceptual artifice and descriptive imagination face the facts of ethnographic minutiae.

EXEMPLARS

Nowadays, there is a constant stream of ethnographic works appearing that might each in its own particular way be appreciated as an exemplar of one or more of the modernist strategies developed in this essay. Most do not advertise themselves as experiments or as having an experimental purpose. Rather, they exhibit aspects or dimensions, more or less well developed, that enact a shift toward modernist ethnography as I have depicted it. Such works are interesting here because of this enactment, regardless of how successful they might be judged, or how good they might be otherwise assessed by the conventional standards according to which ethnographies are currently and soberly evaluated (see Marcus and Cushman 1982).

Other contemporary works are interesting for their mere acknow-ledgement or recognition of alternative possibilities for developing their projects, aside from the ones that they actually pursue. These acknowledgements are usually to be found in the reflexive 'spaces' that are increasingly reserved in contemporary ethnographies – in footnotes, anecdotal asides, prefaces, appendices, epilogues, and the like. Paul Willis's *Learning to Labour* (1976), for example, is an early and pioneering example of such a work in the current tendency toward modernist ethnography. This study of the genesis and fixing of working-class identity among a group of non-conformist boys in an English grammar school setting is highly conventional in its rhetoric and development (ethnography is a method of gathering and constituting data on which analysis is then performed), but it is also keenly sensitive and self-critical as to what is elided and finessed by its manner of construction. On its margins (in footnotes, asides, and the afterword), there is a sort of 'negative image' of the text which I would see as a prologue to a more experimental effort. For example, even as he focuses exclusively on a particular situated group of boys at school, Willis makes it clear that the genesis of class culture should encompass several settings of activity, and that the resistance to capitalist culture as manifested in school experience among the non-conformist boys should be juxtaposed to the same process occurring among other students with a different class identity emerging. He recognizes the challenge, then, of giving up the overly place-focused nature of conventional ethnography without actually taking it up.

So, fitting the requirements that I outlined to exemplars discov-ered in contemporary ethnography is not so much a classificatory exercise that cannot, in any case, be accomplished mechanically or with any sort of precision, but is rather a framework for coherently documenting, interpreting, and arguing about the diverse range of moves in the construction of works that markedly depart from the traditional objectivist and realist project of ethnography at the core of anthropological practice. Thus, the requirements I have posed are as much a way of reading novelty in contemporary ethnographies, as a plea for rethinking the ways that they might be written.

If at the time of writing this paper I were to choose a selection of exemplary texts to discuss, these might be Fischer and Abedi's *De-bating Muslims: Cultural Dialogue In Postmodernity and Tradition* (1990), Herzfeld's *Anthropology through the Looking-glass: Critical*

Ethnography in the Margins of Europe (1987), Kapferer's *Legends of People, Myths of State: Violence, Intolerance and Political Culture in Sri Lanka and Australia* (1988), Latour's *Pasteurization of France* (1988), Rabinow's *French Modern: Norms and Forms of the Social Environment* (1989), Siegel's *Solo in the New Order: Language and Hierarchy in an Indonesian Town* (1986), and Taussig's *Shamanism, Colonialism, and the Wild Man: A Study in Terror and Healing* (1987). I hope that readers might be stimulated to have a look at these texts to judge for themselves the plausibility of classifying them each as enactments of one or more of the modernist strategies that I have proposed. Even more, I hope that this exercise might suggest to readers other even more appropriate and more complexly realized exemplars from among the works with which they are familiar.

CONCLUDING NOTES

Different senses of contextualization and comparison in modernist ethnography

Ethnography, realist or modernist, provides interpretation and explanation by strategies of contextualizing the problematic phenomena focused upon. Once we see how something exists embedded in a set of relationships we understand it. The realist ethnography contextualizes with reference to a totality in the form of a literal situated community and/or a semiotic code as cultural structure. The referent of contextualization for the modernist ethnography, which denies itself any conventional concept of totality, are fragments that are arranged and ordered textually by the design of the ethnographer. The rationale or argument for this design is often the most compelling dimension of the modernist work. The whole that is more than the sum of the parts of such ethnographies is always in question, while the parts are systematically related to each other by a revealed logic of connections.

Because modernist texts are not built upon the idea of little worlds in and of themselves – of community or an autonomous and spatially discrete locus of social activity – they, unlike realist ethnographies are aware of and often explicitly incorporate in analytic designs the comparative dimensions which are inherent in their conception. A realist ethnography is usually developed as a potential case for controlled comparison in a geographic areal perspective, where the comparative synthesis of cases is a discrete, specialized task. In contrast, comparison is inherent to analysis and argumentation within modernist ethnographies because they study processes that cross-cut time frames and spatial zones in quite uncontrolled ways (from the conventional areal perspective). In the modernist revisions of both the temporal and spatial dimensions that we discussed in the section on remaking the observed, comparative juxtaposition of quite disparate but related fragments of the past in memory and of situated sites of social activity in space is a key technique of analysis in these works. Also, as noted in the discussion of the remaking of the observer, modernist ethnographies tend to foreground the comparative bifocality that is inherent in all ethnography but remains submerged in most. And in pursuing a thought experiment of critical intervention, the modernist ethnography also, by juxtapositions, compares the various discourses and identity constructs that are present (dominant, residual, possible, and emergent) in any site of study. So, there are at least three senses of comparative analysis embedded within the single project of modernist ethnography, and they differ markedly from the projects of comparative analysis which are external to any realist ethnography and in which the latter may eventually be integrated.

A constructive use of deconstruction in modernist ethnography

The general notion of deconstruction derived from the work of Derrida that has come down to us now through various commentaries and applications as a shared intellectual capital is particularly useful in the modernist design for the ethnographic study of identity formation, since empirically this process seems to exhibit basic characteristics of a deconstructive critical process in action. Constructed and migrating through a grid of sites that constitute fragments rather than a community of any sort, an identity is a disseminating phenomenon that has a life of its own beyond the simple literal sense of inhering in particular human agents at a particular site and time. Its meanings are always deferred in any one text/site to other possible loci of its production through the diverse range of mental associations and references with which any human actor can creatively operate, literally through the contingencies of events, and sometimes through an explicit politics for or against the establishment of identities in particular places. In the modernist vision, deconstructive process stands for the human condition itself and is an elaborated restatement of the famous modernist sentiment in Marx – all that is solid melts into air.

However, the potentiality for the endless play of signs exists, and could be pursued by the analyst, for whatever critical purposes, even after certain human subjects would will it to stop. (A Derridean, for example, might want to show that the idea that an identity can be fixed through the will is a self deception, however convenient or satisfying, by playfully continuing the demonstration of dissemination without end.) Yet, identities do seem to stabilize, do resist the modernist condition of migration and dissemination in situations of both great tragedy (racial violence) and liberation (nationalism out of colonialism). To document the stabilizations of identity in any domain or across them in an essentially deconstructive world is a primary task of all ethnography. The modernist ethnography only asserts that such resistance in the struggle to establish identity does not rest on some nostalgic bedrock of tradition or community, but arises inventively out of the same deconstructive conditions that threaten to pull it apart or destabilize what has been achieved.

The treatment of power and ethics in modernist ethnography

In the elaborate and programmatic discussions of this essay about the design of modernist ethnography there has been little direct reference to power, class struggle, inequality and the suffering that has moved history. But modernist strategies focused on problems of describing identity formation in any contemporary site(s) of ethnographic research are indeed so obviously directed toward looking at processes of contestation, struggle, etc. among discourses arising from objective political and economic circumstances that this could go without saying. Far from ignoring 'objective conditions' such as processes of coercion, the play of interests, and class formation, the focus of modernist ethnography on the experiential and access to it through language in context is a direct engagement with and exploration of such conditions – without, however, the usual obeisances to the given social scientific frameworks for their discussion. The modernist strategies for ethnography articulate with Foucaultian and Gramscian ideas about the playing out of power relations in cultural cognitions, ideologies, and discourses (apprehended as voices here). In relation to the concerns of political economy with the operations of states, markets, and productive capacity, they seek to display critically the voices/alternatives present at any site of political contest, and to define the politics and the alternatives addressed and not addressed by it in a cultural frame. The great promise of such ethnography is indeed the possibility of changing the terms in which we think objectively and conventionally about power through exposure to cultural discourses.

But while modernist ethnography operates fully cognizant of the history of the political and economic circumstances in which identities have been formed, it is not built explicitly around the trope of power, but rather of ethics, that is, the complex moral relationship of the observer to the observed, of the relevance of the observed's situation to the situation of the observer's own society, and ultimately the exploration of the critical purpose of contemporary ethnographic analysis. These ethical concerns are never resolved in any ethnography, and they expose the kinds of contradictions embedded in the doing of ethnographic research and writing that make the ethnographer vulnerable to a diverting critique of his or her own ethics. But the risk of some readers not seeing anything in this but narcissism and handwringing is well worth taking, since the shaping of modernist strategies through a kind of ethical awareness (about the distinctive grounds of knowledge generated through ethnography) is essential to pursuing the traditional ends of ethnographic realism in the late twentieth century. This is what the modernist remaking of the observer and observed in ethnography stands for.

NOTES

1   Other formulations of the same general problematic that I have recently come across or been reminded of are, for example, Ahmad 1987: 22–5; Clifford 1986a: 24; Rabinow 1986: 258; and Jameson 1987: 40.

2   Thus, to my mind, the tendency to label the current ongoing critique of anthropology as the 'postmodern turn' or 'postmodern' anthropology is misguided. True, the nature of contemporary artistic production and the debates about it have powerfully fed the appetite for controversy in the humanities and the human sciences in the United States during the past decade, but the critique of ethnography and the experiments that follow from it can in no way be closely identified with aesthetic postmodernism. The provocations of the latter have merely created the conditions for appreciating the worth among some anthropologists in research and writing strategies of aspects of classic modernism rethought and revived for their continuing, rather traditional purposes.

3   This play has been facilitated by a rhetorical, literary-style critique of ethnography perhaps best represented in the volume that Jim Clifford and I edited, *Writing Culture* (1986). In my view, the main value of this critique is that it has made possible the exploration of new problems and even methods in anthropology by allowing for the possibility of alternative frameworks and terms in which its traditional problem areas could be rethought. This has been the most important contribution, thus far, of the so-called literary turn

in anthropology, which some have unfairly charged with leading to hermeticism and narcissism, among other academic disorders. Whatever one might think of the use of the textual metaphor in the actual interpretation of ethnographic materials, or of reflexivity as an analytic strategy, the contribution of the textual critique of ethnography itself can hardly be denied.

4   The renewed and focused interest in local determinations of identity (and, by extension, in the traditional topic areas of ethnicity, race, and nationality) is just one of a number of areas of social scientific study which are being rethought through assimilation for its own purposes of aspects of the current debate over modernism/postmodernism. Identity formation is the one that most proximately affects the traditional subject-matter and methods of anthropology. Other social scientific arenas which are being especially influenced by attempts to describe a contemporary modern/postmodern world are urban and regional planning; the emergence of global post-Fordist production processes and political economy; the media and mass cultural productions; and the so-called crisis of 'foundations' in the intellectual work of experts and academics generally (for a survey of such applications, see the special double issue of the journal *Theory, Culture and Society*, 1988, on postmodernism).

5   Of course, Victor Turner's influential notions of anti-structure and liminality (1969) are related to the 'space of experimentation' that I am delineating here. Indeed, Turner is ancestral to the contemporary spirit of experimentation, but the 'anti-structure' tendency in modernist ethnography is significantly different from the similar notion in Turner's work. Turner did not attempt to theoretically do without or dissolve the idea of structure. Liminality fitted easily into a broader scheme of order and derived its definition in relation to it. Modernist anti-structure has a much more uneasy relation to concepts of order, and is more radically deconstructive of the latter. In contemporary experiments, order is not so easily disambiguated in theory and concept from deconstructive process (or disorder). It is in relentlessly sustaining an ambiguity about such distinctions that modernist ethnography clearly distinguishes itself from Turner's liminality, which has its own sphere, and assumes a contrast with structure.

REFERENCES

Ahmad, Aijaz 1987: 'Jameson's rhetoric of Otherness and the "National Allegory"', *Social Text* (Fall), 3–25.

Berman, Marshall 1982: *All that Is Solid Melts into Air: The Experience of Modernity*. New York: Simon & Schuster; 1983: London: Verso; 1988 (2nd edn): Harmondsworth: Penguin.

Bright, Charles, and Geyer, Michael 1987: 'For a unified history of the world in the twentieth century', *Radical History Review*, 39, 69–91.

Clifford, James 1986a: Introduction, in Clifford and Marcus 1986.

Clifford, James 1986b: 'On ethnographic allegory', in Clifford and Marcus 1986.

Clifford, James, and Marcus, George E. (eds) 1986: *Writing Culture: The Poetics and Politics of Ethnography*. Berkeley: University of California Press.

Fabian, Johannes 1983: *Time and the Other: How Anthropology Makes Its Object*. New York: Columbia University Press.

Fischer, Michael 1986: 'Ethnicity and the post-modern arts of memory', in Clifford and Marcus 1986.

Fischer, Michael, and Abedi, Mehdi 1990: *Debating Muslims: Cultural Dialogue in Postmodernity and Tradition*. Madison: University of Wisconsin Press.

Herzfeld, Michael 1987: *Anthropology through the Looking-glass: Critical Ethnography in the Margins of Europe*. Cambridge: Cambridge University Press.

Jameson, Fredric 1987: 'Regarding postmodernism – a conversation with Fredric Jameson', *Social Text* (Fall), 29–54.

Kapferer, Bruce 1988: *Legends of People, Myths of State: Violence, Intolerance and Political Culture in Sri Lanka and Australia*. Washington, DC: Smithsonian Institution Press.

Latour, Bruno 1988: *The Pasteurization of France*. Cambridge, Mass.: Harvard University Press.

Marcus, George E. 1986: 'Contemporary problems of ethnography in the modern world system', in Clifford and Marcus 1986.

Marcus, George E. 1989: 'The problem of the unseen world of wealth for the rich: toward an ethnography of complex connections', *Ethos*, 17, 110–19.

Marcus, George E. n.d.: 'Imagining the whole: ethnography's contemporary effort to situate itself', *Critique of Anthropology* (forthcoming).

Marcus, George E., and Cushman, Dick 1982: 'Ethnographies as texts', in *Annual Review of Anthropology*, vol. 2, 25–89. Palo Alto, Calif.: Annual Reviews, Inc.

Marcus, George E., and Fischer, Michael 1986: *Anthropology as Cultural Critique: An Experimental Moment in the Human Sciences*. Chicago: University of Chicago Press.

Rabinow, Paul 1986: 'Representations are social facts: modernity and postmodernity in anthropology', in Clifford and Marcus 1986.

Rabinow, Paul 1989: *French Modern: Norms and Forms of the Social Environment*. Cambridge, Mass.: MIT Press.

Siegel, James T. 1986: *Solo in the New Order: Language and Hierarchy in an Indonesian Town*. Princeton: Princeton University Press.

Taussig, Michael 1987: *Shamanism, Colonialism, and the Wild Man: A Study in Terror and Healing*. Chicago: University of Chicago Press.

Theory, Culture and Society 1988: 'Postmodernism'. Special double issue, 5/2–3.

Turner, Victor 1969: *The Ritual Process*. Chicago: Aldine.

Williams, Raymond 1977: *Marxism and Literature*. New York: Oxford University Press.

Willis, Paul 1976: *Learning to Labour: How Working Class Kids Get Working Class Jobs*. New York: Columbia University Press.

Wolf, Eric 1982: *Europe and the People without History*. Berkeley: University of California Press.

14

Narcissism, roots and postmodernity: the constitution of selfhood in the global crisis

Jonathan Friedman

INTRODUCTION

Is there a relation between the world system, roots and postmodern culture? Can one ask such a preposterous question? This is certainly nothing for an anthropologist! Certainly not, it would appear, in today's world of 'writing of culture'. I have on several occasions made a plea for exactly such an exercise (Friedman 1987a,b,c, 1988, 1989), and I shall continue to indulge in this vein in what follows.

Anthropology has shifted broadly, as reflex of changes in the specular relation between the West and the Rest, from a position that was explicitly theoretical and ethnographically 'realistic' to one that has narrowed itself increasingly to a discourse limited to the ethnographic act itself. This has been accounted for very generally by a decline in 'ethnographic authority' (Clifford 1983) and a general critique of many of the taken-for-granted categories of anthropological description. Now there is no doubt that this internal critique has been positive for our understanding of the previously little discussed issues of translation, writing and the social context of representing the Other. But little has been said about the context itself, about the historical conjuncture in which such questions emerge as crucial. We have suggested elsewhere (Ekholm-Friedman and Friedman 1980; Friedman 1987a,b) that the context is indeed pertinent since the issues debated by anthropologists are generated by problems of anthropological identity. Thus, as much as one might agree that a more dialogic approach to the representation of others is a potential improvement over Baron von Münchhausen ethnography, our change of heart is not an act of pure altruism or of methodological or even epistemological supersession; not, then, a process of intellectual development. The decline of ethnographic authority is an immediate expression of the fragmentation of the hegemonic structure of the world system. This is a question of politics, of the politics of ethnography as well as the politics of identity in a more general sense than the mere 'writing of culture'. As ethnographic description is the practice of writing the Other for us, here at home, it precludes, by definition, the voice and the pen of the Other. Ethnography, thus, embodies the authority to represent and, by logical implication, the authority to maintain the Other in silence. Now this is a serious political act since it identifies the Other for us. It also, ultimately, through colonial and post-colonial apparatuses, returns that identity to the Other so that it becomes, by hook or by crook, the latter's own identity. So the issue is not merely a disciplinary one, but strikes at the heart of the general relation between power and representation.

> Les luttes à propos de l'identité ethnique ou régionale, c'est-à-dire à propos de propriétés (stigmates ou emblèmes) liées à *l'origine* á travers le *lieu* d'origine et les marques durables qui en sont corrélatives, comme l'accent, sont un cas particulier des luttes des classements, luttes pour le monopole du pouvoir de faire voir et de faire croire, de faire connaître et de faire reconnaître, d'imposer la définition légitime des divisions du monde social et, par là, *de faire et de défaire les groupes*: elles ont en effet pour enjeu le pouvoir d'imposer une vision du monde social à travers des principes de di-vision qui, lorsqu'ils s'imposent à l'ensemble d'un groupe, font le sens et le consensus sur le sens, et en particulier sur l'identité et l'unité du groupe, qui fait la réalité et de l'identité du groupe. (*Bourdieu 1980: 65*)

Identification is the rendering to someone of identity. Ethnography renders the Other's identity to ourselves and, via the conditions in which it is executed, back to the Other. By speaking of him, or for him, we ultimately force him to speak through our categories. This works adequately in conditions of empire, or stable hegemony and a clear hierarchy of identities. But where such conditions begin to disintegrate, its correlative discourses lose their authority, not only because we ourselves come to the realization that we can no longer simply re-present them, but because they will not let us do so. Their self-identification interferes with our identification of them.

The problem for anthropologists is trivial by comparison with the larger issue of which it is but an index. Academics argue back and forth about ways in which to solve the problem and there is a strong tendency to try and reinstate ethnographic authority, by either subsuming dialogue within Western monologue or by resorting to other tactics, such as poetry and what are self-assertedly called postmodern forms of representation (Tyler 1989).[1] But by not understanding themselves as anthropological objects in the world they lose all perspective and run the risk of becoming ensconced in the autistic contemplation of their own experience.

And the problem would appear to be as follows: the ethnographic space of anthropology has imploded. Its centre/periphery reality is crumbling, thus eroding the basis of the West's ability to represent the rest.[2] The metaphor of autism, of narcissistic retreat from objectivism and theory to the exclusive contemplation of field experience, of the encounter with Otherness and the tenacious identification with ethnography: these are part of a concrete transformation of the world that are evident across vast domains of our social existence. If the anthropological situation is a mere symptom of a larger-scale phenomenon then anthropological self-reflection ought to lead us to a broader perspective.

THE VICISSITUDES OF THE GLOBAL SYSTEM

We shall postulate that in the kind of system in which we live, a system based on the reproduction of abstract wealth via the production of means of production and consumption, which in its purest form is industrial capitalism, there is a strong functional relation between changes in the flows of and accumulation of capital in the world arena and changes in identity construction and cultural production. These relations can be subsumed in the relation between material processes and the cultural space of modernity, and in the dynamic and shifting relations between the differently constituted modernities that make up the global arena.

Stable hegemonic phases in global systems are characterized by strongly hierarchical relations between dominant centres and their peripheries. They are characterized by a centralized accumulation of capital and a resultant division of labour that tends to take the form of supply zones for both raw materials and labour in the periphery and industrial manufacture of finished goods in the centre: the world's workshop syndrome.

In counterpoint to such phases are periods of decentralization of capital accumulation, in which centres that have become both rich and expensive from the point of view of production export massive amounts of capital to specific areas of the system. New small and rapidly expanding centres emerge, outcompeting central production, leading eventually to a situation in which the centre becomes increasingly the consumer of the products of its own exported capital. Decline in the centre is a complex and uneven process. While there is a tendency for industrial areas to decline, the vast amounts of capital that are freed from production and repatriated from export are invested in more mercantile projects: real estate, stock market, the arts, luxury goods etc. This phase takes on the paradoxical appearance that combines deindustrialization and gentrification, increased poverty and increased wealth. Slumification and yuppification, the increased stratification of the 'really declining' centres, is a single systemic process. What appears as the emergence of a 'postindustrial' society, characterized by the dominance of the production and control of information, is largely, perhaps entirely, the product of deindustrialization and its concomitant shifts in class structure. In this period, there are new upwardly mobile groups in the centre and there is an appearance of progress due to the increase in commodification and the appearance of escalating luxuriousness of consumer goods and spaces.

> From housing for artists 'living poor' outside the mainstream of society to luxury housing for an urbane 'artistic' bourgeoisie, living lofts reflect an interesting expansion of middle-class culture. By this point in the twentieth century, the cultural style that is associated with loft living – the 'lost lifestyle' – shows a middle-class preference for open space and artistic forms of production, as well as a more general nostalgia about the 'smaller past' of the great industrial era... The integration of an industrial aesthetic into the new cult of domesticity also reflects the commercialization of cultural change, besides obvious social changes like the end of the 'mechanical age' of industrial society, the professionalization of leisure activities, and the dissociation of many middle-class women from household chores. (*Zukin 1982: 81*)

If the main markets for capital investment are land, housing, art and the stockmarket, then there is a clear shift from real to what Marx terms fictive accumulation, that is, the accumulation of paper values whose only effect is increasing stratification via differentiation of wealth and increased pressure on accumulation in general via inflation and its inbuilt liquidity problem.[3] This has happened before, before the 1920s, before industrial capitalism, before the decline of the Mediterranean, perhaps before the decline of Rome and even before the disintegration of the Athenian hegemony.

The decentralization of hegemonic accumulation implies increasing

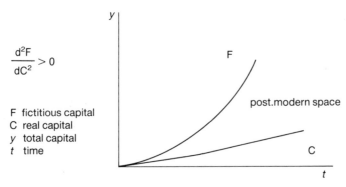

Note: The equation states that fictitious capital grows faster than real, i.e. productive capital, and at an increasing rate. This occurs in periods of decentralization of capital accumulation in the system, accompanied by investment in non-productive sectors in the centre. The postmodern space of investment lies in the gap between real and fictive growth curves.

Figure 14.1 Fictitious capital and postmodernity: tendencies in the system

competition of capitals and a potential shift of hegemony. In the former centre it implies a movement of wealth into consumption and speculative accumulation with its accompanying changes in social structure, and, as we shall see, culture.

There is a relation between economic processes and cultural processes, at any rate in a system based on the accumulation of abstract wealth, that is ultimately dependent on the process of material production. The very organization of consumption and thus of demand is dependent on the distribution in time and space of capital accumulation (Figure 14.1). Demand is not fixed by a well-defined code of consumption, but is driven by the Goethian spirit of modernity. It is thus variable and open, in principle, to infinite variation. In order to grasp this relation it is necessary to understand the nature of the modern self on a comparative basis, a subject to which we shall return. If we are to remain within the rubric defined above, we must limit ourselves to the tendencies of capital accumulation itself. These are characterized by the following apparently contradictory processes:

1 The decentralization of capital accumulation in space and the accompanying appearance of new centres of accumulation as well as shifting centre–periphery relations.

(a) Selective rapid 'development' in some areas, the emergence of 'modernities' and world market consumption centres.

2 The intensification of commodification in the centre – the 'capitalization' of social relations and the increasing transformation of aspects of the social world into commodities, producing what is taken for a postindustrial or postmodern evolution.

3 The general movement of capital in the centre from industrial production into fictitious accumulation, real estate and the 'culture' industries.

NARCISSISM AND THE CONSTITUTION OF SELF

None of this material process should startle us postmoderns if we are true to the practice of 'blurred genres' (Geertz 1980). The economics of global systems is merely a material aspect of a process that is equally culturally constituted, that is, constituted *of* but not *by* culture. Our aim is to discover the connections among the aspects, not to dissolve one into the other.

The construction of identity space is the dynamic operator linking economic and cultural processes. It is the source of the desire and thus the specific motivations that generate representational schemes.

It is not necessary to be an advocate of Freud in order to appropriate such a basic concept as narcissism. It is not necessary to assume, in other words, that there is a universal structure of the human psyche containing id, ego and superego. One may accept the existence of the kinds of activities to which these topoi refer without assuming that they must necessarily exist in a fixed relation to one another within the human individual. The term 'primary narcissism' refers to a condition of dependence of acts of self-definition upon the Other during the period of infancy. This basic human take-off point has been the subject of much discussion and has been most systematically explored by structuralist psychoanalyst Lacan in what he refers to as the mirror stage. There are, of course, clear parallels with the more cognitively biased work of G. H. Mead, as well as much of the early phenomenological psychology of Sartre, which is clearly a source, even if via a critique of the existentialist subject, of much of Lacan's own work.

From a Freudian perspective, the narcissistic state is one characterized by a lack of inner experience or, more correctly, of the kind of experience that defines the self as an autonomous being. The subject is here totally integrated into a larger unity, primarily in relation to the mother; and the constitution of the ego is the gradual internalization of narcissistic mirroring in such a way as to produce an autonomous self. In other terms this consists of the formation of an identity capable of self-realization, that is, with its own project. This development, apparently natural, is, in our terms, very much culture-bound. It is a description of a particular type of socialization characteristic of the formation of the modern individual. It is this cultural specificity that engenders the possibility of 'secondary narcissism' defined as the failure of individuation, 'incomplete mourning in the wake of inevitable individuation, separation and abandonment' (Levin 1987: 502). In a great many 'non-modern', non-capitalist social forms, the combination of dependency and mutuality is elaborated upon as a cultural core. In *Oedipe Africain* (1966), the Ortigues discuss the way in which what is normally internalized in the process of Western individuation is here a constantly external frame of reference for the subject who remains dependent upon the authority and life-project of the ancestors, that is, of the dead. In modernity, the converse situation prevails: by removing the ancestral organization, the establishment and maintenance of personal projects can only have an internal source, and their lack of socially established fixity decentres the project and loosens it from its cosmological foundations. The result is the constant transformation of projects and competition among them, so that in the end the project itself becomes the principal project, that is, the abstraction of movement in and for itself.

Where the modern has his self, or ego, as the locus of his life-project's authority, the tendency in traditional societies is that the project and its authority exist external to the human subject, in the larger social network and its cosmological principles. But in both cases, these encompassing instances can disintegrate, laying bare a common human narcissistic foundation. The disintegration depends on external conditions that occur at different times in different sectors of the larger system. Thus, expansion of a hegemonic centre may entail a crisis for a 'traditional' structure of self in the centre, with accompanying reactions of religious character, just as a similar crisis may later occur in those areas that are successively incorporated into a formative centre–periphery structure. The disintegration of kin and community networks may produce millenaristic reaction in the centre although the context is one, in the case of Europe, of a fully developed peasant society in which higher 'political' orders of kinship have disappeared altogether, replaced by both church and state. In many parts of the periphery where there is a kinship organized polity, there is a tendency to orientate oneself to the modern in such a way that the strength or force, the *mana* that reproduces society, appears to come ultimately from the conquerors, the outsiders and 'stranger kings' who come from the very source of power. As individualization proceeds in the centre it generates a modern cosmology while in these peripheries there is a tendency for the local hierarchies to be encompassed by the higher order of the modern.

The stable cultural situation of hegemony is one in which areas incorporated into the system maintain a value hierarchy commonly described in terms of the devaluation of local culture and the necessity of identification, where possible, with the dominant Western model that is defined as the modern. Colonial mentality and the consciousness of the colonized are both formed in this context.

THE POSTMODERNIZATION OF HAWAII

Hawaii is a special place in the world and the system that integrates the world. It is dominated today by a tourist economy that is heavily capital-saturated. It is, furthermore, counter-cyclical with respect to the mainland because of Japanese investment.

Hawaiian history

Hawaii was rapidly integrated into the world economy after the eventful arrival and death of Captain Cook at the hands of a local chief. Beginning as a provisioning port, it became a prime source of sandalwood in the China trade. The traditional political system, after expanding to encompass the islands with British help, disintegrated as an internal response to rapid economic transformation; the movement of the aristocracy to Honolulu, large scale dislocations in social arrangements, epidemics and demographic collapse, and the virtual bankruptcy of the ruling chiefs ensuing upon the sandalwood trade itself. The kapu system, the religious foundation of chiefly power, collapsed as chiefs became increasingly tied to European and American traders and their military support system. The arrival of congregationalist missionaries, the whaling trade, the development of sugar plantations, the import of Chinese, Japanese, Filipino, and other labourers, the forceful introduction of private property and the eventual expulsion of the Hawaiian monarchy and incorporation into the American empire, created the foundations of modern multi-ethnic

Hawaii, in which Hawaiians, whose numbers had greatly diminished during the first hundred years of contact, (from 600,000 to 40,000) became a low-ranking minority in their own land.

The history of the islands reflects a cycle of increasing hegemony that has now passed into a dehegemonization that is partially offset by Japanese investment. It is to be noted that Japanese investment is no mere perturbation of a more general trend, but a central aspect of the dehegemonizing process itself. Lest it be assumed that the current imbalance is somehow the result of a particular culturally informed economic strategy, rather than a truly world systemic process, it ought to be recalled that 40 per cent of Japan's trade surplus with the US is due to American-owned companies buying or making things in Japan, then exporting them back to the United States. Similarly, up to 60 per cent of American imports from both Singapore and Malaysia come from US-based firms. Furthermore, US companies producing in Japan sold more to Japan than the total American trade deficit in 1985. In other words, the rise of Japan and South-east Asia is an organic expression of the decentralization of American capital accumulation.

As Hawaii, throughout the nineteenth and twentieth centuries, became increasingly integrated into the US economy, the dwindling Hawaiian population found itself in a situation where its language was forbidden, its dance and much of its culture were considered to be a barbaric expression totally at odds with civilization. A combination of stigmatization and social disintegration led to the formation of modern Hawaiian communities, few in number, surrounded by larger multi-ethnic communities generated by the sugar economy and from the late 1950s a rapidly expanding tourist industry that has turned the *Great Gatsby* style of Hawaii into *Miami Vice* in the space of two decades. With the entrance of the islands as a state of the union, dominated by the largest ethnic group, the Japanese, Hawaiians were reduced to insignificance. Mass tourism and a Japanese-American dominated government and educational apparatus, combined to marginalize the Hawaiians even more than the former sugar economy that had little place for them. Throughout the twentieth century, this process of integration has led to a loss of Hawaiian identity. 'Get out, marry a *haole* (white), don't speak Hawaiian. Our old religion is full of the evil magic. To be a good Christian is the only good way; no, the Hawaiian religion is dangerous ... that's why I don't practise it.' Of course, given the economic and political situation, getting out was no easy task. But those that did now find themselves in a curious situation. 'Those people,

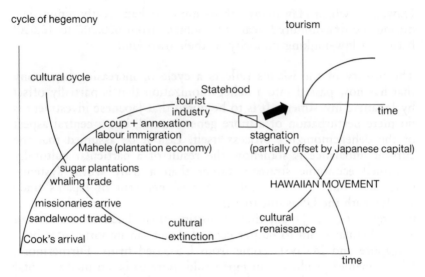

Figure 14.2 Hawaii's history in the global system

coconuts, you know . . . brown on the outside, but white on the inside.'
Such people, good community leaders, they might have imagined.
But they are traitors to the rebirth of Hawaiian identity that has
occurred since the mid-seventies.

Hawaii today is a crossroads in many senses. Here American and
Japanese tourists have had their separate hotels even if Japanese
capital now owns 80 per cent of them. During the sixties, Waikiki
was transformed into the mass tourist centre of the Pacific. Today,
after the crisis of the seventies when tourism declined, unemployment rose, and Hawaiians began to organize, the old hotels are being
renovated as luxurious replicas of the turn-of-the-century or of a
more postmodern mixture of eras, all very much tinged with a
nostalgia for a more aristocratic past. Gentleman ranches and Disney
versions of Old Hawaii are sold to those who can afford it. A recent
report by T. Horton on the subdivision of Hawaii's largest ranch
(the largest private ranch in the United States) runs as follows:

NEW RIDERS OF THE RAINBOW RANGE:
HAWAII'S URBAN PANIOLOS

They're leaving the cities to roam free among the cattle and the
four-bedroom homes. New York and Philadelphia were never

like this. Neither was Waikiki, nor even Maui. For David Kahn, native New Yorker who had to work his way through Philadelphia, Waikiki and Naanapali before he reached the home of his dreams on the island of Hawaii, cowboys and horses and cattle were something you only saw in the John Wayne movies.

Now Kahn is a part of all that, living the life of the wide open spaces with white-faced cattle grazing on his land and neighbours waving hello from their horses and real cowboys punching cattle.

Best of all, Kahn can enjoy all of this without getting any of it on his shoes.

These are the new wranglers of the Hawaii range, executive riders in the sky who are jetting out of the cities to take up life on the range, where never is heard a discouraging word, unless the Dow Jones falls or the phone in the Jeep Cherokee fails. (Spirit of Aloha: Aloha Island Air Magazine, *14, 1: Jan./Feb. 1989*)

There has also been a large-scale influx of Japanese, not least of members of the Yakuza, the Japanese mafia, who are among the major purchasers of Hawaiian buildings and land. It is the major producer of marijuana in the United States, with all the syndicate activity entailed, and the islands are still dotted by small Hawaiian, or part-Hawaiian, local communities struggling to survive while engaged in all of the above activities. Nor can it be overlooked that Hawaii is the major atomic weapon arsenal in the Pacific and centre of operations for an entire hemisphere. And in the midst of all this, a Hawaiian movement or movements increasingly consolidated around the issue of sovereignty, the regaining of lands lost by an unconstitutional coup d'état in 1893, lands amounting to half of the islands, and the reestablishment of Hawaiian culture in the islands. For the cynical Westerner, a fabulous pastiche of postmodernity. For the local Hawaiian, a question of social life or death.

The Hawaiian movement began in the early seventies. It coincided with much of the political activity in other parts of the Western world. Some say that it drew many of its ideas from the Black Power Movement, but there is ample evidence that it had roots in Hawaiian rural areas that had for years opposed the encroaching destruction reaped by American-style development. While there are clear Hawaiian roots, the early years of the movement are best characterized in terms of its incorporation into the student-dominated political left. Its ideology linked Hawaiian rights to the question of peace, ecology, and opposition to destruction of the islands by tourist

capital. There were numerous actions, from the opposition to building resorts to the occupation of land formally owned by the state but
which was claimed by Hawaiians as their rightful heritage.[4] As the
left declined, a separation occurred. The Hawaiians came into their
own. Their identity became solidly established and their focus
shifted to exclusively Hawaiian issues, the control of land, the re-
establishment of Hawaiian culture. A number of nationalist trends
began to consolidate in the late seventies and they intensified in the
eighties. One of the groups claimed independence from the United
States, issued Hawaiian identity papers to its members, and tried to
reinstate the former royal territorial organization. At its head was a
woman who claimed close kinship with the royal lineage. But as
membership was only in the hundreds, little came of this.

While local actions and occupations of land have continued
throughout the eighties, the leadership of the various groups have
converged on the issue of sovereignty with a land base as a solution
to Hawaiian problems. The two major parties involved in this emergent strategy are the Office of Hawaiian Affairs, at present a state
department dealing with Hawaiian issues whose members are directly elected by Hawaiians and part-Hawaiians, and the Kalahui
Hawaii ('The Nation of Hawaii'), a conglomerate of a number of
parties that have been involved in the day-to-day struggles of
Hawaiians. The latter have argued for the return of ceded and Home
Lands to the Hawaiians and the establishment of a sovereign nation.
There are, of course, conflicts between the Nation and the Office of
Hawaiian Affairs, and the latter has taken over many of the former's
ideas and defined itself as the logical state apparatus for an eventual
Hawaiian government. People involved in the movement express
scepticism about the ever-present schisms, but it is nevertheless the
case that a shift in the level of strategy has occurred. No longer is it
merely a question of local struggles to defend Hawaiians against
modern development, but a 'final solution', political autonomy. And
this goal has in principle been recognized by the federal government,
a great step for a people whose existence was barely recognized two
decades ago. Even the configuration of state politics has been
affected. The current governor, John Waihee, is the first Hawaiian
governor of the state, and his election, if not his politics, are a clear
expression of an ideological shift, one that recognizes the rights of
Hawaiians and that recoils from the most extreme effects of tourist
development.

This general shift is shaped by the decline of modernist identity,
and an opening up of the option of roots. Hawaiians, as the indige-

nous people of the islands, however mixed with other immigrant groups – Japanese, Chinese, Filipino, Korean – are the representatives of a local Hawaiian culture that has emerged over the past century and a half. The recognition of an indigenous identity has played a critical role in the emergence of the Hawaiian movement. In the period between the censuses of 1970 and 1980, the number of Hawaiians who identified themselves as such increased significantly, from 130,000 to more than 190,000.[5] But in the same period the population of North American Indians increased from 700,000 to 1,400,000. This is not a fact of biology. Many Hawaiians and a great many Indians who were formerly 'mixed' enough to be able to identify themselves as something else have now begun to assert their identities as indigenous peoples. Hawaiian identity has consolidated during the past decade. It is no longer necessary to hide it or to call oneself Chinese or Korean, as people did during the fifties and even the sixties.

The members of the movement are both young and old. The elders, fewer in number, have struggled for Hawaiian identity for a lifetime. They are among the most radical of the movement. 'Not enough to do like the Navaho. It's always the same. If we go federal we goin' to have the same kind of problems with state power. The only solution for us is real independence.' These are the words of a 75-year-old member of the sovereignty movement, opposed to the federal solution advocated by the Nation. The young members present a definite profile. Most of them, especially those most active, have followed a standard route. They have joined the military at a relatively young age, been to Europe and/or Vietnam. They have returned disappointed with the larger society and have become involved with the movement in a search for something different. They are against modern American society, often against Christianity. They have fought to get subsistence land, to start Hawaiian language schools for themselves and their children. They have begun to reinstate the ancient Hawaiian temples, the *heiaus*. They complain about the Christianity of their parents and the latter's negative view of their own religion and culture.

The Hawaiian movement, born in an economic recession, has now to face a new wave of investment, this time from the Japanese. The latter has consisted in a massive purchase of hotels and resorts, the renovation of old and construction of new resorts, golf courses with exorbitant membership rates ($50,000, for example), inflation of land values and taxes, a state surplus, the elimination of visa requirements for visiting Japanese.

Two roads to the national media

The contrasts are intense. In *Time* magazine we can read of the $360 million resort, the Hyatt Waikoloa.

> Times must be tough for jaded travelers. There are not many places left on this earth that still confer bragging rights now that Katmandu has as many package tours as Atlantic City and darkest Africa is bright with flashbulbs. So just in time comes the spanking-new Hyatt Regency Waikoloa on the lee shore of the Big Island of Hawaii ... To reach their rooms, guests can board a bullet-nosed monorail tram or take a boat along the canal that runs the mile-long stretch of the resort. ... 'Disneyland changed the way people view entertainment,' muses Amy Katoh, who is visiting from Tokyo with her husband Yichi. 'And this place will change the way people think about resorts.' ... The Hyatt hunch is that today's travelers are in desperate search of an Experience, a made-to-order memory, and are willing to pay $265 a night for the average room to $2,500 for a presidential suite in order to find it. (Time, *27 February, 1989: 49*)

This hotel fantasy land, where guests can swim with dolphins, and take their exclusive meals in the artificially made tropical paradise that was once a lava plain situated at the bottom of the largest private ranch in the United States, today in the throes of subdivision for yuppy investors, is surely reminiscent of the larger-scale gentrification that has characterized the Western centres during the past years. And it sports the added attraction of the nostalgia and tradition that, extracted from their life processes, can fill executive lives with the rich experiences of Hawaiian cowboy (*paniolo*) life, a dinner in a former royal palace, or the excitement of a live volcano. There are other hotels and planned complexes. One, at the south of this apparently underexploited island, is scheduled to become a five-hotel complex, 2,500 acres of replicas of Old Hawaii and Old Europe, meant to attract the upper crusts and *nouveaux riches* of Europe. Hawaiian Riviera is its proposed title, a veritable simulacrum of a world that never existed, the imaginary landscape of the historically uninformed new wealth.

Simultaneously, a great row has appeared in the US national media concerning the mass disinterment of a Hawaiian burial place on the island of Maui in conjunction with resort construction:

> The discovery of 900 skeletons at an ancient burial ground has led to a temporary halt in building an $80 million beachfront

hotel on Maui island and to calls for changes in state laws that could slow Hawaii's construction frenzy... Residents are anything but united on how to balance development and preservation... 'It's a religious and spiritual issue for us' said Edward Kanahele, spokesman for an organization called Malama Na Kapuna, or Caring for Our Ancestors. 'In our culture we believe that the exposing of bones is one of the worst things a human can do. It's worse than murder, because it interferes with that person's after-life, which lasts much longer than life on this earth.' (New York Times, *4 January 1989: A11*)

The local Hawaiians who protested over the activities of the contract archaeologist won their case. The developers have backed down, agreeing to move their construction site, and the county has been forced into the option of buying the land in order to ensure historic preservation, an activity that is to be entirely in the hands of Hawaiians.

Fishing in Paradise

There is a small fishing village on the west coast of the island of Hawaii, often referred to by both outsiders and insiders as the last village on the island and the last fishing village in the state. It lies at the end of a somewhat treacherous winding road that descends some 1,500 feet from the main highway to the lava-covered coast. From one of the many scenic views along the road the village can be seen in the distance, an oasis of palm trees and greenery in a desert of black heat. For local outsiders the village is thought of as dangerous. There are stories of mean Hawaiians and there is a famous case of the murder of a tourist to concretize the image. Yet there is a state park right in the middle of this village of at most 200 where people come at a constant rate to camp out and see the 'other' Hawaii. The village itself consists of a string of wooden shacks and two very modern houses belonging to two of the more successful families. There is no electricity, except for private generators, and no running water. One of the shacks, perched over the boat landing, was Elvis Presley's house in the film *Girls, Girls, Girls*, and if the road is paved it is not unrelated to the film studio's needs for rapid and relatively safe transport to and from the village. The ostensible activity of the village is fishing, for local mackerel and yellow-fin tuna. The rate of endogamy is high enough that the expression 'we are all family here' is quite literally true. The atmosphere is one of isolation and serenity, disturbed only by occasional tourists and invading film studios (two other educational films about the village have been made). The idyllic fishing village is a symbol of all that has been lost for urban activists. But there is more here than meets the eye. Villagers are accused of drug-dealing and gambling; they are under siege by developers who would turn them into copies of themselves, or rather, what traditional Hawaiians are supposed to be, selling trinkets and being quaint, while their land is sold off to the highest bidders.

There is even a novel written about this *Last Village in Kona*, published in 1986, the work of one of Hawaii's well-known journalists, who reveals himself, on the book jacket, to be a true descendant of French Hawaiian stock, one of the radicals who supported the Hawaiian movement. The 'last village' bears only oblique resemblance to the real.

> A white coral roadway meanders through the sprawling coconut grove between low walls of lava rocks poled stone upon stone by ancient villagers who lived here centuries ago. Since the roadway was laid down in those ancient times, the general plan of the village is much the same as it was then. Wooden houses stand in the same clearings among the palm trees where thatch huts once stood on stone platforms. (*Altieri 1986: 8*)

The reference is surely to the asphalt road paved by Paramount Studios that meanders through the shacks built here by refugees from the 1926 lava-flow that buried the neighbouring village, and whose rights to the land were not recognized until a few years ago, following decades of sporadic Hawaiian agitation. This is a novel that sets out to describe the Hawaiian struggle to re-establish a cultural identity, and this last village, a core symbol for many, plays a key role in the constitution of a living tradition. The struggle between the modern world of crime, marijuana and virulent tourism and the idyllic life of a Hawaiian past is the driving tension of the work.

> Solomon looked at him for a long time, silently, then said quietly, 'Kawika thinks he can go back. At least part of the way. He thinks he can go back at least far enough to recover some of the culture, some of the feeling of being Hawaiian, that feeling of being truly a part of the land and the sea, part of the whole life and spirit of the place. That's what we lost, you know. That's what it meant to be Hawaiian.' (*Altieri 1986: 7*)

For years it has been said that there is no way back, 'you can't stop progress', etc. And yet the core of the Hawaiian movement is precisely the gut feeling that now is the time. Altieri continues: 'Then maybe he wasn't born at the wrong time . . . maybe he is very right for this time.'

Now the people of this little fishing village have their own very dynamic social life, one that bears little resemblance to the arcadian image of the movement, since it is part of a certain modernity that cannot be grasped in terms of simple oppositions. But the discourse of identity is one of tradition against modernity, and villagers are just as versed in it as are landless urban Hawaiians.

What we have here is a multi-layered and mutually interpenetrated reality: a village with a specific form of life and accompanying strategies, embedded in a discourse of Hawaiian identity that identifies the village with a tradition that is to serve as a model, surrounded by an aggressive tourist industry that would convert the entire local population into hotel workers and Hawaiians-for-visitors, a dying sugar industry, macadamia nut farms, coffee, marijuana: a vast world of perils and opportunities.

The postmodernization of Hawaii refers to the way in which the fragmentation of Western modernist identity is expressed in simultaneous processes, including the nostalgic turn in the gentrification of tourism, the increasing clout of Hawaiianness and the potential new identifications that emerge for villagers that are classified as traditional while at the same time being up to their ears in modern activities. With the breakdown of the homogeneous model of hegemonic identity, the continuum from backward if quaint Hawaiians on the bottom of a progressive modern society that strives to assimilate them, has given way to a polycentric system of identity formation. The two major 'attractors' in this process are the tourist industry that is the cornerstone of modern Hawaii and the Hawaiian cultural movement that opposes such development.

The identification process generated by the tourist industry is one in which Hawaii and Hawaiians are represented as cultural objects having definite contours and which are on display in the hotel *luaus*, staged hulas, boat races etc. Actual Hawaiians are not often represented in the cultural events, although their appearance has been on the increase. Earlier, it was Tahitians and other islanders who often played the role of Hawaiians. This is combined with the powerful representation, by developers and those visitors and residents sharing their ideology, of present day Hawaiians as a mongrel, lazy, criminal race who have nothing in common with their forebears.[6] These images all interact with villagers' self identification. And the new tourism is out to create or really re-create a nostalgic vision of a former Hawaii, the plantation aspect, for the comfort of the new luxury tourist, and the replicated Hawaiian and even European forms that are associated with glorious consumer pasts. In this form of identity, Hawaiians are defined by the image projected by the modern sector. There is a demand for a culture or image of a culture that bears no relation to current Hawaiian realities. If they are to have a role in such development, it is as representatives of 'themselves', as bearers of authentic cultural pasts. The Hawaiian movement is likewise in search of a past, and, if there is any overlap between the nostalgic turn in tourism and the movement, it lies in the focus on roots, on authenticity. But for the movement, that authenticity is totally at odds with tourism, since it is not meant to be an image for others to gaze at, but a way of life, a material solution to the current social predicamemt; the lack of a future in the modern world, and the reduction to playing a role in someone else's image of the past.

A particular aspect of Hawaii in global structural terms is that Hawaiians are focused on their own cultural selfhood and do not look to the outside world as a source of strength or identity. This is especially true of members of the movement and it is perhaps a logical outcome of the strategy of construction of a specific cultural identity. But even in a village like Miloli'i, where the outside world is invoked as a source of power, it is represented in strictly modern terms, as political power and money. And if Hawaiians are to identify with this outside it is because it represents progress with respect to Hawaiian conditions.

THE HYPERMODERNIZATION OF CONGOLESE IDENTITY

The African case is quite the opposite to the Hawaiian. Here the outside is not only a source of power but the very condition of existence of the inside. Money, medicine, development as it is manifested via the state that channels it downward is life-force, and in the Congo its source is usually Paris.

The tourist to the Congo, and there are few indeed, confronts a real, if transformed, Congolese society that he must live inside of during the time that he is resident. It is only in the hotel lobby and certain night spots that he is entirely at home. The white, postcolonial society is indeed an enclave in the larger black world. The tourist in Hawaii does not leave home. It is the Hawaiians that are the enclave, surrounded by a white world saturated with images of the former. In order to get to the Hawaiians one must leave the surrounding world and enter into one of the enclaves. The visitor to the Congo is a superior being in a position of potential patron. The visitor who gets through to the Hawaiians finds himself in a position of suspect equality. Hawaiian identity lies at the centre for the Hawaiian, whereas Congolese identity is intimately bound up with Paris.

Les Sapeurs: *modernity as cargo*

Congo-Brazzaville represents a symmetrical inversion of the situation of the Hawaiians. The Congolese have their own state, whatever its problems may be. They are not surrounded by a white society, but surround it. They have been trafficking with Europe since the fifteenth century. The slave trade dissolved the ancient political system and numerous cultural transformations ensued, including the emergence of witchcraft as we know it today, and of divine 'anti-kingship' as known to the early days of anthropology (for example Frazer).[7] The French colonial period knew plantations and expanding commerce as well as politico-religious movements and political repression. Since independence a very effective system of education has been developed, even if there has not been much employment to absorb the educated. The oil boom that began in 1979 made the country a very successful place from the point of view of state-sector employment and consumption, but the decline of the oil producers' economies has led to a massive crisis since oil allowed the consumption of the elite to increase astronomically without notice as everyone was getting something. In economic terms, most local production has been outcompeted by the inflationary effects of oil. It is cheaper to buy frozen chicken smuggled in from Belgium via Zaïre than that which is locally produced.

In spite of a close association with the Soviet Union, now on the wane, the People's Republic of Congo has been very dependent on its former colonial patron. In identity terms, French and European wealth can be said to emanate from Paris, via the French colonial centre of Brazzaville, the current capital, and the only city whose name was not changed to Congolese after the revolution (De Brazza was the conqueror of the French Congo).

The state class maintains very close relations with France, and spends vast amounts of 'aid' money on the consumption of luxuries that define its position. All such goods are, of course, imported. The most expensive supermarket, in the very centre of the old colonial town, is filled with French imports. It is called Score, an English word whose meaning is irrelevant, if at all known, but its foreignness signifies status. Here, all sorts of government officials can buy their *entrecôte* and brie. All consumption is ranked in scalogram fashion according to social position.

It can be suggested that there is a strong historical continuity in Congolese strategies for success, for while the political and 'economic' structure are totally transformed, the definition of power, as externality, has been maintained. And this definition is not restricted to a specified political sphere but pervades the general matrix of personal existence. Power is a 'force' that provides both health and wealth and its differential presence is expressed in the hierarchy itself. This is truly the land of *la distinction*.

During the seventies, there grew up, in Brazzaville, a number of clubs called 'clubs des jeunes premiers'. Their members were primarily from the lower classes, although, owing to the hyper-developed system of education, they were quite familiar with the literate world of French modernity. These clubs expressed a strong desire to consume the fruits of civilization, whose most important source was France. The members of such clubs were called *sapeurs* from the verb *saper*, which means to dress elegantly. The unemployed *flâneurs* had as their goal the appropriation of symbols of refinement which are also symbols of power. Following the yellow brick road to their source, the institution La Sape emerged, the new meaning of the word, by Congolese logical extension: Société des ambianceurs et des personnes élégantes. Clothing represented the fundamental realm of self-identification for the *sapeur*, and in the continual escalation of fashion, it was obvious that a pilgrimage to Paris would be an absolute necessity in the career of any elegant person. The market for fashion clothes was limited in Brazzaville, so a system of emigration developed. Money was scraped together by hook or by crook, and the young men began to make their way to the city of light. Here they lived in misery, scrounging at the bottom in order to gain access to the symbols of the top. And the mode quickly went beyond the famous French designer labels (griffes): Gianni Versace, Ventilo, Jenfer Mani, Ongane, Uomo, Valentuomo, and shoes by Weston. *Sapeurs* know their *haute couture* and there is no settling for less than the most prestigious names. But the accumulation might well pass through intermediate stages, St Laurent and the like. The movement from Brazzaville to Paris is a move from making one's own clothes out of purchased cloth to safari-style clothing to ready-to-wear copies of European couture, and then the great leap to the custom-tailored luxury attire of civilization. This is a movement through a series of age-classes, or status-classes, until one has attained the position of *parisien*, or elder. Throughout the long apprenticeship, one may on occasion return to Brazzaville in order to demonstrate just how far one has come in the accumulation of 'la gamme'. Such visits are referred to as *descentes*, and there is a special dance, 'la danse des griffes', where the famous labels that have been sewn into a single jacket are displayed in all their splendour. Prestige is thus established, but there is a constant pressure to return to Paris.

One might be tempted to see all this as a cynical statement about the relation between clothing and power. One explanation runs to the effect that the Congo has been too rapidly integrated into the modern sector, provoking extreme reactions such as La Sape (Gandoulou 1984). There are indeed cargo-like aspects of the movement, but they cannot easily be interpreted as statements about consumption. They may, instead, represent authentic strategies that elaborate on a language of power in which modern trappings are encompassed within local hierarchy. The marginalization of portions of the population may easily result in the kind of Sape strategy outlined above. On the surface it might well look like the classical strategy of the *flâneur*, but there is an underlying project of another sort here, the accumulation of 'force', of well-being that emanates from a centre and flows downward via the chosen representatives of the centre. Clothes make the man, it is said, and this is perhaps truer in the Congo than in most other places.

If there is an overlap here it is to be found in the narcissistic tendencies of the European *flâneur*, one who was totally dependent upon the *regard de l'autre*. Campbell has made an important point of the difference between the standard European romantic and the dandy:

> The dandy's striving did not derive from an imaginative dwelling upon ideal models, with a consequent guilt-driven dynamic, but from the shame-driven one which stems from other-directedness. Such an ethic, with its Veblenesque overtones, facilitated the spread of fashion, but cannot be regarded as providing the intellectual origins of the modern fashion pattern as a whole. (*Campbell 1987: 121*)

On the surface, the dependence on externalities, the 'Veblenesque' competition for status via ostentation, do coincide. But in the African material, the latter is not an individual variation. It is a social structure. The *flâneur* was recognized as such, as something different. The dandy was not like ordinary people. He didn't enjoy his consumption for itself, but only for how it appeared to others. It might indeed be argued that the postmodern condition is primarily driven by narcissistic desires in a period where the abstract principles of ego goals are disintegrating. But the narcissist in Western civilization lives in a void, while the pre-modern narcissist is enveloped in a universe of determinate meaning. Thus, clothes for the *sapeur* are not just a means of gratification via the recognition of the other. They are also the definition of political power, and of a place in the social hierarchy.

In this sense they are, for us, a statement concerning consumption in relation to political position. The *sapeur* represents a challenge to the political order insofar as he invades the field of expression of power, thus challenging the legitimacy of the state-class, or at least their monopoly over the sumptuary sphere. Now the specific history of the Congo clearly plays a role here.

The opposition between North and South is one between the Kongo-speaking groups who were most associated, first with the colonial system and its accompanying commercialization, and then with the first independent government that connected itself directly to France. The Northerners (led by the Mbochi) have been associated with the external areas and barbary. Their conquest of power, consisting of a movement of the North to the Centre of Brazzaville, where a new palace has been constructed facing, moiety fashion, the old colonial construction that was inhabited by the former Southerner government, has forced Bakongo identity into alternative solutions. More accurately, perhaps, the term 'Southerner' has become a symbol of alternative sources of status.[8] 'We are the most civilized population of the country. Our appearance ought to vouch for that.'

The *sapeur* is not a *flâneur* because he is, in structural terms, authentic, that is, his identity is univocal. The outward appearance that he appropriates is not a mere project to fool the public, to appear as something other than himself. It is his very essence. The narcissist without a cosmology is a cynic, however desperate. The narcissist whose identity is integrated into a larger system of meanings is an authentic clothing freak. This difference is of absolute importance if one is to understand the relation between the premodern and the postmodern forms of narcissism. The former is part of the constitution of the universe of a particular kind of social life, the latter is the effect of the disintegration of an individualistic experience whose only meaning was the project of modernity, of self-development. The narcissistic condition in the world of modernity is one where the subject continually strives for others to create and support his existence. In the Congolese case, such support and a stable structure of meaning are the foundations of social existence.

The recent sharp decline of the Congolese oil economy has put an inordinate amount of pressure on the kin networks that dominate social life, and on the strategy of prestige accumulation and distribution that is the linchpin of the local system. It has resulted in a veritable deluge of religious movements, most, if not all, of which consist in attempts to intensify or re-establish functioning relations to the sources of wealth and health.[9] The threat of narcissistic decline is met via re-engagement or re-enforcement of the encompassing strategy of the group and its lifeline link to the source of life-force which is always external.

Comparative cargo

If we interpret the notion of cargo, not in its formal ethnographic sense, but with respect to a certain essence of the externality of social selfhood, then there are underlying similarities between the systemic clothes mania of the *sapeurs*, as a cult-like expression of a more standard social strategy, and the kinds of phenomena one finds today in the less 'modern' reaches of Melanesia where the cargo concept was first 'conceived'. In many areas one finds a phenomenon that might be designated as post-cargo. In the Sepik River region, beneath a mountain called Hurun in the foothills of the Prince Alexander Range, an area called Yangoru, there emerged a cult called the Peli Association. 'The Hurun cult seems to date back to about 1969 when two men, Matias Yaliwan and Daniel Hawina, became convinced that a number of cement survey markers placed on top of Hurun were preventing material benefits from flowing to the people,' (May 1982: 35).

Now this is an area that has been in contact with the West since the early years of the century. It had a Catholic mission from 1914. Gold was discovered and brought white settlers and in the 1950s cash cropping; coffee, rice, peanuts, cocoa and cattle were gradually introduced. Labour recruitment expanded and perhaps 40 per cent of the population was absentee. There was only a minimum increase in social and economic benefits for the local people and a great deal of new hardships.

> What development did take place in the Yangoru area, however (and this is equally true of the Sepik Provinces generally), fell well short of people's expectations. Their disappointment was reflected in continued high rates of outmigration, the recurrence of cargo cults ... and a good deal of antipathy towards local government. It probably contributed, also, to the popularity of Australian Bonanza and other chain letter schemes promising easy wealth, which flourished in the late 1960s and early 1970s before being outlawed by the government. (*May 1982: 35*)

In such conditions, it might be expected that the reaction would be as is described above. As in many cults of this type, there is an inherent ambiguity. There is a recognition that the colonial power or national elite is not beneficial for the people and ought to be removed and replaced by locals who have the same interest as those they represent. One of the cult leaders publicly disclaimed that it was a cargo cult, insisting that all wealth was the result of work. But there is simultaneously a self-defining strategy that is inextricably linked to external power. The inferior position of the Papuans is explained as their having been deceived by the missionaries into not heeding the word of god. As a result they were denied the well-being of the Europeans.

> In the early stages of the cult activities there were reports also of people burning money and rubbing the ashes on their faces or cuts on their wrists in order to make their money increase and of people cleaning up graveyards and burying suitcases which they expected to have filled with money. At the time of the ceremonies on Hurun there was in Marambanja village a 'power house' (paua haus) in which were stored certain magic objects of the cult leaders and the money they had collected. Subsequently the word spread that it was in such paua haus, or 'banks' that money was created and there was a move to establish paua haus in a number of villages. In these paua haus the 'workers' and 'flowers' carried out an activity referred to as 'washing money' or 'fighting the dishes' in which sums of money collected by Peli members were tipped back and forth between two large enamel basins; if this was performed correctly, it was claimed, the activity would bring about an increase in the amount of money in the basins. (*May 1982: 46*)

And while the movement is very focused on its local roots, there is no question as to the source of the sustaining life force of society: 'while the association prided itself on its indigenous nature there seemed to be a common desire to have European members' (1982: 44).

There is no real contradiction here. The practice of self-identification and the practice of self-sustenance belong to two different domains. The former is an act of self-objectification, the latter is an expression of the objective self. If there is a potential intellectual confrontation between the two, no synthesis or solution is possible. The same situation was pointed out earlier for the Hawaiian villagers, whose existence is objectified by the movement but whose objective cultural existence is in no sense coterminous with that identity. Traditionalist Hawaiian culture, while a model of selfhood and a political reality, does not map onto the modern village culture as practised by the same people.

Cultural strategies in global perspective

In the West, the decline of modernist identity has led to a new search for salvation. Here it is a search for roots, for a permanence and internal peace that is totally foreign to the Congolese or the Papuan. Religions, even if imported from the East, are the key to human salvation in general because they embody universal truths about human nature. The attraction of collectivist solutions is built into the construction of Western individualism. But the latter are certainly not transcendent. They partake fully in the universe of modernity which contains, by definition, every kind of identity conceivable (in modernist terms).

For Hawaiians, whose official identity was demolished and even legally forbidden, there are similarities with both the Western and the Congolese situations. Cultural identity is something that has to be re-established, and it is thus organized, as in the West, as a search for roots, not a reinforcement of the inflow of health and wealth from the West via 'supernatural' controls. On the other hand there is no need to experiment in collective solutions, because the immediate experience of most Hawaiians is one in which the individual is integrated into a larger group in social, if not in cultural terms, as there is no collective cosmology corresponding to modern Hawaiian social groupings. Thus the Hawaiian movement is a search for an adequate socio-cultural framework for institutionalizing the collective experience that is already present in Hawaiian everyday existence, an existence that is stigmatized and implies a social solution of radical proportions, a land base and a lifestyle that would allow the implementation of a collectivist or holistic identity. For Westerners, superficially similar movements concern, rather, the integration of individuals into experiential collectivities and not the formation of new societies.

MODELS OF CULTURAL CHANGE

I have, in the above, tried to outline the contours of the variations in strategies of identity in a continuum, however curved and punctuated, stretching from societies where individuals are integrated into larger social units and provided with a self-evident set of meanings attributed to selfhood, to societies in which the individual is endowed with a truly autonomous self, detached from all such social and cultural totalities, and whose universe is ordered by the principle of change itself, the principle of all cultures, of generic culture. We now pass to a consideration of how to grasp the simultaneity of different and changing strategies.

The kinds of phenomena that are referred to in this analysis include: the emergence of postmodern cultural trends, the re-emergence of religious fundamentalisms, the emergence of inter-nationalist religious movements (if that is a good term), ethnic movements, subnationalist movements; all of which is characteristic of the West. In those areas of the East characterized by rapid economic growth there are new forms of modernism. These have to be seen in relation to the declining dominance of the West in order to understand the difference between their particularistic cultural character and the universalistic evolutionism that they embody. On the one hand they have emphasized the moral core of the Confucian order, expressed in neo-Confucianism, an order that stresses the ethics of the bureaucratic public sphere, an abstract morality, but one extracted from the ideals of the family and elevated to a set of generalized social principles. This has been linked to the notion that the NIC (Newly Industrializing Countries) lands, for example, have some special culture that is conducive to development, and even superior to Western individualism. There have, on the other hand, been numerous discussions of the relation between Confucian de-velopmentalism and Western models. Neo-Confucianist ideology stresses the goals of democracy and rationalist development above practically all else. The particularistic property of this self-conscious programme of modernity is related to its ethnic base in Chinese civilization. There is an interesting logic in this new modernism. It might be argued that the problem with Western modernity is that its individualism tends to erode the moral values that render the entire project of modernity a genuine possibility. Such a view would dove-tail with Bell's analysis of the dialectical contradictions of modernity that generate, all by themselves, the postmodern dissipation that now has taken form in the West. In the Eastern model with its weaker, if clearly present, individual, entirely oriented to the project of the group, such disintegration ought not to be possible. It would not be wise to overlook, in the face of all this philosophizing on cultural supremacy, that England once sported a kindred morality of super-iority of the race and of the self-evident nature of the Empire. In this sense, it might be said that neo-Confucianism appears as a cultural movement, and is a cultural movement from the point of view of the declining hegemon, but in the same sense that Renaissance Europe was a cultural movement with respect to the declining centres of the East, and in the sense that Englishness arose as a particular cult of modernity in opposition to the rest of the world, not least the rest of Europe. But in such terms, it belongs to the family of modernist cosmologies. The primary difference for us Westerners is that, while stressing all the properties of the rationalist development orientation, it does so without invoking the individualism typical of the Occident. But it is still, I would argue, a question of degree and not of kind. The public morality of the heyday of British dominance, stressing loyalty to the company or to the larger social unit in general, is certainly comparable to neo-Confucianism, even if the West places equal stress on the relation between the individual and the higher principles of morality that are said to transcend all social concerns (but here, again, there are clear parallels in the East). There are even academic statements claiming a deep affinity between the philosophy of Confucius and that of the arch-modernist Habermas (Tran Van Doan 1987).

Religious movements, which have increased logarithmically in the West, have been analysed in world systemic terms by authors such as Wuthnow (1978) and Robertson (Robertson and Chirico 1985). The latter have stressed the processes of relativization of self and of society in the world arena, producing a new kind of identity and awareness, one that stresses mankind, that is, humanity as a boundless whole, and a world system or arena that stresses the obvious need for integration. This process of real international integration is said to produce a religous experience that transcends local national context and begins to institutionalize mankind as a whole, a universalism without hierarchy. But such movements must not be confused with modernist universalism. As religious movements they emphasize the identification of the individual with humankind, a form of species-consciousness that is just as concrete in its essentials as more local religious or ethnic identifications. Tendencies to broad-based, yet concrete identity formation certainly do exist. Even beyond the realm of religious experience, the Europe fever that has spread throughout the continent is evidence of the same tendency. There are clear attempts to establish a specifically European identity, using the old but nevertheless trustworthy instruments of archaeology, history and linguistics. But the more powerful development is toward the local, the national and the fundamentalist. The main characteristic of the recent explosion of religious feeling is its fragmenting effect on national and international hegemony.[10] And there is a common basis to these different forms of identity, insofar as they all, whether 'mankind', Europe, Germany, or Hawaii, seek after authenticity, roots, a concrete identity that is absolutely fixed with respect to the flux of modernity. And if this appears as a 'misplaced concreteness' for diehard modernists, it is no more misplaced than their own quite complementary 'abstractness'.

This world of shifting loci of capital accumulation, of shifting political hegemonies, of new peripheralizations and increasing integration, and of delinking and political autonomization, does not produce a mishmash of formerly pure cultures in some world systemic pot-pourri. It generates a set of contrasting situations and self-identifications. And the latter engender contrasting cultural strategies in their turn, and discourses that cannot communicate among themselves because rooted in such differing conditions of existence. I have argued that the common denominator in all of this divergence is the dissolution of the self. And if the latter process differs according to the way in which the self is culturally constituted, it leads none the less to a universal core of narcissistic experience in which dependence on the defining gaze of the Other becomes the lifeline of personal survival. The reactions to this state depend similarly on the cultural context in which they occur, and this essay has attempted to supply some positions in a suggested continuum of resultant social practices.

The differences that are pertinent here are generated in the articulation between the local dynamics of world-systemic processes and specific cultural constitutions of personhood as they are distributed among the different positions in local social structures. Thus, the individualizing effect of commercial intensification in a system characterized by strong embeddedness of the subject, in a larger social and cultural scheme that elaborates upon a narcissistic dependence, may well lead to explosive witchcraft, where such dependence is defined in terms of a hierarchy of ancestral spirits connected to the subject by lines of force that constitute the body in all its visible and invisible aspects. Where such structures remain intact, they pervade the strategies and their practitioners so that phenomena connecting health and wealth to external, imperial, sources of supernatural power achieve dominance. Witchcraft prevails, and the response to crisis takes the form of attempts to ameliorate the flows by means of cult activities, money magic etc.

In areas where the individualization has been more if not completely successful it is almost inevitably associated with the stigmatization of colonial and postcolonial ethnic–class structures. Here the integration of the subject into the larger group is not often accompanied by an integration into a functioning cultural scheme, since the hegemonic schemes of the dominant elites tend to dismember, if not repress, politically subordinate cultural schemes, by education and by law, and by the everyday usage of cultural schemes that naturalize a specific social arrangement. The individual in such situations may demonstrate many of the Other-dependent emotional tendencies, but there is a lack of any cultural strategy aiming at the accumulation of life-force from abroad. Crisis for the larger society implies a weakening of the power and identity of the dominant groups, and thus a potential strengthening of formerly repressed cultural identities. The response in this case is emancipatory cultural movements, the attempt to re-establish previous forms of existence, rather than reinforce the flows of wealth in the system. This 'Fourth World' strategy is essentially the opposite of the 'Third World' strategy depicted above.

The two strategies may and often are combined, as ought to be expected in the complex situations produced by world processes in local places. Melanesia combines Third and Fourth World strategies in politically explosive ways. It is not unusual that the formation of national elites creates perfect conditions for the redefinition of originally Fourth World ideologies as Third World developmentalism. This area of cultural production deserves a great deal more attention than it has received. The variation and combination of these strategies can only emerge, however, in a substrate characterized by the relatively strong integration of the subject into the group. Movements to establish cultural identity in places like Melanesia, where local social dynamics are still vital, are often, if not always, the work of those who have left their societies and been integrated as individuals into the modern sector. Such movements do not have the same force as the political–religious movements that are so common in Papua New Guinea. In fact, cultural movements invariably appear as aspects of political–religious movements, that is, as the immediately political feature of such movements. In Hawaii, by contrast, where most Hawaiians occupy a position comparable to the small minority of Melanesian activists, the same kind of movement has a greater significance. If for the latter the religious is encompassed by the practice of cultural identification, for the former, cultural identity is encompassed by political–religious praxis.

CONCLUSION

It might seem difficult, if not wrong, to attempt to find unity in a world that is increasingly described in terms of fragmentation, disintegration, meaninglessness and cultural mix. I have tried, nevertheless, to locate the strands of what appears to be a single complex process of global transformation. This is not to say, of course, that there are no local structures, no autonomous cultural schemes, but that their orchestration occurs via a score whose principal theme is the decline of Western hegemony, which takes different forms in different parts of the global arena. Modernity moves east, leaving postmodernity in its wake; religious revival, ethnic renaissance, roots and nationalism are resurgent as modernist identity becomes increasingly futile in the West. In the structural confusion that characterizes the period, the periphery and margins of the system also react, in ways that I have referred to as a complex combination of Third and Fourth World strategies. In a transitional era where the individual, no matter where he or she may be, is out to save him or herself, the different configurations that I have described might be profitably reduced to a number of major cultural strategies differentiated and recombined according to the specificity of global as well as local social position. These are life-strategies, models for satisfying the structures of desire that emerge in the different niches of the global system.

Panorama of cultural strategies

0 modernist:

(a) progressive evolutionist, development of self and society and world. Deviations from this life-strategy are classified as pathological or as just plain undeveloped or infantile, in the sense that all non-modern states are ultimately reducible to a lack of the necessary means to achieve modernity: intellectually, technologically, motivationally.

1 modernism, can be expressed in general cultural terms; in terms of political institutions conducive to democratic solutions and efficient moral governance; in terms of economic growth; and social modernization, that is, modern institutions.

(a) political debates in modernist discourse focusing on variant interpretations of the implementation of the modernist strategy; for example whether social democracy is more efficient and fair than liberalism, the role of the private vs. public sector, etc. marxist vs. other approaches, etc.

2 Asian modernism displays most of the basic characteristics of the Western model, the main difference lying in the

role of the individual as an instrument of the group rather than as an autonomous agent.

In the decline of modernist identity:

1 postmodern–modern–consumptionist:
 (a) cynical distancing from all identification, but an acute awareness of the lack of identity.
 (b) consumptionist: narcissistic dependency on the presentation of self via the commodity construction of identity. Highly unstable and can easily switch over to religious or ethnic solutions.
  1 variation on the above is the consumption of roots as commodities, the creation of a life space reminiscent of a nostalgic vision or some pastiche of eras based thereupon.
2 traditionalist–religious–ethnic:
 (a) solution to lack of identity, the failure of the modern project. The individual feels the acute need to engage himself in a larger project in which identity is concrete and fixed irrespective of mobility, success and other external changes in social conditions.
  1 traditionalist refers to the general aspect of this strategy, the emphasizing of concrete values and morality, social rules and cultural practices.
   (a) religious: usually traditional, fundamentalist in form, sometimes tied to ethnicity.
    (i) local based, community oriented
    (ii) international, mankind oriented, anti-ethnic yet concrete, i.e. species oriented.
   (b) ethnic: the constitution of concrete regional or historical–linguistic-based identity–not so much connected to a value system as to a set of distinct cultural practices and beliefs.
  2 closely connected with the traditionalist strategy is the ecological or green strategy. If the former bases itself in culture the latter bases itself in nature: the correct relation between man and the ecosystem. The overlap is clear and occurs in the evolutionist cosmology where traditional = close to nature = adapted to nature (that is, ecologically sound).
3 Third World – strategy of attracting wealth flows, strategy of attachment and dependency:
 (a) state–class ranking system with chains of clients in which sumptuary consumption plays a central role in defining position.

(b) strategy is unequivocally orientated to the centre as source of wealth, and to the modern as the form of power to be appropriated in the rank-strategy described above.

(c) strategy is thus pro-development defined not in terms of infrastructural growth but in terms of the consumption of modernity or its products that function as symbols of prestige and, as such, power.

4   Fourth World – strategy of exit from the system, the formation and/or maintenance of culturally organized communities that are self-sufficient and politically autonomous:

(a) strategies usually take the form of cultural movements for the re-establishment of a formerly repressed identity and lifestyle.

(b) strategies usually reject all forms of modernity and especially the notion of universal development. They are traditionalistic, and attempt, further, to establish a functioning social order based on particular world-views and/or religious schemes.

(c) tendency to egalitarianism, since there is no basis for ranking in such movements: often local history is re-envisaged so that an original state of existence without any form of social hierarchy is posited at the beginning of time. If leadership is posited, it is invariably in the form of the charismatic leader who is the saviour or father or mother of his/her people and is the embodiment of their values.

If these are the conscious strategies that emerge in the different zones of the world-system, they are not, of course the whole story. They are not the strategies of everyday life, even if they display a certain family resemblance. But they are generated in the same conditions of existence and so are homologous, and partake of a larger set of logical possibilities. The Fourth World cultural strategy is often produced by communities that already have their backs to the world, that have a set of local strategies that are consciously opposed to those of higher political and economic instances. This may be the case whether or not a cultural movement emerges instead of simple accommodation. Third World strategies, on the other hand, are produced in situations where the local structures are encompassed by higher social orders. Third World situations produce weak local identities. Fourth World situations produce strong local identities. But the situations can change into their opposites and the identities and strategies follow suit.

So, the modernist is the natural ally of the Third Worldist, just as the traditionalist or ecological fundamentalist is the natural ally of the Fourth Worldist; and this irrespective of the results of such an alliance. The postmodernist stands alone insofar as his potential allies are all fantasies, primitives-for-us, full of wisdom and close to nature in a way that deprives them of their humanity except as a humanity-for-us. And that form of the postmodern strategy that consists in constructing worlds out of images from past eras and exotic places for the identityless *nouveaux riches* and wealthy seekers after adventures to call their own needs only the products of the world and of world history. Such a strategy is self-consuming and neither needs nor seeks allies.

The fragmentation of the world-system implies a heightening of social activity; of seeking, of finding, of opposing, and of a frenetic creativity in the adaptation to changing conditions. As these lines are written the Soviet Union is undergoing the largest strike in its history, China is attempting to recover after violently putting down a major revolt, not just of students, but of a large section of the urbanized intellectuals and young workers. The revolt was aimed at the overthrow of the organization of state–class power in the face of increasing stratification, itself due to the introduction of massive foreign capital investments and the possibility of large-scale accumulation of wealth. All of these local impulses, practices, movements and strategies, are, I have argued, implicated in global processes that distribute fields of immanent identification in the world arena.[11]

Those who characterize the present as the culture of narcissism, as postmodernity, as late capitalism, as postindustrialism, as information society are all, I would argue, emphasizing particular aspects of a unitary process at the global system level, one that, if we leave our own Western self-absorption, includes the increase of fundamentalisms, ethnicities, of cultural nationalisms, of Third World cultism, and Fourth World liberationisms. If they play rummy for big bucks in some self-isolating village in Hawaii while surrounding tourists search their home tracts for another authenticity that they might capture for their condominium living-rooms, this is not to be understood as a world gone crazy, as cultural creolization, but as a reality that we must try to grasp without the cynical defences of our intellectual cultural schemes that would classify this as garbage and that as cultural pea soup. Only people go crazy, not cultures, not societies. Even the chaos of identities, and of strategies, in the world today is the effect of real, and highly structured, forces that are constantly felt in the lives of those trying to get from one day to the next.

NOTES

1 This, of course, assumes a rather 'old-fashioned' correspondence between our modern poetic mode and a supposed 'primitive mentality'.

2 At a recent academic congress on the Middle East in Copenhagen a presentation by an eminent scholar dealing with tradition and identity in Iran was rebutted by a member of the Muslim Brethren seated in traditional attire in the back of the seminar room. The latter spoke for quite some time and was clearly well versed in his own culture but from a very different interpretive standpoint. Interestingly enough, his discourse provoked total silence.

3 Increasing ratios of fictive to read accumulation implies increasing ratios of debt to means of payment, i.e. declining liquidity ratios.

4 There is an interesting complication here insofar as it can and is being argued that much of the land of Hawaii legally belongs to the Hawaiian people even though it is at present being leased out for resorts, airports, military uses etc. The sum total of the Ceded Lands, lands ceded by the royalty to the territorial government, plus the so-called Home Lands, set aside for Hawaiians in 1920, accounts for almost half of the land of the islands. This is a legal situation that is unique in its political implications.

5 In 1984 one estimate has the Hawaiian population at 208,000. Of all births on the islands, 30% are estimated to be within the Hawaiian population. It is also to be noted that there are at least 70,000 Hawaiians living in mainland USA, either temporarily or permanently. This is a rather low estimate, as is to be expected from the Federal census.

6 One developer, himself a Lebanese, asked scoffingly if we had found any 'pure breeds down there' in Miloli'i.

7 African sacred kings of the nineteenth century were, unlike their forebears, powerless figures who were often killed or castrated as a sign of their being the mere instruments of society.

8 Regional or ethnic identity is not, however, a strong determinant of such alternative sources. While the *sapeurs* began among the Bakongo, the movement, as a basis of social identity, cut across ethnic boundaries, expressive, as it is, of a more general strategy of accumulation that is more closely bound to class than ethnicity.

9 In 1985, 77 religious sects applied for state licences in order to carry out their work in public. That number is apparently closer to 100 today.

10 And it might well be argued that the attempted fusion of Europe is itself an aspect of the fragmentation of a former world hegemony, the formation of a new political and economic sphere and a corporate force in world competition.

11 Via of course the processes of articulation between local and global processes. A global approach does not, of course, assume that the only relevant social processes are themselves global, but that the multiple local social praxes are integrated into such broader processes. Nor do the properties

of the latter liquidate those of the former. On the contrary, global social processes are constituted largely by local strategies and their local and global non-intentional properties.

REFERENCES

Altieri, M. 1986: *The Last Village in Kona*. Honolulu: Topgallant.

Bourdieu, P. 1980: 'L'identité et la répresentation', *Actes de la recherche en sciences sociales*, 35, 63–72.

Campbell, C. 1987: *The Romantic Ethic and the Spirit of Modern Consumerism*. Oxford: Blackwell.

Census of Hawaii 1985.

Clifford, J. 1983: 'On ethnic authority', *Representations*, 1, 118–46.

Ekholm-Friedman, K., and Friedman, J. 1980: 'Towards a global anthropology', in L. Blussé, H. L. Wesseling and G. D. Winius (eds), *History and Under-development*. Leiden/Paris: Center for The History of European Expansion, University of Leiden.

Frazer, J. G. 1905: *Lectures on the Early History of Kingship*. London.

Friedman, J. 1987a: 'Beyond otherness or the spectacularization of anthropology', *Telos*, 71.

Friedman, J. 1987b: 'Prolegomena to the adventures of Phallus in Blunderland', *Culture and History*, 1.

Gandoulou, J.-D. 1987: *Entre Paris et Bakongo*. Paris: Centre Georges Pompidou.

Geertz, C. 1980: 'Blurred genres: the refiguration of social thought', *American Scolar*, 29, 2.

Gillis, N. 1989: 'Wait 'till we tell the folks back home', *Time*, 27 Feb.

Hawaii Statistical Reports 1985: 'Racial statistics in the 1980 Census of Hawaii', Report 80.

Horton, T. 1989: 'New riders of the Rainbow Range, Hawaii's urban paniolos', *Spirit of Aloha: Aloha Island Air Magazine*, 14, 1.

Kouvouama, A. 1989: 'Religion et politique', MS.

Lacan, J. 1966: *Ecrits*. Paris: Seuil.

Levin, D. M. 1987: 'Clinical stories: a modern self in the fury of being', in Levin (ed.), *Pathologies of the Modern Self: Postmodernism Studies on Narcissism, Schizophrenia, and Depression*. New York: New York University Press.

May, R. J. 1982: 'The view from Hurin: the Peli Association', in May (ed.), *Micronationalist Movements in Papua New Guinea*. Canberra: Dept. of Political and Social Change, Monograph 1.

Mead, G. H. 1934: *Mind, Self and Society*. Chicago: Aldine.

Office of Program Evaluation and Planning 1984: 'The present Hawaiian population and projections through the year 2000'. Kamehameha Schools/Bishop Estate.

Ortigues, M.-L., and Ortigues, E. 1966: *Oedipe africain*. Paris: Plon.

Robertson, R., and Chirico, J. 1985: 'Humanity, globalization and worldwide religious resurgence: a theoretical perspective', *Sociological Analysis*, 46.

Sartre, J.-P. 1936: 'La transcendance de l'ego: esquisse d'une description phénoménologique', *Recherches philosophiques*, 4.

Tonda, J. 1988: 'Pouvoir de guérison, guérison et pouvoir dans les Eglises hors-la-loi', MS.

Tran Van Doan 1987: 'Harmony and consensus: Confucius and Habermas on politics', in *Proceedings of the International Symposium on Confucianism and the Modern World*. Taipeh, Taiwan, 2–38.

Tyler, S. 1991: 'A post-modern instance', in P. Pels (ed.), *Reflexivity and the Deconstruction of Academic Authority: Perspectives from Anthropology*. London: Sage.

Wuthnow, R. 1978: 'Religious movements and the transition in world order', in J. Needleman and G. Baker (eds), *Understanding the New Religions*. New York: Seabury Press.

Zukin, S. 1982: *Loft Living: Culture and Capital in Urban Change*. Baltimore: Johns Hopkins University Press.

Index